CAMBRIDGE LATIN AMERICAN STUDIES

GENERAL EDITOR
MALCOLM DEAS

ADVISORY COMMITTEE
WERNER BAER, MARVIN BERNSTEIN,
AL STEPAN, BRYAN ROBERTS

48

MINERS, PEASANTS AND ENTREPRENEURS

MINERS, PEASANTS AND ENTREPRENEURS

REGIONAL DEVELOPMENT IN THE CENTRAL HIGHLANDS OF PERU

NORMAN LONG

Department of Rural Sociology, The Agricultural University, Wageningen

and

BRYAN ROBERTS

Department of Sociology, University of Manchester

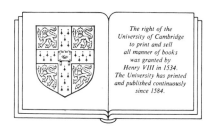

The right of the University of Cambridge to print and sell all manner of books was granted by Henry VIII in 1534. The University has printed and published continuously since 1584.

CAMBRIDGE UNIVERSITY PRESS

Cambridge

London   New York   New Rochelle
Melbourne   Sydney

Published by the Press Syndicate of the University of Cambridge
The Pitt Building, Trumpington Street, Cambridge CB2 1RP
32 East 57th Street, New York, NY 10022, USA
296 Beaconsfield Parade, Middle Park, Melbourne 3206, Australia

First published 1984

Printed in Great Britain at the University Press, Cambridge

Library of Congress catalogue card number: 83-20899

British Library Cataloguing in Publication Data

Long, Norman
Miners, peasants and entrepreneurs: regional development in the central
highlands of Peru. — (Cambridge Latin American Studies; 48)
1. Regional planning — Peru
2. Peru — Economic conditions
I. Title   II. Roberts, Bryan
330.985′0633   HC227

ISBN 0 521 24809 4

CE

Contents

PILAR CAMPAÑA and RIGOBERTO RIVERA, *Grupo de Investigaciones Agrarias, Academia de Humanismo Cristiano, Santiago, Chile*

JULIAN LAITE, *Department of Sociology, University of Manchester*

TEOFILO ALTAMIRANO, *Departamento de Ciencias Sociales, Pontificia Universidad Católica del Perú, Lima, Peru*

v

Tables

Figures

Maps

Preface

This volume is the second of two that bring together the main findings of field research carried out in the central highlands of Peru between August 1970 and December 1972. The project was financed by a British Social Science Research Council (SSRC) grant made to Norman Long and Bryan Roberts of the University of Manchester. Its aim was to undertake a regional study of social change and development in an economically diversified area of highland Peru.

We were joined in the project by two contributors to this volume, Julian Laite and Gavin Alderson-Smith, both of whom were independently financed, the former by the SSRC and the latter by the Canada Council. Subsequently, Norman Long continued with his research in the central highlands and, in 1980, was awarded, together with Jorge Dandler, a further SSRC grant to extend the themes of the original project to include the Peruvian Department of Huancavelica and the Cochabamba region of Bolivia. Some of the preliminary findings of the latter research have been incorporated into the present volume, allowing us to update the material of the early 1970s.

Throughout the earlier research we were ably assisted by Teófilo Altamirano who, following his appointment to the Pontificia Universidad Católica in Lima, continued with work in the central highlands but broadened it to cover regional associations in Lima, the results of which are reported in this volume. The research effort was also aided by two Chilean anthropologists, Pilar Campaña and Rigoberto Rivera, whose investigations among highland *puna* communities are likewise contained in this book. They were based at the Universidad Católica and later studied with Norman Long and Jorge Dandler at the University of Durham.

In the early project, as in its sequel, we have been very lucky to have such excellent collaborators who have helped us intellectually and have become good friends. We have also enjoyed the help of Peruvian research institutions, their staff and students. In the recent period, we would particularly like to thank the

Department of Anthropology of the Pontificia Universidad Católica del Perú, and especially Juan Ossio, Teófilo Altamirano and Oswaldo Medina, for shouldering much of the responsibility for implementing the new research in Huancavelica and for being such good-humoured companions on visits to the field. We also acknowledge the continuing interest and support of the Universidad Nacional del Centro, Huancayo, particularly the assistance given by Juan Solano.

In the central highlands, we enjoyed hospitality from many people: too many to mention individually. We found the area a dynamic and exciting one to work in, but also one in which it was pleasant to relax. However, we would like to express our gratitude for the special help we received from the Mayer family of Huancayo. They provided us with many contacts throughout the region and helped us and our families to settle into the life of the area. Guillermo Mayer was a fund of information and much of the historical analysis of this volume draws from his own memories of the early days of the exporting economy, although of course we alone are responsible for the interpretation.

During the final stage of preparing the manuscript for publication we received generous help from Valpy Fitzgerald (now at the Institute of Social Studies, The Hague). He scrutinized the argument closely and made a number of probing observations that required us to re-work some parts of the analysis. We are most grateful to him, even though his comments occasioned much more work than we had at first anticipated!

Finally, we must thank our families for their forbearance during the period we have been writing this manuscript. The writing involved considerable travelling between Durham and Manchester and, more recently, between Wageningen in Holland and Manchester. Since we had relatively little time to spend together, we worked intensively and our families saw little of us. Although the logistics of completing this second book have been difficult, the experience has been intellectually most rewarding to both of us and has cemented an already close friendship.

Manchester, December 1982   NORMAN LONG
                                                              BRYAN ROBERTS

1

Regional development in an export economy

Introduction

This book explores a controversial issue in the analysis of development –
whether integration into the international capitalist economy entails relative
stagnation for underdeveloped economies or the possibility of sustained economic growth and diversification. We focus upon one provincial region of Peru
– the central highlands – whose economic and social structure has been shaped
by involvement in the international economy from the latter half of the
sixteenth century and which, in recent years, has become peripheral to the more
dynamic growth pole of Lima.

Our conclusion is that significant growth and diversification has taken place
in the region and that this is directly attributable to capitalist expansion.
Throughout our analysis we emphasize the social and political dimensions of
this process since the local dynamic of capitalism has involved important
changes in class relationships consequent upon the emergence of a wage labour
force and new entrepreneurial groupings.

This conclusion is particularly significant since the economy of the central
highlands has been closely linked in this century to the fortunes of large-scale,
foreign-owned mining enterprise. At first sight, the mining complex had the
characteristics of an economic enclave with few dynamic linkages with the area's
economy. This is precisely the situation that is supposed to prevent economic
growth at the periphery. However, we will seek to show that such an
interpretation fails to take account of the significant but small-scale processes of
accumulation resulting from the exchanges between the enclave and a peasant
population which, for centuries, had been involved in labour and commodity
markets.

The central highlands is the most densely populated and economically
differentiated of highland zones. It includes large-scale capitalist mining

companies, Peru's largest livestock estates (now expropriated under the 1969 agrarian reform), peasant and commercial farms, small industry of various kinds, and trading and transport enterprise. The area is notable for its strong sense of regional identity, even evident among migrant groups in Lima who have formed clubs based on village and regional commitments. The region is also well known for its community co-operation and patterns of mutual aid, which have flourished in the face of increasing integration into the national economy. This integration has been accompanied by a high level of peasant protest and political activity.

In a previous volume (Long and Roberts, 1978), we concentrated on examining the types of peasant organization characteristic of the area; in particular we explored the significance of co-operative and collective forms of organization in both town and village. In a series of case studies, we and our contributors showed how apparently 'traditional' forms of community and interhousehold co-operation were shaped and at times created in response to changes in the regional and national economy. Our main focus was the impact of export-oriented, capitalist expansion from the late nineteenth century onwards. The absence of a strong centralized state in Peru encouraged a devolution process whereby local community institutions played a major role in capitalist expansion, facilitating the provision of labour and foodstuffs to the mining and urban sectors, as well as contributing to the processes of internal differentiation within communities.

From at least the end of the nineteenth century, there were clear signs of the emergence of a richer class of peasant farmers eager to seize the new economic opportunities. Frequently, they were able to gain control over community institutions and achieve positions of political influence at district and sub-district levels. Many of the peasant movements of the early part of the twentieth century were based on the strategies of this local entrepreneurial class who sought to resist hacienda control as well as that of rival district authorities. Our analysis also demonstrated how these village-based class struggles continued to influence local development and organization even during the recent period of agrarian reform. Thus, we explained the dilemmas facing state-sponsored co-operatives in terms of competition between different rural classes seeking to defend or advance their particular interests.

In the present volume, we take a more explicitly regional focus, exploring the linkages between the different economic sectors and social groups located in the area. We give special emphasis to the impact of the mining economy, arguing that this was the single most important factor underlying the evolution of distinctive patterns of social and economic organization in the area. Indeed, mining in its heyday helped create a regional identity and structure which left its imprint on social life and which affected the actions of local groups when the area became more fully drawn into the metropolitan orbit of Lima-Callao.

A regional focus is a necessary complement to national and international levels of analysis which tend to dominate theoretical discussions on development. This focus enables us to 'disaggregate' the analysis of development by taking into account the more immediate life circumstances of the populations of underdeveloped countries. These life circumstances often vary significantly from one part of a country to another because underdeveloped countries are frequently made up of regions shaped by contrasting historical experiences of colonialism or by different types of incorporation into the international economy through, for example, mining, plantation agriculture, or smallholder cash-crop production. The concept of region can thus be used to refer to those geographical areas, such as the central highlands, where, over time, class interests and social relationships have developed in a particular way because of a spatially specific pattern of economic change. Hence, even apparently individual decisions, entailing, for example, migration or economic investment, are best analysed in terms of the socio-spatial pattern of interrelationships and opportunities that have emerged.

Looking at the development of a provincial region also enables one to better assess the planning strategies used to counteract the excessive concentration of population and resources in the metropolitan zones of underdeveloped countries. Most planners and governments seek to promote regional development through decentralization and growth pole policies. However, if it is not to be counterproductive, such government intervention needs to take serious account of well-established local relationships and interests. For example, as is shown later, the one major state intervention of the modern period in Peru – the agrarian reform law of 1969 – was, to a great extent, undermined by local interests and power structures, even though its main objective was to promote a more balanced and equitable pattern of regional development.

The next section of this chapter provides an account of the perspective we use in regional analysis. We then give a brief outline of the national economic and political developments that have shaped the recent history of the central highlands. This is followed by a description of the regional setting; and an outline of the organization of the volume concludes the chapter.

An approach to regional analysis

Throughout the volume we use a regional framework of analysis for organizing and interpreting the data. One of the main advantages of such a framework is that it enables the researcher to identify patterns of activity that result from the spatial distribution of economic resources, settlements and social classes. National-level analysis of class, for example, inadequately depicts the structural contradictions that arise from the varying contexts in which classes relate to each other. A region provides one such important context because both agricultural and industrial production is often organized in terms of regional concentrations.

Our definition of region is not based simply on the presence of similar or complementary forms of economic enterprise and occupation or, for that matter, on ecological criteria, the functional interrelationships of settlements, administrative boundaries or notions of cultural heritage.[1] These factors, as we shall see, play their part in shaping a region's identity, but our approach emphasizes the way in which this identity is forged through conflict and alliance as different classes seek to enhance their material and political interests in the face of existing patterns of resource distribution. Consequently, we use region as a heuristic concept in order to capture the shifting nature of socio-spatial relationships.

In the early part of this century, the attempts of mine owners and merchants to impose control over the economy of the central highlands resulted in a distinctive pattern of relationships between mine, town and village. Later, however, other classes, responding to the new opportunities generated by export-oriented production and by changes in the national economy, were able to create new economic and social relationships and thereby contribute to the evolving regional pattern. As Massey (1978: 116) suggests, 'the social and economic structure of any given local area will be a complex result of the combination of that area's succession of roles within the series of wider, national and international, spatial divisions of labour'. It is for this reason that we stress the necessity of adopting a historical approach for understanding the contemporary organization of the central highlands.

When we first drew up our research project, our aim was to explore the role of socio-spatial variables in regional development (Long and Roberts, 1969; 1974). We thought that by looking at the interrelationships of places and people we could avoid some of the shortcomings of the rural–urban dichotomy implicit in local-level community studies, whether urban or rural. But, during the course of the research and in the analysis of the data, we came to doubt the usefulness of the type of regional analysis that we had originally envisaged. These considerations form the basis for the present attempt to develop a different approach to the regional issue.

To state the issue briefly, we feel that our original research, like many other projects, concentrated excessively on systems of exchange and distribution as the key factors in shaping relationships between social groups and in determining the development of local communities. In the course of the research, we became convinced that not only did our analysis require greater historical depth but also that it was more useful to focus on production and, in particular, on the regional system of production that had evolved in this area in order to understand both past and present developments (Long, 1980; Roberts 1980).

It is important, however, to appreciate the contribution made by studies focussing on exchange and distribution. Carol Smith (1976, II: 310), for example, in presenting her version of regional analysis argues that 'production variables are not ignored but are placed within a regional economic framework where the critical variable is the mode of exchange. Stratification is seen to result from differential access to or control over the means of exchange; and variation in stratification is related to types of exchange between producers and non-producers as they affect and are affected by the spatial distribution of the elite and the level of commercialization in the region and beyond'.

What she has in mind is basically the control of commerce exercised by small- and large-scale merchants, and the role of merchant capital in the early stages of capital accumulation. This control is partly a question of access to capital which enables traders to buy in bulk, offer ready cash and so on. But more interestingly, as Smith points out, this control is often achieved through non-market mechanisms as when administrative power is used to force producers to buy and sell on the market. From this perspective, then, a system of markets is also a system which provides differential opportunities for controlling exchange. Certain marketing systems are relatively competitive, giving small producers freedom of choice as to which market and buyer to sell to; while others are more restrictive so that the producer may have little or no choice as to where or to whom to sell his product and are therefore subject to merchant monopolies.

Different levels of market control are, as Smith argues, often reflected in ethnic or class differences: foreign-born traders of the capital city control the importing–exporting businesses; local elites, resident in the provincial centres, own some of the large-scale production units and do business with the foreign houses; *mestizo* or *ladino* traders run local stores and buy and sell at local markets, but also depend on the foreign houses; small-scale Indian producers living in the villages or farmsteads have little alternative but to sell to middlemen of higher ethnic status. Ethnic differences, then, may reinforce market inequalities as has been reported in the Chiapas area of Mexico where *ladino* townsmen use their social superiority and their control of local administration to force Indians to sell at low prices (Stavenhagen, 1965; see also Burgos, 1970). Such chains of exploitation run from the smallest producer to the large importing–exporting houses of the capital city and through them to the foreign metropolis beyond.

According to this view, then, social and economic inequalities within a region can be traced to institutionalized inequalities in the system of marketing and of credit for production. The region itself tends to be defined in terms of a major marketing centre and its sphere of influence. It follows from this that a more equitable income distribution entails improving access to markets and credit by breaking monopolies, improving transport, creating new market places and so on.

A central element in this approach to regional analysis is the focus on the pattern of hierarchical relationships that develops between places within a region. Some places (central places) provide specialized services for the whole region, thereby attracting clients such as traders from smaller centres (Berry, 1967:59–73; Bromley, 1974).[2] Other places may serve simply as basic retailing centres for a surrounding farming population and are dependent both administratively and commercially on the larger centres. Central places have a larger population, a greater range of facilities and institutions and are better connected to metropolitan centres both in terms of communication and through networks of influence. Moreover, the spatial location of elites reflects this system of hierarchical relationships with the dominant regional elites living in the most central place (as Preston (1975 and 1978) documents for pre-agrarian-reform Bolivia). Elite power and wealth is consolidated through the various chains of political and economic dependence that develop between peripheral locations and the major centres. Thus, the major markets, the most specialized and largest stores and the important administrative and judicial authorities are found in the most central places. The facilities associated with major centres create better life opportunities for their residents through education, through better information concerning outside opportunities and through improved health and social services. These advantages of central location are one factor leading to migration to these towns.

The patterns of spatial relationships within a particular region can be viewed therefore as an important element in shaping the nature of social and economic inequality. This we take to be a main contribution of the studies by, for example, Smith (1972, 1976) in the western highlands of Guatemala, and Poggie and Miller (1969) in the south of Hidalgo, Mexico, who base their work on an earlier project by Frank Young (1960, 1964). In Peru, too, there has been a relatively long history of research of this kind, expressed, for example, in the paper by Julio Cotler (1967–68) on the mechanics of internal domination and in the work of many of the Cornell and Instituto de Estudios Peruanos anthropologists and sociologists who carried out research in the

Chancay and Mantaro valley areas (Matos Mar et al., 1969; Alberti and Sanchez, 1974).

The chief limitation of this form of analysis, as Smith (1981) has recently underlined, is that it neglects the class dynamics of regional structures. Regionally powerful classes, such as merchants, plantation owners or indus-trialists, often have conflicting interests. Merchants or 'traditional' landowners may seek to tie down labour locally and to monopolize the marketing of peasant production; whereas industrialists or plantation owners, who are reliant on seasonal labour, may seek to create a competitive regional labour market and are unlikely to oppose independent petty commodity production among the peasantry. Also, interests change over time as shifts in the national or international economy create new regional opportunities for the different groups. In this way, Smith explains the growing complexity of the regional structure of western Guatemala where a mercantile elite changed its mode of operation to become truckers and labour traffickers, but used its administrative power to restrict the entry of peasant entrepreneurs into the urban economy, thus preserving a monopoly over trade and services. In contrast, competitive small-scale enterprise has flourished in the small towns servicing the plantation enclaves of the western lowlands.

The significance of focussing on the dynamics of regional structure is brought out in Appleby's (1976) analysis of the regional system of the Puno area of Peru. He shows, for example, how changes in the scale and organization of wool production for export led to changes in the regional pattern of marketing and urban settlement. The concentration of wool production in large haciendas, along with the development of the rail network, undermined traditional urban centres and concentrated commerce along the railway line and in the largest urban centres (Appleby, 1976, II: 298–300).

This emphasis on the significance for regional structure of change in the wool export economy is also the subject of Orlove's (1977) study in the Sicuani region of southern Peru. Here, relations between economic sectors and the classes within them are explained by the evolution of the wool economy and by its implications for class alliances and conflicts in both rural and urban areas. In contrast to Puno, the late incorporation of Sicuani into the export economy meant that the expansion of the local economy occurred in the context of a relatively strong national government which restricted the power of local large landowners. Consequently, small-scale enterprise had greater opportunity to flourish in the Sicuani area than in Puno.

The analysis of the class dynamics of regional structure needs then to be based on an understanding of the distinctive features and historical context of the development of agricultural and/or industrial production. The basic issue, it seems to us, is that, in areas affected by the rapid expansion of export production, the dominant force for change in local economies has been the requirement that this production has had for labour, land and essential infrastructure. An analysis of exchange and distribution is inadequate for understanding the impact of these demands because changes in production have entailed not only an expansion of commercial opportunities but changes less likely to be fully reflected in exchange and distribution practices, such as modifications in the household economy and in the rural division of labour. For example, villages have become organized around regular labour migration, often of a seasonal kind; local economies have diversified into new craft and trading activities; and women and children have come to play a different and central role in agricultural production.[3] Moreover, such changes are likely to result in, or at times be produced by, new forms of administrative and political control. Indeed, it is often through the political reorganization of rural society that the expansion of the export sector is facilitated and surplus extracted from a peasantry that nevertheless retains control of its land.

As we argued elsewhere (1978: 322–3), the creation of new districts in the central highlands at the end of the nineteenth and the beginning of the twentieth centuries was in great part produced by the activities of commercially-oriented haciendas, plantations, mines and peasant farmers which were aimed at bypassing the existing urban hierarchy. The result, over time, was to increase the possibilities for direct negotiations between even the smallest village populations and the central government authorities. In this type of situation, the basis of the regional class system is unlikely to rest merely upon the control of the means of exchange. Instead it will depend upon the degree of access to the resources of the dominant sector of production and/or control of the labour process.

We emphasize production because it provides a holistic view of the forces making for change. Although, at the most basic level, production simply involves the bringing together of material resources, instruments and labour power, the maintenance of a given form of production, as well as its possibilities or limitations for expansion, depends upon a complex set of institutions. The latter include ideas and definitions of property relations and the means for their enforcement; even aspects of social organization, relating to religious or kinship affiliation, become integral elements in maintaining the labour processes necessary to a given form of production (Meillassoux, 1972; Godelier, 1977: 15–69).

Clearly, then, the development of new forms of production can entail far-reaching changes in local society, leading to the emergence of new interest groups and often heightening contradictions between old and new organizational forms. This type of analysis is especially useful in the Latin American context since, from the sixteenth century onwards, indigenous patterns of social and economic organization have been confronted by the expansion of mercantile and later industrial capitalism.

In the mercantile stage, the exchange and distribution system was one of the main mechanisms by which surplus was extracted by the metropolitan powers from indigenous populations. Yet, even in this period, the economy relied upon state power and institutions to create markets, as in the *reparto de efectos* (the forced sale of commodities to indigenous populations), and to enforce labour services in the mines through the *mita* (labour service). These practices radically restructured indigenous society. Thus, the dynamics of change in the different regions of the continent increasingly came to depend upon the degree and form (i.e. through markets or by supplying labour) of integration into the export economy. Fluctuations in the state of this economy became important sources of change at the local level.

At the same time, pre-existing forms of production, such as community- and household-based agriculture and craft activities, continued and evolved to provide a subsistence base for the mass of the population. The relationships that were established between these pre-existing forms of production and the expanding capitalist system formed part of a complex socio-economic system that varied from region to region and modified both new and old forms of production. We emphasize, however, that this issue is not one concerning the *articulation* of capitalist and non-capitalist modes of production (see Long and Richardson, 1978; Foster-Carter, 1978). Such a conceptualization tends to exaggerate the autonomy and internal coherence of the various forms of production found in Latin America, for example peasant types of communal and household production, the 'semi-feudal' hacienda system and the 'capitalist' plantation or mine. It is more useful, we find, to focus on the interrelations and interpenetration of different forms and units of production within the context of an increasingly commercialized economy. This will be the focus of the chapters that follow.

Peruvian economic development

Export production and regional development are essential elements in understanding the pattern of Peruvian national development. Peru has been closely integrated into the world economy through the export of primary materials since the beginnings of colonial rule. Furthermore, these forms of production have been organized on a regional basis. In the colonial period, the precious metals that fuelled the European economy were mainly located in upper Peru (present-day Bolivia) and in the central Peruvian highlands in the Cerro de Pasco area. The main deposits of mercury in the Americas, necessary for the amalgamation process for extracting silver, were found in Huancavelica, to the south of the central highlands. This export production gave rise to a regionalized system of production based upon servicing the mines with foodstuffs, primary materials like timber, various manufactured products (both locally and externally produced) and labour. The system was articulated through an elaborate network of trading links which encompassed an area spreading from present-day Ecuador to Santiago, Chile and Buenos Aires, Argentina (Assadourian, 1982: 109–221; Larson, 1972; Long, 1980). The dependence on the export economy made this system of economic activities highly susceptible to fluctuations in the international economy, resulting in periodic changes in the importance of wage as against non-wage labour relations and in the degree of market orientation among agricultural producers (Tandeter, 1980, 1981).

After the civil wars of the early Independence period Peru became, from the mid-nineteenth century, a major exporter to the world economy. The first major export product was guano but this was replaced from the end of the century by a range of products which made Peru an unusually diversified exporter of primary materials. These products were sugar, cotton, sheep and alpaca wool, coffee, silver, copper, rubber and, subsequently, oil, other non-precious metals such as zinc and lead, and later fish meal. The volume of exports rose steadily with some fluctuations from the mid-nineteenth century until the present. Thorp and Bertram (1978: 4–6) show that this long-term trend was divided into three major growth phases. From 1830–70 the volume of exports grew at an average annual rate of nearly 7 per cent. A similar rate was achieved between 1890 and 1929 in terms of both value and volume; and from 1942 to 1970 the growth in volume was also high with export earnings increasing at about 10 per cent each year. Indeed, Thorp and Bertram (1978: 321) remark: 'No "engine of growth" other than export earnings emerged to provide the basis for self-sustaining capitalist development'.

Exports have come from all of Peru's major regions (coast, highlands and tropical lowlands), with different areas specializing in different products. Thus sugar is mainly concentrated along the northern coast, cotton in the central coastal area of Cañete and Ica, rubber in the tropical lowlands of Iquitos, and coffee in the semi-tropical valleys of La Convención and Chanchamayo. Mineral production is mainly located in the central highlands and, recently, important deposits have been developed in the southern regions close to Arequipa. Wool has been exported from the southern highlands and, to a lesser extent, from the central highlands. The rise and decline of these export commodities have shaped the development of Peru's regions, although all regions were adversely affected by the following periods of relative export stagnation: from 1870–90, at the time of the Chilean War; from 1930–41 when the main effects of the world recession were felt; and finally in the late 1960s when again there were problems in the export sector.[4]

The relative success of Peru as an exporting economy has been a mixed blessing. Recent economic commentators argue that the dynamism of the export economy meant that there was little government or private sector commitment to developing food crop and industrial production for internal markets. The control of much of the export sector by foreign capital and the propensity for the national capital involved in these sectors not to invest in other productive activities resulted in a dualistic economy. This dualism is characterized by marked inequalities in income distribution between the mass of the population engaged in semi-subsistence craft and food production and those, mainly resident in Lima and the coastal area, who are involved in the export-linked economic sectors.[5]

Peru has been relatively slow to industrialize compared with other Latin American countries of comparable size (Thorp and Bertram, 1978: 261–73). In 1960, agriculture and forestry still contributed a greater share of the Gross National Product (GNP) than did manufacturing industry (21 per cent as against 17 per cent). By 1965 manufacturing was, however, more important: 19 per cent of the GNP compared with 17 per cent for agriculture (Thorp and Bertram, 1978: 258). Industrialization was also closely linked to the export sector through the processing of export goods or through the production of inputs for the export sector. By the end of the 1960s, import substitution industries were becoming important. Industry was concentrated in the Lima-Callao metropolitan area where, by 1975, between 50 per cent and 70 per cent of the value of industrial production was estimated to be located (Gonzales, 1982: 262).

The increase in industrialization, combined with the relative stagnation of domestic agriculture, meant that from the 1940s onwards urbanization in Peru increased rapidly. Large-scale migration movements transferred substantial numbers of the highland population to the coastal region, in particular to Lima. This migration, together with a high rate of natural increase, produced a massive growth in the population of Lima-Callao at an annual rate of just over 5 per cent between 1940 and 1961 and a similar rate between 1961 and 1972 (ONEC, 1974). By 1972, approximately 28 per cent of Peru's total population of 13,500,000 were living in the Lima-Callao area. Although just over half of this growth from 1961 to 1972 was due to natural increase, migrants in 1972 still constituted almost 43 per cent of Lima's population (Ponce, n.d.: 60). The Departments which contributed most migrants to Lima were mainly highland ones, the three major sources being Ancash, Ayacucho and Junín, in that order. In recent years migration to Lima has increasingly been drawn from more distant Departments such as Puno, Arequipa and Piura. The uneven pattern of recent economic development is shown by the fact that only five of Peru's twenty-two Departments apart from Lima-Callao showed a net gain from migration. Two of these were Amazonas and Madre de Dios, tropical lowland areas where colonization was taking place. Two others, Tacna and Moquequa, are located in the extreme south of the country and have become important in recent mining ventures. The remaining Department to gain from migration, Lambayeque, is a centre of sugar production. All five Departments, however, showed quite small net gains (Gonzales, 1982: 158).

Junín, the major Department of the central highlands, was one of the first to contribute migrants to Lima and, in 1972, some 116,000 residents of Lima-Callao had been born in Junín. Junín has also been a major focus of in-migration so that, in 1972, 112,000 residents of Junín had been born elsewhere in Peru, mainly in the neighbouring highland Department of Huancavelica and the Department of Lima itself (ONEC, 1974: Vol. 1, Table 5).

The political context of Peruvian development

The dominance of exports in Peruvian economic growth has had significant implications for national politics. Until the 1960s, the Peruvian political system was effectively controlled by national and foreign interests involved in export production and linked services (Bourricaud, 1970: 38–57). Thorp and Bertram (1978: 323) argue that export-led growth necessarily led to the political dominance of a coalition of local and foreign capitalists, 'eager to sustain the boom as long as possible without interference'. Indeed, a character-istic of Peruvian political development from at least the Independence period has been the slow development of the functions of the state and of its capacity to regulate the economy and society. Neither local nor foreign capitalists had particular need to pressure government into providing an economic and social infrastructure throughout the country; nor, for most periods, did these interests depend on the state for the maintenance of law and order. The owners and managers of the export enterprises, which were often located in relatively unpopulated areas, found it easier to provide their own infrastructure and develop their own forms of control over labour.[6] They certainly had little interest in paying taxes for improved government services.

In the absence of a strong fiscal base and of interests demanding a more effective administration and infrastructure, Peru's government remained highly decentralized until the 1960s. Provincial councils were left very much to their own devices for the collection of taxes and the funding of development projects. The main source of revenue for national government was taxation on imports and exports and on certain consumer items, such as tobacco, sugar, alcohol and matches. Public spending, including that of the Belaunde government of the 1960s, was constrained by the reluctance of political parties to commit themselves to policies involving an increase in direct taxation. Much public expenditure was, in any event, concentrated in Lima and in the expansion of the government payroll (Thorp and Bertram, 1978: 4–5, 115, 290).

The major challenge to the dominance of export capital in Peruvian politics came initially through the formation of APRA (Alianza Popular Revolucionaria Americana). This party originated in the 1920s and early 1930s on the initiative of Victor Raul Haya de la Torre, a lawyer and student leader from Trujillo (Hilliker, 1971: 15–18). APRA drew its early support from amongst the workers on the sugar plantations and the residents of the local towns of the northern coast whose farms or service enterprises had been adversely affected by the monopolization of land, trade and services by large-scale sugar companies (Klaren, 1973: 123–31). APRA rapidly extended its base both socially and territorially to include the mining centres and factory workers and employees, mainly in the textile industry, in Lima and provincial towns. APRA also gained support, as we shall see, among the small traders and commercially-oriented, small-scale farmers of the central highlands. Yet, APRA never gained effective political control in Peru. In 1962, when its candidate, Haya de la Torre, finally won the presidential election by a narrow majority, the military intervened to veto the election. However, APRA retained considerable political influence by the size of its parliamentary representation and through its control over Peru's major trade unions. In the late 1950s, for example, it allied with a member of the oligarchy, Manuel Prado, in support of his presidential campaign in return for concessions over social and labour legislation.

By the 1960s, Peruvian politics were characterized by stalemate and a general malaise. The exporting groups had begun to lose both self-confidence and popular support. Their traditional means of retaining control – a combination of government patronage and repression – became increasingly inadequate in the face of industrialization, mass urban migration and the faltering of the export economy. On the other hand, APRA was unable to maximize on this situation. Its fundamental weakness, apart from the hostility of the military, was its lack of solid support from the peasant population. APRA's revolutionary programme did not envisage, for example, far-reaching agrarian reform (Hilliker, 1971: 154–6). The party became identified with the small- and medium-scale entrepreneurs of rural and urban society. It was committed to the Peruvianization of the economy but less committed to structural reform.

The last president before the military government of 1968 was Fernando Belaunde who was to be re-elected president in 1980 following the ending of military rule. In 1963, Belaunde, the leader of the recently formed Acción Popular party, drew his support from a wide range of social groups: highland peasants seeking agrarian reform; urban professionals and white-collar workers; the self-employed urban workers, who were often recent migrants; and the industrialist class who, as Wils (1979, 174–9, 233) shows, saw themselves, on the whole, as a 'modernizing' entrepreneurial class. Belaunde implemented a series of reforms. He took under direct government control the collection of taxes, which previously had been farmed out to private companies. He also initiated agrarian reform and the nationalization of the International Petroleum Company. Although he increased public spending, he also relied on self-help programmes to develop the provincial areas. An important example of this approach was the Cooperación Popular programme which was promoted in villages and small towns to encourage local inhabitants to provide labour and some materials for the construction of public services, such as schools, clinics and a water supply. Belaunde also made it his policy to extend communications to the remoter areas, including a road linking the Amazonian provinces with the rest of the country.

The Belaunde government of 1963–8 failed both politically and economically. The weakness of the export economy meant that resources were inadequate to finance the reform programmes and this, inevitably, made Peru more dependent on foreign capital. Belaunde thus vacillated on the question of agrarian reform and the nationalization of oil. These factors, and the increasing signs of popular disturbances in both rural and urban areas, were the ostensible reasons for the military intervention of 1968. As many commentators have argued, the basic problem was that no class in Peru was strongly enough organized at this time to impose its will politically. At the same time, the economic difficulties meant less opportunities for work in the expanding cities, while peasant farmers found it more difficult to extract a living from diminishing land resources.

The military government was to remain in power until 1980. The early period of military government, up to 1975, was the most radical, when, after the nationalization of oil, extensive reforms were implemented, such as the agrarian reform of 1969, the nationalization of copper production, the creation of industrial communities (a limited form of workers' control) and the introduction of a social property sector from which private capital and individual profit were excluded.

Various interpretations of the underlying rationale of the military's early reforms exist which vary in the degree to which these reforms are seen to be independent of class pressures (Fitzgerald, 1976; Cotler, 1975; Quijano, 1971; Ferner, 1977; Slater, 1979). From 1975, however, a marked policy shift occurred. The reform programme was slowed down. Co-operation with foreign capital was increased and incentives were given to encourage small- and medium-scale capitalist enterprise in agriculture. The burden of foreign debt had become considerable by this date and, in the absence of fiscal reform, the government adjusted the economy by wage reductions and relied once again on improving primary exports (Fitzgerald, 1981: 9–10).

A striking feature of the history of recent government policy in Peru is the relative absence of explicitly formulated regional development programmes. Prior to the military government, there had been some isolated attempts to stimulate industry in provincial centres such as Arequipa. With the Velasco government of 1968, regional planning was given more emphasis. Thus, industrial parks were implemented for Trujillo and Arequipa and it was proposed to shift the priorities in state investment and credit for industry, agriculture and infrastructure to the regions (Cabieses et al., n.d.: 105–39). The outcome of these policies was, however, not impressive, generating few economic linkages within the regions. Thus, between 1971 and 1974, the bulk of public investment in the tropical lowlands and in the south of the country was in oil exploration and capital-intensive mining (Slater, 1979). In the central highlands, 70 per cent of investment was in energy – to develop the generators that supplied Lima with power. There was more diversification in the north where 25 per cent of the total investment was in agriculture, but 85 per cent of this was destined for the capital-intensive agricultural sector of the coast; much of the rest of this regional investment was made in the development of the iron and steel complex in Chimbote (Wilson, 1975). Gonzales (1982: 208–11) provides statistics on government regional investment between 1968–80 which show that, although it was not as concentrated as is sometimes thought, the coastal Departments received the bulk of public investment.

Regions in which peasant farming has predominated, such as the central highlands, have received little direct benefit from government investment programmes. Land reform did little to promote the productivity of the peasant farmer or, for that matter, to make more resources available to him (Caballero, 1981). Indeed, government policies have tended to have negative effects on the development of the peasant highland zones. Policies of subsidizing the imports of basic foodstuffs and controlling the prices of internally produced crops have reinforced the already unfavourable terms of trade for the peasant farmer. Figueroa (1980) estimates that between 1973 and 1975 peasants lost about 50 per cent of the total income transferred by the entire programme of agrarian reform through government pricing policies.

The basic point is that the export-dependent growth of Peru has created economic commitments that hinder balanced regional development. Hence, governments have been unable to redistribute national income through policies aimed at improving conditions for peasant farming and at industrializing the interior. The central highlands is a case in point. Over time, there has been no government intervention to halt the decline of its industries. The major infrastructural project of the region is the hydro-electric project on the Mantaro river. This massive generating complex was initiated by the Cerro de Pasco Corporation primarily to ensure power for its mining complexes (Peruvian Yearbook, 1956/7). Subsequently, the project was taken over by the state ostensibly to provide power for stimulating industrialization in the central highlands. This last objective, however, was not realized and the main outcome of the project has been to provide power to Lima-Callao.

The central highlands

Throughout this book we use the term 'central highlands' flexibly to include the Departments of Junín, Pasco and parts of Huancavelica. This area is situated about 300 kilometres due east of Lima with a good road and rail connection to the capital (see Map 1). Most of our own data are drawn from a more limited area, however: primarily, the Mantaro valley, its adjacent highland zones and the refinery town of La Oroya. Huancayo, Peru's eighth largest city in 1972, is located in the Mantaro valley and is the capital of Junín. In 1980, its population was estimated to be almost 200,000 and its rate of growth in the last twenty years has in fact been higher than that of Lima (*Plan Operativo*, 1980). The city of Huancayo has drawn its population mainly from the Departments of Junín, Huancavelica, Pasco and Lima and is the commercial and administrative centre of the central highlands.

In 1980, the Department of Junín had a population of approximately 860,000 inhabitants. The rate of population growth in recent years has been estimated at 2.7 per cent which, while somewhat below the natural rate of increase for the Peruvian population as a whole, still makes it the highland Department with the greatest capacity to retain its population. This population growth, however, has been unequal. The major growth areas have been the tropical lowlands of Satipo and Chanchamayo where agricultural colonization

Map 1   Peru: Location of research

DEPARTMENTS:
1 Tumbes
2 Piura
3 Lambayeque
4 Amazonas
5 San Martin
6 Cajamarca
7 La Libertad
8 Loreto
9 Ancash
10 Huánuco
11 Pasco
12 Junín
13 Lima
14 Huancavelica
15 Ica
16 Ayacucho
17 Abancay
18 Cuzco
19 Madre de Dios
20 Puno
21 Arequipa
22 Moquequa
23 Tacna

has been proceeding apace. The larger towns and villages of the Mantaro valley have also shown above average growth, while the villages in the *puna* (high altitude zone) have shown negligible growth or even a loss of population.

Apart from mining, the major economic activity of the Department of Junín is agriculture. In 1970, Junín was the fourth Department in terms of the level of agricultural production, accounting for 7.6 per cent of national production and following the coastal Departments of Lima, Piura and La Libertad (Gonzales, 1982: 263). In 1976, cultivation was concentrated in the four traditional crops of the region (wheat, barley, maize and potatoes). Industrial crops, particularly coffee, had become important in the tropical lowlands. The traditional crops accounted for 55 per cent of the value of production. Vegetables accounted for 15 per cent, fruit, 13 per cent and coffee, 11 per cent (*Indicadores estadísticos*, 1981: Table 10). This production is a significant part of the national total. Potatoes from Junín, for example, constituted, in 1973, 19 per cent of Peru's total production, barley, 18 per cent and coffee, 28 per cent (Sanchez, 1979: Table 11). Livestock production is also important with about 200,000 sheep and approximately 35,000 cattle, which together represent about 3.4 per cent of national production.

The structure of landholding in the region is predominantly family-controlled smallholdings, in both the valley region and the *puna* communities, supplemented by communal land, mostly pasture; while large landholdings (ex-haciendas) dominate the highland zone (Long and Roberts, 1978: 10–11). This structure is similar to that which Caballero (1981: 96–109) delineates for the Peruvian highlands as a whole: 76 per cent of agricultural holdings are below five hectares and these take up 42 per cent of rain-fed cultivated land and 50 per cent of irrigated land. Holdings of less than fifty hectares constitute about 86 per cent of cultivated land. The same predominance of the small-holding is found in livestock production. Thus units of less than five hectares control 58 per cent of cattle and 53 per cent of sheep.

This pattern of landholding contradicts the stereotype of the highlands being dominated by large landholdings with a dependent peasant populace. In Junín, as we shall see, the large landholdings were never the most important units of production for arable farming. However large estates did develop in the *puna* highlands and, before the 1969 agrarian reform, probably accounted for the majority of pasture land in Junín. As Caballero's figures on livestock (given above) suggest, possession of land did not necessarily mean that the large estate owners controlled the livestock. The estates were dependent on nearby peasant communities for labour and peasants often grazed their own sheep on hacienda pasture (Long and Roberts, 1978: 12–13). The large livestock estates in Junín, as elsewhere in the highlands, were transformed by the agrarian reform into government-controlled co-operatives, SAIS (Sociedades Agrarias de Interés Social).

One important limitation on agricultural production in Junín is the relatively poor quality of soil and the climatic uncertainties. Only 2.8 per cent of Junín's land is suitable for intensive cultivation compared with the national average of 8.6 per cent. In the Department of Arequipa, Peru's major provincial centre and an important dairy farming zone, 10.4 per cent is suitable for intensive cultivation. In Junín, an additional 18.6 per cent of land surface is suitable for less intensive cultivation and a further 31.5 per cent for pasture. Nearly half of Junín's land surface (47.1 per cent) is inappropriate for farming, as compared with 37.9 per cent nationally (*Plan de Desarrollo*, 1967).

Most of the best land is found in the temperate valley zones, particularly that of the Mantaro valley. It is here that traditional food production is concentrated. The region lies twelve degrees south of the equator and the most densely inhabited parts lie between 3,000 and 4,000 metres above sea level. Consequently, there are only slight seasonal differences in temperature. In the central highlands, winter temperatures (October to April) range from 1°C to 21°C while in summer (May to September) the range is from 6°C to 23°C (average 8°C to 11°C). Almost all the rain (about thirty inches per annum is the average for the central valley zone) falls in winter, particularly in January, February and March. July, August and September are months of very low rainfall when maximum demands are placed on irrigation supplies. They are also months when the phenomenon of temperature inversion can cause sudden local frosts and considerable damage to crops. For example, in 1972 almost the entire maize crop was destroyed by frost. These climatic uncertainties, together with market fluctuations, mean that there is considerable uncertainty in agricultural production, and crop yields vary in any given year in different parts of the region.

Soil conditions in the valley vary greatly within short distances, due primarily to the effects of glaciation. Most of the agriculture is carried out on three sets of natural river terraces located between one and two hundred metres above the river bed.[7] Soils on these terraces range from coarse gravels to rich loams. Land close to the river is badly drained and subject to flooding in winter; the soil on the steep slopes of the valley sides tends to be thin and infertile. The most productive agricultural land is that which is irrigated by the two major canals, one on each side of the valley. The longest one (sixty-four kilometres in length), which runs down the eastern margin of the valley, was completed in 1942 and now irrigates 4,200 hectares.

Manufacturing industry, excluding the refinery at La Oroya, is a much less significant part of the region's economy than agriculture. Even if refinery production is included, industry's contribution to the regional product of Junín

Table 1 *Economic activity by sector and value of production: Junín, 1976*

Sector of activity	Percentage of economically active population[a]	Percentage value of production
Agriculture and fishing	48.5	22.4
Mining	2.7	15.7
Manufacturing[b]	10.7	27.3
Electricity	0.2	2.1
Construction	4.0	4.8
Commerce	11.4	7.2
Transport	5.3	4.7
Financial establishments	0.9	8.3
Services	16.3	7.5
Total	100.0	100.0

[a] Proportions of economically active population are estimated for 1976 on the basis of the 1972 census.
[b] This includes the large industrial refinery at La Oroya, classed as a basic metal industry and accounting for probably three-quarters of the value of manufacturing production but only one-quarter of employment in this sector.
Source: Indicadores estadísticos, Instituto de Planificación, Junín, 1981.

in the 1970s was approximately 27 per cent (Table 1). This compared with 12 per cent for commerce and transport and about 15 per cent for government and personal services. We will see later that most industry and private commerce is very small scale.

The Department is well connected to the coast by rail and asphalted road from Huancayo to Lima (see Map 2). However, although the network is extensive, linking many of the peasant communities by dirt road or track to the main communication routes, only 5 per cent of the roads in the Department are surfaced. Buses and taxis are the major means of transport within the region and between Huancayo, the mines and Lima-Callao. Nevertheless the railway, completed to Huancayo in 1908, transports a considerable tonnage of minerals and other primary products to Lima-Callao and also carries over 300,000 passengers each year (that is, about 1,000 each day). The heaviest passenger rail traffic in 1976, however, was between Huancayo and Huancavelica with almost 2,000 people travelling each day. The railway extension to Huancavelica was completed in 1926.

The organization of this volume

This book is the outcome of a joint British/Peruvian research project. Even those chapters not written by ourselves are based on data gathered within the

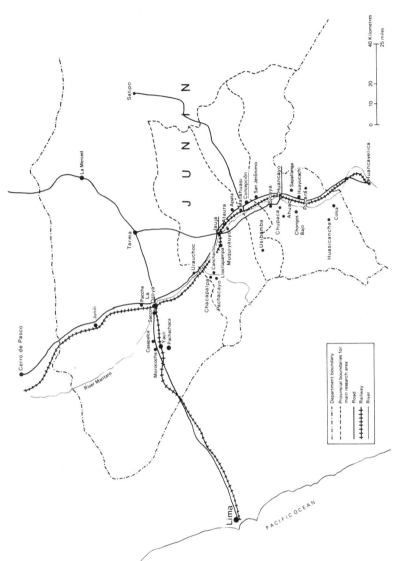

Map 2 Central highlands region: Department of Junín

21

framework of the project. In the processing and writing up of the materials, we have tried to develop a similar analytic perspective. The various chapters aim to cover the key changes in the social organization and interrelationships of village, mine and city to illustrate the workings of the regional system. In the final chapter and conclusion, we will return to the issue of regional development and to an understanding of the patterns that are to be found in Peru and elsewhere in Latin America.

Chapter two provides a general historical account of the evolution of the central highlands from colonial times until the beginning of the twentieth century. We focus in the third chapter on the mining economy as it expanded as a result of the investments by the American-owned Cerro de Pasco Corporation. We analyse economic statistics on mining, agriculture and industry between approximately 1920 and 1960, exploring the specific ways in which a dominant system of production shaped the region's institutions. We examine the way in which forces set in motion in one period influence the evolving regional system of another. Although our focus is on the complementary relationships of the mining economy and village institutions, we show that these relationships alter over time and are not to be understood as a static system.

In the following three chapters, we provide an account of the changing class relations and patterns of class conflict that have transformed the regional system. Chapter four looks at the characteristics of the regional elite, resident in Huancayo, during the period 1920–60 when the modern mining economy was at its apogee. The aim is to show, as Cardoso and Faletto (1979) have suggested, that the locally dominant classes are weakly organized when the major production resources are externally controlled. We look, however, at the implications of this situation for the organization and strategies of other classes in the area, particularly the richer peasant farmers, small-scale traders and industrial workers. Chapters five and six examine social differentiation among contrasting village populations. The crucial distinction is between the highland pastoral villages and the agricultural villages of the valley floor. These latter have a long history of independence from the haciendas and of market-oriented agricultural production. In the modern period, both types of villages have become heavily involved in labour migration to the mines and, to some extent, to the coastal plantations.

As Laite shows, in the valley villages where land is short the village becomes mainly a service centre and a subsistence base for the mining economy. Internal differentiation is not marked. Where land is more abundant, however, internal differentiation based on commerce, small business and farms of different sizes is apparent. There is internal conflict over resources, and earnings from wage labour are reinvested in the village economy. In most valley villages the impact

of the mining economy has been to accentuate internal processes of differentiation and conflict. These conflicts have been important factors in blurring the
class structure of the area: hence, for example, many industrial workers also
belong to the richer peasant/small entrepreneurial class.

The situation is quite different in the pastoral *puna* highlands described by
Campaña and Rivera in chapter five. There, the impact of the mining economy
has been more devastating in that the farming base of some of these villages has
almost disappeared. On the surface, these highland villages provide the classic
case of a rural reserve providing cheap labour for the mining industry. The
villages furnished a basic subsistence for the families of mine workers. Their
continuing poverty ensured that successive generations would seek similar
work. Yet, even in these cases, there are significant differences between villages
and also evidence of economic diversification and growth.

From chapter seven onwards, we focus on the contemporary patterns of social
and economic organization in the central highlands as the influence of the
urban–industrial economy of Lima-Callao increases. From approximately the
1960s, the influence of the mining economy wanes relative to that of the coast.
Migration movements include less labour migration and more rural–urban
migration of a relatively permanent nature. Population from even the smallest
villages becomes involved in direct migration to Lima and, to a much lesser
extent, to Huancayo. Huancayo begins to attract greater proportions of its
migrants from the neighbouring and economically poorer Department of
Huancavelica. In chapter seven, we look at the urban economy that has
developed in Huancayo as a result of these changes. In the contemporary period,
small-scale enterprise, alongside government employment and welfare payments, has become the mainstay of the city's economy. This small-scale
enterprise connects the city to the villages of the region. In the main, the local
entrepreneurs are people who have gained experience and small amounts of
capital from work related to the mining economy.

We argue, then, that the previous system shapes the present situation
through social relationships and institutions which help to organize an efficient
regional network of small-scale enterprise. The city's economy has a vitality
that belies its apparently peripheral position with respect to the coastal region.
We extend this argument to the rural sector in chapter eight and study a case in
which a 'traditional' institution – a fiesta club – is an important element in
organizing entrepreneurship at both village and regional level. In this chapter,
we also examine the types of household economy that underpin small-scale
enterprise and even the substantial commercial farms that have developed in
recent years. Chapters seven and eight show the artificiality of the rural–urban
distinction for understanding contemporary social organization.

In chapters nine and ten, the persistence of a regional identity in the area is examined by looking at what happens to migrants in Lima. Altamirano compares regional associations from the Mantaro valley with those from a much less economically developed highland region – that of Andahuaylas. This comparison shows how the significance of regional associations differs, depending on the nature of the region of origin and when migration to Lima first commenced. The comparison also serves to highlight the special characteristics of the Mantaro valley, many of whose migrants have achieved a comfortable standard of living in Lima. Despite their 'success', however, these migrants retain a continuing interest in their villages of origin and have a strong feeling of regional identity.

In chapter ten, Smith examines the patterns of economic enterprise and rural–urban networks among migrants from one of the poorer of the region's villages – Huasicancha. Unlike the Matahuasi migrants who figure in chapter nine, these Huasicanchinos are less successful economically, living mainly in the slum tenements of Lima or in squatter settlements. Yet, amongst this group, too, village links and village-based institutions, such as the fiesta system, continue to be an important basis for managing the household economy.

The final chapter emphasizes that the central highlands should not be regarded as a unique case. Similar accounts of local enterprise and migration could be given for other regions in Peru or elsewhere in Latin America. The significance of a regional approach to these issues lies in uncovering the systematic relationships between the different economic sectors and social classes. This helps us to understand the rationality of what might otherwise appear to be discrete and unconnected patterns of social action. At another level, our aim is to understand how a peripheral region like the central highlands survives in the face of the centralizing tendencies of modern capitalist development.

2

The development of a regional economy in the central highlands

In this chapter, we outline the major social and economic processes that created a regional system in the central highlands. Our main interest will be to examine the linkages that developed between the mines and the agrarian sector during the colonial period and into the nineteenth century. An important part of this process was the strengthening of village institutions and the consolidation of small-scale economic enterprise in trade and agriculture. The expansion of local economic enterprise prior to the twentieth century and the class interests to which this gave rise show some important continuities with the effects of large-scale modern mining which we analyse in the next chapter.

The colonial economy of the central highlands

Almost from the beginning of Spanish colonial rule, mining shaped the social and economic organization of the central highlands. From the seventeenth century, the Cerro de Pasco area developed as an important producer of silver and by the late eighteenth century it was the major South American source, replacing Potosí (Fisher, n.d.: 21). In addition, the Santa Bárbara mine at Huancavelica, to the immediate south of the area, was the primary American source of mercury, which was essential to the amalgamation process of silver extraction. The central highlands and especially the Mantaro valley provided labour, fodder, foodstuffs and timber for these mining complexes.

The relationship between mining and agriculture in the Peruvian Andes developed differently from the system of production that Palerm (1976) describes for colonial Mexico. The Mexican system was essentially based on large-scale mining enterprises which were serviced by haciendas, often owned by the mine owners, which in turn depended on the skills, labour and land reserves of the Indian communities. In Peru, mining was based on relatively small-scale enterprises which were not so closely integrated with agrarian or

25

merchant capital as was the case in Mexico (see Brading and Cross, 1972: 566–8). Thus, at the end of the eighteenth century, the average number of Peruvian mine workers per productive unit was 13.3, while in Mexico the industry was dominated by ten large enterprises, each with about 1,000 workers and fixed investments of one million pesos (Fisher, n.d.: 16–17). Unlike the situation in Mexico, mine owners in Peru were generally regarded as the social inferiors of merchants and landowners (Fisher, n.d.: 17).

A further factor differentiating the situation in the central highlands from that of Mexican mining regions such as Zacatecas and Guanajuato was the relatively dense settlement of the indigenous population close to the mining centres. In Mexico, the mines were worked from the beginning by migrant wage labourers who settled in the mining towns. The need to provide this population with foodstuffs, clothing and other necessities became the basis for large-scale agricultural, industrial and trading enterprises (Brading, 1971; Wolf, 1957). However, in Peru the proximity of the Mantaro valley to the mines of Huancavelica and of Cerro de Pasco made possible a mining economy based on more temporary migration patterns in which mine workers returned to their villages seasonally or after a period of years. These workers could be fed and clothed from village production and, consequently, their consumption needs were not such as to stimulate the rise of large-scale enterprises to service them.[1]

The system of production that developed around mining in the colonial period in Peru was therefore less centralized than Mexico. Nevertheless, the impact of mining on the central highlands was, we argue, the decisive factor in the development of its colonial social and economic organization. This impact can be seen most clearly in the agrarian structure since it led, directly and indirectly, both to the protection of indigenous institutions and to the growth of individualized, small-scale farming. In this situation, village and town jurisdictions, as well as the *puna* hacienda, became, by the end of the eighteenth century, the key components in regulating the area's economy and distributing its resources.[2]

The colonial organization of the area was consolidated at the end of the sixteenth century when the viceroy Toledo instituted a set of measures designed to boost mining production (Samaniego, 1980b). One of these was the reorganization of the *mita*, which forced a proportion of all adult males to work for a period, such as four months, in the major mines of Potosí (Bolivia) and Huancavelica (Wachtel, 1977: 101–22). To facilitate the administration of the *mita* and the collection of taxes, the population was concentrated into *reducciones*. The policy of *reducciones* encouraged the nucleating of settlements, with the identities of the scattered population often being retained by *barrios* (administrative sub-divisions) within the new villages. A typical pattern was a central settlement and several smaller ones nearby that were administratively subordinate to the central one. The central settlement became, in effect, the seat of power in its district with the right to use all the resources of the district, whereas the subordinate settlements had more restricted rights.

It was in the central nucleus that the Spanish and the local *curaca* (indigenous elite) families settled. The *curacas* became the authorities of the reorganized jurisdictions. In the central highlands, this policy created the village organiz-ation that, with modifications in jurisdictions, has persisted to the present day (Samaniego, 1980b). Each village was assigned an area of land by the crown, which was liable to tax and *mita* service, to maintain its population. This population (*los indios tributarios*) administered its resources through its own officers who allocated land to each family, oversaw communal work projects and ran the village institutions. It is clear from several of our village archival sources that the agricultural land allocated to families was passed on from generation to generation, although this land was, in theory, communal property.

Two other forms of land tenure acquired significance in the colonial period. The maintenance of the Catholic church and its ritual was assured by land grants from the crown and from individual endowments. These church lands came to be administered by religious brotherhoods (*cofradías*) who also accumulated properties by purchase and, at times, rented out the lands to individual farmers in return for a fixed income (Celestino and Meyers, 1981). Also, from the first days of the Conquest, Spanish immigrants settled in certain villages of the Mantaro valley and were granted land by the crown. Likewise, certain members of the pre-Conquest indigenous elite were given private possessions of large tracts of land in return for their co-operation with the Spanish authorities.

These different forms of land tenure coexisted within the same village jurisdictions and, indeed, boundaries of the different types of land were frequently ill-defined. Apart from being a frequent source of litigation, the intermixing of these different forms of landholding permitted the development of varied and flexible strategies of land utilization, involving, for example, the renting or share-cropping of both communal and private land.

This pattern of village organization developed partly in response to the extensive trading networks connecting the mines, the colonial entrepot, Lima, and the northern and southern highlands. This trade, along with most of the mining enterprise, was financed by relatively small-scale middlemen (*aviadores*) (Fisher, n.d.; Gongora, 1975: 163–4). Acquiring their capital from Lima-based merchants, these *aviadores* offered small, short-term loans to the mine owners and supplied, on credit, tools and other manufactures. The *aviadores* were based in the provinces and served as links not only with Lima, but also with village-based agricultural and craft producers. They also helped to organize the extensive mule trains that serviced the mining economy and connected the central highlands with the southern highlands and the coast.

The shipment of mercury from Huancavelica to Cerro de Pasco was essential to silver production and the Mantaro valley was the corridor that connected the two points. The rearing of mules, production of fodder for the animals and employment as muleteers provided important economic opportunities for the peasant villages along the route. Although there were fluctuations in the mining economy, and therefore in the demand for labour and inputs, it is likely that, like Potosí, this pattern of commercialization survived mining recessions, often generating alternative sources of livelihood in other sectors of the economy.[3]

In the central highlands, and especially in the valley zone, the mine-based colonial economy was conducive to the emergence of a system of medium and small-scale commercial farming, together with trade and craft production based on a differentiated peasantry. The lack of development of agricultural haciendas in the Mantaro valley is probably best explained by the fact that the requirements of mining operations took precedence over estate-based agricultural production. Thus, it was in the interests of the colonial state to protect the subsistence base of temporary migrant labour and to guarantee the survival of communal lands and a certain autonomy for village institutions. There was differentiation within villages, based on ethnic status criteria and on landholdings of different size. However, the relatively low returns on large-scale foodstuff production for the domestic market, when compared to the commercial possibilities in trade and transport, did not encourage the consolidation of landholdings. Thus, in comparison with areas that were less closely linked to the mining economy, the valley areas of the central highlands showed relatively little development of agricultural estates based on a system of share-cropping or servile labour. Alternative wage labour opportunities outside the villages made such systems of labour exploitation relatively non-viable.

One consequence of this economic situation was what appears to have been a relatively early process of *mestizaje* (becoming assimilated to *mestizo* culture) in the valley villages. For example, by the late eighteenth century, the village of Sicaya, though listed as a *pueblo de indios*, had a population containing numerous *mestizos* (Escobar, 1973: 35–7). The significance of these changes in ethnic identity is illustrated by a set of documents concerning land conflicts in Sicaya that occurred between 1788 and 1811 (Archivo municipal de Sicaya). These documents consist of the petitions of the Sicaya authorities to the provincial governor in Jauja, a counter petition of a land claimant to Lima and the official response of the governor.

The dispute appears to have begun with a member of the Sicaya community

(Manuel Aliaga), classed as an *indio tributario*, who fled from his lands as a result of murder charges against himself and his family. The lands were then taken over by a resident of the neighbouring village of Chupaca, which had superior administrative jurisdiction. This man is described in the various documents alternatively as an 'indio vecino de Chupaca', as 'el mestizo Manuel Aliaga, vecino de Chupaca', as 'cholo libre del pueblo de Chupaca', and, finally, as 'este cholo Aliaga'. The first description ('indio vecino') appears in Aliaga's appeal to the Real Audiencia at Lima. The other terms are used by the authorities of Sicaya.

Aliaga attempted to present himself as an *indio* with consequent rights to land belonging to a *común de indios*. The Sicaya authorities based their case on the claim that Aliaga was violating the rights of the *común de indios*. They claimed that after seizing the land he had rented it to others, including *mestizos* (i.e. a category that cannot claim rights to land belonging to the *común de indios*). They pointed out that, as a consequence, the 'poor indians of Sicaya are deprived of sustenance'. This problem, they said, was grave because 'today more than ever we need land'. The reason for this, they argued, was that improvements in health care, especially vaccination, had increased population. They stressed that the acts of these *mestizo* outsiders were harming the interests of the tribute-paying population.

To add to their troubles, the Sicaya authorities had to defend the disputed border lands against the Chupaca authorities. An official boundary commission was set up and in the official report it was made clear that neither village had clear documents and that the final decision was based on the consent of the two parties. The Sicaya authorities insisted that the decisions, which were in their favour, would not affect those lands which they customarily rented to people in Chupaca. However, the Chupaca tax collector proceeded to allocate some of the lands in dispute to *indios tributarios* who had no lands, whom the Sicaya authorities then opposed, claiming that they were *mestizos* and *indios* of Chupaca.

The dispute became more complex because the wife of the man who originally fled his lands decided to claim them back. The Sicaya authorities vigorously denied the claim on a variety of grounds: that, as the widow of a deceased *indio tributario*, she had rights to only a small plot; that, as the mother of an absent *indio tributario*, she had no rights; that anyway she was not born in Sicaya and nobody knew to which town she did belong. They ended with a statement 'if they [she and her sons] are not from Sicaya, but from another town, or if they are *mestizos* and consequently do not pay tribute, then let them go to the *montaña* [tropical lowlands] where unoccupied lands can be obtained'.

The rights and wrongs of the claims and counter-claims are not our concern.

The case, however, highlights the important, but ambiguous, status of communal institutions by the end of the colonial period. As this case shows, communal institutions continued to flourish until the end of the colonial period, being used as the basis for claims to rights to land by all the parties to the conflict. In the petitions, the ethnic status of *indio* is used positively to justify claims to land, while the term *mestizo* or *cholo* is used negatively to exclude people from land. The significance of such claims is indicated by the fact that all the resolutions of the provincial governor favoured the communal rights.

The emphasis on communal institutions masked considerable social differentiation within the villages, based on individualized commercial production. Aliaga, we learn from one document, was away trading flour that had been processed locally. His allies in Chupaca were among the largest landowners of the southern part of the valley. Renting out land was clearly a common practice, even when it was communal land. The Sicaya authorities were themselves relatively prosperous peasant farmers and the inhabitants of Sicaya were by the end of the eighteenth century, predominantly classed in parish documents as *mestizo*. Chupaca was, at this time, the administrative centre of the southern end of the Mantaro valley. Its authorities were landowners and traders who used their position to further the economic dominance of Chupaca. Sicaya was a relatively prosperous agriculturally-based village and sensitive to the pretensions of its powerful neighbour.

Celestino and Meyers (1981) show, on the one hand, how communal institutions, especially the *cofradía*, served to reinforce processes of economic differentiation at village level. The *cofradías* allowed, for example, village elites to develop economic enterprises based on the renting out of *cofradía* land and on marketing the agricultural products. On the other hand, these communal institutions functioned to protect village lands from the incursions of larger landowners and other village units, particularly as in the *puna* region *cofradía* land was often located on the borders between village and hacienda territories.

The proximity of the mines made such counterbalancing tendencies more evident in the valley areas of the central highlands than in other zones. The crown had an interest in protecting one of its major tax bases, the Indian community, and, although the labour *mita* was rarely used, it had been replaced by the communities paying tribute money to subsidize the mining operations. At the same time, the opportunities provided by the mining economy reinforced the process of economic and social differentiation within the villages of the area.

This late colonial period was in fact a boom period for the Cerro de Pasco mines which stimulated economic activity throughout the central highlands

(Fisher, 1970: 137–8). Fisher (n.d.) charts the fluctuations in the mining economy at the end of the eighteenth century and concludes that mining recovered in production and value after the decline of the earlier part of the century. In the 1791 official statistics of the mining sector, the mines of the central highlands (the Tarma Intendencia) are listed as employing 3,926 mineworkers out of a total of 8,875 mineworkers in the whole of Peru. In addition, the mines employed large numbers of seasonal workers (Fisher, n.d.: 18–19).

Wilson (1978) reports social and political tensions in the Tarma district of Junín during this period. There, the Spanish intendant was viewed by the local elite as too protective of Indian institutions. This elite was engaged in multiple enterprises in agriculture, mining and trade; but, in order to take advantage of the expanding economic opportunities at the end of the eighteenth century, the members of the elite needed to control communal land and contract labour. This led to a series of confrontations between the Spanish colonial administration and local economic interests.

The system of production that developed around the mining economy was thus full of contradictions and open tensions. Communal institutions had developed under crown protection, although they also permitted a degree of internal social and economic differentiation. The small-scale nature of mining production and the scatter of its operations opened up a wide range of opportunities in trade and agriculture which were often most viable for small-scale entrepreneurs. Such entrepreneurs, as well as the large landowners and merchants, depended on access to labour and other resources which were controlled by communal institutions. Despite these centrifugal tendencies, the social and economic structure of the region remained hierarchical and ethnically differentiated during the colonial period. The importance of mining meant that the crown intervened to maintain existing jurisdictions and, ultimately, to support the political and economic power of both the Spanish and native landowning classes.

The nineteenth century: the decline of the mining economy

When independence from Spain was achieved in 1821, the Department of Junín, comprising the provinces of Huancayo, Jauja, Pasco and Tarma, already exhibited a monetized and economically differentiated economy. Following Independence, the mining sector (mainly located in Pasco) lost its former economic importance. Some of the factors in the decline were long-standing, such as the inadequacy of the technology, especially concerning drainage, to deal with increasingly complex mining operations. The Napoleonic wars also disrupted communications and the demand for silver. In addition, the wars of independence and the subsequent civil strife destroyed much of the mining infrastructure, including essential pumping machinery. Labour and capital flows and trade routes were also interrupted in this period. The combined effect of these factors was to close down many mines and substantially reduce the output in others. It was small-scale mining operations, often conducted by village entrepreneurs, that characterized much nineteenth century mining. DeWind (1977: 99–101), for example, describes the *busconeros* (scavengers) who reworked the old mines of the Cobriza region. These were peasants who worked long hours mining small quantities of ore in order to obtain some cash income.

Independence soon brought a weakening of centralized state control. The civil wars of the nineteenth century – the struggles of the *caudillos militares* – meant the decentralization of political control. The provinces of Jauja and Huancayo were an arena for these conflicts since the Mantaro valley was the largest inter-Andean valley close to Lima. It served as a key strategic point for the contending parties and played a crucial part in all the military campaigns of the nineteenth century (Arguedas, 1957: 19). Huancayo's location on the major routes out of the southern end of the valley was to make it an important base for military operations and was a major factor in its rise to prominence. In 1854, Huancayo was one of the focal points of Ramon Castilla's campaign against Echenique and it was there that Castilla published the decree abolishing slavery in Peru (Tello Devotto, 1971: 32–5). Elsewhere in the area, towns such as Tarma and Jauja became the seats of rival political groups who maintained a considerable independence from central government control. In 1873, there was a formal decentralization of Peruvian government which gave greater powers to local municipal administration. Our own research in the archives of the Huancayo municipality and Wilson's (1978) research in those of Tarma indicate that, until the early twentieth century, local affairs were conducted without much reference to the government in Lima and without significant intervention by that government in local affairs.

The decentralization of political control was accompanied by the liberalization of land tenure arrangements. The protection given to communal land-holdings was substantially reduced by the Bolivar decrees, which permitted the redistribution and sale of such lands, and this opened the way for a free land market. The situation, then, was one which tended to further the economic interests of locally-based village and town elites. They were no longer restrained by a central government interested in maintaining communal institutions. Our own research, that of Wilson (1978) for Tarma and that of Alberti and Sanchez (1974: 33–41) for Jauja indicate that it was the larger landowners and merchants who controlled local political office since, in the absence of opportunities in the mining sector, control over agricultural resources became more crucial.

There were, however, important limits to the domination of the central highlands by a class of larger landowners. Until the end of the nineteenth century, the crops produced in the area were predominantly for the internal market. Climate and poor soils combined to make production levels unpredictable. Also, the freeing of restrictions on land transfers at the beginning of the Independence period contributed as much to differentiation within the villages as it did to furthering the consolidation of large landholdings.

A further factor in shaping the pattern of development was the increase in population during this period. The Sicaya document, which mentions demographic growth at the end of the eighteenth century, reflects a general increase in population in Peru, which was growing at a rate of 1 per cent by the end of the eighteenth century. There was a slight decline in that growth rate in the first three decades of the nineteenth century, but thereafter growth accelerated (Chavarría, 1978: 43). By 1750, the population of the provinces of Jauja and Huancayo was approximately 30,000 (Adams, 1959: 12). It had reached 119,714 by 1876, out of the total for the Department of 209,871 (Espinoza, 1973), and by 1900 it was 200,000 (Adams, 1959: 12). Samaniego (1974) provides figures for villages and districts at the southern end of the Mantaro valley that show a similar increase. Thus, in 1778, Chupaca had a total of 3,082 inhabitants, while in the national census of 1876 the population occupying the same territory was 12,157. As both Adams and Samaniego emphasize, this population increase meant, for the first time, that there was serious pressure on available land resources, especially in the arable zones.

The nineteenth century in the Mantaro area can therefore be characterized as a period dominated by struggles over the control of local productive resources – mainly land. These struggles acquired a variety of forms. Some were between landowners eager to expand their domains at the expense of village communities. Others related to conflicts that occurred between households within the same village: for example, richer villagers used their control of political office to exploit the lands and labour of their poorer co-residents. Yet other conflicts took place between villages as, for example, a politically dominant village attempted to intensify its control over the labour and land resources of subordinate ones.

These processes varied between ecological zones. The major commercial resource of the region in the nineteenth century was wool, the demand for which had been stimulated by the Industrial Revolution in Europe. In his report on the economic situation in the Mantaro area of 1874, Norberto Padilla cites several examples of 'progressive' haciendas, such as Laive, using important thoroughbred stock (Tello Devotto, 1971). In the high *puna* zone of the central highlands, livestock haciendas were consolidated during the nineteenth century, often at the expense of contiguous village communities. By 1872, Sicaya had lost a substantial part of its *puna* pastures to the neighbouring hacienda Laive, which was owned by landowners based in Concepción and Huancayo. In 1811, these pastures (the hacienda Cacchi) had been registered as belonging to Sicaya to provide for the welfare of the *común de indios* and of the church. There is a detailed account, in that year, of the stock (some 7,000 animals) and boundaries of the property as part of a rental contract with a Huancayo-based landowner. Sicaya was able to use this 1811 document to contest Laive's control of the pastures.

Wilson (1978) provides data on similar processes of estate consolidation in the Tarma *puna* and in the hot lowland zones. The Tarma elite, who dominated the provincial council, used their administrative control over Tarma's extensive and well-populated *barrios* to obtain labour services which, at times, were channelled to benefit their own estates. In Jauja, a group of landed families mainly owning estates in the adjoining Yanamarca valley, expanded their estates at the expense of communal lands (Hutchinson, 1973: 20–21; Tullis, 1970). These families exercised close control over the economic activities of the province, making use of labour services from subordinate districts and acting as the judicial and administrative authorities of the area (Alberti and Sanchez, 1974: 33–41).

In the valley area, the conflicts over resources occurred mainly within villages and between villages. Sicaya's long struggle with the hacienda Laive was followed by one with the inhabitants of the small village of Cacchi. This village belonged to Sicaya, but claimed the exclusive right to the remaining *puna* pastures. In this case, as in most other cases of inter- and intra-village conflict, the tensions arose as local farmers and traders sought to extend their enterprises either by encroaching on the lands of subordinate villages or by trying to use political office to obtain free labour. Conversely, those in subordinate villages sought political independence as a means to more effectively control their own resources, avoiding taxes and restrictions on markets and pastures (Samaniego, 1978: 49–52; Roberts and Samaniego, 1978: 246–55; Favre, 1975).

Underlying these conflicts was the vitality of small-scale commercial enterprise at the village level during the nineteenth century. With the decline in mining opportunities, villagers adjusted by taking advantage of the opportunities created by economic and political instability. Many of them made money by supplying foodstuffs, fodder and clothing to the armies that went through the valley. The needs of the garrisons are cited by Arguedas (1957) as a major factor in the development of Huancayo's Sunday fair. This fair, established in early colonial times, grew rapidly as a market for a vast range of industrial and agricultural products that drew in buyers and sellers from miles around.

Small-scale enterprises were well suited to the economic and political conditions of the time. These enterprises were often organized on a multiple basis, combining agricultural and non-agricultural pursuits, and were run by a group of kin-related households. Such enterprises facilitated the transfer of labour and other resources among the various branches of economic activity thereby maximizing the use of scarce resources and also spreading the risks. Wilson's (1980) analysis of the strategies of the Tarma landed elite suggests that this pattern of multiple enterprise was found not only at the village level but also among the members of the regional elite. Landed families combined agriculture with mining and trading. They also shifted resources, such as labour, from one branch of activity to another. Wilson cites the shortage of capital, the scarcity of inputs, particularly labour, and the general climate of economic uncertainty as the reasons for these strategies. This Tarma elite was not completely successful, however, in controlling the resources of the nearby peasant villages. One reason appears to have been that the villages, like those of the Mantaro valley, were socially and economically differentiated with a flourishing commercialized economy.

The vitality of the village economy of the central highlands is attested by Norberto Padilla's report of 1874 (Tello Devotto, 1971: 50–3). He stated that the Sunday fair of Huancayo brought together between 25,000 and 30,000 traders. The nearby village of Sapallanga is characterized as full of 'Indians and ancient customs' but was also said to be the provider of woollen thread and woven cloth for the Sunday fair. Chupaca is described as having a flourishing agriculture based on the hard work of its inhabitants who have developed irrigation. San Jerónimo is seen as very progressive with its inhabitants travelling to Lima to engage in trade in foodstuffs and provisions. Padilla also made special mention of the investments in public works being made in several of the valley towns, and described how communal landholding persisted in valley villages.

The Rise of Huancayo and the Commercial Economy

As the nineteenth century progressed, the focus of economic activity in the Department gradually shifted to the southern end of the Mantaro valley, with Huancayo becoming the predominant town (Espinoza, 1973: 344–6).[4] Huancayo occupied a strategic position at the head of the valley and was surrounded by relatively fertile and extensive agricultural land. It was the most convenient stopping place for the mule trains from Huancavelica and the southern highlands on their journeys to the northern highlands and the coast. Routes to the tropical lowlands and to the *puna* crossed through Huancayo and its nearby districts. Huancayo became the capital of the southern province of Junín in 1864. By the end of the century it was the place of residence of government officials, landowners, with haciendas in the tropical lowlands and in the *puna*, and craftsmen and merchants.

The social and political structure of Huancayo contrasts, in certain aspects, with that of towns such as Jauja and Tarma where landed elites were dominant. Huancayo was the place of residence of important landowners: their interests in protecting their rights and rents do not have a prominent place, however, in the administration and judicial concerns of the Huancayo authorities (Tello Devotto, 1971: 71, 79). There were relatively few haciendas within the province of Huancayo: 21 were registered in 1876 compared, for example, with 110 in Tarma and 168 in Pasco (Espinoza, 1973: 339). The agricultural enterprise of the Huancayo landowners appears to have been of a different order from that of the hacienda owners of Jauja. The estates of the Huancayo elite were dispersed in different regions of the highlands – often outside the jurisdiction of Huancayo – and involved different types of economic activity. Some were cattle ranches, others were mainly used for the production of sugar, but relatively few were agricultural or involved a resident dependent peasantry.[5] Unlike the elite of Jauja or Tarma, the Huancayo landowning class had relatively little interest in enforcing its control over the immediate region of the city. In contrast to those of the Jauja or Tarma councils, the proceedings of the Huancayo council, in three selected years of the nineteenth century, do not show a single instance of the council compelling the districts within its jurisdiction to provide labour or services.[6] Also, the types of agricultural enterprise and the characteristics of the landowners appear to have permitted less social pretensions than was the case amongst Jauja's elite who were well connected with prominent Lima families (Alberti and Sanchez, 1974: 43).

Huancayo's landowners were essentially involved in commerce and their town houses often served as depositories for agricultural produce. Huancayo was an important centre for distilling liquor; there were seven official stills in Huancayo by 1880 and the sugar for these came from tropical lowland estates (Tello Devotto, 1971).

A fuller understanding of Huancayo's rapid growth is obtained by looking at the particular types of relationship that the town maintained with the surrounding area. Huancayo was set in an area in which there existed an abundance of small-scale opportunities. The population in the province was 60,000 in 1876 and the main occupational group were the farmers. This farming population was also internally differentiated, with perhaps 15 per cent of the population in both agricultural and stock-raising villages producing a sufficient surplus for marketing. These richer peasants often diversified their houshold economies through trade and/or craft activities (Samaniego, 1974). Many of the farmers produced alfalfa to sell to the muleteers along the trade routes. This farming was often complemented by the cultivation of plots of land in the fruit-, sugar- and coffee-producing region of the tropical lowlands. There had long existed a tradition of colonizing this region from the valley and many of the valley's richer peasant farmers had rights to plots of land there, which they farmed with the help of their children and relatives, or by share-cropping.

Mining operations in the latter half of the century were small-scale, each employing perhaps only one or two workers, and they were not greatly profitable. Nevertheless, the mine labour force of the central highlands in the mid-nineteenth century was probably over two thousand workers and a good proportion of these were drawn from the villages of the Huancayo province (Laite, 1977; Wilson, 1978). For many villagers and small-town residents, mining represented a further possibility of extending their economic interests. In several of the villages of the valley, such as Muquiyauyo in Jauja province, prominent local families were reputed to have made fortunes through judicious mining investments (Grondin, 1978a).

Part of the significance of these developments for Huancayo can be appreciated by considering the enrolment in Huancayo's main school, Santa Isabel, which, by the end of the century, was probably educating about sixty students each year. The school was founded in 1852 and provided an education which could lead to training for the professions (Espinoza, 1973: 323). It was the school to which the children of Huancayo's elite were sent and a son of General Cáceres, a former president of Peru, was educated there. By the end of the century the school registers show that most pupils came from outside the city of Huancayo. In many cases, these children travelled to school each morning or they boarded in the city (Roberts, n.d.: 143–4). Between 1892 and 1898 the large villages in the province of Huancayo provided a substantial number of these students: some 27 per cent of the total. Another important group (16 per cent) came from the province of Huancavelica and a further 11 per cent came from other provinces, mainly Jauja. The relatively high costs involved in such an education – especially for out-of-town residents – indicate the existence of a class of fairly wealthy farmers and entrepreneurs in the villages and small towns of the Huancayo area.

In this respect, the contrast with Jauja's school, San José, is instructive. San José had approximately the same number of students as Santa Isabel but, in contrast with Huancayo, Jauja educated a smaller proportion of village students. Between 1869 and 1900, over 60 per cent of the students were drawn from Jauja itself. However, like Santa Isabel, San José also educated the children of the villages and small towns of its region. These villages, too, were evidently well developed economically in this period. Prominent amongst them was Matahuasi – the village which is the topic of several subsequent chapters and which lies at a distance of twelve miles from both Jauja and Huancayo. Matahuasi was, in the nineteenth century, a centre for the organization of pack-animal transport. As early as 1869, Matahuasi children, from different families, were enrolled in Jauja and, by 1900, there were twenty-six children from the village studying in either San José or Santa Isabel. The names of the families from Matahuasi who were sending children to school in the towns are, in the main, names no longer known in Matahuasi, which suggests a possible out-migration of these 'richer' village families.

A further indication of the economic differentiation of this region is the substantial number of qualified voters registered at the end of the nineteenth century. Some of the villages such as San Jerónimo, Chupaca and Sicaya had as many, or more, qualified voters than did Huancayo itself (Table 2).

These data show the importance of the small towns and villages around Huancayo. They were less differentiated economically than the city; but they were the place of residence of a group of commercial farmers. The other principal occupations listed for these literate householders were chiefly craft activities, although all the villages had some full-time resident traders. To this day, the size of their churches, their impressive central squares and large, well-constructed, though dilapidated, houses, attest to the presence in the past of families of high social standing.

Norberto Padilla's accounts of each district in the province confirm this picture of relative prosperity. The towns which in 1897 had a substantial number of voters (Chupaca, Chongos Bajo, Sicaya, San Jerónimo) are characterized by Padilla as having a flourishing agricultural economy and a large number of 'whites' (*blancos*) and *mestizos*. In contrast, Sapallanga is said to be dominated by traditional customs because it is made up of the 'aboriginal race' and its agriculture needs improvement. Likewise, the majority of inhabitants of Colca are said to be Indians who have emerged from an abject state and bad ways. Pariahuanca, lying on the eastern slopes of the mountains in the tropical lowlands, is described as being dominated by large estates specializing in fruit and sugar production (Tello Devotto, 1971: 50–3).

The suggestion is, then, that Huancayo, more than either Jauja or Tarma, was simply a *primus inter pares* among the towns of its province. Huancayo did not monopolize either the political or economic power of its region; nor was it the undisputed place of residence of the social elite of the area. Indeed,

Table 2 *Qualified voters in the districts of the province of Huancayo: 1897–1907*

District	No. of voters	Percentage of voters in agriculture	Population in 1876	
Colca	42	83	5,410	
Chongos Bajo	160	75	3,692	
Chupaca	343	93	12,157	
Huayucachi	75	60	—	
Pariahuanca	15	87	5,100	
San Jerónimo	276	86	6,327	
Sapallanga	31	58	10,284	
Sicaya	259	87	3,193	
Huancayo	278	27	10,592	(5,948 urban)
Total	1,479[a]		56,755[b]	

[a] Available literacy figures from the census of 1876 correspond fairly closely to the number of qualified voters. There were 1,810 literate persons recorded for the province as a whole.
[b] This total excludes the district of Jarpa which was abolished in 1891. The full total for all districts of the Huancayo province in 1876 was 60,236. The district of Huayucachi was created in 1896.
Source: *Registro electoral*, 1908; Tello Devotto, 1971: 55.

Chupaca, which lay only a few miles distant from Huancayo, remained, at the end of the century, the principal residence of one of the most important landowners of the central highlands – Bartolomé Guerra – who was also a national political and military figure.

There are few signs, at this period, of substantial migration from these villages and towns to Huancayo. The electoral registers show that 7 per cent of literate heads of household resident in Huancayo in the period from 1896 to 1900 were born in the villages of the province. The fact that most migrant households came from Huancavelica and the southern highlands (12 per cent of total households), or from Lima (8 per cent), or were of foreign origin (7 per cent) is indicative of Huancayo's position as an urban centre 'open' to external relationships. Three per cent of all literate householders in Huancayo were born in other provinces of the Mantaro valley (Jauja and Concepción) and 9 per cent were born elsewhere in Peru. Just over half of Huancayo's voters were born in that town.

By the end of the century, Huancayo was mainly a commercial town. In a directory of 1880, there were listed three Chinese restaurants, one hotel, seven lodging houses, two icemaking factories, six liquor factories, two ham curers, fifty-two shops in the permanent market, eight general stores, five leather goods stores, nine shoemakers, nine tailors and three barbers (Tello Devotto, 1971: 56). The proceedings of the council also indicate an awareness of Huancayo's commercial importance: in a meeting of 1895, the council took measures to ensure a water supply for the 'numerous flour mills in the city', to tax the 'profitable' commerce of eggs with Lima and to tax commercial travellers because 'for the last ten years, the commercial houses of the capital send to all the provinces of the coast and of the interior and especially to Huancayo, agents who bring a large number of samples, and who profit considerably but pay no local tax' (Actas: 27.6.1895). Huancayo was evidently a centre for trade on a regional basis.

Moreover, by the end of the century, a lower proportion of town councillors were born in Huancayo than had been the case in 1875 and 1885. These newcomers were quickly incorporated into the political structure of Huancayo and, in this sense, there was no sharp change in the characteristics of the political 'elite'. Landowners continued to play their part in councils and, indeed, the same families often continued to occupy council positions.

Developments in the national economy at the end of the nineteenth century favoured the expansion of trade in the provinces. After the ending of the war with Chile, Peru began a period of rapid economic growth. Although this growth was led by exports, it resulted in considerable industrialization, especially in textiles and other basic consumer goods industries (Thorp and Bertram, 1978: 32–6). Most of the production was based in Lima and was initiated by immigrant groups, such as the Italians and Germans. The central highlands became an important market for these producers, and for the importing houses who benefited from the boom. In both Huancayo and Jauja, the larger trading concerns began to be dominated by Lima merchants or by those of foreign origin (Alberti and Sanchez, 1974: 45).

Wilson documents the economic forces at work in the tropical lowlands of Tarma that were undermining the established pattern of elite control during this period. Large-scale commercial production of sugar for *aguardiente* (rum) and, later on, coffee cultivation attracted investors from outside the province. Several of these were recent immigrants to Peru and others were from Lima. Gradually, the newcomers displaced the Tarma elite who had a more conservative attitude to landholding and investment, preferring to live off rents and spend profits on luxury items (Wilson, 1982). Once the lowland estates ceased to be controlled by the Tarma elite, the towns of the tropical lowlands sought and gained independence from Tarma's political and economic control. Wilson shows that the immigrant entrepreneurs, who came to exploit the new economic opportunities in alcohol and coffee, developed much stronger business relationships with members of the peasant population (shopkeepers, bar owners and muleteers) than had the established landed elite. They also had stronger ties with the business houses of Lima and Europe.

Commercial agriculture was stimulated in these years by the growing demand for animal fodder, for tropical crops, such as sugar and coffee, and by the demand for foodstuffs for the mines which were also beginning to develop rapidly. This stimulus benefited the numerous small- and medium-scale commercial farmers in the villages and small towns of the area, but was of limited incentive to large agricultural landowners in areas where the uncertainties of the temperate high altitude climate made large-scale production of foodstuffs and fodder a risky venture.

As Wilson (1978) points out, the diversified and differentiated village economies of the region were an obstacle to the consolidation of large agricultural estates. The villages absorbed local labour supplies, diminishing the pool of reserve labour necessary for the expansion of labour-intensive agricultural enterprise. This last factor probably explains the limited interest that established landowners showed in the development of estates in the tropical lowlands. They neither controlled sufficient labour, nor did they have the ready cash with which to hire it. It was the immigrant entrepreneurs and medium-scale commercial farmers (who were also often immigrants, for example, the Chinese) who were better placed to exploit the new opportunities. These immigrants had access to credit and to distribution networks that were linked into the larger towns and into Lima; they also had the necessary cash reserves with which to contract labour when needed (Wilson, 1982: 203–10).

The livestock haciendas of the *puna* zone were intensifying their production at this period, but they did not require much labour. Gradually they were combined together to form large companies, both at the Jauja and Huancayo ends of the valley. These companies were mostly controlled by families resident outside the region and, thus, represented less of an investment potential for locally resident landowners than did the smaller haciendas they replaced. Sociedad Ganadera de Junín was formed in 1906 out of a number of small locally owned haciendas in the Jauja area and, in 1910, Sociedad Ganadera del Centro consolidated many of the haciendas of the highlands around Huancayo. Both companies included non-resident members of the Lima oligarchy and both aimed at rationalizing production. This consolidation 'displaced' provincial hacienda owners who had resided in Jauja, in Huancayo and in the smaller towns such as Concepción. This change only partially affected the village economy, producing conflict mainly with the highland pastoral villages in which already there was emerging a group of commercially-oriented peasant farmers interested in expanding their own herds (Samaniego, 1978).

In this context, the class that had become dominant in Huancayo sought to expand their influence by improving communications and developing commercial links rather then by attempting to transform the agrarian structure through investment in large-scale commercial farming. Indeed, the most prominent landowners resident in Huancayo at the end of the century had substantial interests in trade and urban property. Many of them were of foreign or Lima origin and had begun their careers in Huancayo in a relatively modest way as postmasters, muletraders or shopkeepers. Those landed families who had been established for a longer time, such as the Penaloza family, retained strong ties with Lima and spent most of their lives there. Thus, despite the continuing importance of agriculture and small industry, the dominant economic tone of the city of Huancayo, and even of Jauja and Tarma, at the turn of the century was that of selling goods and services and seeking out new markets for these.

Conclusion

By the end of the nineteenth century, the struggle between different classes for the control of the resources of the central highlands remained unresolved. There were conflicts at many different levels: between hacienda owners and peasant communities; between 'prosperous' valley villages and 'poor' *puna* villages, which latter were often aided and abetted by the haciendas; between *comuneros* with little land and richer peasants who were usually also the local political authorities; between established landed families and immigrant entrepreneurs who often supported the village farmers and traders in their struggles against the nearby haciendas. In a previous volume, we and our contributors documented these conflicts and analysed the revitalization of communal institutions in this period (Long and Roberts, 1978). We argued that communal resources, such as pastureland, and community institutions, such as the *faena* (communal work party) or fiesta system, provided the means by which local entrepreneurs could expand their resources through mobilizing the political and economic potential of the village.

These historical processes can also be depicted using Adams' conception of power domains (1975, 68–93).[7] During the colonial period, the power domain was essentially unitary, with the colonial state concentrating power, while the subordinate levels, such as the differentiated Indian communities, the Spanish hacienda owners and the traders, were approximately coordinate in relative power. In the nineteenth century, a major input was removed from the system, the wealth and central economic role of the mining sector, which had sustained the concentration of power at the top. Thus, in the central highlands the power domain became fragmented and no superordinate level (e.g. landowner, merchant, military figure, rich peasantry, etc.) could command sufficient resources to impose a unitary domain.

The legacy of the colonial mining economy was, then, a multiple domain structure. The colonial period had created a complex and differentiated economy in the central highlands, but the decline of mining meant that this economy decentralized, creating the basis for multiple power domains. It did not lead to the emergence of some other type of unitary power domain, for example, one dominated by a prosperous hacienda class.[8]

The next chapter explores the subsequent injection into the regional system of massive economic resources, consequent upon the restructuring of the mining economy by the American-owned Cerro de Pasco Corporation.

3

The Mining Corporation and regional development

From the early twentieth century, the central highlands became an integral part of Peru's expanding export economy, being the principal location of the mining industry and an important contributor to the development of wool production and, through the supply of seasonal labour, to the operation of the coastal cotton estates. The impact of the export sector on the economy of the central highlands was, as we shall show, substantial both in terms of the wages spent locally and in terms of the linkages that developed between the export sector, agriculture, commerce, transport and local manufacturing industry. These linkages did not result, however, in a significant regional accumulation of capital in agriculture and industry. Such an accumulation, in terms of industrial plant and infrastructure, of the consolidation and modernization of farms and of the linkages between these sectors, could have provided the basis for a pattern of self-sustained regional development. Why such a development failed to materialize is the focus of this chapter.

At the beginning of the twentieth century the central highlands region had the resources needed for growth. The largest deposits of silver, copper, lead, zinc and coal known in Peru were located in the Department of Junín. Timber was available from the tropical lowlands, while there was extensive arable and livestock farming in the valleys and surrounding *puna*. Junín was, at this time, the single most important national source of barley, potatoes and wheat and, after Puno, was one of the major national centres of wool production.

The human resources for development were also considerable. It was, in relation to the rest of Peru, a densely populated area, containing, in 1900, some 400,000 people. Furthermore compared to other highland Departments, education levels were high. The proportion of the population attending primary school in Junín was double that of Departments such as Cuzco, Huancavelica, Ayacucho or Puno. However the numbers attending school were small. In 1924, there were just over 10,000 pupils in Junín, but this level of attendance was only surpassed by Lima, Arequipa and Ancash (*Extracto estadístico,* 1924:34). By 1926, Junín was second only to Lima in the number of pupils who had completed primary and secondary education, with, 1,178 pupils graduating from primary school in that year and 305 from secondary school (*Extracto estadístico,* 1926:133). The great majority of these graduates would have come from the valley areas. Another indicator of the level of literacy was that, throughout the 1920s, Junín was second only to Lima in the number of periodicals published within its borders, twenty-three newspapers and magazines by 1929.

In this chapter we will examine the growth of the regional economy from the 1920s to 1960, with particular reference to the major economic sectors and their interrelationships. These dates approximate the period in which the modern mining economy exerted its maximum influence on other local economic activities. Within this period, there are important sub-periods marked by the world economic depression, 1929–32, and the Second World War, 1939–45. Both the Depression and the War affected the region, in the former case through sharp drops in mining production and the laying-off of labour, and in the latter case through the freezing of metal prices resulting in lower profitability for mining and shortages in imported goods leading to import-substituting industrialization (Thorp and Bertram, 1978: 155–7, 193–5). This period was a relatively homogeneous one in the economic history of the central highlands, representing the time when the region was most fully integrated into Peru's export economy. In the following three chapters, we will complement the economic analysis of this chapter with an account of social organization, analysing the role played by changing class interests in shaping the patterns of economic development.

The development of the modern mining sector

In this section, we have attempted to document the enormous economic importance of modern mining investments for the central highlands, identifying its major direct linkages with other sectors of the economy.

The stagnation of the mining sector ended in the last two decades of the nineteenth century. Initially, the revival was based upon an increasing demand for silver and improvements in technology and exploration. This led to a more intensive exploitation of several important mines in the central highlands, such as Morococha, Casapalca and Yauli, and the establishment of a number of smelters. A more fundamental reason for the revival of mining was the switch to non-precious metals, especially copper, in the 1890s. The demand for such metals on the part of the industrialized countries ensured both profitable markets and substantial sources of finance for improving technology and developing the infrastructure for large-scale mining enterprise. Foreign capital was to finance the building of the railway to the central highlands. It had reached La Oroya by 1893. In 1889, the US engineers, Backus and Johnston, established a modern smelter at Casapalca whose output was being transported by rail from 1894. In Cerro de Pasco, there were eleven smelters operating by 1900 and a further four in the surrounding area. The combination of improved transport and better smelting increased the scale of operations. Between 1892 and 1893 production of copper at the Cerro de Pasco mine increased by two-thirds (Laite, 1981: 56).

Peruvian capital was gradually displaced from the mining sector. In 1902, the Cerro de Pasco mining company (later called the Cerro de Pasco Corporation) was formed in New York and bought 80 per cent of the concessions in the Cerro de Pasco area for over 500,000 pounds sterling. (Thorp and Bertram, 1978: 81–2). These purchases were facilitated by the fact that mine owners had found it difficult to make profits in the face of high transport and installation costs. However, when the company extended the railway to Cerro de Pasco in 1904 transport costs were reduced to about 20 or 30 per cent of the pre-railway era (Miller, n.d.: 31–2). By 1914, two major companies, Cerro de Pasco and Backus and Johnston, accounted for 92 per cent of Peru's copper production. In 1919, Backus and Johnston sold out to the Cerro de Pasco Corporation.

The Cerro de Pasco Corporation became the major producer of the central highlands. Its smelter at La Oroya, built in 1922, processed ore from its company mines and also ore bought from independent producers in the region. Throughout this period until 1960, copper, silver, lead and zinc were among Peru's major sources of export earnings. However the diversification of Peru's exports meant that, despite its importance, the mining sector and the interests associated with it did not dominate the national ecomony (Table 3).

The Cerro de Pasco Corporation made possible a vast expansion in mining production in Peru through innovations in technology and organization that resulted in high profits on investment. Net profits as high as 31 per cent were obtained in the 1920s and the 1930s, although the Depression also resulted in losses in some years (DeWind, 1977: 61–2). Thorp and Bertram (1978: 87–9, 91) estimate that, between 1916 and 1937, the Corporation's gross earnings in Peru totalled 375 million dollars, compared with a total initial investment of the order of 16 million dollars in the period 1901 to 1907. A substantial part of the figure for gross earnings, however, was reinvested in Peru in the form of wage payments, taxes and payments to suppliers. The percentage of the gross earnings that were returned in this way to Peru were high relative to mining operations at this time in other countries, such as Chile, or when compared with

Table 3 *Composition of exports by value (percentage shares)*

	Silver, copper, lead, zinc	Sugar and cotton	Wool and coffee	Fish products	Petroleum	Other
1920	12.0	72.0	2.0	—	5.0	9.0
1930	26.9	28.5	3.3	—	29.7	11.6
1940	25.4	28.2	5.2	—	24.8	16.4
1950	21.1	50.5	4.6	2.9	13.1	7.8
1960	36.4	27.8	5.9	11.5	4.1	14.3

Source: Thorp and Bertram, 1978: 40, 153, 208. These authors point out that the figure for 1920 is very approximate since export valuation practices are unclear. The exports under the 'other' category include rubber. Production of minerals was heavily concentrated in the central highlands, so that in 1940, for example, Junín produced 89 per cent of copper, 74 per cent of silver, 86 per cent of lead and 99 per cent of zinc (*Extracto estadístico*, 1941).

the Peruvian oil companies. Thorp and Bertram (1978: 87) show, for example, that between 1922 and 1937 the returned value on the Corporation's earnings in Peru was 139 million dollars, or approximately 55 per cent of their total sales earnings in this period. Of this sum, 48 per cent was paid in wages and 42 per cent in payments to suppliers of ores and sundries, while only 10 per cent went to the government in taxes. The bulk of the Corporation's payments in Peru are likely, then, to have gone to people living in the central highlands, although some of the suppliers of ore, such as the Fernandini family, were based in Lima. In the 1950s and 1960s, the value returned by the Corporation to Peru was higher still, rising to 76 per cent of their gross earnings. This was mainly due to the increase in the Corporation's local purchases of ores and materials (Thorp and Bertram, 1978: 215).

The importance of the independent producers was a result of the economic conditions created by fluctuations in the world commodity market due to recession, price freezing by major purchasers such as the United States and preferential tariffs for their colonies operated by European governments. Copper was particularly badly affected. It fell in price by 69 per cent from 1929 to 1932 during the Depression and its recovery was slow until the end of the Second World War (Thorp and Bertram, 1978: 161–2). A consequence of the uncertainties of the international commodity market was that the Cerro de Pasco Corporation was itself unwilling, after the 1930s, to extend its operations by direct investment. Its copper production decreased throughout the 1940s but at the same time it increased the amount of ore purchased from independent producers so that in 1947 one-third of the Corporation's production at La Oroya was based on purchased ore (DeWind, 1977: 395). The independent producers included some important Lima-based families, but there were also smaller operations whose owners resided in the central highlands, forming the local elite together with the landowners and large-scale merchants. Zinc and lead prices were less affected by the Depression and recovered their 1929 prices earlier. However, these ores were mainly mined by Peruvian entrepreneurs and could be produced by locally available technology. From the 1940s onwards, almost without a break until 1962, the Cerro de Pasco Corporation purchased most of its lead from independent producers (DeWind, 1977: 396). By 1946, 64 per cent of zinc was being produced by independent producers (Thorp and Bertram, 1978: 160).

The existence of independent producers and the links between them and the operations of the Corporation had widespread ramifications for the regional economy. Transport of minerals to the railheads was central to the whole mining system. Many of the mines, especially the smaller ones, were at some distance from the railway so that, although the bulk of mineral shipments to the coast was handled by the central railway, truck transport was used to bring the minerals down to the railhead. The mining companies did not usually provide this transport. This was supplied by small-scale, often village-based, operators who used savings derived from periods of labour migration or from returns on commercial investments to purchase a truck.

Registrations of trucks in Junín indicate the importance of this transport sector: from 1929, when 353 trucks were operating in the Department, the number rose steadily to reach 3,760 in 1956 (*Extracto estadístico*: various years). In these years, Junín was second only to Lima-Callao in the number of truck registrations. Junín's trucks made up 7.5 per cent of the national stock in 1929 and 8.5 per cent in 1956. Transport was also needed in these years to facilitate the increased movement of goods and people to the mining and production centres. Bus services expanded particularly rapidly and, by 1956, there were 1,033 buses in operation in Junín, or 18.3 per cent of the national stock. The functional nature of this transport boom is revealed by the relative scarcity of passenger cars, which by 1956 comprised only 2 per cent of national registrations. The presence of independent small-scale mines, and the Corporation's own tendency to seek local suppliers of construction materials, machinery and provisions, also stimulated the development of commerce and small-scale manufacturing. In the next chapter we will provide a detailed account of how these particular linkages developed in Huancayo.

The most direct linkage between the mining sector and the regional economy occurred in relation to agriculture. In 1926, land purchases by the Corporation, including the estates of the Sociedad Ganadera de Junín, were consolidated into the Corporation's farm division which at one time owned 322,000 hectares and was one of the most efficient meat and dairy producers in Peru. The reasons for the Corporation's investment in large-scale farming estates are varied and complex (Laite, 1978). The poisonous fumes from the La Oroya smelter had severely damaged surrounding farm land, and litigation led the Corporation to buy up much of this land as a means of settling claims. The damage was not, however, permanent. The Corporation's farm division was able to develop livestock production successfully, providing it with a means of provisioning the mine population, as well as of selling wool in the national and international markets. Some commentators have attributed the Corporation's actions to a deliberate attempt to deprive local peasant farmers of their lands, thus forcing them to make a living by selling their labour to the company (CIDA, 1970).

The farm division was an important source of innovation, developing new high quality breeds of sheep and improved methods of pasture management. From the 1950s, the average yields of mutton and wool from the farm division rose consistently and by 1966 were more than double the yields obtained on other farms in the province of Junín (De Wind, 1977: 247–8). In the 1950s and 1960s, the Corporation's farm division was selling approximately one million kilos of meat a year to their workers at prices that were about two-thirds of those charged in Huancayo (DeWind, 1977: 250). As DeWind points out, the ability of the farm division to sell meat and dairy products cheaply and still to make a profit was based on the very low wages paid to farm workers in a predominantly peasant farming economy. In 1951, farm workers were paid, on average, half as much as miners, although rights to use land owned by the farm division for grazing their own animals and cultivating their own crops partly compensated for these low wages.

With the increasing rationalization of farm production, the workers' access to land was reduced but their wages, relative to those of the miners, were increased. By 1969 they earned 80 per cent of the mine workers' wage (DeWind, 1977; 254). This increase in farm workers' wages was a deliberate policy to enable the Corporation to stop their shepherds using company land for their own animals. Farm wages elsewhere in the region remained low. As chapter five will show, this rationalization process was not fully successful since local peasant farmers continued to pasture animals on company land in the 1960s (Martínez-Alier, 1977).

The organization of mine production

The organization of mine production was basically divided between extraction and smelting activities.[1] The mines were underground workings which

Miners, peasants and entrepreneurs

required considerable labour both to sink the shafts and to extract ore. It was only much later, in the 1960s, that open-pit mining was introduced into the central highlands and, even then, it was on a much smaller scale than was the case in southern Peru. Consequently, productivity in the mines of the central highlands was low throughout the period, since there were limits to the amount of mechanization of mining in the underground system.[2] Indeed, until the 1940s there was considerable use of hand labour not only in drilling operations underground, but also in the construction of access roads, railways and infrastructure. De Wind (1977: 36–7) cites the example of the Yauricocha mine whose railway took five years to complete in the early 1940s, employing between 500 and 2,000 men daily on the construction work.

The Cerro de Pasco Corporation did introduce important technological innovations, primarily by generalizing the use of electric power. Electric power soon replaced animal and human power in hoisting and was used to drive air compressors, blowers, and water pumps, as well as providing telephones and electric lights that made possible 24-hour-day operations. These technological developments did not, however, replace much labour. Whatever was saved in substituting hand labour by inanimate power was more than compensated by the demand for labour created by the expansion in operations made possible by these developments. The labour required for these various mining operations was primarily unskilled and semi-skilled: to operate the hand drills; to load and unload the wagons; and to help with construction activities. The labour requirement of the mines of the central highlands was, consequently, enormous when compared with other industrial processes. In the late 1930s and 1940s, the average number of workers employed in extraction probably came to close on 16,000 a year.[3] Of these workers probably more than 60 per cent were employed in the Corporation's mines, according to their records for the years 1920–70 (Laite, 1981).

The other crucial components in the mining process of production are concentration and smelting. As the metal content of the ores declined, so the company found it necessary to concentrate the ore before smelting. Concentration plants, which remove the waste from the metals, were developed close to the mines. These used a flotation principle with chemicals and water for separating the fine-crushed ore into its various components. Smelting operations were, however, increasingly centralized in the large smelter in La Oroya, built originally in 1922.

The La Oroya plant was highly complex technologically, operating two major circuits, one for copper and the other for lead (DeWind, 1977: 52–3). These circuits each had four steps within them, resulting in an integrated production process producing high-quality ore direct for export. The operation of the smelter demanded a greater range of skills and organizational control than was needed in the mines. Thus, the numbers of both skilled workers and white-collar workers was higher in La Oroya than in any of the other mining centres owned by the Corporation. In the late 1930s and during the 1940s, the workforce of La Oroya fluctuated between 3,000 and 5,000 workers, of whom 6 per cent were white-collar workers.

Mine labour

The expansion of mining did not bring about the formation of a full-time wage labour force. The Corporation faced serious initial problems in meeting its massive labour requirements. Local recruits were not easily obtained because the predominance of peasant agriculture occupied the population in subsistence activities for most of the year. At the beginning of the twentieth century, households appear to have had adequate amounts of land for family subsistence. Their members were not readily attracted by the wages and poor working conditions of the mines. Labour shortage was thus produced by the combined effects of the local agrarian structure and inadequate incentives to seek permanent wage work. The difficulties that the mining companies experienced in obtaining workers led to the extensive use of the *enganche* system for labour recruitment for the mining operations of the Corporation.

The *enganche* system involved a cash payment, in advance, to a prospective worker or to his or her head of household, which was redeemed by working-off a contracted period in the enterprise. The system was also used to recruit labour for the cotton plantations of the coast. The success of this system depended upon a network of local intermediaries who were themselves advanced money by the Corporation and who had sufficient influence with local authorities to enforce the contract that had been made with prospective workers. By its nature, then, *enganche* was a highly decentralized system of labour recruitment that both depended on local politico-administrative jurisdictions and encouraged the activities of local middlemen. *Enganche* thus helped to create the highly developed system of traders and transporters who supplied the mines and urban centres and who now convey workers to and from centres of employment. DeWind (1977: 166) cites a North American visitor to the mines at the beginning of the 1920s who reported that the Corporation employed 4,000 *enganchados* or more than half of the workers at the time. *Enganche* remained in practice in the mines as late as the 1940s, although by that date it seems to have been used mainly to recruit people for work in high altitude underground mining (Bonilla, 1974: 42–5).

The gradual replacement of the *enganche* system by direct contracting was due mainly to the pressure of increasing population on the existing land resources. Smallholder agriculture was the predominant form of tenure among the peasants of the central highlands and, with the increase in population, the average size of plots was decreasing to below the level adequate for a household's subsistence (Samaniego, 1978; Grondín, 1978a). The relatively poor soils of the region, lack of irrigation and the stagnation in food prices (see below) meant that wage labour other than in agriculture increasingly became a necessary complement to the village economy.

Mining was not the only possible outside source of income but, in the period between 1920 and 1960, it was the largest and most accessible source of full-time wage labour for those villagers without capital resources or relatively high levels of education. There was little large-scale commercial farming and, although there were opportunities to work on the cotton harvests, these were seasonal. Factory employment was beginning to develop in Huancayo, but job opportunities were few and the levels of pay depended on seniority of service (Roberts, 1978a: 139). Jobs in Lima were sought in this period by people from the central highlands, but these were mainly the best educated people from Huancayo or the richest agricultural villages of the valley.[4] Commerce and transport were expanding, as incomes rose in these years, but these opportunities were entrepreneurial ones, requiring some capital and good contacts in the region (Long, 1979). Many of these opportunities, as Laite's analysis of the case of Matahuasi in chapter six shows, were generated by the expansion of the mining economy.

It seems that, in many villages, the mines remained an unpopular choice for those seeking work. Bonilla (1974: 44–5) emphasizes the continuing reluctance of villagers to work in the mines when other income opportunities were available, citing the 1946 report of an *enganchador* who went from village to village in the Mantaro valley trying to recruit labour for the Cerro de Pasco Corporation. He was offering the equivalent of 4.2 soles a day (1.9 soles in the prices of Table 4) for unskilled workers for the mines, but encountered difficulty in finding recruits. The *enganchador* wrote: 'They say that they prefer to work in their village or other neighbouring villages, because they are paid from 3 to 4 soles with food, coca, cigarettes and lime and that these jobs are not in the mines where they can get ill with pneumoconiosis'. (44.) In other places, villagers preferred to work on the irrigation canal of the left bank of the Mantaro for between three and five soles a day and on road construction projects.

However, low earnings in agriculture and the shortage of other income opportunities enabled the mining companies to recruit workers for relatively low wages. For example, calculations of the average salaries paid by employers during 1949 show that, in the mining sector, workers received 1,733 soles per

Table 4 Daily wage-rates of workers ('obreros') in different sectors of employment in various years[a] (at constant prices in soles)[b]

	Average rates: central highlands				Average rates: national			
	Mining	Agriculture	Manu-facturing	Commercial agriculture	Manu-facturing	Construction	Transport	Services
1933	2.1	0.71	—	1.42	—	—	—	—
1942	1.77	0.61	2.08	1.65	3.0	1.9	2.5	—
1945	1.54	1.14	2.01	1.98	3.38	3.5	1.9	—
1948	2.15	—	—	1.37	3.34	3.17	2.99	0.67
1950	2.88	—	2.49	—	4.15	3.4	3.46	1.92
1955	2.94	—	—	—	4.37	4.58	3.66	2.78
1960	4.2	—	—	—	5.89	5.88	6.94	3.45

[a] The daily wages have been adjusted by the cost of living index for workers in Lima with 1934-6 = 100 (Boletín de estadística Peruana, 1962: 235)

[b] The wages cited for the different years are averages for workers in the relevant category. They are not strictly comparable since they are taken from different volumes of the Extracto estadístico and the basis of calculation is not always the same. The 1945 figures contrast with the others in that they are based on individual occupations, such as underground miner (lampero) in mining, weaver (tejedor) in national manufacturing, labourer (peón) in construction and porter (cargador) in transport. The 1950 figure for highlands manufacturing is based on our own data for the Manufacturas mill in Huancayo.

Sources: Extracto estadístico, 1942: 554–5; Anuario estadístico del Perú, 1955: 512; Boletín de estadística Peruana, 1962: 757–60.

annum compared with 4,457 soles for workers in textiles and 3,090 soles for leather industry workers (*Extracto estadístico*, 1949: 600–1).

In Table 4 the relatively low pay of mining as against urban occupations is demonstrated, as is the low pay of highland occupations when compared with those in Lima. These data from official sources are only rough indicators of the relative wage levels of different sectors of employment in different locations. Apart from problems of the reliability of this information, there is also the difficulty that the data do not reflect overtime or piecework earnings, or, conversely, the fact that workers in some sectors (e.g. agriculture and even textiles) do not work the year round. The pattern is corroborated, however, by Laite's analysis of the wage levels reported by his sample of work histories of miners and villagers (1977: 208–20). As the data in Table 4 show, the relative stagnation of wages in the mining sector came to an end in the 1950s when union pressure, and the impact of the greater world demand for metals accompanying the Korean War, led to high wages. Informants confirmed this trend in their reports of earnings in this period which compared favourably with earnings in other sectors of the economy of the central highlands.

The relatively low wages paid in mining and other occupations in the highlands were probably insufficient to meet the full subsistence costs of workers and their families. The cost of living in urban centres, such as Huancayo, was only a little less than the cost of living in Lima, despite much lower salaries. In 1944, for example, meat and agricultural products were only a little cheaper in Huancayo than in Lima, but manufactured goods were more expensive and housing prices were approximately the same (Pareja, 1979:11; *Extracto estadístico*, 1944). In the mining townships, housing and food were subsidized but there, too, evidence suggests that wages barely met the local subsistence costs of workers. Grondín (1978b: 102–4) interviewed villagers in Muquiyauyo, who had worked in the mines around 1930, who claimed that they had been unable to send much money home. They earned between forty and seventy soles a month and had to pay food and lodgings of between thirty and fifty soles a month which left little to meet other necessary expenses, such as overalls at seven soles, a shirt at eleven soles or a pair of shoes at seven or eight soles.

In 1948, a government survey of the budgets of mining families was carried out in five of the major production centres of the central highlands (*Extracto estadístico*, 1948–9: 676–81). This survey showed that, among 114 families interviewed, the average weekly expenses for a family of five were 96.42 soles of which 61.5 per cent was spent on food and 17.3 per cent on clothing, with the remainder spent on such sundries as furniture, transport, hygiene, health, entertainment and schooling.

However, at this date, the average daily wage of a miner was 5.56 soles and of a skilled worker 8.1 soles. Clearly, then, it was only by working long hours of overtime or by not having to support a family in the mine centre that subsistence could be met. Another possibility was that other family members would supplement the mining wage through seeking additional sources of income in, for example, petty trade or craftwork. The same survey shows that, of the families in La Oroya, one-third owned sewing machines, although only 10 per cent had radios, suggesting that purchases of consumer durables were mainly confined to those that might supplement family income. DeWind (1977: 223) suggests that as late as 1972 the wages were not adequate to cover more than the bare day-to-day family necessities and these were met only with difficulty. Almost half of the wage was spent on food and much of the rest on clothing, allowing little for furniture and other expenses.

These data suggest that mining labour was, in effect, cheap labour in that wages did not meet the full subsistence costs of the workers. As was noted above, the Cerro de Pasco Corporation provided cheap foodstuffs for their employees and thus kept wage demands down. Also, as we will see in this chapter and in chapter six, the village economy provided a significant subsistence base for the family members of miners. These subsidies lessened worker pressure on the Corporation to pay higher wages, but the basic constraint on wages was the fact that the mines of the central highlands were highly labour intensive both in production and in construction activities. Furthermore, they did not easily lend themselves to mechanization. This constraint and the conservative investment policy of the Corporation, noted earlier, meant that mining profits were boosted by maintaining a cheap workforce.

It was only in the 1950s and 1960s, when the Corporation began to mechanize production more widely, partly through the introduction of open-pit mining, that wage levels began to increase. In this period, wage increases for *obreros* in the Cerro de Pasco Corporation consistently outstripped the increases in the cost of living index (DeWind, 1977: 183). An important factor in raising wage rates in the Corporation and, consequently, in stimulating mechanization, was successful labour union organization, particularly after 1944 (Laite, 1981). However, mechanization raised productivity to such an extent that workers could be paid higher wages; yet the wage bill still declined as a proportion of total costs. In 1951, wages paid to *obreros* were 10.1 per cent of sales (De Wind, 1977: 181). By 1968, the worker payroll had declined to 8.96 per cent of sales, but even this was higher than the payroll of workers in the highly mechanized, open-pit operations of the Southern Peruvian Copper Corporation. There, workers were, on average, paid more than in Cerro de Pasco, but their payroll constituted 4.12 per cent of sales (DeWind,

1977: 186–7). One of the implications of higher productivity was that the Cerro de Pasco workforce in the 1960s and 1970s did not increase substantially, despite large increases in output, remaining at between 13,000 and 15,000 employees.

The peasant miner

We argue that until the 1950s, at least, a series of factors combined to limit the formation of a permanently resident industrial labour force in the mines. Firstly, the labour power required for mining was relatively unskilled and it could easily be recruited from the villages of the central highlands. Secondly, much of the labour in the mines, as in mining construction activities, was either temporary or seasonal in nature. Thirdly, fluctuations in international commodity prices resulted in sharp contractions and expansions of labour demand, defining mine labour as essentially non-permanent. For example, total employment in the Cerro de Pasco operations fell from 13,066 in 1929 to 5,686 in 1930. Informants told us that most of this workforce was drawn from the Mantaro valley region and returned to their villages of origin. Employment in the Corporation did not reach 13,000 again until 1955 and continued to fluctuate from year to year. Fourthly, and most importantly, wages were, as we have seen, insufficient to provide a permanent subsistence for workers and their families.

The available evidence indicates that the workforce in the mining sector was, indeed, a relatively unstable one. Laite calculates on the basis of the 1972 company records that, on average, men had started working for the Corporation thirteen years previously, but he points out that this average conceals the fact that a substantial number of workers (one-third) had begun work less than five years before. Also, the workers who had stayed longer had often interrupted their work for alternative opportunities in their home villages or elsewhere. He calculates that the average number of years in company employment was five years for his sample of current and past employees of the Corporation (Laite, 1981). DeWind (1977: 189), basing his conclusions on turnover indices provided by the Corporation, estimates that in 1958 the average length of stay in the mines was a little over three years and by 1969 it had risen to five years.

The career of one of our informants in the village of Muquiyauyo illustrates graphically the types of mobility that underlie these statistics. This man began to work for the Cerro de Pasco Corporation in 1941 at the age of eighteen to help maintain his mother and siblings, the father having abandoned the family. He worked in the mines for four years before moving to the provincial town of Jauja to study at secondary school. After two years of study, he returned to the mines for a further two years, before spending one year in Lima as a construction labourer and one year in Huancayo where he helped his mother's brother in a bakery. In 1952, he was back in the mine where he stayed until 1968 ultimately working in the mine stores as an *empleado* (white-collar worker). He used his savings and separation pay to buy a tractor and set up a store in Muquiyauyo, and is currently a relatively prosperous farmer in the locality.

There is also clear evidence that workers leave some or all of their family in the villages while they work in the mining sector, returning at weekends and holiday periods or for village festivals. We identified such cases in our studies of the villages of the Mantaro area. Laite (1978) shows that in the town of La Oroya, one of the most habitable of all the Corporation towns, the size of the resident population was much smaller than would have been expected had the Corporation's employees been accompanied by their families. Some of this was accounted for by young bachelors who made up 21 per cent of the *empleados* and 17 per cent of the *obreros*. However, the Corporation's own records for dependants of La Oroya workers show that they have 18,520 children, while the census of 1972 counted only 9,080 children living in the town. Since the Corporation's employees constitute only 40 per cent of La Oroya's adult male population and non-Corporation adults will also have families and dependants, it is evident that a large number of La Oroya workers leave their families at home.

These statistics simply confirm what observers of the living conditions of the mining centres would conclude. Neither the barrack-like company housing located in desolate and smoke-affected barren hillsides, nor the slums of the old town of La Oroya offer a favourable environment for bringing up a family, when compared with villages which, at least, provide space and the opportunities for growing crops and raising animals. Many villages nowadays are well serviced by educational, health, water and electricity services.

The different categories of employees, the *empleados* and the different skill levels of the *obreros*, stayed for similar periods of time with the Corporation. Most employees were drawn from peasant backgrounds, although there were contrasts between the types of village which supplied the different categories of company employees. The unskilled miners tended to come from the poorer *puna* villages, while the more skilled workers and those in La Oroya came from the agricultural villages of the Mantaro valley. These contrasts reflect the difference in educational levels between valley and *puna* villages, with those in the valley villages having benefited from the earlier establishment of primary and secondary schools (Long and Roberts, 1978: 32–3). Even within the valley, as chapter six shows, there was differentiation with some villages supplying *empleados* for the mining sector and others supplying *obreros*, although some *empleados* came from Lima and other coastal and highland cities.

However, migration to the mines has been a predominantly short-distance movement. Laite's analysis of the company records shows that, in the smelter town of La Oroya, 16 per cent of *empleados* and 10 per cent of *obreros* were born in the town itself, while 49 per cent of *empleados* and 64 per cent of *obreros* were born in the Department of Junín, mainly coming from villages. A further 8 per cent of *obreros* and *empleados* originated from Cerro de Pasco. Only 3 per cent of *empleados* and 1 per cent of *obreros* were born in the city of Lima. Most of the remaining workers came from the highland Department of Huancavelica. In the mining centres, workers are also recruited from the Departments of Junín and Pasco. The few people born in the provinces of Lima and Callao were concentrated in the larger mining centre of Cerro de Pasco (DeWind, 1977:261).

The links maintained with the villages and small towns of the region are crucial to understanding the various ways in which the mining economy stimulated regional growth. In the period from 1920 to 1960, the workforce in the mining sector was predominantly made up of migrant peasants, who would eventually return to agriculture or establish themselves on a small-scale in commerce and transport. Even in the period since 1960, workers of all categories (*obreros* and *empleados*) have maintained active links with their villages of origin and with family members living elsewhere, in towns such as Huancayo and Lima. There has, however, been some stabilization of labour in the recent period with the improvement of wages and social conditions in the mining centres. A mobile labouring population, frequently unaccompanied by family, constituted a large, but narrow, urban market for manufactured goods and foodstuffs. Such markets, had they also included the substantial purchasing power of the expatriate administrative staff of the mining complexes, would have been an important stimulus to regional industrial and agricultural production.[5] Instead, the wages paid by the mining sector were, in the main, fed back into the village and small-town economy throughout the region.

These cash flows maintained the peasant semi-subsistence economy (Grondín, 1978b; Long and Roberts, 1978: chapter 11; Laite, chapter 6 in this volume). Savings from mine work were invested in purchasing and improving houses, in helping the villages to improve their infrastructure and in establishing small businesses of a retail or transport type. Some investments were made in agriculture by purchasing land, cattle or a tractor and improving the resource base through use of fertilizers and other modern inputs. The overwhelming impression, however, is that wage labour in the mining sector constituted a complement to small-scale agriculture, enabling households to maintain themselves despite an inadequate and fragmenting resource base. There is little evidence of a major consolidation of land, with the poorer peasants being forced off the land to seek work elsewhere. By and large, most households in this period managed to retain a land base and to combine small-scale agricultural production with other economic activities.

This pattern was reinforced by the labour contribution that the central highlands made to the cotton export sector. Cotton was mainly produced on the central coast of Peru, in the valleys of Cañete and Ica. From 1920 to the 1950s, cotton rivalled petroleum as Peru's major export commodity by value (Table 3). In 1920, Peru was producing 38,386 tonnes of cotton and by 1947 the tonnage had risen to 65,069 tonnes (*Extracto estadístico*, 1947: 139). In 1920, 38,704 workers were employed in cotton production, of whom 63 per cent worked in the Departments of Ica and Lima. By 1944, when cotton production had passed its peak, 79,526 workers were employed, of whom 70 per cent were working in these two central Departments.

These workers were mainly migrants, employed seasonally for the harvest which ran from about May to October. Their daily wage rates averaged around 1.50 soles during the 1930s and rose a little in the 1940s, making them several times higher than wages in highland agriculture (Table 4). Employment in the cotton harvest was an attractive source of income for families from the central highlands, especially since men, women and children could do the work. The harvest period of cotton coincided with the quiet period in highland agriculture and thousands of people went down to the coast every year. Labour migration to the cotton harvest was organized by *enganchadores* who, like those in mining, were often traders and were well-connected with the local authorities of highland villages. *Enganchadores* organized each year the mass exodus of village families, first on foot and subsequently by train. This type of work was sought after most by villagers living on the western side of the Mantaro river close to the passes leading down to the coastal plain. Our surveys in the villages of Sicaya, Chupaca and Ahuac showed that almost all their households had participated in this form of wage labour until the beginning of the 1950s (for more details, see Samaniego, 1978: 61–2).

The development of agriculture until 1960

The development of agriculture throughout this period was constrained by the lack of capital investment. Yet, at the beginning of the century, conditions had seemed to favour the expansion of agricultural production in the central highlands. The advent of the mining economy and the opening-up of the area through the development of rail and road networks created increased market possibilities. Indeed, one of the stated government objectives in building the railways was to stimulate agricultural production in the highlands to serve the growing needs of the urban and mine populations. However, as Miller (n.d.) has demonstrated, there was no evidence in the early years of railway operation that substantial quantities of agricultural goods were being transported from the central highlands for sale in Lima. By the late 1940s, when some foodstuffs were transported to Lima by road, the central railway was carrying insignificant amounts of produce. Between 1946 and 1949, for example, it carried an average of 2,477 tonnes of agricultural produce per year, which constituted only one-half per cent of the total carriage, excluding shipments of ore. The bulk of cargo was concentrated in manufactured goods, provisions, timber and petroleum.

Agricultural produce could find markets in the mines and growing towns of the region. But these were likely to be limited by the non-market exchanges between the peasant villages and work centres mentioned in the last section. However, the absence of a strong local market stimulus is not in itself an adequate explanation for the poor performance of agriculture within this regional economy. We need to know why it was that the central highlands failed to become an important supplier of foodstuffs to Lima and why food processing industries did not develop within the region.

One important conditioning factor was the movement of agricultural prices from the 1920s to 1950. From 1928 to 1946, the wholesale price index for vegetables, cereals and meat and dairy products increased more slowly than the general index for all products, including manufactured goods. Indeed after its high point in 1926, the price index for vegetable and animal products fell and did not reach the 1926 level again until 1942 (*Extracto estadístico*, 1947: 291). The relatively low price of food products was a major contributor in this period to reducing the cost of living. The cost of living index based on Lima prices was lower for food than for housing, clothing and miscellaneous items throughout the 1920s and for most of the 1930s, with food prices increasing relative to other prices only in the 1940s (Table 5). Even in the 1940s, clothing prices were still rising more quickly, and thus providing a stimulus for the development of the textile industry in Huancayo and other places.

Food prices were not, then, favourable enough relative to those in other sectors of the economy to provide much incentive for investment. This situation did not result, as has been the case elsewhere, from a dynamic peasant production that kept prices low, hence subsidizing the costs of urban development. As Fitzgerald (1979: 143) argues, there is no evidence that low food prices were the result of large numbers of peasant cultivators in Peru selling their surpluses cheaply in the urban market. Instead, these low prices seemed to have resulted from government free trade policies which, in these years, led to

Table 5 *Relative movement of price indices in Lima, 1920–47 (1913 = 100)*

Year	Food price index/ Other indices	Food price index/ Clothing price index
1920	98	78
1923	84	67
1926	81	76
1929	80	72
1932	89	90
1935	93	87
1938	96	88
1941	99	82
1944	100	73
1947	117	80

Source: Extracto estadístico, 1947: 296. This cost of living index is for worker expenditures in Lima. The other items included are housing (18 per cent of total expenditure), clothing (12 per cent of total expenditure) and sundry expenditures (15 per cent of total expenditure). Food is calculated as 55 per cent of total expenditure.

large per capita food imports, particularly of cereals (Thorp and Bertram, 1978: 139–40, 197–200). Furthermore, government stimuli for domestic agricultural production were directed towards encouraging coastal farming in products which competed with those of the highlands.

From 1934–8, Peru imported every year, on average, 125,800 tonnes of wheat (FAO, 1955: 47). Using 1937 as the base year, the index of wheat imports rose steadily throughout the 1940s, with one decline in 1946, to almost double by 1950 (*Extracto estadístico*, 1950). Thereafter, wheat imports increased even faster. The significance of these figures can be appreciated by comparing them with the total national production of wheat which, in 1937, was 90,258 tonnes. Junín produced 24,190 tonnes of the national wheat total.

Although wheat and flour were the main imports, other basic food products were also imported when necessary. Barley, which was used for brewing beer as well as for domestic consumption, was imported in increasing quantities. The 1937 index of barley imports had more than doubled by 1950 (*Extracto estadístico*, 1950). Even potatoes were imported during these years. 146,692 kilos were imported in 1937 and similar quantities thereafter. These quantities were relatively small compared with national production but, again, indicated government unwillingness to impose tariffs in order to foster local production. Rice was the only produce that was, to any extent, protected by government tariffs and producer subsidies, resulting in some expansion of rice production in the northern coastal region (Thorp and Bertram, 1978: 199–200).

Government policy towards non-export agriculture concentrated on keeping prices down to benefit urban consumers, both by permitting the import of cheaper products especially from the United States and Canada, and by price controls (Thorp and Bertram, 1978: 132–40, 198–200). In these circumstances, there was little incentive for the development of agriculture either in smallholdings or large-scale farms.

At the beginning of this period, the agriculture of the central highlands was concentrated in precisely those products that were most affected by this national policy. The four principal crops of Junín from 1929 to 1960 were potatoes, barley, wheat and maize. In 1929, these products occupied 27.9 per cent, 21.2 per cent, 12.3 per cent and 10 per cent respectively of the Department's total cultivated area (Censo Agropecuario, 1930, cited in Renique, 1978: 112). Junín's production of these crops relative to national production had sharply declined by 1969 (Table 6). Initially, there had been some absolute growth in production levels, mainly by bringing more land under cultivation and with only small increases in productivity concentrated chiefly in potato production. By 1959, however, even the yields on potatoes had declined from the 1950 levels.

The climate and relatively poor soils of the central highlands made cereal production a hazardous enterprise. Nevertheless, investments in irrigation, fertilizers and the use of hybrid seeds, together with new cropping patterns, could, in this period, have increased agricultural production significantly. However, unfavourable prices for non-export agricultural commodities and the weakness of the urban market made investment in agriculture less attractive than in trade or transport. Our case studies in different areas of the Mantaro valley – in the Jauja, Concepción and Huancayo provinces – showed only a few cases of land consolidation with the major trend being towards land fragmentation in response to increased population levels.

The improvement in potato production during part of the period was concentrated in the less densely populated zones at some distance from Huancayo (*Extracto estadístico*, 1944). The potato was the one major crop in the central highlands which required little investment to improve productivity; it was a basic local food and faced little competition from imports. It thus became the main agricultural crop in terms of value. However, the potato did not generate significant linkages with industry or commerce. Unlike wheat and barley, the potato was marketed directly to the consumer, involved no processing, nor was it transformed into an industrial food product. However, by 1960, and partly because of deliberate government policy, potato pro-

Table 6 *Junín's production of selected crops as percentage of national production*

	1929	1950	1950–6	1959
Potatoes	9.5	22.0	19.8	5.9
Wheat	12.4	16.7	13.6	2.5
Barley	18.5	15.6	13.6	7.2
Maize	4.0	11.0	8.7	5.9

Source: Extracto estadístico, 1930, 1950, 1959.

duction in Lima was already rivalling that in Junín, thus challenging highland producers for their largest potential market.

During the 1950s, and especially in the 1960s, the pattern of agricultural development in the central highlands began to change. Wheat and barley production diminished sharply and were replaced by fodder, vegetables and dairy farming. We will discuss these changes in chapters seven to ten when we consider the contemporary period, but we can note here that the new pattern was still based on a highly fragmented pattern of landholding, and on the direct marketing of products to urban centres and, increasingly, to Lima.

There is no evidence, then, that the cash flows generated by the mining economy consolidated agricultural enterprise and generated important regional linkages between agriculture, industry and commerce. As we shall see in chapter four, the control of land and of agricultural production was not, in fact, a significant factor in the political and economic power of the class that was dominant in the region during the period up to the 1960s.

Industry and commerce

The mining economy had a more decisive influence on the development of manufacturing industry and on that of commerce than it did on agriculture. Between 1920 and 1960 the economy of the central highlands was one of the most highly commercialized regional economies in the country. One indicator of this are the sales of the Estanco de Tabaco. For most of the years from 1943, when the figures are first available, until 1950, Junín was second only to Lima-Callao in the value of sales (*Extracto estadístico*, various years). The concentration of consumption in Lima is shown, however, by the fact that half of these sales occurred there, while Junín accounted between 1943 and 1950 for only 5.4 per cent of all sales. The comparison with Lima demonstrates the concentration of consumer markets in the capital. Thus, while the market for

Table 7 *Economically active population by sector of activity:*
Junín 1940 and 1961 (percentages)

Branch of activity	1940	1961[a]
Agriculture and livestock	61.4	51.8
Mining	8.4	10.1
Construction	1.8	2.6
Transformative industry	12.4	11.2
Transport	2.1	2.7
Commerce	4.3	7.2
Administration and social services[b]	2.6	4.1
Domestic service	4.0	3.9
Other personal (e.g. restaurants)	1.4	2.6
Others	1.5	3.5

[a] These percentages include the new Department of Pasco created in 1944 whose capital was the mining centre of Cerra de Pasco. They have been included with those of Junín to allow comparisons with the 1940 figures when Pasco was part of the Department of Junín.
[b] Part of the increase in administrative services is due to the rise of Huancayo as the dominant organizing centre of the region.
Source: Dirección General de Estadística, 1944, 1966.

tobacco was twelve times greater in Lima than in Junín, the population of Lima-Callao was only four times greater than that of Junín.

In this period, the regional economy increasingly diversified into non-agricultural activities, with especially significant growth occurring in commerce and administrative services (see Table 7). The development and dynamic of the region is also manifested in the growing importance of the town of Huancayo which had become the most important commercial and administrative centre of the central highlands. Huancayo increasingly concentrated the population of Junín to become, by 1961, Peru's sixth largest city after Lima-Callao, Arequipa, Cuzco, Trujillo and Chimbote (Table 8).

The growth of Huancayo was based upon its function as an organizing centre for the mining economy. It became a bustling commercial and industrial centre whose housing and urban infrastructure rapidly expanded. The relative growth of Huancayo can be appreciated from the revenues of the provincial councils and their associated welfare institutions (Beneficiencia Pública). These revenues give some indication both of the scope of municipal initiative in public works and welfare, and of business and real estate activity, since they are based on revenues from taxes on property, commerce and the sales of certain commodities.

Table 8 *Population growth of Huancayo and Junín: 1876–1961*

	1876	Per- centage of total	1940	Per- centage of total	1961	Per- centage of total
Junín						
Huancayo (urban zone)	5,948	2.8	26,729	6.2	64,000	12.3
Total	209,759		428,855		521,210	
Peru						
Lima-Callao	155,436	5.8	619,934	9.3	1,902,024	18.4
Total	2,699,106		6,680,500		10,319,527	

Sources: Extracto estadístico, 1923: 1–2; Dirección General de Estadística, 1944, 1966.

In the 1920s, the revenues of the provincial council of Huancayo, including that for welfare, was less than 1 per cent of the total national municipal and welfare revenues of provincial councils. The Lima-Callao provincial revenues, in contrast, made up half the national total. However, the other provinces of Junín, such as Tarma and Cerro de Pasco, had revenues that, in these years, often exceeded that of Huancayo. The change in Huancayo's relative position began at the end of the 1930s. The revenues of the provincial council became 1 per cent of the national total at this time. In the late 1940s and early 1950s, they fluctuated between 3 and 5 per cent of the national total. Compared to the other provincial councils of the Department, Huancayo's revenue was by far the largest, representing 66 per cent of all provincial revenues in Junín in 1955.[6]

The contrast with Arequipa, Peru's most important regional centre is instructive. In the 1930s, Huancayo's revenues were only about one-tenth of those of Arequipa, although the populations of the two provinces were approximately the same. By the late 1940s and 1950s, however, Huancayo's relative status changed. Its revenues rose to about one-half of those of Arequipa; and in 1955 reached 54 per cent of Arequipa's total revenue of just over 16 million soles or approximately 408,000 dollars (1951 exchange rate). By 1955, the population of Huancayo province was estimated to be 154,518 and that of Arequipa, 160,300 (*Anuario estadístico*, 1955: 42–3).

In the period 1920 to 1960, Huancayo became a centre for manufacturing industry. The analysis of the industrialization of Huancayo will be undertaken

in more detail in chapter 4, but here we will briefly outline its relative importance in the national context. It is difficult to provide reliable data on
industrialization since national statistics do not give a systematic regional
breakdown until the 1960s. However, in 1943, the figures for industrial
establishments were published on a regional basis in the *Extracto estadístico*. In
that year, Junín was third in importance in the number and capital value of
industrial establishments, after Arequipa and Lima, where the majority of
industry was concentrated. The factories reported to exist in Junín at this time
were one woollen and one silk factory, ten small garment workshops, one
ribbon factory, two tanneries, twelve soft drinks producers and two breweries.
Most of these establishments were located in Huancayo itself.

In the first economic census of 1963, Junín was again third, after Lima and
Arequipa, in the number of industrial establishments reported, Of the 4,195
recorded in that year, Lima reported 2,593, Arequipa 224 and Junín 147. The
average size of these industrial units was 38 employees in Lima, 32.5 in
Arequipa, and 19.4 in Huancayo. The calculation for Huancayo excludes the
smelter plant at La Oroya (with some 5,000 workers).

Junín's industrialization was closely linked to the evolving regional
economy. The textile factories, for example, were supplied with wool from local
estates. In 1931, the largest textile firm (Los Andes) was established in
Huancayo, mainly on the initiative of the director general of the Sociedad
Ganadera del Centro, the largest livestock estate in central Peru. The Sociedad
Ganadera del Centro took this action in response to price fluctuations in the
international wool market and in order to reduce its freight costs by marketing
in Huancayo (Pareja, 1979: 8). The other main industries in Junín, such as the
tanneries and the breweries, were also dependent upon local products. Other
incentives to the establishment of industry in Junín were the relatively low
labour costs of the region (see Table 4).

Given these incentives to industrialization, and the circulation of cash
deriving principally from the mining economy, it is surprising that Junín and
Huancayo did not develop a more solid industrial base. Data from the register of
businesses of the different Departments of Peru indicate this relative inability of
entrepreneurs in Junín to invest locally. These registers do not contain reliable
estimates of the total value of businesses registered in a particular Department,
but they do provide an indication of the relative propensity of businessmen to
establish formal enterprises and to invest capital. From 1938 to 1960, Lima
accounted for approximately 90 per cent of the total capital declared by
businesses established in these years (*Extracto estadístico*, Registro mercantil:
various years). Arequipa accounted for 2.9 per cent and Junín for less than 1 per
cent. Some Junín-based commercial and industrial companies were undoubt-

edly registered in the Lima office, but our own examination of the Junín records in Huancayo indicated that most of the important companies of this period were registered there. The contrast with Arequipa is also significant and indicates that the entrepreneurs of the southern city were more prepared than their Junín counterparts to invest locally. Arequipa was more distant from Lima than Huancayo (see Map 1), although the surpluses generated in the Arequipa region by the wool-producing economy were less than those created by the mining economy in the central highlands.

Conclusion

The mining economy of the central highlands was not an enclave economy in the narrow sense of the term. Important linkages developed between the various sectors of the regional economy. These were fostered by the surpluses generated by mine production. The central highlands do not exhibit, then, the economic stagnation that Klaren (1973) reports for Trujillo, consequent upon the implantation of large-scale, export-oriented capitalist agricultural enterprises and their monopolization of production and associated services.

The main economic impact of the Cerro de Pasco Corporation was through the wages paid to its workers which were spent locally, and through the supplies and services which it purchased in the region. The chief characteristic of these inputs was that they were numerous, but small in amount. Workers did not earn enough to accumulate significant amounts of capital and their wages were spent mainly on consumer goods. The traders, truckers and local manufacturers who supplied the goods and services also had relatively few opportunities to accumulate capital. The markets of the central highlands were extensive, but based on a population with low purchasing power. The costs involved in travelling to cover these markets, competition over supplying them, especially given the proximity of Lima, and the risks associated with fluctuations in demand made businessmen loathe to expand their enterprise. The result was a numerous class of small-scale entrepreneurs and very few large-scale businesses, most of which, as we shall see in chapter 4, were controlled by Lima-based commercial firms.

In this context, the regional economy evolved as a loosely integrated one in which different and, at times, conflicting economic rationalities coexisted amongst different sectors of the population. Hence, we find in the agricultural sphere, capitalist farmers, peasant entrepreneurs and smallholders dependent on communal resources. In the urban/industrial sphere, large-scale capitalist enterprises were often administered by foreigners and manned by workers who retained rights to land and returned regularly to their villages. Likewise, trade and finance were organized, as we shall see in chapter four, by ethnic and social groups with different types of commitment to the region. Furthermore, the weakness of government administration at regional level meant that there was no reason for the persistence of class-based forms of political organization aimed at capturing local power.

In contrast to the nineteenth century, there is less evidence of concern on the part of local groups for the expansion of local agriculture. Instead, income opportunities were sought in wage labour and in service activities. These opportunities made it possible for families to retain a land base in the village despite increasing demographic pressure on resources. Some of the implications of these processes are brought out in chapters four to eight (see also, Long and Roberts, 1978). The main implications were the reorganization of the household in order to manage and take advantage of spatially-dispersed income opportunities, the increasing investment in education with the aim of securing external jobs, and the reshaping of village institutions, such as fiestas and village associations, to bridge urban and rural areas. These changes in village institutions helped consolidate the links with the mining sector, both by facilitating wage labour and by providing a framework for the organization of life in the mining camps.

The transformations that occurred in the central highlands were partial ones in that they did not result in the complete integration and rationalization of the economy at regional level. Thus, small-scale enterprise in farming, commerce and industry survived and proliferated alongside the growth of large-scale capitalist mining operations. This structure was basically a dualistic one reflecting at regional level the pattern described by Fitzgerald for the national level (Fitzgerald, 1979: 91–9). The mining sector was closely linked to the international economy both in terms of its exports and for inputs of machinery, technology and expertise. It was also the dominant source of surplus generation in the region. In contrast, the small-scale sector had no direct links with the international economy, its markets being predominantly local. In farming, industry and the services, the small enterprise tended to be labour intensive, lacked modern inputs and had low levels of productivity.

This dualistic structure was not based on the separation of economic sectors, but rather on a pattern of exchanges and interdependencies between them. The large-scale mining enterprise benefited from cheap labour and supplies subsidized by peasant agriculture; this limited the consolidation of landholdings and the expansion of agricultural production. It also hindered the development of an industrial proletariat since even the unionized mine workers retained links with their villages and had land there. A similar 'peasant-worker' phenomenon appeared, as we will see later, among the unionized textile workers of

Huancayo. An important contributing factor in maintaining the region's unbalanced pattern of development was the local class structure that developed during this period of the mining economy. It is to this issue that we turn in the next three chapters.

4

Class relations, local economies and large-scale mining

In this and the next two chapters, we look at the implications of the dominance of the mining economy for the class relations that developed in different types of rural and urban location. The expansion of mining created opportunities and constraints and stimulated a diversity of responses from a highly differentiated peasant sector which was closely interrelated with local towns and cities. The struggles that took place focussed on the appropriation and control of the new resources generated by the mining economy.

The cases that follow have been chosen to illustrate this complexity, contrasting the impact of the mining economy on economically differentiated, agriculturally based villages in the valley with its impact on less differentiated, predominantly pastoral villages in the highland zone. The valley villages have a history of 'independent' smallholder production, complemented by crafts and commerce; whereas the livelihood of the highland *puna* villages has been more dependent on external factors, such as relations with the owners of the large livestock estates bordering them and with the valley merchants and farmers.

In the present chapter, we focus upon Huancayo, the administrative and service centre of the central highlands. Huancayo illustrates, more than any other location in the region, the workings of the mining system of production since it is the place through which a great deal of the inputs and outputs of the mining sector are organized. We analyse the class composition of Huancayo at the height of the dominance of the mining economy. By this time, Huancayo had become the main centre of the central highlands and was the place of residence of a regionally important class of businessmen. We examine the characteristics of this class and their relations with other urban classes. Although the business class profited from the mining economy, they did not own or control this major regional productive resource. We seek to understand the difference that this situation made to class conflict and to the dynamics of political change in the region.

70

Huancayo and the mining economy

Huancayo's dominant position was consolidated and given a definite form when Huancayo took on the characteristics of an entrepot city. The notion of 'entrepot' is usually restricted to those port or capital cities that serve to link an underdeveloped country with the metropolis, acting as administrative and commercial centres that help to organize the exploitation of the primary resources. The case of Huancayo is distinct in that the city became an integral part of the effective and profitable working of the agro-mining economy.

From the 1920s, Huancayo became an important centre for the recruitment of labour for both mines and plantations. Even the livestock haciendas, which did not require a large workforce, used Huancayo as one source of recruitment and also as a supply centre. In 1919, the Sociedad Ganadera del Centro advertised in the Huancayo newspaper *La Patria* for skilled workers. By 1937, six of the large hacienda companies had offices in Huancayo.

The transport of seasonal workers to the coastal cotton plantations of Cañete was organized from Huancayo. In the early years the recruits travelled by foot to the coast but, with the arrival of the railway, they were sent down from Huancayo in specially organized railway coaches. After the completion of the road in the 1930s, bus transport was increasingly used.

One of the main *enganchadores* of the area, whose family originated from the villages of Sicaya and San Jerónimo, became permanently resident in Huancayo because of the facilities that it offered as a transport and trading centre. He set up several businesses in Huancayo and bought a large house. The importance of Huancayo to him, as to other *enganchadores*, was that, as a banking, judicial and communication centre, it made the work of advancing money and drawing up and enforcing contracts easier. Huancayo also played some part in the organization of the workforce for the mines. It served as a place where family and relatives could, in times of need, receive cash advances on the salaries of mine workers, or where mine supply and construction contractors could pay bills or advance credit.[1] One Huancayo businessman reported receiving a budget of some £20,000 to handle such transactions in the 1970s.

The most important service that Huancayo provided for the mines was that of organizing the provisioning of the goods and services on which these enterprises depended. Huancayo was the headquarters of the Cercapuquio mining company, had agencies of the other mining companies and was the location of one of the government mining offices. The stores of the Cerro de Pasco Corporation were, to a large extent, stocked by Huancayo merchants who acted as agents of Lima factories and importing houses. One Huancayo businessman supplied not only soap powder to the Corporation but was also contracted to supply mattresses manufactured by a small Huancayo workshop which had some five workers and which used the wool and cotton waste of the Huancayo textile factories.[2]

With rising timber prices after the First World War, the Cerro de Pasco Corporation also encouraged the development of the eucalyptus industry for pit props and rail sleepers and an agent was installed in Huancayo to organize the buying of timber from the peasant farmers of the area. This man, a Canadian, was made mayor of Huancayo in 1927 and served for three years in that post. The timber which was bought in minor quantities was stocked in Huancayo and became the basis of a small-scale timber industry. As a railhead and the junction between the broad-gauge central railway and the narrow-gauge Huancavelica railway, Huancayo became important for the trans-shipment of minerals from the southern mining area. These were sent to the smelters at La Oroya. The city also became a purchasing centre for minerals from small-scale miners. Although the large companies like Cerro de Pasco appear not to have made substantial profits from this purchasing activity, it was in their interest to keep alive small-scale mining as a potential reserve.[3] Until at least the 1950s, two Huancayo firms bought ore for the large companies and made cash advances to the small-scale miners.

Of perhaps even greater significance for the economy of Huancayo was the business of transporting ore and constructing roads and buildings for the mines. Several of the large mines (Cobriza and Cercapuquio) sub-contracted the shipment of their ore to local truckers; these truckers often combined this business with that of transporting agricultural produce. All this stimulated the development of large repair workshops in Huancayo, as well as providing a lucrative business for the agencies that sold the trucks and buses. The construction work involved in building roads to the Cercapuquio mine and to some of those of Cerro de Pasco was organized from Huancayo, and the small Huancayo manufacturers provided much of the building materials that were needed.

These examples could be multiplied but, unfortunately, it is not possible to give a more precise estimate for the amount of mine and hacienda business that was conducted in Huancayo. In the case of the largest of the hardware merchants, his personal estimates suggest that, in the years immediately following the Second World War, something like half of his business depended on supplying the mines and, to a lesser extent, the haciendas. Much of the rest of this kind of business depended, indirectly, on these enterprises since they also sold to the shops and craftsmen of the villages and small towns that provided the bulk of the labour migrants.

One consequence of Huancayo's increasing integration with the agro-mining enterprises was the diversification of its urban economy. In 1915, the city's economic activities were heavily commercial, with 74 per cent of the council's tax assessment on businesses being levied on traders. By 1947, trade formed 43 per cent of the city's tax revenue and small factories, bakeries, transport and such services as restaurants and hotels made up 48 per cent. At this date, the city also had four large-scale textile mills whose total workforce was over one thousand.

The first of these mills was established in the late 1920s and the others in the 1930s, following the Depression. By 1947, the textile workforce, including the smaller factories and workshops, was probably about 1,500 workers out of a total urban workforce of some 8,000 workers. The other industries in Huancayo were small-scale and, with the exception of the tanneries and the brewery, each employed less than ten workers.[4] By 1953, the textile workforce had risen to over 3,000, which constituted 80 per cent of the economically active population of the city (International Development Service, 1953). The stages in the diversification of the city's economy are revealed when we consider the period of registration for different types of businesses in Huancayo (see Table 9). These businesses represented the larger, formally established businesses whose directors included the most prominent Huancayo businessmen of each period. Industrial businesses were registered mainly in the 1940s and this is also a period of intensive commercial activity. However, by the 1950s, transport enterprises dominate the registrations.

Migration and urban growth

The economic diversification of Huancayo was accompanied by an expansion of the urban population to a size of 27,000 in 1940 and 64,000 in 1961 (Dirección General de Estadística, 1966). A large part of this population increase was due to in-migration. This migration had two clearly distinguishable components. The first was the increase in the migration of people originating from Lima (often foreign-born) who came to establish businesses or to fill clerical or professional positions. Although this kind of migration was a feature of Huancayo in the 1900s, by the 1940s it had come to characterize the composition of the city's business class. Huancayo had always been a city open to migrants; now the migrants moved to take over the city.

The increasing importance of the immigrant population can be appreciated by comparing the situation in later years with that in 1920. In 1920, the number of literate householders born in Huancayo was 52 per cent, a proportion of natives identical to that reported in 1900. Indeed, the percentage of natives of Huancayo reporting their occupation as trader was higher in 1920 than in

Table 9 *Numbers and types of businesses registered: 1930–59*

Years of registration	No.	Industry	Commerce	Transport[a]	Hotels, restaurants, banks	Mines	Agriculture
				Type of business (percentages)			
1930–9	60	22	29	17	12	8	12
1940–9	86	26	39	17	7	—	11
1950–9	65	2	31	40	6	—	11

[a] Transport covers bus companies, car and truck agencies and shops for spare parts.

Note: The enterprises registered with the Registro Civil are chiefly the larger ones and those which involve partnerships. Excluded are family businesses; but we found that most of the larger Huancayo enterprises were recorded. Many of the enterprises registered had a very short duration. What these data indicate is where economic interests were directed at a given period, as local businessmen combined to exploit what they saw to be promising new opportunities.

Source: Registro Civil, Patrón de Comerciantes, Huancayo.

1900, with 46 per cent of traders born in Huancayo in 1900. By 1935, however, of the twenty-five prominent citizens who formed a commission to collect funds to erect a monument to 'Fatherhood' only four or five were from Huancayo. The remainder were almost equally divided between foreigners – Chinese, Japanese, and Europeans – and merchants from Lima (*La Voz*, January, 1935). In 1947, 40 per cent of the large commercial establishments were owned by people with foreign surnames – mainly Chinese, Japanese and European Jews (Registro Civil, Patrón de Comerciantes, 1947).[5] A large proportion of the other big establishments were branches of Lima firms, or were owned by businessmen originating from Lima.

The foreign presence in Huancayo's economy was a source of comment in the local council and several of the Huancayo-born councillors drew attention to the number of foreigners owning businesses and to the fact that many of them had not complied with the laws about naturalization (Actas: 19 June 1935). A resolution required that any new foreign establishment should first be reported to the trade inspector to ensure that the number of such establishments did not exceed the quota (Actas: 4 December 1938). After the Second World War, it was claimed that the Japanese were avoiding restrictions by registering businesses in the names of Peruvians (Actas: 24 February 1945).

The second component in migration was the large-scale influx of people from the nearby villages, who came to work in the growing textile industry. In the 1940s and 1950s, over 40 per cent of the textile workforce was recruited from the villages (Roberts, 1978a). Of the remainder, nearly 30 per cent were born in Huancayo itself. The data on the textile workforce are based on one company's records of its entire workforce during these years and thus are a direct sample of this section of Huancayo's working population. This migration from the villages contrasts with the situation at the beginning of the twentieth century when there was little migration between the nearby villages and the city. This migrant workforce of the 1940s and 1950s was relatively well educated, though they were not the wealthiest villagers. The more prosperous farmers and those who had achieved high levels of education were just as likely to migrate directly to Lima as they were to move to Huancayo (Laite, 1977; Long, 1973; Roberts, 1973; Samaniego, 1974).

It is more difficult to reconstruct the origins of sections of the city's population other than the textile workers since suitable statistics are not available. However, in our survey of the population of Huancayo conducted in 1972, we included life-histories of respondents and, on the basis of these histories, it is possible to isolate those who first came to the city in the 1940s and 1950s and to analyse their origins and occupations.[6] The analysis of the survey, supplemented by reports from informants, indicates that the labour force of Huancayo in the period of the dominance of the mining economy was mainly recruited from the areas adjacent to the city (i.e. the valley, its highlands and Huancavelica). The professional and managerial classes, however, tended to come from Lima and the coast.

Within the labour force there was some differentiation. Migrants from the fairly large and prosperous villages around the city tended to colonize the relatively well-paid factory and craft jobs, whilst migrants from the remote and poorer villages provided the more casual labour force and were involved in petty trade and personal services.[7]

Class relationships in the city

In comparison with the beginning of the twentieth century, Huancayo's economy became more closely controlled by Lima-based capital in the period from the 1920s to the 1960s. The mechanisms by which this increasing dependence was enforced were the banking houses and the growing importance of credit for the expansion of business in the area. A branch of the Bank of Peru and London (later known as the Bank of London and South America) was established in 1919 and branches of the other major banks were established by the end of the 1930s. More significant for the nature of local social relationships, however, was the increasing importance of the importing houses and their agents. By 1919, Grace and Company had established an office in Huancayo to sell textiles, dry goods and sewing machines. This company was shortly followed by another American agency, Wessel, Duval and Company, by the British companies of Duncan Fox and Milne and Company, by the Japanese firm of Susuki Hermanos and by several Chinese and German importing houses. Some of these firms were interested both in selling imported manufactured products, or those manufactured in their Lima factories, and in purchasing the products of the region. Grace and Company traded wool and one of the German houses purchased wheat for flour.

The predominance of foreigners and migrants from Lima among the most important businessmen of Huancayo was a direct result of the policies of the importing houses and of the agricultural and mining enterprises. The importing houses showed a preference for recruiting agents of their own nationality or who were married to someone of their nationality. Several of the banks were foreign-owned and managed. The prominence of Italians in Huancayo's economy owed much to their links with the Banco Italiano of Lima (later called Banco de Crédito). The development of an economic climate that was dominated by the export–import business meant that those who had family and friendship links with Lima and abroad were in a favoured position. Their credit was assumed to be better than that of local people and their political contacts with Lima were also usually advantageous. The Chinese and Japanese groups in Huancayo retained a strong cultural identity, forming their own associations and establishing links with Lima associations and with various importing houses of their own nationality.[8]

The importing houses and their agents dominated the economy of Huancayo, and they did so without the necessity of investing profits to establish a close-knit network of local relationships. The mode of operation of these importing houses gave their businesses the characteristics of monopolies. Most of the larger houses – with Grace and Company taking the lead – established factories and bought haciendas to achieve a vertical integration of their businesses that ensured maximum profitability (Yepes, 1972).[9] Some of the Chinese businessmen rented commercial farms and shipped the produce directly to Lima. In this situation, it was only the local agents of these houses who were able to make large-scale purchases of regional products for Lima and for export.

The Huancayo agents were supplied in bulk and on a regular consignment basis. Their goods were then sold directly to the public or through retailers. The agency of a particularly scarce product, such as cement, was sought after by Huancayo merchants and was often obtained only after paying an extra commission to the Lima company who supplied it. Not only could the local agent make an extra – and often illicit – profit from such a scarce product, but he could also use it to stimulate the sale of his other products. In one incident in 1945, for example, the mayor of Huancayo, who was also the administrator of one of the large textile factories, proposed an administrative regulation to secure the purchase of cement directly from the Lima cement company for himself and for the city council. He was aided in the negotiations with the company by his brother, the local manager of the Banco Popular, who had excellent contacts in Lima. This manoeuvre was apparently used when the mayor was unable to bribe the Huancayo cement agent to give him extra cement for the expansion of the big textile mill (Actas: 1 March 1953).

Such was the importance of these agencies that a successful business career in Huancayo depended upon securing and accumulating profitable agencies. One important foreign merchant began in Huancayo in 1938 as an employee for a Lima-based German importing house. Acting as their local agent, he travelled throughout the highlands establishing contacts as far afield as Huancavelica, Ayacucho, Huánuco, Tingo María, Pasco and Chanchamayo. Later, he became independent of the importing house and set himself up as the agent for a flour mill, a local textile factory, a Lima shoe factory and another German firm, while still retaining the original agency as a supplier of paper and school materials.

The flour agency involved collecting wheat for their mill in Lima, and in the same way he bought up wool for textile firms in Lima.

One indication of the importance in Huancayo's economy of these links with importing houses in Lima is the composition of the Chamber of Commerce in Huancayo in 1927.[10] At this time, the president was a merchant originating from Lima who had once been an employee of Grace and Company and was still co-owner of a Lima dry goods firm which had branches in the highlands, including one in Huancayo. The vice-president was the manager of the local branch of the Bank of Peru and London and the treasurer was an Italian merchant who held several importing agencies. Of the five committee members, three were managers of the local offices of importing houses. In this same year, the mayor of Huancayo was a Canadian, who was an employee of the Cerro de Pasco Corporation.

It proved relatively easy for Huancayo businessmen to obtain credit from the Lima banks and importing houses. Indeed, one of the greatest economic assets of this Huancayo business class was their access to credit.[11] Very little cash savings were invested in their various enterprises, and the formally established firms declared little capital assets. Nor did they attempt to raise any by selling stock to the public. The fact of a partner contributing cash is unusual enough for it to receive a special mention in the Patrón de Comerciantes (Registro Civil). The common practice in commerce, industry and land purchases was for bank loans to be taken out almost immediately, with the fixed assets – land, buildings or machinery – being mortgaged for the loan. Given the expanding market of this period and the high level of interest paid to the banks, the predominant strategy was that of maximizing profits on sales rather than that of building up and improving assets.

The development of Huancayo's industries illustrates this process. The 'owners' of the assets were usually the banks who financed the operations. The entrepreneurs who set up the industries made their profits from their sales and, since labour was cheap and abundant and the markets in the mine townships and villages were expanding, showed little interest in modernizing production.

The majority of Huancayo's industrial enterprises were established by merchants. The largest textile factory – Manufacturas del Centro – was founded by a Central European Jew who had traded in cloth to the growing markets of the mine townships. Facing difficulties in obtaining an adequate imported supply, he started a textile mill with the help of Lidio Mongilardi – the manager of the first of the textile mills in Huancayo. The textile machinery was second-hand and was not substantially improved during the whole lifetime of this privately-owned factory. As one of the ex-administrators of Manufacturas recalled, the whole emphasis of the industry was on sales. Large numbers of workers were hired in order to keep up high levels of production, and additional jobs were done on a putting-out basis.

Conditions of work in the early 1940s appear to have been extremely bad, with male and female workers expected to work, at times, for sixteen hours continuously (Pareja, 1979). Pareja documents carefully the various abuses to which these first textile workers were submitted, including the use of the local police to intimidate or imprison those involved in labour union organization. However, the textile union, which was organized by APRA, became strong in the late 1950s, partly because of the collaboration of the party with President Prado. In this later period, the strategy of management was to avoid strikes by agreeing to worker demands on wages and working conditions. Top pay among textile workers became twenty times that received by bank clerks (Manrique, 1972).

Also, in the 1940s and early 1950s, when demand was rising and there was little external competition, the textile mills could, without difficulty, sell all they produced. Increased costs because of higher wages were met by acquiring additional bank loans and by lobbying government for protective tariffs. No attempts were made to lower costs by improving machinery. The owners of these Huancayo industries had, by the late 1940s, moved to Lima to look after the commercial side of their businesses, leaving managers in charge of production. In the case of Manufacturas, the company was ultimately taken over by the largest creditor – the Banco Popular.

This Huancayo business class did not involve themselves significantly in those activites which would have required them to compete for and organize local resources. Despite the importance of transport services and the timber industry in the city's economy, the large-scale businessmen remained outside these activities. Both activities involved establishing and maintaining relationships with local people. Timber – eucalyptus – was dispersed in hundreds of small plots throughout the area. Transport was organized by a large number of single units which, given the state of the roads and the number of passengers, required constant repair and detailed care. Of the thirty or so transport enterprises established in the 1940s and 1950s, only three, short-lived enterprises, were established by people from Lima or abroad. The other enterprises were set up by small-scale entrepreneurs from the villages or from Huancayo whose contribution to the enterprise was usually a second-hand truck or bus. The agencies to sell cars, trucks and agricultural machinery were, in contrast, controlled by businessmen who originated from Lima.

An indication of the interconnections among large-scale businessmen is given by reviewing the composition of the partnership structure of the firms registered in the 1940s and 1950s in the Patrón de Comerciantes.[12] Of the twenty-five businessmen who were partners in more than one of these firms, some ten of them were completely interconnected by the network of partnerships. These men controlled the economically most important enterprises in Huancayo; but only three were born in the city or in the area around. There were five 'isolates' who were not interconnected with the other businessmen and these were involved in those economic sectors that required close connections with local people – the timber industry and transport. Three of the 'isolates' were, in fact, local people.

In many cases, partnerships among the business class were short-term and resulted from a temporary coincidence of interests. These businessmen did not develop strong economic and social alliances and never came to form a defined regional interest group. Their links with Lima and the business commitments that many of them had in the capital meant that their residence in Huancayo was also temporary. They spent long periods of time in Lima – often a year or more – with but occasional visits to Huancayo.

Those who became involved in politics and became national parliamentary representatives were to spend most of their time in Lima and showed little regional political commitment. The long-established Huancayo landowner, Augusto Peñalozo, who also owned considerable amounts of urban land, was a national deputy for over twenty years. Other long-term parliamentary representatives were also prominent Huancayo business figures: E. Risco Gill, Lima-born merchant; E. Ráez, Huancayo-born professional and property owner; A. Chaparro, manager of Sociedad Ganadera del Centro; R. Alvarez Calderón, businessman and manager of Sociedad Ganadera del Centro; J. and F. Calmell del Solar, businessmen and property and landowners. Despite the political prominence of some of these people, they gained little that was substantial for Huancayo. Indeed F. Calmell del Solar, when Minister of Labour, was to preside over the closure of Huancayo's textile industry.

The low degree of interest of the Huancayo business class in monopolizing the smaller-scale services of the area or in investing in agricultural production gave a special character to their relations with other social classes in the city and rural areas. The economic interests of the business class did not directly conflict with those of other entrepreneurs. It was in the interest of the business class to encourage enterprise on the part of others. They readily became the patrons of local agricultural initiatives, sponsoring improvements in stock and agricultural technique. Through their agencies or commercial establishments, they extended relatively easy credit to local people who wished to set themselves up in trade, small-scale industry or transport. The preoccupation of these large-scale businessmen was threefold. They favoured an open labour market so that labour could be recruited cheaply for their industries. They needed a constant supply of foodstuffs to feed their workers. They also wanted a constantly expanding market for the sale of the goods in which they traded, encouraging the improvement of communications and the development of networks of traders operating on extended credit.

Members of this class in the city council sponsored regional fairs. Those who were parliamentary representatives lobbied for the interests of local villages in Lima. They pressed for the quick restoration of communications with areas that had been cut off by flooding and acted against jurisdictions or monopolies that restricted the movement of people or goods. It was the Chamber of Commerce – headed by a prominent landowner and merchant – that spoke out in 1935 against the exploitation of the small Indian farmers by traders who bought up regional produce and against the rise in food prices that this occasioned (Actas: 22 September 1935). Furthermore, it was one of the key members of Huancayo society – the lawyer, Sánchez Arauco, who was a partner in many industrial and commercial firms and a close friend of the most important local landowners – who denounced the practice of buying up regional produce which, he claimed, was endangering the city's large Sunday fair (Actas: 13 April 1935).

In the city, a class of smaller traders, craftsmen and small industrialists developed in this period, partly through the economic encouragement of the big business class. The expansion of the smaller and medium-sized textile factories in the city was helped by the sponsorship of the larger operators. The big factories provided raw materials on favourable terms and, in at least two cases, one of the largest of the textile operators actually set up others in production. In interviews with these two minor textile industrialists, they recalled how the large-scale operator – a Palestinian Jew, whom they identified as being, socially, a member of the local business class – had encouraged them to set up independently. One of them who came from a poor Huancayo family had been a foreman in the big factory and the other, a Japanese immigrant, had been a street trader. They recalled the expanding market for local textiles in the 1940s and 1950s which made it seem as if there was room for any number of textile producers. The large-scale operator, whose factory had some two hundred workers at its height in the 1950s, also owned retailing and wholesaling stores and it was important to him to have a steady supply of products for marketing.

Another foreign businessman sponsored many local people to set up in business during his career as the agent for businesses in Lima and for the mines. It was he who sub-contracted a supply of mattresses for the Cerro de Pasco Corporation to a Huancayo workshop. He also supplied, on credit, the imported cloth that set up some of the prominent contemporary cloth traders. He backed an employee to establish his own, rival, hardware store and he sponsored other local people to take over an agency for Volvo cars and trucks. This man, a German Jewish immigrant who came to Huancayo in the late 1930s, was more committed than most of the business class to an explicit policy of encouraging local enterprise. [13] It was in the interest, however, of even the profit-oriented businessmen to encourage local enterprise since their control of credit and finance ensured that they would ultimately gain by it. The relationships of semi-patronage that developed rarely appear to have been consolidated by enduring social relationships. Contemporary accounts recall the social divisions between the foreign and Lima business class and the independent craftsmen, mechanics and small traders of the city.

The relationships between the large-scale industrialists and their workers were less ambivalent. The industrialists opposed any labour union organization and manipulated their political contacts in Lima and Huancayo to thwart worker organization (Pareja, 1979). In the early years of the industry, the owners adopted a paternalistic approach in an attempt to weaken organization among workers who were receiving wages that were substantially lower than those in the Lima textile factories. They set up social clubs, provided free meals at times and often personally recruited the workers. In the case of Mongilardi, the co-owner of Manufacturas and an ex-manager of Los Andes, this policy was explicitly based on his antagonism to the labour unions that were dominating the Lima textile industry at this time. Yet, despite the efforts of the owners, the workers did organize against them in the early 1940s. However, the authoritarian regime of Odría (1948–56) outlawed APRA, the party behind the first successful textile union organization in Huancayo in 1945. In 1953, an international development report was to comment favourably on the prospects of the Huancayo textile industry, explicitly mentioning the absence of union activity (International Development Service, 1953).

After the fall of the government of Odría in 1956, the unions gained strength, forcing the owners to grant higher wages and the extension to the workers of welfare benefits that were operative nationally. There is no evidence in this later period of any prolonged or bitter disputes between workers and industrialists. From the late 1940s, the workers dealt only with managers since the factory owners took up permanent residence in Lima. In Manufacturas, the years after 1956 were marked by an increasing co-operation between the union and the management, extending even to the introduction of worker redundancy. Workers in the co-operative that replaced the private enterprise had been, in the large majority, favourable to both the wages and the personal treatment they had received from the private enterprise (Roberts, 1978a).

Huancayo's industrial labour was neither stabilized nor particularly committed to city living. The turnover of the workforce in the largest mill was several times greater than that in the textile mills in Lima owned by the same company (Roberts, 1978a: 138). Throughout this period, many workers took temporary lodgings in the city and returned to their villages at weekends. With the improvement of public transport in the 1950s, workers began to commute to the city from the nearest villages. In the smaller factories, workers often left their jobs to return home for the busy agricultural period – especially during the harvest. Several owners indicated that this migration pattern had suited, to some extent, their production cycles in which the absence of workers coincided with the seasonal decline in demand for woollen products on the coast. Those textile workers who are still living in Huancayo continue to retain these farm attachments, returning to their villages at weekends and taking an active part in agricultural production.

The instability of Huancayo's industrial labour force is best understood in the context of the regional system of production. The continuance of smallholding agriculture in the areas around Huancayo, and the practice of combining this agriculture with wage labour in the mines and casual work or trade, created an opportunity structure which discouraged lengthy commitment to any one job. The migrants who came in from the villages to take skilled jobs in Huancayo had a multiplicity of aims. Some were saving cash to pay for further education, some to buy land or animals and some to save for a marriage dowry. Furthermore, staying in the city and remaining in the same job depended on events that were often unpredictable, such as the death of a parent or the need to educate siblings.

The range of income in the textile factories also meant that the relative advantages of textile work over other jobs in the area changed over time. As a first job, textile work might be attractive but, unless the worker was promoted rapidly, he could earn more by working in the mines, in transport or in certain kinds of trade. The diversity of the area's economy and the small-scale nature of most of the opportunities made difficult the development of a permanent industrial labour force. In any event, the economic instability of the industry with its absentee owners and lack of investment made many workers doubt that industry represented the dominant future employment of the area. Contemporary textile workers recalled, in interviews, how they had begun to learn other skills or had set up their wives in trade in anticipation of the decline of the large-scale industry.

The characteristics of the industrial labour force in Huancayo weakened their class organization. Although industrialization in Huancayo had led to union and political activity among workers, there was little basis for sustained organization in the face of the decline of large-scale industry and the alternative possibilities open to the workers.

The relationships that developed amongst these different classes effectively limited the development of organizations committed to defending local economic interests. The medium- and small-scale factory owners did attempt to form an association to defend their interests in the 1950s but, apart from occasional and informal meetings, no effective action was taken by this class. The large-scale industrialists and important traders operated at the national level and never needed to use Huancayo as a political base. In their absence, the smaller-scale entrepreneurs – who were in any case closely linked to the larger operators – were an ineffective pressure group.

The history of the Huancayo Chamber of Commerce is illustrative of this situation. Despite its auspicious beginning, founded by one of the most prominent local landowners and merchants and including all the most influential local businessmen, it never once acted as an important source of pressure in the formation of local or national policy. One important businessman described its most important function as circulating lists of those defaulting on bank loans. Even its membership of perhaps one or two hundred was eventually surpassed by the branch of the national commercial association – CONACO – which provides national-level information services for local businessmen.

The municipal government in Huancayo had little revenue in this period and had no say in the distribution of the government services and contracts that did come to the region. It was only with the short-lived Junta de Obras Públicas in 1956 that local people (the Junta was composed of local businessmen and representatives of the villages and labour unions) were entrusted with the distribution of government contracting work in the area. Even in this case, however, it was the Lima-based parliamentary representatives who influenced the assignment of most contracts. In this situation, the Huancayo council became a somewhat unimportant administrative body. Moreover, a change had occurred in the composition of the council compared with the beginning of the twentieth century when the large-scale landowners and merchants were represented. Until the 1940s, the mayors of Huancayo continued to be drawn from the dominant economic class of the city but, after that period, they were more likely to be professionals who were often government employees. This trend also reflects the increasing control and influence of the central government in provincial administration. Council members were themselves aware of this change and, in one meeting in 1952, it was remarked that the councillors should not be criticized for failing to give enough time to support the regional fair since they were not men of independent means but had to work full time (Actas: 2 May 1952).

Party politics did occasionally emerge in the city council especially in those periods when APRA was legal (Actas: 17 September 1945). In general, the councils appear to have been chosen to reflect a variety of political and occupational interests. It became customary to include one or two members of APRA as well as members of the other parties, one or two industrial workers who were often officials of the Textile Labour Union, as well as professionals, clerks and a few merchants. Neither local businessmen nor workers had much confidence in the council as an independent political body. If favours were needed from the government, it was usual to go directly to Lima and to lobby the appropriate minister. The dominant business class had their own direct contacts and even the textile workers, through their union, had direct access to national-level politics.

Regional politics and class relations

The increasing importance of APRA in the Mantaro area and in the central highlands illustrates the political implications of these class relations. Throughout the period, from the 1920s until the 1960s, APRA came increasingly to dominate the politics of Huancayo and its area. The central highlands region was one of the strongholds of the party and contributed, through the strength of its mining and textile unions and through particular personalities, a great deal to the institutional power of the party. Ramiro Prialé, for many years the secretary-general of the party, was the representative for Huancayo and a member of one of the longest established professional families in the city. APRA's strength was that its base was as much in the villages and small towns as in Huancayo or other labour centres. It attracted people with a variety of occupations. The APRA-dominated Unión Sindical of Junín brought together textile workers, transport workers, small shopkeepers and artisans.

The range of places and occupations covered by APRA reveal the migration patterns of the area. In the villages and smaller towns, it was usually the richer peasant farmers who were APRA members. Their sons and siblings were the labour migrants who went to the mines or cities. Some of these families became active in APRA politics. In one case that we studied, the father remained in the village and occupied positions in the village council. One son became an APRA union leader in the mines. Another son was an APRA union leader in the textile industry. Other members of the family were also APRA sympathizers and were professionals or owned small stores in Huancayo.

APRA was a class party, representing the migration experience and the economic interests of the richer, smallholding peasants of the Huancayo area. In appearance, though, the party's basis of support rested on heterogeneous economic interests; richer peasants, miners, shopkeepers, small-scale traders and transporters and textile workers. In the Mantaro area, APRA never seems to have recruited the poorer peasants, who were often the wage labourers of the richer smallholders. Equally, the party was not supported by those members of the business class of Huancayo who were of foreign or Lima origin. APRA's anti-foreign and anti-monopoly position and its emphasis on native, small-scale enterprise, provided an ideology suited to the position of the 'intermediate' economic interests it represented. APRA represented a class which both exploited the labour of the poorer classes and was dependent upon, and confined by, the economic monopolies of the business class.

Nevertheless, APRA was eclectic in its commitments. The economic characteristics of its membership bridged city and countryside and prevented the party becoming strongly committed either to particular forms of urban industrial or rural agricultural development. In the Huancayo area, the party has remained ambiguous in its attitude to agrarian reform and to the co-operativization of landholdings. Neither did the party act consistently as a pressure group in favour of the industrial development of Huancayo. Even during the periods of APRA's political ascendancy in the 1950s and 1960s, Huancayo and the Mantaro area gained little in the way of subsidy or economic stimulus from the central government.

APRA's failure to benefit the region was not a political accident. Its class characteristics made it a party of local, particularistic interests that impeded the formulation of national policies for regional development from the centre. In the central highlands, APRA and the class it represented stood for decentralized government and for local initiative. APRA supporters, as we will see in subsequent chapters, have often opposed and subverted the attempts of national government to impose administrative reforms or changes in the agrarian structure.

In this situation, it is significant that the business class failed to develop a strong political base in Huancayo and in the central highlands during the apogee of the mining economy. We attribute this to their position as financiers and merchants who were not dependent on monopolizing local production, in agriculture or small-scale services. There was, consequently, little overt or consistent class conflict between this class and others seeking to improve or to defend their own economic base. The peasant movements of the area were as much directed against other villages and the smaller haciendas as they were against the large estates, such as Ganadera del Centro and Cerro de Pasco, owned by absentee landowners from Lima or abroad (Smith and Cano, 1978; Roberts and Samaniego, 1978). Indeed, members of the Huancayo-based business class at times supported the villagers in their conflicts with local *hacendados*. As we have seen, a similar ambiguity was present in the 1950s in the relations between the textile union and the Huancayo industrialists. Initial conflicts finally resulted in accommodation at the local level and in the gradual withdrawal of capital by the large-scale industrialists.

In the absence of a strong local political organization controlled by the regionally important business class and linked to nationally powerful classes, regional government remained relatively weak and underdeveloped. One consequence of this was that the villages and small towns had more freedom to develop their own economies. Despite the growth of Huancayo, there was, as we will see in the next chapters, considerable vitality in the smaller towns of the region. This chapter, then, has argued that no clear class hegemony developed in the central highlands during the apogee of the mining economy. This political and social fact is crucial to understanding the subsequent economic development of the region.

5

Highland *puna* communities and the impact of the mining economy[1]

In this and the next chapter, peasant responses to the expansion of capitalism are examined. Peasant communities entered into direct relations with highland mining centres and with commercial plantations of the coastal area where there was a growing demand for labour. Much of this labour, however, retained a base in the village, continuing to own or have rights to individual or communal land and leaving wives and children behind to care for livestock and the upkeep of family property. The situation that developed between the mines, plantations and peasant villages was akin to that characterized by De Janvry and Garramon (1977) who argue that 'cheap' labour is a critical element in the functioning and profitability of capitalist enterprise in peripheral economies.[2]

Although we do not wish to debate the issue here of whether or not the peasant subsistence base is essential to the logic of capital accumulation in the periphery, we claim that the relationship between capitalist enterprise and peasant villages in the central highlands served the interests of both parties. For the first half of the twentieth century, the best available labour force for the mines and plantations was located in the villages of the central highlands; conversely, the increase in village population in relation to land resources made wage labour a necessary complement to agricultural production. In this sense, the expansion of export production shaped the pattern of development of both *puna* and valley communities. This expansion created new resources as well as undermining some existing economic activities. Moreover, it had an uneven impact on the region, depending on the resources available to the villages and their type of integration into the export economy.

In this chapter we look at the impact of export production on the economic and demographic structure of a group of *puna* communities. These communities were directly affected by the expansion of Cerro de Pasco's mining and livestock enterprises.

Capitalist enterprise in the highland zone

Large-scale capital investments brought with them the opening of new roads, new railways and new mining encampments. The resultant demand for labour power led to a crisis in production relations in the central region. The relationships that communities had developed with the mines during the nineteenth century were broken with the arrival of the Cerro de Pasco Corporation, which led to the loss of existing jobs in smaller-scale mining and to the partial elimination of the labour-intensive pack-animal system of mineral transport. According to Flores Galindo (1974), this occasioned economic depression in certain of the *puna* communities.

A further factor in the economic transformation of the communities close to the mining operations was the ecological damage produced by the new large-scale smelter at La Oroya (opened in 1922). Agricultural productivity was gravely affected and, as far away as the Mantaro valley communities, trout fishing was destroyed. The smoke poisoned 700,000 hectares of pasture lands in the *puna* zone. This led the Sociedad Ganadera de Junín to sell some of its haciendas to the Cerro de Pasco Corporation who developed a new branch of production based on thoroughbred sheep reared as much for their meat as for their wool.[3]

Many of the communities of the central highlands felt the ill effects of the expansion of the Corporation's operations. The impact of these operations was greater on the villages of the *puna*, which were directly affected by the expansion of the livestock division of the Corporation, since the rationalization of production denied these communities access to lands over which they claimed right of pasture. As Samaniego (1978) points out, when discussing the conflicts between the haciendas at the southern end of the Mantaro valley and the communities bordering them, the traditional practice of grazing livestock paid little attention to fixed boundaries. When a hacienda fenced off what it believed to be its own land, there was inevitably some disruption to the pastoral activities of these neighbouring communities. The new system of production in the highland estates also brought about a change in the labour system of the haciendas from one of *pastores huacchilleros* to one more dependent on wage labour. As Martínez-Alier (1977) shows, highland estates had depended heavily on using shepherds whose payment consisted largely of the right to pasture their own animals (*huacchas*) on hacienda land. Wage labour had been discouraged by the low profitability of estates. Traditional grazing practices, and the poor quality of the local breed of sheep, led to low productivity. The increase in the demand for wool on the world market and for meat in the urban centres and mining camps made the new wage-based system of production viable.

Table 10 *'Huacchilleros' and workers in the SAIS of the central highlands*

Name of SAIS	Ex-feudatories, *huacchilleros* or share-croppers		Permanent workers and employees		Total
	No.	%	No.	%	
Túpac Amaru No. 1	–	0.0	189	100.0	189
Cahuide No.6	224	41.9	311	58.1	535
Pachacuteo No. 7	178	76.7	54	23.3	232
Ramón Castilla No. 8	222	89.5	26	10.5	248
Harinas Toledo No. 31	28	65.1	15	34.9	43
Mariscal Cáceres No. 25	22	100.0	—	0.0	22
Huancavelica No. 40	1,172	100.0	—	0.0	1,172

Source: Ministry of Agriculture, *Dirección de Asentamiento Rural*, September, 1974 (cited in Caicho, 1977: 32).

However, its adoption varied considerably, with the haciendas that belonged to the Corporation being the most affected and others less so. Employees of the Corporation's haciendas were reduced, over time, to some two hundred workers, including shepherds, foremen and technical staff who were trained to breed and rear seventeen different types of sheep in a flock of 150,000 animals.

The extent of variation in the persistence of the *huaccha* system can be appreciated in Table 10, referring to the livestock co-operatives (SAIS) established by the agrarian reform of 1969. The former haciendas of the Corporation constitute SAIS Túpac Amaru No. 1. The Table makes clear that these were unique in the central region in being entirely made up of permanent salaried workers.

Even in the Corporation's haciendas, however, a substantially modified form of the *huaccha* system managed to persist until at least the mid-1970s. Hacienda workers were allowed to rear animals on Corporation land as a supplement to their wages provided that these animals did not mix with the thoroughbred stock.[4] The reasons for these limitations on the development of a wage labour system and on the consolidation of large-scale capitalist enterprises are varied. As Martínez-Alier (1978) would argue, there was considerable peasant resistance to the introduction of a new system of labour relations and to the fencing off of estate land. Litigation and violent confrontation between peasants and Corporation employees were a regular irritation to the Corporation's plans (Laite, 1978: 87–92). The Corporation could not rely upon a local elite to control the villages: indeed village authorities often sided with their fellow villagers and, at times, received the support of the provincial authorities in their struggles against the Corporation. Furthermore, it suited the Corporation to stabilize their agricultural labour by allowing their workers to graze their own stock. Hacienda labour was hard to come by, especially in the context of the opportunities offered by mining or through trade with the mining centres. One of the villages in the study (Usibamba) acquired a reputation locally as a 'pariah' community because the Corporation was reputed to have a policy of refusing to recruit people from Usibamba as mine workers. It was said that this policy arose because the Corporation depended upon Usibamba to provide labour for sheep shearing.

It is frequently a characteristic of dependent economies that expansion of capitalist enterprise is accompanied by the persistence of what appear to be 'archaic' forms of social relationship. This is the process, for example, that Marx (1972: 816–18) described in his account of primary accumulation in the European countries and of the formal (as opposed to the real) subsumption of labour to capital. In the absence of an established and generalized free labour market, capitalist enterprise developed strategies of subordinating labour that included coercion and state legislation. Where these latter strategies are not so possible, as in the central highlands, then paternalistic ties and non-wage incentives are used. On estates and in the small and medium-sized mines of the central highlands relationships between workers and employers are strengthened by ties of *compadrazgo*. It is usual for the employer to be the *compadre* to a large number of workers. Since work is often casual, employers help their workers to diversify their activities. A favoured worker, for example, will be given a contract to transport minerals for his employer. He will also get credit from him to assist with the purchase of a truck paid for in instalments.

Such arrangements tend to blur class commitments and boundaries. Class organization is further impeded by the fact that members of the same family or household will generally have different positions in the economic structure: women in the highlands play a crucial role in agriculture, livestock activities and commerce, whilst the husband is often a wage worker in non-agricultural activities outside the community. This leads to the circulation of cash and products between rural and urban locations. In this situation, class locations will be fundamentally contradictory, since members of the same household or the same individuals placed in different socio-economic contexts will be subject to varying pressures, which, at times, unite them with co-workers and, at others, encourage them to seek their own individual or household advantage. Thus Laite (1977) points out that workers in the La Oroya refinery show strong class solidarity in the work situation but, once outside that situation, they identify with their villages and their interests there. Moreover, the longer the worker is in the refinery the stronger his reliance on his village of origin may become, since his children will be reaching school age and will be sent back to the village for education. Also, over time, the worker will have invested in land and housing in anticipation of his final return.

Communal resources and economic change: general tendencies

The vast majority of the *puna* population resided in peasant villages lying outside the jurisdiction of the haciendas. Although villages might be involved with the haciendas through *huaccha* or by providing temporary labour for sheep shearing, villagers were, in theory, independent producers able to sell their labour and products where they wished. Within the *puna* zone a series of factors facilitated the establishment of a complex system of social relations of production between the agro-mining enterprise and the communities of the region. In the last section, we noted the difficulties of the extension of land resources by the communities, of the natural increase in the population and of the damage done by smelting and mining to the communities' own agricultural and pastoral activities. A major factor that differentiated their situation from that of valley villages was the system of land tenure. In the *puna* communities, the community was, above all, a group of families who had inalienable rights to land, pasture and other means of production through birth in the community or as a son of a *comunero* (community member).[5] Although this was also formally true of valley villages, the privatization of rights to land had greater effects there, reinforcing the commercialization of smallholder production. Also, in the case of the *puna*, most land was pasture which remained under the control of the community and not individuals.

The *comunero* does not develop a permanent relationship to the mines and continues to control land and livestock, thereby sustaining the existing pattern of landholding and impeding the development of the internal productive forces of the villages. The villages tend to become centres of residence for people whose source of livelihood is predominantly outside the village or for people who are not economically active. The family becomes the crucial element in articulating service, peasant and mining activities. In the first four decades of the twentieth century there was an intense flow of labour from the *puna* communities to the mining centres. The scarcity of economic opportunities within the communities meant that mine work became the principal source of livelihood for many families, resulting in a flow of cash into their community and the possibility of capitalizing agriculture and livestock production. The salaries paid by the Corporation represented for *puna* families higher returns than could be obtained locally. Despite the poor working conditions in the mines, the poorer circumstances of the *puna* communities meant that the Corporation could always count upon a steady flow of labour.

In the years immediately following the beginning of large-scale mining operations, a large amount of labour was required for infrastructural work. In this period, a sector of workers went to the mines during the slack months of the agricultural cycle (i.e. seasonal migration took place). After 1920, mining operations necessitated a more qualified and, above all, a more permanent labour force. Workers from the *puna* villages had low levels of schooling and of craft skills and few local income opportunities. They tended to find employment as unskilled workers. In contrast, workers from the valley, with high skill levels and more local resources, were better placed to obtain skilled or semi-skilled work in the mining sector and migrated to the smelter town of La Oroya. The impoverishment of the *puna* communities meant that peasants remained working in the mines for a period of some years. In general, *comuneros* spent between six and ten years working in the mines, although those who came from haciendas and the most remote and poorest communities may have remained longer and then often moved to the cities. This length of time was necessary for the migrants to save enough money to expand their herds or to invest in service activities outside the community. Hence, a particular pattern of integration with the capitalist economy was established in which the *comunero* temporarily abandoned his community to go to work in the mines but his economic and social interests remained concentrated in his place of origin where family, land and livestock were located.

Mine wages were not substantially invested in production in the communities, but were used for small-scale land and livestock transactions and also for public works through the activities of the migrant clubs (see chapter nine). Furthermore, savings were often invested in activities outside the village and trade and transport were to become the economic sectors that developed most in the region. Two processes, then, are detectable in the *puna* communities: on the one hand, there is a stagnation in internal agricultural production but, on the other hand, the villages become more internally differentiated due to the relative 'progress' and 'enrichment' of the communities through public works and individual social mobility based on wage labour.

As the next chapter shows, these processes of internal differentiation were more accentuated in the valley villages which had better access to communications and a richer land base. The *comuneros* of the *puna* villages tended to invest in housing, shops or market stalls in cities such as Huancayo or even Lima due to the lack of investment opportunities in their own communities. This pattern of investment did not encourage the local development of large-scale enterprises, but rather became the basis for the prevalence of small-scale activity and petty trade, with *comuneros* often combining simultaneously various activities. This growth of the service sector and its relationship to the fragmentation of agricultural resources is one of the most outstanding characteristics of the economy organized around the mining complexes of the central region.

In the 1950s there were important changes in mining production which resulted in a reduction of the labour force.[6] Although there had been previous periods in which the mines had laid off workers, the 1950s marked a definitive change in the nature of external economic opportunities for *puna* communities. Industrial investment in Lima, together with the increase in strictly urban economic opportunities, was accompanied by a much slower rate of economic growth in agriculture and by increasingly capital-intensive mining operations with less need for manpower. Thus, like other groups, *puna* inhabitants became increasingly involved in urban migration to Lima-Callao and the provincial cities. Although these migrants did not necessarily lose their social and economic links with their communities of origin, where they still retained rights to land or animals, the communities now ceased to be the centre of their economic operations. Once one member of the family migrated a process of chain migration got underway in which the first migrant became the bridge by which relatives and *compadres* established themselves in the city. Thus, from the 1950s, the *puna* communities underwent a gradual process of depopulation which has profoundly changed their economic and demographic structure. Depopulation has meant that agriculture and livestock-raising in the *puna* has become increasingly less intensive and production is often orientated to the needs of those who reside externally.

Althaus (1975) studied the changes in production that occurred from the period of the legal recognition of various of these *puna* communities until 1972.[7] Apart from Canchaillo, which was affected by exceptionally high out-migration, the communities had a significant increase in the numbers of sheep (cattle in Usibamba) in this period. The increase in quantity entailed a systematic decrease in quality of production. Only in exceptional cases were sheep, who were ready for shearing, actually sheared. The marketing system, which was only weakly developed, was reduced to the sporadic sale of livestock. The implication is that production was mainly destined for domestic consumption and household exchange.

The absence of systematic shearing, the high rates of mortality and disease amongst sheep and the poor quality of the pasture show both the secondary role that these activities occupied and a tendency towards a simplification of economic activity. It is clear that the decrease in the number of mules, llamas and alpacas (in Suitucancha the number of llamas has decreased by 41 per cent) is the result of simplifying stock-raising in order to concentrate on sheep.

Differential responses to capitalist expansion

Our study included the sixteen peasant communities which, at present, form part of the SAIS Túpac Amaru.[8] This SAIS was the first co-operative to be established under the 1969 agrarian reform. The SAIS model was intended to integrate peasant communities into commercial production. SAIS Túpac Amaru is made up of the seven haciendas which formed part of the livestock division of the Cerro de Pasco Corporation, a total of 250,000 hectares of land. The sixteen peasant communities possess a total of 175,000 hectares. However, the farming activities of the peasant communities are independent of the SAIS and these communities only receive part of the profits of the SAIS. Representatives of the communities participate in the administration of the enterprise. Our own data are drawn from research in five of these *puna* communities.

The most interesting conclusion of our study is that, where the relationship between the community and the mining sector was stronger, so the deterioration of the village agrarian economy was greater, and the evidence of a peasantry, in the sense of a population mainly dependent on small-scale farming, was less. This latter finding is illustrated by the fact that, although some savings were invested in land or livestock, the principal investments were in trade and transport outside the community.

Table 11 shows the income composition of the population of the sampled communities, indicating that, with the exception of Usibamba, *comuneros* obtained most of their income from activities that lay outside agriculture or livestock-raising, the most important sources being wage labour, trade and transport.

Income composition correlates with differences between the economic and demographic structure of communities. We will use these three variables (income sources, economic and demographic structure) to differentiate the communities and to measure the dominance and effects of the mining economy. We aim to show that the impact of the mining economy on the region is neither homogeneous nor mechanical. Indeed, it is crucial to emphasize the importance of local factors in shaping both the regional system and the internal structure of the local units of that system.

The community of Usibamba is an extreme case of the absence of labour migration together with a high level of development in local agriculture. We will use the case of Usibamba, though atypical, as a negative example to test our basic proposition that the decline in the agrarian economy of the *puna* region is

Table 11 *Sources of income of 'puna' villages (percentages)*

Community	Livestock	Agriculture	Non-agricultural	Total
Usibamba	26.3	52.2	21.5	100.0
Chacapalpa	27.9	12.0	60.1	100.0
Llocllapampa[a]	24.2	6.1	69.7	100.0
Urauchoc	4.7	37.7	57.6	100.0
Canchaillo[b]	28.4	10.9	60.7	100.0
Pachachaca[c]	12.6	11.9	75.4	99.9
Paccha	11.3	—	88.7	100.0
Sacco	1.0	—	99.9	100.0

[a] Llocllapampa has a large silica quarry which the community works as a co-operative.
[b] Canchaillo has the smallest number of inhabitants of all those in the Table. Its relationships are almost exclusively with the agricultural estates where wages are lower than in the mines.
[c] Although Pachachaca has half the population of Chacapalpa, its close relationship with the mines results in levels of income for the community comparable to those of urban areas. The majority of the population received a wage. In the early 1970s, the average salary was approximately 50,000 soles a year per family.
Source: COMACRA, Community Survey, 1971.

a direct result of the extraction of labour for the mining economy. We have classified the communities according to basic differences in income sources and economic activities. Category A comprises Usibamba, where there has been little migration to the mines; Category B includes those communities in which there has been a high level of labour migration to the mines but which have nonetheless retained a reasonably viable productive base; and the third category (C) consists of those communities which exhibit high rates of labour migration, but whose local systems of production are more evidently in decline than is the case of Category B. The major foci for economic activity in Category C are now outside the village economy.[9]

Absence of labour migration: Category A
Usibamba's economy is based upon a combination of agriculture and livestock production. The relative absence of labour migration in this community is associated with a high level of development of the village's productive forces. This is apparent in the intensive production of fodder for livestock which enables the pasture area to support a large number of animals per hectare. With thoroughbred stock it is possible to maintain one sheep per hectare of *puna* pasture (a cow is considered as equivalent to five sheep units) but, with over-grazing and the use of *criollo* (non-pedigree or native) stock, pastures can

Table 12 *Economic activities of heads of household in Usibamba*

	Households	
Economic activities	No.	%
Livestock production	26	9.4
Agriculture	225	81.5
Crafts and trade	12	4.2
Workers/employees	15	5.4
Total	278	100.0

Source: COMACRA, Community Survey, 1971.

maintain three sheep units per hectare. In the case of Usibamba, the production of fodder enables the village to support, on average, eight sheep units per hectare, the majority of which units are cattle. This level of production, however, requires that the *comunero*-farmer remains constantly in the community and does not leave the care of animals to children and women, as happens in other communities.

In this situation, the entire population is orientated towards agriculture and livestock and there is little diversification in other directions (Table 12).

The fact that there has not been any substantial labour migration either to the mines or to urban centres has limited savings from wage labour. As a result there is little infrastructural development in terms of public buildings, schools or water supply. In appearance, then, Usibamba is one of the poorest communities of the zone.

A further consequence of the weak relationship with the mining economy is that the population structure of this community approximates a normal population pyramid. The substantial proportion of population below the age of fifteen indicates that there has, until recently, been little permanent out-migration; although permanent out-migration is now appearing in the 15–40 age categories, especially amongst males (see Fig. 1).[10]

Population density is high when compared with other communities, making available a considerable amount of labour for local productive activities. Usibamba has the worst population/land ratio of all the *puna* villages (0.86 hectares per inhabitant). The need to intensify agricultural production and to specialize in stock-raising keeps the *comunero* in his place of origin. In Usibamba the migration that exists is principally seasonal. There is some permanent migration but, in these cases, migrants have abandoned the community without maintaining rights to any of its economic resources. This outcome is different from that of the migration from richer communities, where rights to land are retained.

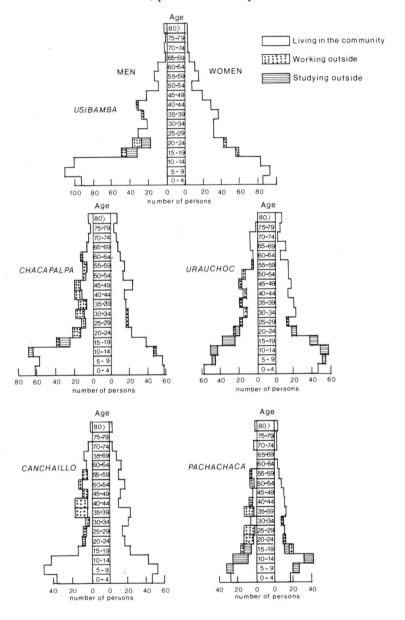

Fig. 1   Age and sex composition of five *puna* communities

98

The people of Usibamba are essentially peasants. They do not have the capacity to accumulate capital and broaden their economy to take in non-agricultural activity.

Communities with migration and viable local production: Category B
The majority of communities within SAIS Túpac Amaru belong to this intermediate category. They are communities whose internal economy is predominantly livestock grazing combined with subsistence-based agriculture. What is characteristic of these communities is that they maintain a close relationship with the Corporation through migration. The peasant-miner spends less of his wages on feeding himself or his family. Instead, he has invested in land and livestock in the community and in developing other economic activities such as trade and transport which are often located outside the community. These communities have also received substantial financial help from the migrant associations in the mines and cities. This cash has been used to construct public works, churches and sports facilities.

In Table 13, we contrast two communities of this category. Chacapalpa has a high percentage of its heads of household primarily working in livestock production, although one-third of them are wage earners. Since the community of Urauchoc is located in the valley of Tarma and is situated close to that city, it has developed its agricultural rather than livestock resources. Although 75 per cent of the heads of household in Urauchoc are either engaged in agriculture or livestock-raising, this percentage is somewhat deceptive because many of these heads of household are women whose husbands remain outside the community, working as traders or wage earners in Tarma or the nearby mines.

In these communities, the rich *comuneros* are usually involved in a variety of economic activities and possess a large amount of livestock and land. However, as they do not remain constantly in the community and, as in most cases, most of the family resides in the city, they must contract labour for their land and livestock. This labour is provided by the poor *comuneros* who work in return for gifts and for the right to graze their own animals on the owner's land. Money wages are becoming more common in this area but are usually accompanied by some form of gift or by rights to graze animals (*huacchillaje*).

Although there is pronounced social differentiation in these communities, clear-cut social classes have not appeared. The rich *comuneros* engage in a varied network of economic activities while the poor *comuneros* do not become proletarianized because they maintain some access to productive resources, however minimal. The situation is different for the *peones*, who are migrants from other regions. These latter are contracted by the rich *comuneros*. They

Table 13 *Economic activities of heads of household in Chacapalpa and Urauchoc*

Economic activity	Chacapalpa		Urauchoc	
	No.	%	No.	%
Livestock	133	48.0	26	13.1
Agriculture	20	7.2	124	62.6
Crafts and trade	32	11.6	5	2.5
Mine workers/employees	92	33.2	43	21.7
Total	277	100.0	198	100.0

Source: COMACRA, Community Survey, 1971.

sometimes own livestock in the community and can be included in the category of the agricultural semi-proletariat.

The field of economic action extends beyond the limits of the community to include nearby towns, cities and Lima. This makes it possible to obtain secondary and higher education, with students being sent to board with relatives in the towns, thus reinforcing the urban migration process while consolidating the relationship between the urban migrants and the community. In the *puna* communities, because of the absence of resources comparable to those of communities in the Mantaro valley, education has become a key factor in the social process. Note, for example, the numbers who are away studying especially in Urauchoc (see Fig. 1). Thus, *puna* migrants often include a number of urban professionals. Indeed, in contrast to the situation in the valley villages, the professions are a more common route to social and spatial mobility for *puna* migrants than are entrepreneurial occupations, such as trading and trucking.

If we analyse the demographic structure of Chacapalpa and Urauchoc, there is a noticeable depression, beginning at age fifteen. Part of the active male population is outside the community, while still retaining residence within it. However, the narrow base of the pyramid, compared with that of Usibamba, indicates that there is a long-standing process of relatively permanent migration. In these Category B communities, the preponderance of women in the economically active age categories is also noticeable.

In our fieldwork, we found that the rich *comuneros* in these communities represent a strong power group who retain the political and administrative control of the community. Their external relationships enable them to operate effectively within the wider power system. This is one of the factors that explains why the process of restructuring the communities, begun under the agrarian reform of 1969, and implementing new criteria of membership, has not been effective in the *puna*.[11] The reforms envisaged the establishment of local production co-operatives and the exclusion from community membership of those not primarily engaged in local productive activities. They have not been effectively implemented in these communities due to the opposition of the richer peasant class.

Migration and decline: Category C

The communities in Category C also have a low proportion of their income derived from agriculture. Like those of Category B, they have provided substantial amounts of migrant labour to the mines and haciendas of the Corporation. In contrast to Category B, however, the four communities of this group show a greater decline in their agricultural and livestock-raising economy. Three of them, Pachachaca, Paccha and Sacco, are very close to the most important mining centres of the central region. The fourth community – Canchaillo – is only two kilometres away from the Pachacayo hacienda, which was the administrative centre of the livestock division of the Cerro de Pasco Corporation.

The poor quality and limited extension of available land also influence the situation of these communities. The land is unable to provide for the subsistence of more than a handful of *comuneros*. The first three communities were also those most affected by the smoke damage from La Oroya. Until 1962, Canchaillo only possessed half of its present-day land extension. In appearance, these communities enjoy a relative prosperity because money coming from mine labour was invested in communal work projects: schools, a medical centre, churches and roads. Substantial amounts of money were also invested in trade and transport. Table 14 shows that a high proportion of the population of these villages is employed outside livestock and agriculture. Yet, even these percentages are deceptive since they include women heads of household (about 50 per cent) whose husbands work in the mines or cities. In Pachachaca, 59 per cent of the heads of household work in agriculture and/or livestock but only 24.5 per cent of household incomes come from agriculture and livestock (see Table 11). In the case of Sacco and Paccha, income from outside agriculture and livestock-raising is even higher (see Table 11).

A large proportion of the farmers and livestock-raisers are women. The population pyramids (Fig. 1) demonstrate fewer men between the ages of twenty and sixty years than is the case for the other categories, while the proportions of women are much higher. Indeed, Pachachaca has almost no resident men in the economically active ages. There are few people of economically active age in these communities to take charge of the agricultural work. The lack of young married couples, a result of out-migration, has prevented normal population increase. There is, thus, a serious threat to the survival of these communities.

Table 14 *Principal occupations of heads of household*

Economic activity	Canchaillo		Pachachaca		Paccha		Sacco	
	No.	%	No.	%	No.	%	No.	%
Livestock	33	44.0	26	20.2	36	24.3	11	6.7
Agriculture	8	10.7	50	38.7	—	—	—	—
Crafts and trade	5	6.7	6	4.7	16	10.8	36	22.0
Mine workers/employees	29	38.6	47	36.4	96	64.9	117	71.3
Total	75	100.0	129	100.0	148	100.0	164	100.0

Source: COMACRA, Community Survey, 1971.

The educational levels of Category C are higher than those of the other categories. Most young people have completed their primary studies, and a large percentage are studying at secondary or professional levels. Since the communities offer them no chance of work, they leave for the cities or the mines. They abandon their plots of land or leave them in the care of elderly relatives, women or migrant *peones*, who come from the even poorer communities outside the central highlands. The majority of economically active men who are registered as resident in the community of Pachachaca work in the mines. Of the total of 44 men between twenty and thirty-nine years of age, 37 of them are wage labourers.

Although these communities have a territorial identity, their members cannot be classified as peasants even when part of the family remains working on the land. The communities have either been abandoned by their economically active population or, as in the case of Sacco, they have become suburban service centres. Sacco is less than two kilometres from the smelter of La Qroya and houses a large number of people who work in the smelter. Of its 200 legally inscribed *comuneros*, only 20 work in agriculture. The other 180 are traders, mechanics, restaurant owners or smelter workers.

The social conflicts which arise in this category of community are not solely based on agricultural or livestock production. Rather they reflect the contradictions that are typical of the region as a whole. For example, in Sacco there are conflicts between farmers and stock-raisers who want to develop the infrastructure for livestock production and other *comuneros* who want to see a further development of urban services. In such a community, even a rich *comunero*-farmer cannot obtain an annual income from livestock that is comparable with that which a skilled mine worker obtains in a month's work.

The shortage and poor quality of land have made it impossible to reinvest

Table 15 *Principal characteristics of the 'puna' communities*

Category A	Category B	Category C
One community only	Majority of communities	Some communities
Weak relationship with mining economy	Strong relationship with mining economy	Strong relationship with mining economy
Intensive development of internal economy	Relatively intensive development of internal economy	Deterioration of the internal economy
Little or no wage labour or savings from mine work	Reinvestment of savings from wage labour both within and outside the community	Reinvestment of savings from wage labour outside the community
Mainly seasonal migration	Strong labour migration with some permanent urban migration	Strong labour migration and strong permanent urban migration
Low levels of education	Medium levels of education	Highest levels of education
Large proportion of economically active population work in community	Medium proportion of economically active population work in community	Low proportion of economically active population work in community
Class composition: peasants	Class composition: rich *comuneros*, peasants, rural semi-proletariat	Class composition: rich *comuneros*, peasants, rural and urban semi-proletariat

savings from wages in agricultural production. Thus, these communities have stagnated in terms of the development of their productive forces and, as a consequence, they show a high rate of permanent urban migration especially amongst the economically active population.

In Table 15, we summarize the major characteristics of the sixteen communities that now form part of SAIS Túpac Amaru.

In fifteen of the communities, the residents are closely linked to wage labour and to the service sector outside the village economy. In contrast, there is the case of Usibamba whose 'peasant' insertion into the regional economy has brought little evident prosperity. We do not know exactly why the population did not seek work in the labour centres; but the result of not seeking work has been the slow but sustained involution of its productive forces, since land could not keep abreast of population increase. The increase in local agricultural production and productivity did not raise the standard of living of the population, nor did it lead to capital accumulation and to economic differentiation. Yet this is the only community in which production has increased in the years of the dominance of the mining economy. Furthermore, Usibamba is the only community of the area to have experienced a rapid increase in production as a result of the 1969 agrarian reform. Indeed, it is often taken to be a model of such development by state officials, while the other communities are seen to have been unsuitable vehicles for the changes which the state wished to impose.

Conclusions

From the end of the nineteenth century, a new phase of capitalist expansion began in the highlands of Peru. This phase consisted of the imposition of production enclaves, based on mineral exploitation, arising from the needs of the industrialized metropolitan countries. The agricultural decline of the colonial period, together with the relationship that the communities had with an extractive economy based on guano, cotton and sugar in the nineteenth century, facilitated their conversion into sources of labour supply for the new mining economy. This labour had been partially displaced from agriculture and came to constitute a relative surplus population (see Marmora, 1975). A permanent relationship became established between these communities and the mining centres, resulting in a powerful migration movement from the countryside to these work centres. The establishment of the Cerro de Pasco Corporation in the area sharpened this situation. This new relationship provided the communities with the key element for changing their social and economic organization. Mining, peasant and urban economies were thus integrated into a single circuit of social relations.

The complex relations of production present throughout the region were shaped by the mining system and by the pattern of land tenure in the communities. These relations were not based on a stabilized mine labour force. Peasants took on 'proletarian' characteristics in order to complement their agricultural interests and to extend their domestic economy to include commerce, transport and artisan activities. This situation, together with population pressure, led to the fragmentation of land within the agrarian structure, so that it is difficult to talk of agricultural enterprise. Instead, the situation was that of family allotments designed to supplement income.

The central factor in understanding the economic process is that of the concrete relationships of production. On the one hand, the family household, both as an enterprise and as an active element in the regional economy, is a key element in this process. It is capable of including a variety of simultaneous economic activities and, within the limitations of an enclave economy, small-scale enterprise can become highly complex. On the other hand, the fragmentation of land, the near impossibility of accumulating land through a fully commercialized agricultural process, and the development of large-scale mining result in an entrepreneurial situation of high risk and uncertainty. In this situation, the flexibility of small-scale enterprises and their diversification enable them to cope efficiently with the permanent crisis in the economic system. This system is highly affected by factors external to its own dynamic, such as the system of international prices for primary materials.

Consequently, an entrepreneur needs to maintain various activities at the same time, since the failure of one enterprise (a restaurant, for example) does not then mean the failure of the entire family business. Variation is thus economically rational and effective when the conditions do not exist to develop large and more formally organized enterprises.

In the agrarian sector, these processes result in a particular type of differentiation which is not based on the internal capitalization of agriculture. Instead, it results from the activity of peasants as proletarians who may later become small-scale entrepreneurs. Social differentiation is based fundamentally on wage-labour experience outside the community and is consolidated through links of kinship and *compadrazgo*. The rich *comuneros* are inserted into a varied network of production relationships which are, in part, contractual and, in part, kinship based. These *comuneros* must respond simultaneously to different group or class interests. For this reason, it is impossible to classify them unequivocally within any one social class.

The poor *comuneros* are those who, for various reasons, have been unable to develop stable relationships with the mines. Instead, they have remained in the community, working in agriculture or stock-raising. They migrate seasonally to the mines or plantations, or work as the *peones* of the richer *comuneros*. The economic relationships between rich and poor *comuneros* are complicated by kinship and *compadrazgo*. These relationships are constantly reinforced in so far as they guarantee the power and political control of the rich within the communities. This control enables them to manage local resources and the communal structure in such a way that the regional system of production is maintained.

The differences in community responses are significant for the development and change of the regional economy. The scarcity of local productive resources and the presence of social groups eager to expand their own household enterprises led to conflict with the dominant system of production. Land invasions and the formation of peasant unions were powerful forces for change in this region in the 1950s and 1960s. Likewise, the mine-based labour unions waged effective struggles against the Corporation for higher wages and better working conditions so that, by the 1960s, the demand for the mine workforce was no longer a particularly 'cheap' one, accelerating the demand for technological change in the mines. The power of the unions was one factor in the Corporation's willingness to cede its installations to the government under nationalization. The bargaining power of unions was, in part, based upon their peasant links which enabled them to sustain lock-outs and lengthy strike action.

Depending, then, on their relationship with the mining sector and on their own levels of resources, the *puna* communities provided a varied set of inputs into the changing regional system, evolving their particular political and economic strategies. This resulted in a situation that was not readily amenable to the imposition of structural reform from outside. Hence, the intentions of agrarian reform were to founder in the face of the complexity of local economies and of the diverse interests represented in them.

6

Migration and social differentiation amongst Mantaro valley peasants

Introduction

The intention of this chapter is to analyse how capitalist expansion in the central highlands has led to increased socio-economic differentiation within the villages of the Mantaro valley, examining closely the role which migration has played in this process. The hypothesis that capitalist expansion in the country-side results in increasing socio-economic differentiation has been much debated. Analysing the Russian experience, Lenin (1967) first argued that capitalism spread amongst the peasantry due to pressures from both external sources, acting through imbalanced exchanges, and internal sources, stemming from the accumulation of capital in the rural sector. As capitalist relations expanded so polarization occurred between richer peasants and landless labour-ers. Challenging this view, Chayanov (1966) maintained that the differenti-ation observed by Lenin in the rural areas was due to processes internal to the peasant economy and that this economy was highly resistant to capitalist penetration. This debate has continued with reference to both the Russian case and the experience of underdeveloped countries today (Goodman and Redcliff, 1981).

Integral to the differentiation debate is the concept of the peasant economy, distinguishable from the capitalist economy by its units of combined pro-duction and consumption, household labour and lack of market valuations (Shanin, 1973). The resilience of the peasant household and extended family, plus the mutual aid practices found amongst peasants, ranging from household exchanges to communal co-operation, result in a dogged resistance by peasants to the polarization process. It is this resilience that I examine in the following pages showing, however, that peasants become economically differentiated and yet absorbed within the capitalist economy in a variety of ways.

In the Mantaro valley in highland Peru there exist the elements that normally

107

characterize a peasant economy but which, in fact, are part of a capitalist economy. The valley contains numerous villages and *comunidades* in which the dominant economic activity is agriculture, practised under a smallholder system and centred on household semi-subsistence farming. In 1961, some 90 per cent of the farm units in the valley were under five hectares and the trend was towards increasing land fragmentation.

In valley agriculture, household farming is the most prevalent activity. The peasant household controls property and organizes production. Usually, it consists of a two- or three-generation household with the senior generation owning the resources, while other family members work them. The transmission of household property is mainly through inheritance and there is a cycle of property dispersal and concentration. Property passes down to both males and females and so is broken up, but is then re-grouped as one inheritor tries to purchase the inheritance of his siblings.

The organizing principle of the household is that consumption needs be met through the mobilization of household labour. Labour is recruited and removed through the cycles of birth, marriage and death, constantly changing the balance between the household's labour inputs and its consumption needs. The household is also the locus of most decisions relating to the lives of its members. Planting and harvesting times and practices are discussed there, whilst the senior members advise on purchases, schooling and marriage. Yet, no one household meets all its needs and so attempts are made to mobilize external resources while maintaining the viability of the household. Occasionally, such attempts lead to the breakdwon of the household as external demands become too great, but usually they do not.

There exists within Andean peasant culture a range of co-operative practices which can be used to sustain household farming (Long and Roberts, 1978, 305–15).[1] Relations between individuals are established by the practice of *al partir* (the sharing of cost and profit on land) and *hipoteca* (the temporary pawning of land). Relations between households are created by the practice of *uyay* (the exchange of household members at times of sowing and harvesting), *minka* (rewarding people in kind) and by *trueque* (bartering). At the village level is the *comunidad* itself, through which peasants engage in common agricultural or construction tasks. *Cofradías*, or religious brotherhoods, organize the working of church lands and see to the disposal of the produce. Such disposal is occasionally through a fiesta, in which all the villagers co-operate through dancing and recreation.

Underpinning these peasant co-operative practices in the valley are their social systems of kin and *compadrazgo* (Wolf, 1950). The villages of the valley may be described as loose kin groupings. In small villages, nearly everyone is related to everyone else. The common street greeting is that of *primo*, or cousin, on the assumption that, even if the other is only an acquaintance, he is probably a kinsman. Kin are an ubiquitous feature of peasant life and are called upon to help in both a variety of life-crises and in everyday village tasks. One aspect of kinship co-operation is the sexual division of labour which exists in Andean villages (Harris, 1978). Men and women perform different agricultural tasks, with the men often specializing in tasks such as the use and care of bullocks whilst the women are responsible for heavy field labour or do the planting and harvesting.

The institution of *compadrazgo*, or ritual co-parenthood, also broadens and reinforces the bases for co-operation. Through rituals, such as baptism and marriage, peasants are obligated to help the children of their *compadres*. In return, *compadres* assist one another when called upon. In the Mantaro valley there has evolved a particular form of *compadrazgo* whereby, without the usual ritual, the close adult relatives of spouses call one another *compadres*. In village situations where kin are abundant this *compadrazgo* terminology gives added status to kin members who have become 'closer' due to a marriage.

However, although all these economic practices and social elements exist amongst the peasants in the Mantaro valley, one cannot identify there a peasant economy that is distinct from, and articulated with, a capitalist economy. Rather these peasant practices are contained within a capitalist framework. Commercialized agriculture exists alongside subsistence agriculture, as well as entrepreneurial activities and industrialized mines. Even subsistence peasants must market some of their crops in order to purchase salt, oil and bread. Until the 1930s, hens' eggs could be used as a currency in village shops, but this has died out except in unusual circumstances. Commercial farming exists in many villages and market-oriented peasants occasionally combine agricultural and trading ventures.

In the agricultural economy of the valley, three broad social classes can be distinguished, defined in relation to the means of agricultural production (Long and Roberts, 1978, 316–18). The first class consists of the rich peasants who have sufficient land to produce a surplus for the market. This class is itself differentiated. Some rich peasants use mainly household labour whilst others rely on employing workers. Furthermore, some rich peasants combine their agricultural production interests with trading, to the extent that some are mainly traders, perhaps using their land and products as insurance against entrepreneurial ventures. Approximately 15 per cent of the households in the valley are rich peasant households.

The second class in the valley agricultural economy is made up of the subsistence peasants. This class has enough land to produce sufficient to meet household necessities, but no more. Consequently, there is little accumulation of capital and therefore little expansion. To supplement their incomes, members of these peasant households engage in craft work, migrate to urban work-centres or work sporadically on the land of rich peasants. The third class comprises the poor peasants and is again differentiated. Some have small plots of land which do not meet their subsistence needs whilst others are landless labourers. These peasants work regularly in the fields of others, migrate, or work in the commercial ventures of the rich peasants as porters or labourers. Also included in this class are *comuneros* who have usufructuary rights to communal land. The subsistence peasants comprise between 40 and 50 per cent of valley peasant households, whilst the poor peasants account for 35 to 40 per cent.

Although all the agrarian classes have available to them the co-operative arrangements of Andean culture, these practices are distributed unevenly between classes (Laite, 1977). The rich peasants gain access to land either by purchasing land or by renting it. Some subsistence peasants may also rent land. The poor peasants, however, use the practice of *al partir* or become members of the *comunidad* in order to gain access to land. Moreover, whilst rich peasants both purchase and inherit land, poor peasants only acquire land through inheritance. Different practices are employed in land use as well as in land access. The rich peasants use paid labour, but it is the poor peasants who rely on *minka*, *uyay* and their extended kin. It is thus the rich peasants who mainly contribute to the proletarianization of the poor peasants. Finally, it is the rich peasants who are mainly market-oriented, selling their agricultural commodities, in contrast to the subsistence production of the poor peasants.

As well as the existence of these classes in the agricultural sector, the villages of the valley also contain other social classes. For example, there are craftsmen and merchants, trading in wood, clothing or other commodities, who have no agricultural base. Some of these traders own large shops. Importantly, there also exists in the region a large mining workforce, drawn from villages in the region who are not fully proletarianized. Hence, today, the stratification system is based on access to land, non-agricultural work and urban wage employment.

One important element in the process of differentiation in the valley has been migration. During the Inca and colonial periods peasants were forced to migrate to the mines. During the nineteenth and twentieth centuries peasants have voluntarily migrated to mining centres, coastal plantations and Lima. Currently, the valley forms part of a migratory process which embraces the highlands, the mining sector and Lima.[2] Seasonal migration from the poorer villages, lying either to the south of the valley or at the foot of the valley slopes, provided female agricultural labour to work in the fields of richer valley villages, as well as supplying male temporary labour to the mines of Huancavelica. The women from these poor villages are recruited both by rich peasants and the families of men from the richer villages who are themselves working in urban centres. These men send home cash to help with the hiring of this casual labour. The worker-peasant in the urban centre may be joined by his wife and family, and so sever his links with the land, or he may maintain these links through keeping his wife and children in the village. The village lands provide security for migrant labourers in the mines and Lima and many migrants return to their villages in times of crisis or at retirement.

Thus, this migratory process is partly a circulatory one. Peasants from poor villages work temporarily in richer villages and then return. Peasants from richer villages work in mines and cities and then return to their villages. Even though they may migrate for decades, many return to their villages. Previous analyses of migration in Peru have been conducted in Lima, which was seen as the nodal point of migration (Matos Mar, 1966; Vandendries, 1975). Undoubtedly the uni-directional flow of migrants to Peru's cities is the most important migrational feature in Peru. However, alongside that migration process is circular migration which contributes to socio-economic differentiation in the rural areas.

Two valley villages

In order to assess the impact of capitalist expansion and migration on the rural economy, two villages in the Mantaro valley were selected for analysis. It is important to stress that these villages were research locations, not analytical units. They had different class structures and so their patterns of migration and socio-economic differentiation differed. However, three qualifications to this must be made. Firstly, the village is a meaningful social location for peasants who will readily identify themselves as being from this or that village. Secondly, social interaction takes place within the village setting and so reinforces the village as a meaningful social arena. Thirdly, the villages are kin groupings and so are unique milieux. These kinship networks often overlap class boundaries, providing alternative bases for social interaction.

Indeed, it is these alternative bases of social interaction in the villages, combined with the continuance of co-operative arrangements between households and the availability of migrational opportunities, which have limited the tendency towards polarization in the rural economy, even though there has been differentiation. As yet, there is no open and widespread conflict in the villages between the agrarian classes even though exploitative relations exist between them. As will be shown, one important reason for this has been the fluid composition of the middle stratum, a consequence of the marked upward and downward social mobility in the agrarian sector.

Ataura and Matahuasi are two villages which lie on the left bank of the Mantaro river, some twenty kilometres from one another (see Map 2). Ataura is small, in terms of land and population, but Matahuasi is large, prosperous and expanding. Migrants from both villages live and work in the mines and in Lima, and both villages have high rates of emigration. Of all the villages in the Mantaro valley, Ataura has the highest percentage of its sons working in the mines, while Matahuasi has the largest number of villagers living and working outside the valley. Only just over half of the adults living in the two villages were born there.

Ataura contains some 1,700 men, women and children and occupies approximately 600 hectares of land, 400 of which are viable for crops or pasture. The main occupational activity is agriculture practised through smallholdings. Ataura is overwhelmingly composed of poor peasants. Four-fifths of the households own or work less than one hectare, whilst it requires from between three and four hectares of irrigated valley bottom land to meet the subsistence needs of households. One-fifth of the Ataura households own more than one hectare, but most of these own between one and two hectares. Only two people in Ataura own approximately five hectares.

All told, there are 107 adult men living and working in Ataura. Nearly all of them have some agricultural interest, but only one-third are solely peasants with no other supplementary occupation. About half are artisans, with shoemakers, house-builders and drivers being the most common types of occupation. Shopkeepers and professionals represent one-tenth of the resident male population, the former often selling the products of their own fields, while the latter are school teachers or retired white-collar workers. Two-thirds of the men are independent workers, one-tenth are mainly independent, occasionally hiring out their services to others, whilst one-quarter are dependent workers. Of these dependent workers, one-quarter worked not for cash but as *partidarios* (share-croppers), splitting the cost and profit of cultivation with the owner of the land. The remainder of the dependent workers work for small concerns, the government, or private landholders. Two-thirds of all the men work in and around Ataura whilst the others work in Jauja, Huancayo, or valley villages.

Matahuasi is a much larger village than Ataura. It contains some 4,000 inhabitants and extends over some 2,000 hectares, most of which is cultivable. Like Ataura, the predominant activity in Matahuasi is agriculture, but the class structure of Matahuasi is more differentiated than that of the smaller village. Nearly all Matahuasi households are engaged in agricultural production. One-seventh of Matahuasi households are rich peasants, owning four or more hectares of cultivable land, whilst nearly two-fifths own between one and four hectares. So, a little over half of the village households are those of rich and subsistence peasants.

The other half of the households are those of poor peasants, a class which is internally differentiated. One group in this class comprises the landless labourers, who make up one-fifth of Matahuasi's households. This group has been growing over time. The second group consists of peasants who own less than one hectare, accounting for one-quarter of village households. At the same time, Matahuasi is a recognized *comunidad* and there is an extension of sixty hectares of communal land. *Comuneros* with usufructuary rights to this land are drawn from the class of poor peasants, there being 120 households with such communal rights.

As well as Matahuasi's agrarian structure being more differentiated than Ataura's, its occupational structure is also more complex. Although in Matahuasi most households are engaged in agriculture, only half of the heads of household are solely peasants. The remainder are shopkeepers and traders, artisans, school teachers and other professionals, and unskilled workers. Each group accounts for approximately one-tenth of household heads repectively. Importantly, the commercial activities in Matahuasi are on a much larger scale than in Ataura. As well as prosperous shopkeepers catering to the large population and outsiders, there are timber merchants, agricultural traders and milk producers. Some members of this commercial stratum are rich peasants with trading outlets, but others are mainly traders who maintain an agricultural base.

To assess the effect which capitalist development and migration have had on class differentiation in the Mantaro valley, aspects of village social structure were investigated. These aspects are the migration patterns of the two villages, their landholding structures, occupational systems and fiestas. Overall, important differences emerge between the two villages. These differences are due mainly to the different class composition of the villages, but the unique characteristics of each village are also a contributory feature. The first aspect investigated is that of the migration histories and processes of the two villages.

Migration patterns compared

Migration affected the valley during the Inca period as the Inca state established colonies, or *mitimaes*, throughout the valley. The Inca state required the valley inhabitants to labour for short periods of the year in the highland mines, through the *mita* system (DeWind, 1970). With the Conquest came the immigration of Spanish settlers and the emigration of valley peasants to work in the mines. The Spanish settlers accumulated land and portions were also allocated to the Catholic church. Thus, land was removed from the control of the indigenous community which occasionally disputed this appropriation. One case in Ataura displays the relation between landholding and migration (Bullon, 1942). In 1749, a son of Ataura, then a Spanish captain, laid claim to some land in Ataura. He himself had moved to a village on the other side of the river and his claim was contested by the residents of Ataura, who argued that they had bought the land in 1694 and now used it to support them while they worked in the mines.

Valley dwellers were required by the Spanish not only to work in the mines but also to render labour-services, or *faena*, in the major municipal centres. Such involuntary migration affected both Ataurinos and Matahuasinos. Ataurinos had to render *faena*, which usually involved cleaning the streets or the bullring, in Jauja. If a man was working in the mines when his *faena* fell due, then his son or his wife went in his place. If they could not go, then the family was fined. *Faena* continued until the end of the nineteenth century and old men in Ataura remember it bitterly, observing that, 'Jauja held us as slaves'. For Matahuasinos, the *faena* was rendered in Apata, of which Matahuasi was an *anexo* (dependent hamlet).

The influx of armies also affected the two villages. Ataura rested on a small knoll overlooking a narrow strip of land and a bridge, both vital to the defence of Jauja. In 1570 the knoll marked the boundary between the Xauxa and Huanca territories. During the nineteenth century, Spanish, Chilean and Nationalist armies fought for control of the hill and of the bridge. Similarly, in the 1890s, when the armies of Pierola and Cáceres clashed in the valley, Matahuasinos supported the victorious Pierola against Apata, allied with Cáceres. In return for this support, Matahuasi was granted its independent status.

During the nineteenth century, the villages provided places for resting and victualling for migrants travelling to and from the highlands, Lima and the jungle. The old Inca highway from Cajamarca to Cuzco ran through the valley and close to the villages and was still used by travellers. Older Ataurinos remember the village at the end of the nineteenth century as being 'like a port', and houses in the village square had a flourishing *pensión* trade. In Matahuasi, peasants were contracted by the nearby monastery of Acolla to transport *colonos* (settlers) down to the jungle. Matahuasi thus became a staging post and there emerged in the village an important group of muleteers.

The late nineteenth and early twentieth centuries witnessed not only the passage of traders and colonists but also the increasing emigration of valley peasants to the nearby mines of Yauli, Morococha and Cerro de Pasco. The flow of Ataurinos to these mines was marked. The Yauli parish register shows that, between 1835 and 1850, seven Ataurinos were married in that mining parish. Their occupations were those of miners and it was noted that they had been resident for some time in the parish. This was the highest number of marriages recorded in Yauli for any one of the Mantaro villages.

As was seen in chapter three, to meet the labour demand in the mines workers were recruited through the *enganche* system. *Enganche* was labour contracting through debt. A labour-recruiter, or *enganchador*, would forward a peasant a small sum of money and the peasant was then required to work off the debt by labouring in the mines. This system was favoured by mine owners since it not only provided labour but also meant there was no contractual obligation between the mine owner and the labourer, only between the labourer and the *enganchador*.

The operation of *enganche* in the villages was based on certain requirements. In order to act as an *enganchador* the generation of confidence and trust relationships was of prime importance both for the negotiations with the contracting company and for the negotiations with the contracted labour. It was while working for a mine owner that a man could build up confidence relations with him to the point that the owner was prepared to lend the money to be used as forward payments. During this build-up the prospective *enganchador* would use his lands and status in the village to convince the mine owner that he was reliable. When sub-contracting for the Cerro de Pasco Corporation such lands and status were essential for the American company did not provide the initial contract money, which the *enganchador* thus had to find for himself through sales, loans or savings. Armed with this cash the *enganchador* then had the problem of negotiating contracts with the peasants.

There were generally three bases for such negotiations. The first was the example of the successful mine worker turned *enganchador* who provided the evidence that fortunes were to be made by working in the mines. The second was the status of the *enganchador* or his 'front men' in the village itself. As landowners and council members they could convince the peasants that the work was neither too hard nor too dangerous, that further payments would be forthcoming and that the contracts would not be broken. Key figures in extended kin groups were contacted to use their family ties and so reinforce these guarantees.

However, the danger of the work and the high accident rate meant that in time the third basis, that of coercion, was more frequently used. When a miner fell ill or died without completing his contract, he left outstanding a debt which could be paid off either by one of his family – his son, for example – working off the requisite number of days, or by his family raising the cash – for instance, by selling land.

When problems of settlement arose the onus for collection of the debt lay not on the *enganchador* but on the *fiador* who had guaranteed the peasant's ability to pay off the debt. Thus, the *enganchador* maintained a distance between the recruitment of labour and the collection of debts in order to minimize the consequences for his future recruiting position. However, it still became necessary for *enganchadores* to use the debt relations that characterize the life of poor peasants in order to gain a supply of labour. By allowing credit relations in their village stores to run on, or by offering cash to solve the life-crises of marriage, death or fiesta finance, the *enganchadores* could bring pressure to bear on people to induce them to work in the mines. Failure to pay the *enganche* debt had the direst of consequences. The *fiador* would contact the family of the debtor and, if they could not pay, then either the *fiador* had to work off the required days himself, or he would have to seize the debtor's lands and house. The latter alternative led to the bitterest of disputes which rankle even today.

In Ataura, the most important *enganchador* was Lucas. He was an Ataurino who had made his fortune in the mines and after his return to the village he continued to contract labour. A village notable and a successful migrant, Lucas had little difficulty in persuading peasants to accept advance payments. A second *enganchador* in Ataura was Isaias from the neighbouring village of Huamalí. Lacking Lucas' social standing, Isaias relied more on debt pressure through his local store. This made him extremely unpopular and one feature of the contemporary rivalry between the two villages is the memory that the fathers of Ataura were hooked (*enganchados*) by the sons of Huamalí.

In the late nineteenth century, the pattern of emigration from the valley to the mines closely reflected the class divisions in the valley. The peasants would migrate to become day-labourers or contract-workers for the larger companies. Some might group together and open a small mine for themselves, sharing costs and profits. These small-scale miners would sell their ores to larger companies for smelting. The cash obtained from such migration could be used to pay off debts or to buy household commodities or even parcels of land. The descendants of Spanish families also migrated. However, their sons went to be clerks, accountants or overseers in the larger mining companies. On their return, they would perhaps set up a mill, buy a shop in Jauja, or invest in some livestock.

With the advent of the Corporation, migration to the mines from valley villages quickened. At the same time peasants began to develop trading relations with the mining sector. In the case of Ataura, the links established with the mines were labour links. Ataura became a provider of mine-labourers. In the case of Matahuasi, however, the village established both labour and trading links with the mines. Because Ataura is a village with little land, composed of poor peasants, there has not been the scope for the accumulation of capital and the development of commerce. In Matahuasi, on the other hand, rich and subsistence peasants have managed to set up trading ventures, while poor peasants have become miners. Complicating this division, however, is the fact that migration has itself been an avenue of social mobility for poor peasants who have been able to capitalize on migration earnings.

For most of the twentieth century, Ataura's migration patterns have been dominated by the mining sector, and by the Cerro de Pasco Corporation. Whereas during the nineteenth century Ataurinos in the mines were either working for a variety of medium-sized mining companies or were self-employed, during the twentieth century the Corporation became the major single employer in the mining sector with the construction of railways and roads (Laite, 1978).

By the end of the second decade of the twentieth century, Ataurinos had gained *empleado* positions in the Corporation. Ataurino *empleados* would then recruit other Ataurinos and thus village networks expanded throughout the Corporation. Several villages 'captured' particular company departments in this way. *Empleados* from particular villages became occupational gatekeepers, the foci of the village networks. Several Ataurinos became *empleados* in the refinery which the Corporation built in La Oroya, some eighty kilometres from the valley.

In the 1920s, Ataura's integration with the wider national scene, and particularly mining, was established.[3] More and more people migrated to the mines while the construction of the refinery gave to some the opportunity to learn skilled trades. The Corporation was probably the largest single employer of migrant Ataurinos. After mining, government construction projects and office work, often in Lima, were an important source of employment. Agricultural employment for male Ataurinos declined markedly during the 1920s. The rapid outflow of men to the mining sector left a village of women, children and aged.

However, the Depression of the 1930s resulted in men moving back into the agricultural sector. As the government cut its workforce and small private concerns laid off men, the migrant wage labourers of Ataura became poor peasants once more on their own plots of land. For many, however, the 1930s was a period marked by endless journeys seeking work. It was not until the late 1930s that manufacturing and construction work expanded. One example of this was the commencement of the construction of the irrigation canal which was to run the length of the Mantaro valley.

With the boom of the 1940s, there was a shift away from mining, characterized by its low, fixed wage-rate, into occupations in Lima. The Ataurinos could earn a living either in construction work or in the informal, self-employed, sector washing cars or selling newspapers, for in these occupations no capital was required. Unlike during the 1920s, however, this resurgence in emigration was not accompanied by a sharp decline in agricultural employment. During the 1950s and 1960s, agricultural employment remained important as Ataurinos established ways of maintaining both external and village interests. Thus, the opportunities opening up in expanding manufacturing and construction work were taken mainly at the expense of mining, which continued its relative decline. Dependent work, however, increased, as migrants moved out of the 'informal' occupations into wage or salaried employment, often as skilled workers.

Some of these changes can be seen in Fig. 2. Looking firstly at the number of people now resident in Ataura who worked in the mines in particular years, we can see that many people from the same village spent their working lives together not in the village, but in a migrant work-centre. The most striking feature of the two graphs, however, is the decline in numbers working in the mines since the Second World War, and the rise in importance of Lima. That the graphs should decline towards the end is due to the nature of the sample, for some of the men interviewed had been resident in Ataura for several years. However, that the graphs should decline at different rates is the interesting feature, and the Lima graph continues to rise for many years after the mining graph has begun to fall.

Thus, Ataura's twentieth century migration history has been one of migration to the mines, return to Ataura and then emigration to a wider range of sectors than before. The existence of a smallholder economy, as well as peasant co-operative practices, enabled the Ataurinos to withstand both the Depression and fluctuations in external employment. When reflation came, Ataurinos shifted away from the low-paid mining sector, which experience had taught them was unstable, and developed a range of interests across a wider variety of sectors, including agriculture.

In the first decades of the twentieth century, Ataurinos migrated to the mines for periods from a few months up to four or five years. Migration from the Mantaro valley was not predominantly seasonal, although at the end of the nineteenth century *enganche* contracts would have fitted more into a seasonal pattern. Apart from the 1930s, when little work was to be had, the length of time spent working away from home has steadily increased. Working away from the village for ten years or more is now the pattern for most Ataurinos, although in this general pattern there remain the frequent returns to the village due to brief pauses between jobs.

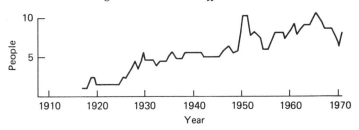

Fig. 2a   Number of people, now resident in Ataura, resident in Lima 1910–70

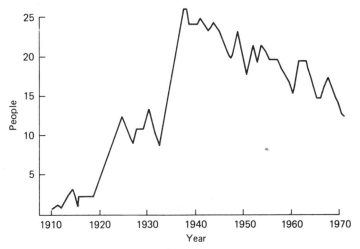

Fig. 2b   Number of people, now resident in Ataura, resident in mines 1910–70

The gains to be had from migration have varied throughout the twentieth century for Ataurinos. Perhaps the most profitable era was the beginning of the century when cash could be used to buy houses and land for the first time. A few of those who became *enganchados* managed to invest the advance payment in land, tools or a house, but most *enganche* histories are ones of accident and debt. But, as more and more of the village economy was brought into the cash arena, the prices of land and houses began to relate to the level of wages and profitable dealings became rarer. During the 1930s, migration earnings only just stretched far enough to cover sustenance. Since the Second World War, wage increases in the mining sector have led to the possibility that some savings can be made and invested in the village. However, migrants generally need an alternative source of income, or subsistence, to be able to do this.

The migration history of Matahuasi contains some similarities and some differences to that of Ataura. Like Ataura, Matahuasi at the end of the nineteenth century was overwhelmingly agricultural, although there were more entrepreneurial activities there than in Ataura. As well as the muleteers and the *pensión* trade, Matahuasi women would bake bread in the village and walk in the early morning to Jauja to sell it as street vendors. The building of the railway in 1908, however, undercut such ventures, bringing cheaper products such as flour into Matahuasi.

With the improvement in transport and the expansion of the mining sector there was an increase in the number of Matahuasinos who migrated.[4] Matahuasinos had previously migrated both to the mines around Cerro de Pasco and to the small mines in Huancavelica. This pattern changed in the early twentieth century as more migrants went to work for the Corporation. As in Ataura, there was a steep rise in the numbers working away from the village during the 1920s and a concomitant decline in male employment in agriculture. Again, similar to Ataura, Matahuasino migrants moved also into manufacturing and construction projects, mainly in Lima.

It was during the 1930s that Matahuasi's migration pattern began to differ from that of Ataura. With the decline in external employment opportunities in the 1930s, Matahuasinos once more turned to agriculture, and this sector's share of employment rose markedly. Mining declined as an employer and was never again to become so important. But, in other sectors there were remarkable increases. The number of people employed in transport multiplied, as did that in small private concerns, and thus it seems clear that the move out of mining and other external employment was followed by a move into agriculture and small transport businesses.

After the Depression, the revival of the 1940s affected Matahuasi as it had done Ataura. Emigration diversified away from the mines and, although mining remained important, there were increases in those working in transport, manufacturing and construction as entrepreneurs, traders and craftsmen. These increases also centred on Lima, which became an important work-centre for Matahuasinos before it did so for Ataurinos. During the 1950s and 1960s, these trends continued as Matahuasi built up links with a range of sectors, more at the expense of mining than of agriculture. Commercial activities, skilled and white-collar occupations increased steadily, while more and more Matahuasi migrants became self-employed or worked for small concerns. While mining declined relatively, and construction and manufacturing fluctuated, agriculture held its share of employment and transport steadily increased in importance.

Thus, in Matahuasi in the 1930s, there was a major shift of resources into transport – a shift that did not occur in Ataura. With the post-1945 boom, Matahuasinos were able to consolidate this diversification away from mining, and they were able to do so through independent ventures. At the same time, as

Table 16 *Migrants' occupational history by village*

Occupation	Ataura		Matahuasi	
	No. of years spent in main occupation	%	No. of years spent in main occupation	%
Peasant	213	18	140	11
Obrero	369	31	506	40
Artisan	196	16	213	17
Empleado	254	21	149	12
Trader	50	5	139	11
Other	107	9	113	9

$X^2 = 104 = HS (N = A + B + C = 76)$
For N see note 5.

in Ataura, the village economy was sustained. In both villages, these rural resources were used to defend the peasants against fluctuations in external employment. In Matahuasi, however, they were also used to underwrite transport and trading ventures which expanded after the Depression. The economy of Ataura could not provide this backing and so Ataurinos returned to wage labour after the Second World War.

The differences in the migration experiences of the two villages are revealed by analyses of the life-histories of villagers now resident in Ataura, Matahuasi and La Oroya, the refinery town.[5] The differences revealed by the analyses stem partly from the different class structures of the two villages and partly from the facts of unique village organization and history. That is to say, village differences, once established, tend to be self-reinforcing, complicating class divisions. One example of this is in migration history. Whereas the poor peasants of Ataura have migrated mainly to the mines, the poor and subsistence peasants of Matahuasi have moved mainly to Lima. The different economic situations in metropolis and mines have separately influenced the occupational careers of Matahuasinos and Ataurinos.

One major difference between the two villages is that, whereas only two-thirds of the Matahuasinos resident in Matahuasi have migration experience, nearly all the Ataurinos resident in Ataura have once been migrants. Consequently, Tables 16–20 represent the life-histories of virtually all Ataurinos, but of only a proportion of Matahuasinos.

Table 16 shows that both sets of village migrants have spent equal amounts of time as *obreros* and *empleados* whilst working away from the village: 52 per cent.

Table 17 *Migrants' sectoral history by village*

	Ataura		Matahuasi	
Economic sector	No. of years spent by migrant group in economic sector	%	No. of years spent by migrant group in economic sector	%
Agriculture	226	20	142	12
Mining	602	54	475	40
Manufacturing	27	2	77	6
Construction	84	8	91	8
Commerce	8	1	57	5
Transport	51	4	238	20
Service	52	5	66	6
Government	71	6	22	2

$X^2 = 242 = HS (N = A + B + C = 76)$
For N see note 5.

However, the Ataurinos have passed more time as *empleados* than have the Matahuasinos. At the same time, Ataurinos have spent more time as peasants than the Matahuasinos, who have spent more years as traders. The reason for these differences are straightforward. In urban work-centres Ataurinos do not have the capital to engage in trading. When Ataurinos return to their village they take up a peasant way of life for the village offers little alternative. Matahuasinos, on the other hand, become traders both in urban work-centres and in Matahuasi. Currently, half of the Matahuasinos resident in La Oroya are traders, whilst all of the Ataurinos there are wage labourers. When Ataurinos and Matahuasinos are working away from the village, it is the Ataurinos who develop long-term industrial strategies, involving both lateral job moves from onerous to acceptable Cerro de Pasco Corporation departments, and vertical job promotion from *obrero* to *empleado*. The reason they engage in these long-term strategies is because alternatives in Ataura are so limited. The sectoral distribution of migrants' life-histories reflects the preponderance of mining in relation to Ataura.

Mining is clearly the most important sector of migrant work for Ataurinos, more so than for Matahuasinos. Indeed, mining and agriculture dominate the Ataurino life-histories and account for three-quarters of the total years worked by the migrants. For the Matahuasinos, however, the picture is different. Mining and agriculture account for just half of the migrants' life-histories, and so Matahuasinos do not simply oscillate between these two sectors, as the

Table 18 *Migrants' work-place by village*

Department	Ataura		Matahuasi	
	No. of years spent by migrant group	%	No. of years spent by migrant group	%
Huancavelica	20	2	–	–
Lima	67	6	189	15
Pasco	107	9	323	3
Junín	987	82	1031	81

$X^2 = 106 = HS$ (N = A + B + C = 76)
For N see note 5.

Table 19 *Mobility rates by village*

Village	Average villager changes following categories every N years of working life					
	Department	Province	Village	Occupation	Employer	Sector
Ataura	12.8	7.6	6.5	5.6	5.7	6.2
Matahuasi	14.3	7.2	6.7	7.3	6.7	7.3

N = A = B + C = 76
For N see note 5.

Ataurinos do. Rather, Matahuasino migrants work in a diversity of sectors, the most important of these, after mining, being transport. Furthermore, the Matahuasinos have worked more in manufacturing and commerce than have the Ataurinos.

Finally, these patterned differences between the two villages are reflected in the places in which the migrants have worked. The Ataurinos, focussing on mining and subsistence agriculture, have remained mainly in the highland Departments of Huancavelica, Pasco and Junín. The Matahuasinos, however, have worked more in Lima, as traders, manufacturing workers and in transport concerns. The patterns of migration within Junín differ between the two villages. Many Matahuasinos have followed the old colonization route down to the coffee haciendas of the jungle. Although these haciendas are in Junín, the Ataurinos never go to work there, having built up their contacts in the mines.

Thus, the life-histories of those Matahuasinos and Ataurinos, resident in both La Oroya and the villages, who have migration experience display

Table 20 *Reasons for migration*

Reason	Percentage of respondents citing reason
To earn more money	39
To join kin already working	25
No work in the villages	12
Work opportunities presented themselves	11
Dislike of village life	11
To be near the village and family	11
To support nuclear or/and extended family	9
Poor	8
To pay for education	7

N = A + B + C = 76
For N see note 5.

significant differences between the villages. And the more evidence that is adduced relating to migration histories, the more these differences are reinforced. Like the respondents themselves, the brothers of these men – some 150 adults – have worked mainly in the mines, in La Oroya and in Lima. Also like the respondents, there are marked differences between the work destinations of the brothers from each of the two villages. Whereas half the Ataurino brothers have worked in La Oroya, very few Matahuasino brothers have done so, and, although one-third of the Matahuasino brothers have worked in Lima, only one-tenth of the Ataurino brothers have done so.

Despite the various differences between villages and classes in relation to migration, it is quite clear that, in general, for valley villagers, migration is an important part of their lives. This importance is shown by the rates of spatial and occupational mobility of the migrant groups resident in the villages and in La Oroya. The mobility rates are clearly high. Ataurinos change occupations every five and a half years, whilst the Matahuasinos do so just over every seven years. Table 19 shows that these valley dwellers are worker-peasants, combining subsistence production with employment that is directly integrated into the national economy. Migration from the valley is not a flight from the land by landless labourers, as is shown by the reasons which migrants give for migrating.

Having to migrate because they had no land at all was not given as an important reason by the respondents. Of course, being 'poor', supporting the family and looking for work are indicative of a situation in which there is little land and few work opportunities in the village. Yet, this is not the massive alienation of poor peasants from the land. In fact, the range of people who migrate and the range of reasons why they do so are more striking features. As well as the poor peasants looking for work to make subsistence possible, there are the subsistence peasants themselves, seeking savings to purchase tools, animals or even land, or looking for training possibilities either in trade or in further education. When asked, the respondents themselves observed that nowadays everyone migrates, whether he be rich or poor. The rich look for professional work not to be found in the village, whilst the poor complement their rural interests with migration.

The main patterns and processes in the migration histories of valley dwellers having been outlined, it is now possible to turn to analyses of changes in landholding, occupational structures and recreation to understand the impact of capitalist development and migration.

Patterns of landholding

The main impact of capitalist expansion and migration on the structure of landholding in the valley has been to bring land within the cash arena. Alongside this commercialization of land has gone increasing differentiation. During the nineteenth century there were four landholding entities in Ataura. The largest landholders were a group of five Spanish families, descendants of earlier colonials who had been granted land. Alongside these was the Catholic church which owned land that was worked by villagers. The land was occasionally rented, but more often worked in common, with villagers and church dividing the harvest. At the same time there was some communal land that was not owned by the church; this comprised forty hectares of land which lay on an island in the Mantaro river, between Muquiyauyo and Ataura. Positioned in the middle of the river, the island was protected from frost, and could produce up to two crops per year. Finally, there were the indigenous landholders, owning or working small plots around the village.

With the increase in migration at the end of the nineteenth century, this pattern was to change as land was brought into the cash arena. The most dramatic change was that produced by one man – Lucas. Lucas was the illegitimate son of a Spanish family and in the second half of the nineteenth century, unrecognized and without land, he searched for work in the mines. During the 1860s he worked near Casapalca and rose to be a mine administrator in Colquipallana. His son managed the mine store and supervised the transportation of the ores, while Lucas, having made his fortune, returned to Ataura in 1891 with sacks of silver.

On his return, Lucas bought out the larger Spanish landholders through the purchase of seven hectares and a mill, and then consolidated his position by further land purchase. By 1920 he owned over twenty hectares, employed three full-time labourers on his land, and had opened a shop in Jauja. He experimented with Argentinian cattle and crop-raising, became known as the 'Father of the Village', and at sowing and harvest time would recruit migrant labour from Huancavelica, directing them from the back of a large white horse.

The families that he had bought-out moved away from the village and became professionals – priests, lawyers and doctors – in Huancayo, Jauja and Lima. Indeed, Lucas' own sons continued this trend to professionalization. On his death, three sons sold their land inheritance and used the cash to become engineers and politicians, while their mother sold the mill and moved to Jauja. The fourth son, however, continued to invest in land, and by 1925 owned nearly forty hectares, which in that year he sold to his son and himself set up a textile shop in Jauja. Eventually, his grandsons have in their turn become professionals and moved from Jauja to Lima.

Lucas' example, the recruitment drives of *enganchadores*, population growth and the possibility of ready cash in the mines induced many men to go to the mines in the 1920s and 1930s. On their return, these men bought the available land in Ataura, either from those who wished to leave the village, or from widows in debt to *enganchadores*. The emigration of these men looking for work meant that, in the early 1920s, the demographic structure of Ataura was one of a resident population of children, old men and women. Women were not represented on the village council until 1930 and so when the municipal agent decided to sell the communal land on the island to Muquiyauyo there was little opposition.

However, as news of the deal passed round the male mining migrants, opposition began to grow and a major conflict loomed. By this time, the refuse dumped by the refinery into the river at La Oroya had made its way into the Mantaro valley, and the villagers realized that the river and the island had become so polluted as to be worthless. Thus, the matter was dropped and a crisis was averted. However, in terms of pressure on land, the damage had been done and immigrants now had to bid for the land on the valley bottom.

Pressure on land began to ease somewhat over the next few years for two reasons. The first was that Lucas' grandchildren began to sell their land and move off to Jauja and Lima. The parcels of land were mainly bought by returning miners. The mill was bought by a miner's wife and Lucas' big house was purchased by a retired refinery worker. Secondly, the sale of church lands during the 1930s brought more land onto the market in Ataura. These sales took place throughout the Mantaro valley in this period, perhaps, as some say, to provide funds for Franco during the Spanish Civil War. In Ataura, the sales provided land which could be bought by returning migrants. They broke the land up into smaller plots and so contributed to the continuance of Ataura's subsistence economy.

Thus, in Ataura, the two processes of commercialization and differentiation succeeded one another. The expansion of the cities and mines led to the migration of both peasants and Spanish families. At first, the purchase of land by returning migrants did not lead to blocks of land being broken up. Whereas the social composition of the landholders in Ataura changed, at first the landholding structure did not. However, increasing pressure on land and the further sales of land led to the fragmentation of the landholding structure, resulting in the numerous small plots worked by the poor peasants of Ataura today.

The structure of landholding in Matahuasi at the end of the nineteenth century was similar to that in Ataura, being composed of blocks of Spanish family land, communal land, church land and private plots. The major differences were two-fold in that, in general, there was more good agricultural land in Matahuasi which could come on to the market and, in particular, there was a prime extension of church (*cofradía*) land which came up for sale in the 1930s.

As in Ataura, money accumulated from migration earnings began to bring Matahuasi land into the cash arena at the beginning of the twentieth century. Further land alienation was brought about by the increase in commercial activities in Matahuasi itself. Then, in the 1930s, the sale of church land throughout the valley opened the opportunity in Matahuasi for the acquisition of land on a large scale. In Matahuasi, the amount of land released was much greater than it had been in Ataura, and its acquisition has had a more marked effect on social differentiation (Winder, 1978).

Since the church land had been communally worked and the produce communally distributed, the villagers felt that negotiations with the church should proceed on a village basis. With many of the villagers concerned away working, a group was elected to represent Matahuasi's interests. Realizing that organized opposition from the dispersed village migrants would be sluggish, this group promptly bought the land for themselves – much of the money used in the purchase coming from working in, or trading with, the mines and Lima. The response of the remainder of the village was to form a committee to contest this and it was through the work of this committee that the legally recognized *comunidad* of Matahuasi was formed.

Thus, the combination of a sudden increase in the supply of land, the absence of many villagers and the availability of cash resources for a small minority meant that in Matahuasi two easily identified land-related strata were created in the village – the large, private landholders, and the members of the *comunidad*.

Not only do these strata continue to exist today, but the effects of the original split are still expressed in hostility between the groups, as they struggle for political office in the village. In Matahuasi, the economic differentiation which has occurred in the landholding structure has laid the basis for polarization and class conflict.

Occupational differences

The impact of capitalist expansion and migration on the occupational structures of the two villages has been similar to their impact on landholding. That is, in Ataura, the occupational structure contains a range of occupations, but these are all either dependent or petty pursuits which do not permit capital accumulation on any scale. In Matahuasi, by contrast, an important commercial stratum has emerged which, in the main, retains its agricultural base. As well as these occupational distinctions in the division of labour in the villages, there is also an important sexual division of labour.

Undoubtedly, occupational differentiation has existed for a long time in the valley, in the presence of muleteers, bakers, cobblers and so on. However, the increased range of occupations is a feature of the twentieth century. Even in the poor peasant village of Ataura, there are teachers, drivers, carpenters, agricultural labourers and many more. Perhaps the best example of differentiation in the village economy of Ataura is given by the rise of the several shopkeepers in the society of the village. This example shows how differentiation has occurred, how it has occurred within village networks, and how limited are the activities of petty shopkeeping. The commercial activities of Ataura occur mainly in the shops and the main body of shops is to be found around the central square. The structure of shopkeeping has become fragmented. The square is flanked by a row of shops in the lower half of what was once a large house owned by a Spanish family. In the first decade of the twentieth century the house was divided into three shops by sons who catered to the traders from Cuzco and Lima. Through the marriage of their sons, the house was divided again, with one new shop passing into a wife's family. Their children, in turn divided the house and exchanged shops among themselves as they tried to move nearer to the new road, which in the 1920s passed on the other side of the square. However, the trade of the early years has gone and the owners of the shops now prefer to sell them or rent them out to other members of the family. The money for such purchases and renting has come almost invariably from migration to the mines.

Of the seven shops that today make up the old house, five are owned by cousins – two of whom rent to cousins, one to a nephew and another to an independent person – while two are owned independently. All the men who run the shops have worked in the mines for long periods and have used their savings either to buy the shop or its stock, while of the two women, one had a husband who worked in the mines. The situation is very similar for the remaining nine shops in Ataura, the owners having worked from two to thirty years in the mines. Of course, the mechanisms of marriage and inheritance still serve as a source of wealth, and enabled one woman in the 1950s to invest in shops and houses in Ataura. Yet this woman was in fact a grand-daughter of Lucas, and it was part of his mining fortune that had passed down to her.

Small shopkeepers, such as those described, exist in Matahuasi as well as in Ataura. In both villages such occupations are limited, 'small-time' affairs. Often, the existence of such shopkeepers is the result of savings and experience gained from migration. For most of those who set up shop it is merely a retirement occupation. An initial investment is required which comes either from the trader's savings from migration, or from a bank, or from the wholesale merchants that supply the shop. Also required is some experience, provided either by the migrant himself or by a friend, and, although the shop may only be a supplementary means of support for the trader, all of them take careful advice before embarking on the venture. The shops are located to attract customers – in the square, close to the road or railway – and are staffed by the trader himself or by his wife. Aiming to capture some part of an already established market, the shops sell very similar products. All are general goods stores (*abarrotes*), selling foodstuffs and beer. The produce comes either from the trader's own fields or, for both Ataura and Matahuasi, from wholesalers in Jauja. Indeed, the operation of these small shops may be described as the management of the wholesaler's outlet.

The limits to commercial activities in Ataura are revealed through the second example of occupational differentiation in the village: the attempts by villagers to establish transport ventures. The failures of such ventures in Ataura contrasts sharply with their success in Matahuasi. In Ataura we have the cases of Alfredo and Armando, failed entrepreneurs who have returned to wage labouring in the mines.

During the late 1950s, Alfredo built a brick house in Ataura with money he had earned from working in La Oroya. He decided to become a trucker and, having only a little land of his own, he persuaded the village priest to lend him the money for the lorry. The priest is a descendant of the old Spanish families of Ataura and over many years he has increased his wealth by surreptitious acquisition of land in the village. He now rents out this land and himself lives in Huancayo. He advanced Alfredo the money, but insisted that, since Alfredo had no land, the house be the guarantee for the loan. Alfredo bought the lorry, but, through lack of contacts and thus contracts, the venture failed and the priest sued Alfredo for the money. The priest won the suit, evicted Alfredo, and the house now stands empty. Alfredo's family are lodged in a small adobe dwelling nearby, while Alfredo is working in La Oroya.

A little later, in the early 1960s, Armando returned to Ataura from the mines of Tamboraque. With the money he had earned there, plus a sum raised from putting their land in *hipoteca* (short-term mortgage), Armando and his brother Flavio raised enough money to put a deposit on a lorry. For three years they became truckers. They hired a driver and worked carrying anything to and from Lima and the valley. Again, however, the venture failed, and the brothers now shake their heads at the inexperienced way they went into the transport business without the necessary contacts. The problem was, they pointed out, that with their land in *hipoteca* they had no supplementary source of income either to pay off the loan interest or to feed themselves when the venture was in a slack period. Unable to pay their debts, the brothers were evicted from their house in Ataura and are now working in La Oroya to earn enough money to redeem their land.

In contrast to these stories of failure by the poor peasants of Ataura are the success stories of rich peasants in Matahuasi. Little land, few contacts and much uncertainty were a fatal combination for Ataurinos attempting to diversify. However, rich and subsistence peasants in Matahuasi have been able to overcome the problems of capital accumulation and diversification. The cases of Gonzalo and Julio illustrate how they have been able to do this. Gonzalo has used migration money to finance his ventures, whilst Julio busily trades with the mining sector.

The son of a large landowner in Matahuasi, Gonzalo studied in Lima and then went to join his brother's timber business in the jungle. The two brothers supplied wood to the mines and railway but, with wood prices falling and transport costs rising, they could not compete with wood produced in the Mantaro valley itself and so they sold the business and bought some land, a house and a lorry in Matahuasi. Gonzalo's brother opened a timber yard in Concepción and Gonzalo became the trucker taking timber to the mines, then mineral from the mines to Lima, and then paraffin from Lima back to the valley. The brothers acquired the transport contract to the mines from their sister, who had a timber yard in Jauja. Then Gonzalo crashed the lorry and was forced to look for wage work. His brother-in-law, who was a chemical engineeer in La Oroya, offered Gonzalo a job and so, for five years, Gonzalo worked as a Corporation *empleado*. He amassed some savings, returned to Matahuasi and bought an old lorry. He now works part-time for his brother in Concepción and part-time for himself, plying his lorry on contract work.

The case of Julio is that of an agro-entrepreneur – a rich peasant who uses his agricultural activities and village links as bases for trading.[6] Julio's father established a timber mill in the 1940s and purchased land for farming. Both mill and land are now controlled by Julio and his wife. The three operatives who work for Julio, one of whom is a cousin, have specified work tasks on the farm and in the mill, but it is Julio himself who travels to the mines to negotiate timber contracts with contacts established by his father during thirty years of operations. Although the farm land is still owned by the father, it is Julio, his sister and her husband who farm it. It is a large tract of land and enables the household to grow crops, rear cattle and keep chickens. The sister does the day-to-day work on the farm, while Julio markets the produce and receives a share of the profits.

Julio's marketing activities are much influenced by his marriage, for his parents-in-law were successful traders who owned lorries and had their own paid middlemen in Lima. Julio's mother-in-law now runs the business and Julio is developing increasingly closer ties with her. He helps her by transporting temporary labour to her fields at harvest time, while it is she who has the market connections in Lima for the sale of the produce. As well, she allows Julio to use her lorry to transport timber to the mines, enabling him to make several deliveries a week. Operating on this scale, Julio is now constantly searching for timber, and his mother-in-law is able to put him in touch with local farmers. Occasionally, Julio is further helped by his affines, who, driving lorries under the direction of their mother, work with Julio at harvest time.

Gonzalo and Julio, then, contrast sharply with Alfredo and Armando. Through the availability of land and the existence of trading networks, these subsistence and rich peasant Matahuasinos have been able to build up independent trading relations with the mines and with Lima. Migration, resulting in money and contacts, has played a part in the establishment of these relations which are complementary to viable household economies in Matahuasi. It is a similar story for the other Matahuasi truckers who were able to capitalize on the commercial opportunities offered by the mines rather than just the employment openings. As well as owning lorries to transport their products, they opened shops and restaurants in the mining centres as outlets for their goods, and controlled sources of supply in the valley through their own or family land. In Ataura, however, the poorer village economy could not underwrite the risks of commercial ventures and there was no history of trading contacts that could be used in the setting-up of such ventures.

A third example of occupational stratification is given by the agricultural sectors of the two villages. Again, the examples given show the general processes of differentiation occurring within the valley, as well as highlighting the differences in agricultural practice between the poor and the rich peasants of Ataura and Matahuasi.

In Matahuasi, Saul is a rich peasant (see chapter 8). He bought church land and now forms a link in the overall migration process that includes poor villages, the valley and work-centres. Many of the able-bodied men in Matahuasi are away, and those that are left are working on their own land. So, to recruit labour, Saul hires a labour contractor. Together with the contractor, Saul goes in his lorry to a poorer village on the valley slopes and picks up a gang of six women. Their own sowing or harvesting period is at an end and they are free to work for Saul. He employs them on specialized tasks, such as the harvesting of oats, for village children can do the easier work, and, in 1976, he paid the minimum sum of four soles per day per worker. The money went to the contractor, while Saul gave directly to the women two soles worth of coca per day, plus food and drink. On top of that, he paid the team one sack of whatever they harvested and gave the contractor an extra five soles per person per week.

Saul would have preferred to use a harvester to gather some crops, like wheat, for it was cheaper. It took six women six days to harvest one hectare of wheat, which cost 150 soles, but a harvester could do the job in one day for only 80 soles rent. The problem is that the land is irrigated, thus has ridges across it, and therefore a harvester cannot be used on it. So, Saul continues to contract labour. He contracts the same team each year and he gets to know their work while they get to know the employer, the land, and the surety of payment. Usually only women come, for their men are working in small mines or in the hydro-electric project, but occasionally a man does come. He then works on an individual task, never joining the women in their work. These activities of Saul, like those of Julio, can support independent, diverse ventures, and stand in contrast to the subsistence activities in Ataura.

The village economy of Ataura is small, divided and subsistence-oriented. It is a 'weekend' economy for migrant miners. The scale of the economy, and the co-operative practices available in Andean culture, support a migrant solution to the problems facing the household. So, typical agricultural scenes in Ataura are of women working the land. Wives and mothers of migrants or of retired Corporation workers, these women tend several small plots of land scattered around the village. At planting and harvest times they mobilize either another female kin member for hand-work, or contract a retired *obrero* who has two oxen. As he ploughs, the woman brings him beer and food which they consume together, gossiping. He receives the flat cash rate for the job and the woman helps him to carry his implements back to his house. This sort of operation does not provide the basis for diversification and so Ataurinos spend their working lives as migrant labourers and poor peasants.

These village scenes in Ataura reflect the fourth dimension of differentiation in the rural economy. Prior to the twentieth century, Andean culture involved a strict sexual division of labour, but it is a division which has been compounded amongst poor peasants by capitalist expansion and migration. Since the beginning of the twentieth century, Ataura's resident population has been comprised of women, youths and the elderly, for the men have been in work-centres. This demographic imbalance has reinforced the sexual divison of labour in Ataura in three ways.

Firstly, the absence of men means that it is the women who are called upon to perform communal tasks. The women performed the *faena* (communal work obligations) of their migrant husbands. It was the women of Ataura who built the church tower, carrying stones from the river bed. After the widening of the franchise in 1930, Ataura did not become, as one old lady insisted, 'almost a matriarchy!', but they did play a prominent role on the village council for many years. Today, there are no women on the council, but they still provide the labour for communal village projects, such as the damming of a spring high up on the mountain side.

Secondly, the absence of menfolk reinforces the tendency for Ataurinas to turn inwards upon their own company and kin. A women's world has developed in the village, organized around a whole range of village affairs from childbearing to agricultural labouring. Kinship is the main basis of the women's world. To the insider, kin provides a readily available pool of contacts from which to establish social relations but, to the outsider, kin can present an almost insurmountable barrier. Thus, many women prefer to remain in their own village after marriage for they know that it is in the world of the village that they will have to make their lives. To make that life in a strange family is too daunting a prospect for many women.

The third way in which the emigration of men contributes to the sexual division of labour is in relation to landholding and land usage. Women inherit land similarly to men and, as men emigrate and die in accidents at work, or perhaps simply abandon the women, there is a tendency for women to appropriate land. At the same time, migrants leave their wives, mothers and sisters in charge of their village land. It is these women who work the land. They do the manual work, or they contract others to plough and harvest with money sent to them by their migrant husbands. So, the women develop a keen landed interest since the responsibility for the working of the land devolves on them.

This sexual division of labour, creating close ties between women and the land, leads to a further dimension of differentiation in the valley villages. The close relation of valley women to valley land probably distinguishes them from other non-valley highland women. The daughters of valley villages are seen as a good marriageable prospect by men from non-valley villages. Immigrating into villages, then, are both returning migrants and the husbands of village women. In Ataura these latter outsiders are viewed with some suspicion by the native-born Ataurinos. The Ataurinos refer cagily to the number of *yernos*, or sons-in-law, of the village, and occasionally speak disparagingly of these men who have married their sisters and captured their land. *Yernos* are only permitted to sit on the village council after several years of residence, while for their part the outsiders recognize this suspicion and try not to aggravate it.

Returning migrants to Ataura and Matahuasi find that the range of occupations available to them in the village milieu differs in each village, even though these migrants may have had similar occupations in urban work-centres. In Matahuasi the market for land is more open than in Ataura. There is more land in Matahuasi and a higher turnover in land ownership. In Ataura small pieces of land come up for sale only occasionally. Consequently, in the small village, migrants who have been *empleados* invest their savings in a house or a small shop and live off their pension. In Matahuasi, however, an *empleado* pension may underwrite other activities as returning migrants there take up dairy farming, or become commodity producers or entrepreneurs. *Obreros* returning to Matahuasi may manipulate their social networks and attempt similar ventures or they may buy small plots of land adequate for subsistence.

Finally, analysis of migrants' occupational preferences shows how migration was regarded differently by the two sets of villagers (Table 21).

The poor peasants of Ataura preferred working in the mines to living in the village. They liked the money, the fringe benefits, the level of skill required by machine work and the relative security of employment in the mining sector. For these poor peasants, Ataura offers neither work nor money. The majority of the Matahuasi sample were subsistence peasants who, while acknowledging that there was money to be had in mine work, disliked the danger and routine necessary to earn that money. They preferred the independence and tranquillity of village life, observing that migration was necessary only to provide a means through which an independent village existence could be established.

Fiestas

The main recreational activities in the valley are the fiestas which are held there (Long, 1973; 1977). Peasants do not 'take holidays' but rather give over time to dancing and drinking in the village, as do migrants who return for these fiestas when they have vacations. As with landholding and occupations, the history and contemporary structures of these fiestas in Ataura and Matahuasi show how the class structures of the two villages differ and how migration has affected them. In Ataura, the fiesta is a recreational moment for poor peasants and

Table 21 *Work preference by village*

Preference	No. of villagers mentioning preference	
	Ataura	Matahuasi
For mine work	12	4
For village work	3	10

N = A + B = 29 $X^2 = 7.6$ = HS
For N see note 5.

migrants; in Matahuasi, the fiesta is an arena for the consolidation of entrepreneurial links.

In the second half of the nineteenth century, Ataura consisted of two *barrios*, that of *arriba* (upper) and *abajo* (lower). *Abajo* in fact ended at the village square and did not transgress onto the agricultural land between the foot of the valley side and the river. Fiestas consisted of street dancing and took place either on 15 January, to celebrate the patron saint of Ataura, or during fiesta weeks later in the year. Each *barrio* would organize a fiesta and the two barrios would finish dancing in the village square amid rivalry and drunken confusion.

At that time, one man would be *padrino* (male sponsor) for the whole fiesta, organizing and subsidizing the event. Since the occasion was usually the ritual consumption of common produce from church land, he would cover his costs from the produce, leaving the rest for consumption. The two *barrios* would be led by two Spanish families and when a third *barrio* was founded, at the end of the nineteenth century, it was again a Spanish family which was involved. During the first decades of the twentieth century, then, dancing was organized on the basis of the three *barrios*, often around trees erected in different corners of the central square.

By the 1920s, the dancing and finance were no longer being controlled solely by the Spanish families, for a new group had emerged – the affluent migrant miners. Wearing western-style clothes and jingling silver money in their pockets, the miners would provide a band and tree of their own. Their presence was an expression of change and tension in the village, and the fiesta was often the occasion for the expression of that tension. The fiestas had never been peaceable affairs, but their history after the 1920s is one of conflict and schism. The old Spanish families resented the threat to their status posed by the migrants and when one Spanish descendant found a migrant dancing (and living) with his wife he tried to knife him, but only struck down his own brother. Such resentment acted both ways, however, for often miners returned only to be faced with dubious land negotiations conducted in their absence by the residents.

The friction and brawling continued until the early 1950s when in one fiesta it finally came to a head. One group dancing in the square was from the area which bordered with Huamalí and, when they complained that their orchestra could not be heard, another group rounded on them. The second group pointed out that the first had no right to be in the square since they conducted their affairs in Huamalí, which, as everyone knew, had turned the fathers of Ataura into *enganchados*. Furthermore, the first group married girls from Huamalí and went to live there while continuing to own land in Ataura. And, finally, they were withholding water from Ataura. The resulting fracas was so serious that dancing in the square was abandoned and each *barrio* retreated to hold its own fiesta.

However, by then, several households had settled on the agricultural land on the valley floor and so they decided to create a new *barrio*, the fourth in Ataura. At first they located the *barrio* chapel, essential to the identity of a *barrio*, near the river, but, when this was washed away, a new one had to be built. The finance for this caused yet another scuffle in the *barrio* and now the one *barrio* contains two separate fiesta groups. The extended family units of the village live near one another, and so *barrio* fiestas are very much kin celebrations. Thus, when the fourth *barrio* itself split, it did so on a kin basis.

The structure of contemporary fiesta groups displays this kin basis. The organization of a fiesta necessitates the provision of a band, food, a dancing place and much beer. If the fiesta is a *corta-monte*, which consists of ceremonial dancing around a decorated tree, then a tree must be provided, decorated and erected in the main dancing area. Such organization requires finance and several *padrinos* of the fiesta agree to pay for the various elements. In the early 1970s, the cost of being a *padrino* could vary from 2,000 to 8,000 soles, and *padrino* offices last for only one day!

There were about forty major participants in the *corta-monte* festival in the fourth *barrio* and all of the forty were closely related to one another. The main features of the *corta-monte* are street dancing, during which dancers are collected from their houses, and then a lengthy dance around a specially prepared tree. As the dancers circulate they are invited to chop at the tree with an axe. They are allowed several blows and then the axe passes to another couple. He who fells the tree is then obliged to finance the *corta-monte* for the next year. The supposition is that it is luck which selects the feller, but the relevant device is in fact the family, who decide beforehand who will chop the tree. Thus, they control the axe towards the end of the dancing in order that the selected person can have the honour. Honour for him, but family knowledge provides the guarantee that the new *padrino* has the financial means to meet his commitments.

It is the family that does the hard work for the fiesta, which includes cooking, brewing and carrying and erecting trees, and it is the extended family of all social statuses who are invited, from the shepherd boy to the village mayor. In the fourth, divided, *barrio* none of the central figures of the rival kin group were invited, even though they were neighbours. Also, it is the more prosperous members of the family who provide finance. In Ataura, the source of this finance is a second common link beside that of kin, for it is money from migration.

Of the twenty organizers and financers of the fiesta, eight were *padrinos*. Of these, three were currently working in the mines, two were professionals in Huancayo, one was a professional in Lima and one was a retired mine employee. Of the twelve *madrinas* (female sponsors), three were the wives and one the daughter-in-law of retired mine employees, three lived in Jauja, two in mining centres and only one in Ataura. The dancers themselves were also mainly migrants and, when the tree had been felled and they moved off to dance in the square, it became clear that this structure was repeated among all the other dancing groups. As evening fell, the square was flanked and lit by mini-buses from La Oroya, buses from Lima, taxis from Huancayo and lorries from neighbouring villages. Thus, the Ataura fiesta is mainly a recreational moment for migrants.

The fiesta of San Sebastián in Matahuasi (see chapter 8) provides a contrast to this. San Sebastián is an important saint in Matahuasi and in his name a club has been established there to organize fiestas on the saint's day. The club is predominantly made up of lorry owners, drivers and businessmen who either live in Matahuasi or maintain close contacts with it. As chapter eight shows, the main function of the club is to serve as an arena in which certain types of relations among entrepreneurs are defined and reinforced. As in Ataura, the fiesta itself takes up a week of dancing and drinking but, in Matahuasi, it is on a larger scale, for there are bull-fights, processions and horseback displays, as well as street dancing.

Conclusions

Capitalist expansion and migration have led to the crystallization of social classes in the valley. During the nineteenth century, the class structure was based on landholding and was composed of two major classes, the Spanish descendants and the indigenous peasantry. The economic changes of the first half of the twentieth century broke down this simple division and expanded the basis of class beyond simply access to land. Economic structures in the valley became more complex. However, out of that fluid situation classes have emerged and are crystallizing. In the agricultural sector rich peasants have emerged who are market-oriented and who engage in trading. Subsistence peasants still remain, although increasing population and consumption demands pressure their subsistence base. Poor peasants, unable to meet subsistence, and agricultural labourers have also increased in number. Alongside these agrarian classes are commercial and industrial classes, existing both in the region and in the villages themselves.

As yet, this class differentiation has not produced marked polarization. This is due in part to the availability of migration opportunities, the potential for social mobility and the fact that population expansion has only recently met ecological limits. At the same time, the potential for conflict is reduced in villages due to the various co-operative arrangements in Andean culture. Much of agrarian production is organized by households for subsistence and these households co-operate with one another. However, it is clear that such co-operation is increasingly class distributed. The poor peasants engage in household exchanges and rely on kin, but the subsistence and rich peasants rely on commercial arrangements, hiring labour and purchasing land.

Thus, even though villages are unique locations with different histories, separate villages form part of the agrarian class structure in the valley. It would appear that the two villages, Ataura and Matahuasi, stand in different relations to the wider Peruvian economy. Ataura is a small subsistence village which cannot support capital accumulation and does not contain sharp socio-economic differentiation. It is a village of dependent worker-peasants, integrated into the highland mining sector. Matahuasi, on the other hand, appears as a village which has established independent trading relations with the wider economy. It is a village in which capital accumulation and socio-economic polarization are present. However, the differences between the two villages stem mainly from their different class structures. In Ataura and Matahuasi it is the poor peasants who become dependent migrant labourers, whilst in Matahuasi it is the rich peasants who turn to trading. Consequently, although there are important village differences in the valley, one cannot speak of a peasant economy, distinguishable from a capitalist economy, in this region. It is not that a peasant economy has been increasingly differentiated by capitalist penetration, but rather that the agrarian classes in the valley are once again changing as the capitalist economy develops.

The migration which occurs in this region is therefore not from a peasant economy to a capitalist one, but forms part of capitalist development. Migration is not an external variable acting·on a traditional economy and transforming it into a modern one. The economies of the region are not dual ones, dichotomized between traditional and modern sectors.[7] The Mantaro valley has long been affected by wider national events and cannot be characterized as containing isolated communities existing in socio-economic equilibrium.

Rather, different classes in the region labour with the resources available to them. On the one hand, this may mean that rich peasants use kin contacts to recruit labour and they may pay that labour in coca. On the other hand, it may mean that the poorest peasant has a long history as a mine worker.

7

Industrialization and the emergence of an informal regional economy

Post Second World War industrialization in Peru marked a new phase in regional development. It resulted in the undermining of the regional system of production based on large-scale, agro-mining enterprise and led to an increasing centralization of population and resources in the metropolitan area of Lima-Callao. In this chapter, we explore the significance of these changes for contemporary patterns of socio-economic activity in the central highlands. We claim that, despite the disarticulation of the region, the previous mine-based system of production continues to influence the ways in which local groups attempt to handle and interpret the significance of these new forces of change. In the following chapters, we identify some of the more important socio-cultural mechanisms and relationships which are characteristic of this process. The present chapter focusses upon Huancayo in the contemporary period, as its role shifts from that of an administrative and commercial centre of the agro-mining economy to that of a centre for government services surrounded by a burgeoning small-scale economic sector.

The period following the Second World War is one in which the Peruvian population increasingly concentrated in the metropolitan area of Lima-Callao. In 1940, the metropolitan area contained 10 per cent of the national population while, in 1972, its share had increased to nearly 25 per cent. This population concentration was due, in large part, to the increasing importance of manufacturing industry and the concentration of that industry in Lima-Callao. By the 1970s, the metropolitan area concentrated a growing and major part of Peru's industrial production (Wils, 1979: 41; Gonzales, 1982: 262). Growth in the industrial product averaged between 7 and 8 per cent a year from 1950 to 1975. In 1950, manufacturing industry constituted 14 per cent of the GNP as compared with 23 per cent for agriculture. By 1968, manufacturing had increased to 20 per cent, while agriculture had dropped to 15 per cent (Thorp and Bertram, 1978: 258).

Provincial regions of Peru, as Webb (1975) shows, became increasingly disadvantaged in this period in terms of their share of the national income.[1] By 1972, however, there is some evidence that the Departments outside Lima had improved their per capita income relative to Lima, probably because the population expansion of the latter had not been compensated by an equivalent rise in the value of production (Gonzales, 1982: 199). The agrarian economy, especially in the highlands, stagnated in the face of population growth and an inadequate resource base. Food imports and the increasing efficiency of coastal agriculture in regard to particular crops further undermined highland farming enterprise (Caballero, 1980: 15–33). The central highlands, and especially the Mantaro valley, were somewhat more dynamic economically. Thus, from the end of the 1950s, there are signs in certain areas of significant improvements in agricultural productivity consequent upon the more generalized use of fertilizers, insecticides, improved seed and mechanization (see chapter eight). Furthermore, there was a gradual shift among many farmers away from low productivity grain crops (like maize and wheat) towards a greater emphasis on vegetables, barley (for beer production) and alfalfa (for livestock).

As we have described elsewhere (Long and Roberts, 1978: 30), these changes in production were taken up by small-scale as well as medium- and large-scale farmers. A major implication of this was that the costs as well as the potential profits of production rose considerably, reinforcing the commercialization of the local economy and making the role of private or public credit more central to the operation of agricultural production itself. Hence, local traders and businessmen came to play a bigger part in determining the types of smallholder production, often vying with government extension services and co-operatives to supply essential production inputs.

These trends have important implications, as we shall argue in this and the following chapter, for the rise and character of small-scale enterprise in the region. This is especially the case when placed within the context of the slow, overall growth of the region's economy from the 1950s onwards. Although mining production increased, it became more capital-intensive and more concerned with the development of newer mineral deposits in the southern regions of Peru, such as Marcona.[2] The city of Huancayo began to 'de-industrialize' with the closure of its large textile factories in the late 1960s: no large-scale manufacturing industry was to replace these factories (Roberts, 1978a).

Population growth in the central highlands was relatively rapid, increasing from a Departmental total of 521,210 in 1961 to 696,641 in 1972 (Dirección Nacional de Estadística, 1966; ONEC, 1974). The population growth of Huancayo was more rapid, registering an annual rate of almost 7 per cent, which rivalled that of Lima. In 1961, the population of the city of Huancayo (made up of the contiguous urban nuclei of the districts of Huancayo, Chilca and El Tambo) was 64,153; in 1972, the same urban zone had a population of 116,052. Like Lima, this growth was based largely on migration from the immediate rural hinterland and from other parts of the highlands, particularly from the Department of Huancavelica.

These population increases in the region as a whole, and in Huancayo in particular, were not accompanied by the expansion of job opportunities in industry and mining. In the intercensal years, 1961–72, there was a drop in employment in the mines of the Department of Junín from 10,687 to 5,898. In the same period, employment in manufacturing industry in the Department showed a slight decline from 19,843 to 19,785. Agriculture increased its employment somewhat, from 84,557 to 87,814, but, at the same time, the average size of landholdings decreased. The major points of growth in employment were in transport, commerce and the other services, which together, by 1972, made up some 28.2 per cent of the economically active population of the Department, as compared with 46.3 per cent in agriculture and 10.4 per cent in manufacturing industry (ONEC, 1974),

This process is a familiar one in the literature on urbanization in developing countries: job creation in the large-scale sector of the economy does not keep pace with employment demands from the growing urban population. Even in Lima, ILO estimates suggest that the amounts of both unemployment and under-employment grew in the years from 1960–1970. The situation in Huancayo has been more drastic due to the failure of large-scale industry really to take root. The question, then, that we wish to pose is how could Huancayo continue to grow and attract migrants despite the deterioration in its industrial base.

Small-scale enterprise and urban development

These changes in the regional economy suggest that the central highlands are being increasingly marginalized by the concentration of capital-intensive production in the metropolitan centre. Thus Quijano (1973: 267–9) points out that the possibilities of capital accumulation in provincial areas have been diminished by the concentration of modern industry in the large cities: factory production in the provinces is being displaced and economic survival depends more and more on small-scale, labour-intensive activities of low productivity.

We will seek to understand this proliferation of small-scale enterprises in terms of the distinction between the formal and informal sectors of the economy, suggesting a dualism in the economic structure that permits less productive activities to survive even where large-scale capitalist enterprise dominates the national economy.[3] This dualism is evident in the difference between large-scale firms, based on capital-intensive technology, and employing a minority of the labour force, and the multitude of small-scale businesses or independent workers who use little capital or technology. The first sector can pay relatively high wages because of its productivity, while the second has few barriers to entry. Consequently, the second sector absorbs labour, has low productivity and produces little income.

The importance of this distinction is that it suggests that capital accumulation will not occur in the small-scale sector, where activities will produce a subsistence income rather than profit for reinvestment. However, as Fitzgerald (1979: 19–20) points out, the linkages between the two sectors are crucial, especially since the low production costs and the labour absorptive characteristics of the small-scale sector may, in fact, contribute both directly and indirectly to capital accumulation in the large-scale sector. The small-scale or informal sector permits the putting-out of less profitable activities. Also, the informal sector can serve to produce food supplies, some manufactured goods and personal services on terms of trade favourable to the formal sector, while also marketing cheaply the (expensive) goods of that sector.

The informal sector, therefore, is an integral part of capitalist expansion. Moser (1978) points out that the activities identified with the informal sector are similar in kind and function to those of petty commodity production in Marx's account of the transition to industrial capitalism. Thus, petty commodity production is increasingly subsumed by capital and put to use, as in the case of the cottage industry or the thousands of 'independent' craftsmen who worked in the cellars and garrets of the nineteenth century British towns. Small-scale enterprises and the self-employed are placed in a situation in which they compete intensively with each other to produce goods or to offer services at very low cost, thus contributing to capital accumulation. Also the large number of self-employed and under-employed urban poor act as a 'reserve army of labour', keeping wages low in the formal sector and providing readily available additional labour when shortages occur.

Several commentators have made the further point that capital scarcity in underdeveloped countries makes the urban informal sector a convenient means of cheapening labour costs for the large-scale sector (De Janvry and Garramon, 1977; Portes, 1981). Formal sector enterprises are able to pay much lower wages to workers than in industrial capitalist countries because their workers, unlike those of Europe and the United States, are able to obtain a large part of their subsistence outside the formal market economy.

The emphasis on the functionality of the informal sector for capital accumulation requires an important rider when applied to provincial centres such as Huancayo. The small-scale sector is less likely to be controlled directly by its linkages with the large-scale sector because such centres are not significant locations for large-scale productive investment and capital accumulation. It is only in the more dynamic industrial and commercial cities that it is possible to have a highly developed structure of sub-contracting by industrial or merchant capital (see Bromley and Gerry, 1979). Where this does not exist, as in Huancayo, the pattern of small-scale enterprise probably exhibits greater diversity, with considerable movement between different types of economic activity.

There is, also, a crucial difference in the process of primitive accumulation as described by Marx in the nineteenth century from that taking place in Peru. The state is more directly involved in both the economy and in providing social services than was the case in early nineteenth century Britain. The importance of the state in Peru is, in part, based on the weakness of the national capitalist class and the necessity for direct state investment in the creation of large-scale economic enterprises. A second aspect is that the state has a crucial role to play in creating the basic social and political conditions for capitalist development. Uneven development contains powerful centrifugal forces threatening the unity and integration of the national system. Regional and ethnic divisions often challenge the central authority and lead to social fragmentation, while non-capitalist forms of production slow down the integration of the national market. In this situation, the state in Latin America has, in varying degrees, sought to impose a uniform order throughout the national territory, not only through a coercive presence, but also through the extension of education and other social and administrative services.

There are two major implications of this process that interest us: firstly, the state's presence is a major factor giving significance to the informal/formal distinction. Hence, economic and social security regulations impose costs and limits on the activities of enterprises that are considered part of the formal sector. These costs are more than compensated by the various privileges received by the large-scale enterprises through monopolies, tax and tariff concessions. However, it often benefits large-scale enterprise to put out labour-intensive parts of their operations to smaller informal firms. Conversely, the price competitiveness of the small-scale sector comes to be based on avoiding government regulations.

The extent of state regulation is a variable which needs to be studied in the context of each Latin American country. In Peru, since the 1950s the regulation of the formal sector has been quite extensive and has often favoured those working within formal enterprises. The military government's industrial reform legislation in 1970 was, in this respect, an extension of previous interventionist strategies aiming at protecting certain groups of workers against arbitrary dismissal and at enforcing social security obligations on employers. The Peruvian state accommodated the demands made by organized workers because, it can be argued, the industrial bourgeoisie was weakly developed.

The second implication of the role of the state is the extension of educational, health and other social services to areas like the central highlands. In the 1950s and 1960s, Peruvian governments increasingly pursued an explicit policy of integrating and modernizing highland areas through public education, community development, legislation restructuring peasant communities and, finally, agrarian reform (see Long and Roberts, 1978: 297–328).

The situation of Huancayo is, in many respects, similar to that described by Lopes and Brant (1978) for the town of Parnaiba in Piaui in Brazil. There, the decadence of the extractive export economy meant the collapse of the old regional system based on large landholdings and a flourishing entrepot town. In its place, state funds, in the shape of pensions, social security payments and salaries for state officials, became the major basis of the town's economy. Commerce and services of various sorts flourished on the basis of these revenues, providing the means of integrating the fragmented, small-scale peasant sector into the wider economy.

The account that follows will explore these themes, showing the extent to which small-scale economic activities have now become a central characteristic of the urban economy of Huancayo and of its hinterland. The organization and linkages of small-scale enterprise provide a new pattern of regional inter-relations. Entailed in this new economic order are changes in the patterns of migration and in the relationship of local populations to the state.

The fragmentation of the urban economy

One significant change in the distribution of economic activities in Huancayo is the rapid increase in male employment in the services, including government services, so that 39.2 per cent of economically active males are employed in these activities (Table 22).

Another important change is the proliferation of small-scale enterprises, so that approximately 76 per cent of employed males are employed in enterprises where there are less than ten other workers (Table 22). There is also a considerable amount of self and family employment amongst all branches of economic activity whether professions, commerce, craft, transport or unskilled labour, amounting to 49.4 per cent of the employed male population (Muñoz,

Table 22 *Branch of activity of economically active males: Huancayo, 1972 (as percentages)*

Branch of activity	Economically Active	Working in establishments with		
		Less than 5 workers	Between 5 and 10 workers	More than 10 workers
Agriculture	8.8	35.2	58.5	6.3
Mining	6.3	31.9	59.6	8.5
Manufacturing[a]	14.6	65.6	22.4	12.0
Construction	6.5	40.1	20.1	39.7
Commerce	18.3	68.7	16.4	14.9
Transport	6.3	54.5	15.4	30.1
Services	23.9	49.4	28.9	21.7
Domestic services	4.2	—	—	—
Government services (education, bureaucracy)	11.1	19.7	24.3	56.0
Total	100.0	45.6	30.7	23.6

[a] Manufacturing includes all processing and conversion activities, such as shoemaking, carpentry, tailoring as well as factory work. Services are mainly repair work, restaurants, hotels, bars, personal services and professional services (lawyers, accountants). There were few cases of professionals employed in manufacturing or commerce.
Source: Muñoz, 1982: 24. The Table uses our 1972 survey of Huancayo, based on a stratified probability sample of 811 males between the ages of twenty and sixty. The stratification has been adjusted to give the actual distributions of the economically active.

1982: 27). In the manufacturing sector, it is striking that as much as 72 per cent of workers are independent or family workers.

Some idea of the extent of this proliferation of small enterprises is given by the register of businesses in the city. In 1972, there were nearly 2,000 registered businesses that were economically active, ranging from small grocery stores to car and truck agencies.[4] Apart from these businesses, and, probably, an equal number registered in the other jurisdictions of the city, there were also over 1,000 permanent stalls in the city markets. Employment in these different types of enterprise is small-scale and ranges from an average of 7.1 workers in the city's factories to 1.2 workers in the grocery stores (Table 23). Most of this labour comes from the immediate family or kin and even enterprises, such as bakeries, which employ a relatively high number of workers are chiefly manned by family labour.

The 1965 and 1972 data from the municipality's tax assessment of businesses provide information on another aspect of this evolution of the city's economic

Table 23 *The structure of business in Huancayo in 1972*

Type of business	Average number of people employed	Percentage of workers who are family workers	Percentage of owners born in Huancayo or resident for 20+ years
Grocery stores (69)[a]	1.2	89	55
Restaurants, bars, hotels (28)[a]	3.0	59	50
Barbers, beauty shops (22)[a]	1.5	35	50
Bakers, butchers (15)[a]	4.0	67	87
Mechanical repairs (15)[a]	2.3	46	80
Tailors, carpentry (63)[a]	2.4	63	59
Small businesses[b]	1.4	57	65
Formal businesses[c]	6.4	22	82
Factories (excluding large textile) (19)[a]	7.1	13	79

[a] No. in sample.
[b] Small businesses include hardware stores, electrical repair shops, newsagents, small cloth merchants, etc.
[c] These are businesses that are listed among the 560 largest businesses in Huancayo in the 1972 municipal tax assessment; they include agencies of Lima firms, large hardware and general goods stores, radio shops and cinemas, furniture stores, large cloth merchants. They exclude the factories which are listed separately.
Source: Survey of sample of businesses in Huancayo, 1972. Sample taken from list of approximately 2,000 businesses.

structure.[5] Comparing these data, commerce (44 per cent) and small-scale craft industry (20 per cent) have a greater share of the capital assessed in 1972 than was the case earlier when commerce had 41 per cent of capital assessed and craft industry had 7 per cent.

This fragmentation of Huancayo's economic structure is so marked because of the almost total disappearance of the large-scale textile industry. The 3,500 textile workers of the 1950s became the 200 workers of the remaining textile mill, Manufacturas del Centro. This de-industrialization was due to a series of factors, including the increasing inefficiency of production in factories whose machinery had not been renewed and competition from more modern Lima-based factories and from contraband imports (Roberts, 1978a: 146–53). In the face of declining profits and increasing fiscal responsibilities for their workers, the Lima-based owners declared bankruptcy, transferring stock and some machinery to coastal factories. No private capital showed interest in re-opening these factories or re-establishing any other large-scale manufacturing plants. Indeed, the remaining workers of Manufacturas del Centro were only able to secure help to establish a co-operative with the advent of the military government of 1968 which, in its early years, sought to encourage co-operative enterprise and worker participation in industry and agriculture (Roberts, 1978a: 153–60).

The disappearance of the large-scale textile industry has meant an increase in the number of smaller textile workshops that employ few people and are mostly concerned with the making-up of garments from cloth or yarn. This material is often synthetic and comes mainly from Lima. There are at least 438 garment workshops, mainly located in the outlying districts of Chilca and El Tambo (Alberti and Sanchez, 1974: 66).

The transport sector remains numerically as important as it was in 1965, but its contribution to the municipal tax assessment has become overshadowed by the increasing numbers of commercial firms with a relatively high assessed capital value. The gradual ending of the dominance of the importing houses and of their agencies has had the effect of encouraging local merchants to carry stock which they can now often obtain directly and on credit from Lima. The important exception to this trend is the increasing commercial dominance of a branch of the Lima company, A. Milne and Company. This branch – Auto-motores San Jorge – has come to almost monopolize the sale of cars, trucks and agricultural machinery.[6] These are the only manufactured goods sold in Huancayo that still require large-scale financial backing.

The weighting of the different sectors of economic activity in the assessment is not proportional to employment in these sectors. Whereas 30 per cent of the male population is employed in non-government services, this sector accounts for 11 per cent of the declared capital value of the largest firms in the 1972 municipal tax assessment. The relative employment figures for businesses in Huancayo (Table 23) also indicate that those sectors of activity where more capital is likely to be invested (factories and formal businesses) do not create substantially more employment than ventures with little capital. The tax data on the largest firms and the survey data on businesses refer only to the city of Huancayo; the metropolitan districts of El Tambo and Chilca are not included. Comparing our own data with those of Alberti and Sanchez, which refer to the whole metropolitan area, it is clear that the bulk of the small food stores, bars, restaurants and other service establishments are found in the outlying districts (Alberti and Sanchez, 1974: 66).[7]

The complexity and labour-absorbing capacity of small-scale enterprises

Much of the contemporary economy of Huancayo would fit Geertz's description of the bazaar economy. In activities ranging from market trading to transport and to the small textile workshops there is an elaboration of economic detail, a proliferation rather than consolidation of enterprise and a dependence on family relationships (Geertz, 1963b: 30–47). Many of the small traders make a profit which, at best, only contributes to their subsistence; the rest is provided by family or kin living together and sharing expenses. Of the traders we sampled in the large wholesale market of Huancayo, we estimated that at least 20 per cent were earning below what would be required for subsistence in the city and that perhaps another 40 per cent were earning a bare subsistence income.[8] This subsistence income, covering all the necessary facilities and food that must be purchased, was estimated in 1972 to be a monthly income of about 1,500 soles. For many of these traders, however, much of their subsistence was 'free', in the form of accommodation, food from the countryside and perhaps surreptitious use of such services as electricity and water.

A study of the market traders was undertaken at the request of the association of traders which was planning to form a co-operative; most of the members were, in fact, retailers. In interviewing these traders, it became clear that, for many, their businesses constituted a particular 'way of life' in which economic rationalization was a minor part. One small trader arrived early in the morning and remained much of the day to sell perhaps eight pounds of potatoes at one sol (one penny) profit per pound. She was elderly and evidently enjoyed the social companionship of the market. Other traders had no clear idea of whether they were making profits or not; their yardstick was whether they had enough cash left to replenish their stock, allowing for the cash and goods taken out for their own needs. For example, we spent several hours in the company of some of the co-operative leaders, attempting to obtain a clear idea of the profitability of the business of one of their members – a genuinely helpful trader. We constructed balance-sheets of products bought and sold and arrived at a clear loss when expenses had been allowed for. This puzzled the trader as much as it did ourselves; but he remained adamant about the quantity of his purchases and of his sales, saying that anyway it did not matter since he got by. Our reluctant conclusion in estimating the feasibility of the co-operative was that this group of some 500 traders did not make sufficient profits to justify the costs involved in investing in a new building and in the complementary services. The co-operative had to be justified on social, not economic, grounds.

The turnover of retail businesses was relatively high in our sample, with some 10 per cent of registered businesses having closed down within the year. Some of these closures were temporary – especially in the house-front shops; the owners, when interviewed, said that they had closed for lack of present funds but expected to open again when they had more capital. The activity that went into these ventures was quite complex. Purchases of goods were made in different places, depending on fluctuations in 'offers' and in supplies; some-times purchases were made from travelling salesmen, sometimes from super-markets or large traders, sometimes directly from Lima. A considerable amount of time was spent in making such purchases, checking on prices and travelling. Often the sale of scarce goods would be used by traders to persuade customers to buy less scarce items. Urban retailers or producers would themselves, or through a family member, sell in the rotating markets of the villages, in the Sunday market of Huancayo or make arrangements with travelling traders to exchange one kind of good for another – for example, contraband razor blades or scissors were exchanged for locally-made jumpers. Much of the bustle and 'colour' of the commercial life of Huancayo is made up of these small-scale deals and movements, creating an impression of a highly disordered and fragmented economic life.

A similar complexity, and tendency to an intensive use of labour, is found in the transport and repair industries of the city. Investing in a car, truck or bus has been one of the most common ways in which villagers as well as city people have used their savings from wage labour. The small-scale transport business has also been facilitated by the credits granted by the motor agencies. Huancayo has eighty-one bus companies that operate from the city. Most of these service the villages of the Mantaro valley. Eleven of these companies worked within the city and sixteen were primarily long-distance transport, operating from Huan-cayo. These companies had a total of 249 buses, 92 collective taxis and 86 microbuses registered in the transport office of Huancayo.[9]

The dominant characteristic of these transport companies is that they are formed through the partnership of a large number of individual bus or taxi owners. The majority of these companies have more than ten people listed as co-owners and some (the urban services) as many as forty people. Even long-distance transport is organized through the association of individual bus owners who are, also, often the drivers. The large firm La Perla de Junín, which runs services to the coast and distant parts of the highlands, is owned by 233 people who are registered as living in addresses that range from Huancayo to the important small towns on the bus routes. There is no large-scale trucking company in Huancayo, and the 635 trucks registered in the province are mostly individually owned by people in the city and the surrounding villages. Most of the trucks operate from the villages directly to Lima or the mines, but they still use the repair and service facilities of Huancayo.

The responsibility for the car or bus usually rests with its owner-driver. He sees to its maintenance and repair. This maintenance and repair is itself a complex and time-consuming operation as the driver shops or searches around for the necessary spare parts – sometimes making use of a friend's trip to Lima to obtain them more cheaply there. If he cannot effect the repair himself, the car or bus is taken from one repair shop to another, looking for a good price. Workshops tend to specialize in one particular branch of repair – tyres, bodywork, painting, welding, motors etc. – and 'specialist' workmen move from one workshop to another in search of work contracts. There are more than one hundred such workshops in Huancayo and the spare parts outlets constitute one of the major retailing activities of the city.

Business strategies in the informal sector

The individual ownership of transport is, in part, a product of the reluctance of small-scale businessmen to build up their enterprises. This reluctance is as characteristic of their activity in the villages as it is in the city, as the next chapter shows. In the cases we documented of reasonably successful contemporary traders and industrialists, we noted a tendency for them to reach a certain size – employing perhaps seven workers or owning two trucks – and then to set up others in a separate enterprise. This tendency is illustrated by the case of the largest of the wholesale traders of the Huancayo market. His recent expansion has taken the form of setting up kin as partners in the enterprise. Furthermore, he has given his lorry drivers a percentage of the profits in return for their taking full responsibility for the repair and maintenance of the vehicle. This case is significant because, of all the market traders, this man had one of the most stable bases for his enterprise. He was an ex-miner from the neighbouring province of Huancavelica and he used his contacts with the mines and with the potato farmers of Huancavelica to undertake large-scale contracts to supply the mines with agricultural produce. This supply made up some 80 per cent of his business, giving him a turnover that allowed him to offer competitive prices and to help other traders out – especially his kinsmen – when they needed supplies.

Diversification is another strategy used to spread risk, as Long (1979) demonstrates in his analysis of multiple enterprises in the Mantaro valley. One of the remaining and successful medium-sized textile factory owners in

Huancayo, who once employed nearly thirty workers, is now content with his present workforce of seven and more modern machinery. He could increase his output by taking on more workers and machines; but he chooses instead to develop the retail outlets of his business and other interests he has in Lima.

One important element in this readiness to proliferate enterprises rather than to consolidate them is the set of welfare and tax obligations to which an employer is liable. In theory, the size of the enterprise should not make a difference to this but, in practice, enterprises employing less than ten people, especially where there is family labour involved, are able to escape liability. In the 1972 survey of the city's population, we found that 52 per cent of the economically active male population were not registered, as they should have been, with the social security. The variable that best correlates with this informal *economic activity* is size of the enterprise (Table 24).[10] These obligations were cited by the larger traders and businessmen as one reason for their lack of interest in expansion. The extent of these obligations on industry was often mentioned by those involved in textiles as a reason for the failure of the Huancayo textile industry.

In the 1960s, the Peruvian government increased the protection given to employees and workers and placed much of the burden of this protection on the individual companies which were made responsible for pensions as well as for payments to the social security system. From 1968, the military government modified these obligations by assuming responsibility for pensions, but initiated a variety of experiments in worker control and participation. Under the most prevalent form – *the comunidad industrial* – the firm was obliged to put aside part of its profits into a workers' and employees' fund which would buy shares in the company until workers owned half the company (Alberti et al., 1977). These proposals affectd firms above a certain size (six workers, or with an income of more than one million soles) and effectively acted as a further restraint on expansion. One medium-sized textile industrialist in Huancayo specifically gave this as the reason for not expanding further.

The profits of enterprise

Under these conditions, it is not surprising that the small, informally organized enterprise proliferates. Such enterprises rely heavily on family labour, which is often unpaid and is unlikely to demand its full rights. Indeed, contrary to conventional wisdom, the importance of family ties in recruiting to jobs may actually have increased in the city over time, as a result of the changes in the economic structure.[11] More than half of the present adult male population said, in the survey, that they obtained their actual jobs through kinship or friendship links or had assured work on arrival. Textile workers who had obtained their

Table 24 *Sector of activity, size of enterprises and whether registered with social security*

No. of workers	Percentage of respondents not registered						
	Manufacturing	Construction	Commerce	Transport	Services	Government services	Total Percentage not registered
Alone	87 (16)[a]	71 (17)	60 (40)	100 (8)	70 (37)	75 (20)	78 (138)
2–5 others	56 (25)	100 (5)	75 (40)	73 (11)	64 (50)	56 (23)	66 (154)
6–12 others	47 (19)	30 (10)	43 (35)	30 (10)	24 (34)	30 (23)	34 (131)
More than 12 others	26 (19)	14 (14)	19 (21)	60 (5)	13 (30)	12 (17)	19 (106)

[a] No. in parentheses represents number of cases in category.
Source: Sample survey of Huancayo, 1972.

jobs at the height of Huancayo's industrial boom in the 1950s reported more frequently than did later entrants into the workforce that they obtained their job through their own initiative. These latter cite family and friends more frequently as the means by which they secured employment.

The prevalence of informally organized enterprises had, however, another more fundamental cause. Under the economic uncertainties of the area, such enterprise provides the necessary flexibility for survival. Enterprises with no firm commitments to employees, to plant or to buildings, can resist temporary depressions by cutting down severely on their overheads. Formally established businesses, like the hardware store described below or a large factory, are stuck with their costs. Indeed, it seems as if the failure of Huancayo's textile industry was not simply that of competition from Lima factories, but also of competition from the more informally organized textile workshops that sprung up in the city in the late 1950s. Several of the medium-sized textile industrialists commented on the difficulties this informally organized textile industry posed for them. The low overheads of the informal industry enabled their owners to produce a cheap article for local consumption and for sale in the extensive low-cost markets of both coast and highlands. The medium-sized producers, with expensive machinery and high wage and tax obligations, had found it difficult to produce low-cost items. Increasingly their market was confined to the urban middle and upper classes, where there was severe competition from Lima factories and imports. Hence, basis for the informally organized textile industry was, in part, the dissolution of the large-scale industry. In some factories, workers were given machinery as compensation at the time of closure and used this to set up small workshops. Furthermore, easy credit had made possible the widespread purchase of knitting and weaving machines.

Uncertainty in operation is not simply a question of national economic fluctuations, it is built into, and reinforces, the predominance of small-scale enterprise. The large number of small farmers producing foodstuffs for the market makes the collection and transport operation a complex one. It is an operation that, on the part of the trader or transporter, depends on the skilful combination of kinship, friendship and work obligations to ensure continuity in the loads and to fulfil contracts. It is for this reason that the bulk of the agricultural trade in the area is conducted directly from the villages to Lima and, in the main, by village-based intermediaries. The Huancayo foodstuff traders transport, at the most, 5 per cent of the area's produce to Lima, often specializing in produce from areas with which they themselves have social contacts.[12]

We have mentioned the case of the largest potato trader who obtains his produce from Huancavelica; another two of the large-scale traders in produce are also of village origin and obtain produce from their areas of origin. Some of the Huancayo traders rent land, or buy up crops in advance, to ensure the contracts they have with Lima wholesalers. Only two or three make a practice of this and their operation is a small part of the region's trade. The wholesale traders of Huancayo do not make great use of the circulating markets (*ferias*) of the area to buy up and accumulate produce. Indeed, in our studies of these markets, very little concentration of agricultural produce occurred. An important indirect effect of the years of wage labour has been to develop a commercial and transport infrastructure that enables villagers to market their products directly, using the good road communications to Lima and the easy credit terms to purchase trucks to do so. Also, out-migrants from these villages are now stallholders in the Lima wholesale markets, often providing the necessary contacts and Lima credit to finance the operation.

Small-scale operation involves detailed local knowledge and a variety of local relationships. It encourages the devolution of responsibility onto the actual operator: the truck driver who makes arrangements for loads or for roadside repairs with other drivers, the individual trader who seeks out the best buys and most likely markets, the small-scale industrialist who exploits family labour when a market possibility opens up or who produces a new type of garment on demand. The situation makes of Huancayo a city where you can get anything done, or made, at short notice and low cost. It is also a pattern of economic activity which suits a situation where markets are neither predictable nor easily fitted to standardized production or services. In the central highlands, the vigour of this 'informal' economic activity does not seem to be an indigenous cultural phenomenon to the extent that Geertz claims the bazaar economy to be for Indonesia or North Africa (Geertz, 1963b; 1979). In Huancayo and its surrounding area, the triumph of the small-scale over the large-scale, of intricate economic activity over rationalized activity, is clearly part of the evolving pattern of dualist capitalist development in Peru.

An idea of the risks and small rewards attending fairly large-scale and formally organized businesses under these conditions is given by the 1971 balance-sheet of one of the city's largest single-owner businesses. This is a large hardware and general goods store that is also an insurance agency and employs seven staff.[13] The total sales of the year were of the order of £84,000, yielding a gross profit of £24,000; but of this profit only £6,000 was left after the various expenses had been met. Of these expenses 30 per cent were taxes, 26 per cent general expenses such as the renting of the shop, repairs, payment to sub-agents, insurance and vehicle maintenance. Thirty-four per cent consisted of salaries, since seven non-family employees were occupied full-time in attending the job, delivering orders and stocking the warehouse.

This man paid relatively good salaries and was unusually scrupulous in meeting his obligations. Few had better contacts or a larger clientele. Perhaps one-fifth of his credit sales were to government agencies and he sold widely outside Huancayo. He has also been an agent for mining and international construction companies. The £6,000 with which he was left was an ample salary, but not exactly the profit that might be expected from a capitalist venture of this order. It was not sufficient to allow for further investments, whether in industry, commerce or urban land. Half his sales were on credit and his obligations to his employees could not legally be quickly curtailed. Thus, it only needed a temporary difficulty in supply, illness or slowness in payment by clients to wipe out most of these gains. He subsequently sold out this business, retaining only the insurance agency which he runs by himself.

The small-scale activity that increasingly characterizes Huancayo consequently does not encourage the accumulation of capital. The high cost of overheads, such as credit, and weakly developed markets restrict both formal and informal enterprise. The earnings of informal enterprises are almost entirely spent on the subsistence of their workers and owners. Even the larger operations make profits that provide little more than a reasonable living for their owners. In the cases for which we have detailed information – three of the largest wholesale traders and a medium-sized textile industrialist – their profits were no higher than the salary of a professional or managerial employee. One of the wholesale traders had a gross monthly turnover of about £1,000 and an estimated net monthly income of £130. He employed five people, ran two trucks and his wife's brother managed part of the enterprise for a share of the profits. The industrialist had a monthly sale of £900 and a monthly profit of £550, after the costs of production and the wage of seven workers. This sum had to cover the overheads of the factory, such as rent and repairs, taxes and the social security of the workers.

Incomes of this size were mainly used for house construction, home improvements and for establishing the family with a suitable education and style of life. Naturally, the 'ideal-type' Protestant entrepreneur might forego such luxuries to continue to reinvest. Significantly, these businessmen were aware of the choice but, despite their different backgrounds and activities, had basically the same attitude to reinvestment – that, beyond a certain point, it was not likely to yield better returns given the limitations of the economic situation.

This orientation also characterized the last remaining large-scale industry of Huancayo – the co-operative textile mill, Manufacturas del Centro. The owner-workers showed considerable reluctance in the early days of the existence of the mill's co-operative to commit themselves to plans for the permanent expansion of production, through new machinery and taking on additional members. They preferred to co-opt members of their family to work as contracted labour, which was ill-paid and was not covered by social security. In the interviews, they claimed that this contracted labour represented the safest way to expand production and also allowed them to do favours to kin and friends. Many of the members used loans from the co-operative and their right to buy goods at cost price to help family or kin to set up businesses which, at times, competed with the co-operative's own retailing outlet. In these ways, the prevalence of small-scale activities in Huancayo and the orientations that characterized them influenced the mode of operation of even the largest and most formal of the city's enterprises.

The success of a family enterprise

The preceding points concerning the workings of small-scale enterprises can be concretely illustrated by the following case. The example concerns one of the largest of the wholesale trading businesses in the Mercado Mayorista of Huancayo. The scale of this enterprise, which specializes mainly in fruit trading, is indicated by the fact that in 1972 the annual volume of sales was around £100,000, giving an approximate profit of £10,000. This volume of business, together with the large number of persons gaining a livelihood from it (approximately eleven individuals each of whom works in some part of the enterprise), makes this one of the largest commercial enterprises in contemporary Huancayo. The original capital for the founding of this business came from the marketing of agricultural products in the potato-growing zone of the highlands above the Mantaro valley. This contrasts with other large-scale trading enterprises, which we studied, where the initial capital came from savings obtained through mine work.

The father originally traded his own and other villagers' agricultural surpluses to Huancayo, the mine towns and, through intermediaries, to Lima. The fact that he and his wife had inherited a reasonable extension of land in one of the most important potato-producing zones, and were later able to purchase additional plots, enabled them to extend their business, buying a second-hand truck in 1959. In 1950 the eldest daughter had been given money by the father to cultivate coffee in the lowland area of Satipo. She stayed there nine years, eventually shifting into fruit cultivation and purchasing land. After this, she moved to Huancayo and bought her way into a stall in the Mercado Mayorista, using her contacts with the Satipo fruit growers to set up trading links. By 1963, and with the help of her father, she was able to buy her own truck, although this was registered in the father's name. A younger sister came to assist with the selling and gradually began to trade on her own account. By 1968, this sister had managed to acquire her own stall in the market and in the following year, again with the father's help, she purchased the third truck of the family enterprise, at a cost of £3,200.

Finance for these vehicles was partly obtained through hire-purchase arrangements which involved heavy monthly repayments. In order to clear these debts, the enterprise signed a contract in 1969 with a Lima-based, soft drinks multinational company to supply 12,000 kilos of oranges every week for a period of two years. The company employed three other sub-contractors to bring citrus fruits from the peasant farms of the Satipo and Chanchamayo areas. This was advantageous to the multinational company since product and transport prices were cheaper than for the more commercially produced and higher grade coastal varieties of orange. The disadvantage was the fragmentation of production in the Satipo zone which made supply irregular.

The family enterprise continued with this contract for two years making substantial profits, but they found it difficult to keep up deliveries and to compete with other traders who also made bids for the contract. At the end of the two-year period, the family again concentrated its efforts on the Huancayo wholesale market. They were able to use some of the profits from the contract to buy a bus for carrying passengers to and from Satipo. This bus was run for them by a bus company that provided the driver and office arrangements, in return for 20 per cent of the ticket receipts. The family complained that these receipts represented only half the true revenue, since passengers and luggage were taken on at different points without issuing tickets. The family had decided not to invest in the establishment of a company of their own because of the large investment required. During this period, the agricultural investments of the family continued both in Satipo and in their home village, where they used the most up-to-date methods of cultivation.

In 1972, the multiple enterprise was organized as follows. The wholesale fruit business was run by the two daughters from Huancayo where they both owned substantial and well-equipped houses. The husband of the eldest daughter and a brother acted as drivers; they handled negotiations in the fruit-producing areas and carried on a little trading of their own. Both were assisted by non-family *ayudantes* (assistants). The father had a house in Huancayo, but spent a great deal of his time in the village, helping his eldest son with the farm and trading in potatoes to Huancayo and Lima. The mother remained in Huancayo and took charge of supervising the revenues from the bus. The eldest son lived permanently in the village and showed no desire to move from there. Another daughter and son resided in Huancayo and helped with the market business.

The farm in Satipo was managed by a trusted worker who also had his own land and who hired labour when needed for agricultural tasks. The activities of these various people were closely, but informally, interrelated. Although there was a rough division of labour, individuals would help each other out as and when needed, regarding the trucks, for example, as joint family property. There was no fixed division of profits among the family members, each apparently taking from the circulating capital what they needed for their expenses. However, the father and the two daughters, being those who received the bulk of the revenue of the enterprise, kept some control over individual expenditure and probably over major investment decisions.

This complex business is built upon a core of close kinship ties and utilizes a network of trading links with peasant producers both in the village of origin and in the new colonization area of the tropical lowlands. Thus, fruit purchases were made mainly from long-established contacts. We observed that the traders that came to buy from the wholesalers also often had long-established ties with the family. In turn, the daughters purchased vegetables from other traders in the wholesale market to ship down to Satipo to be sold to local contacts there. Indeed, the daughters were well embedded in the social life of the market. In May 1972, they were co-sponsors (*priostes*) of the three-day Fiesta De La Cruz for the wholesale market of Huancayo.[14] This fiesta, like the San Sebastián Fiesta described in the next chapter, serves partly to enable the *priostes* to pay off social obligations and, in general, to consolidate their prestige within the market. In 1972, there was competition between two groups representing, respectively, the potato and fruit traders; yet, despite the rivalry, members of the two groups collaborated with each other, making gifts of beer and attending each others' celebrations.

Several important processes can be identified from this case. There is a slow process of capital accumulation based upon the use of family labour, informal social networks and upon a strategy of economic diversification. There is also a flexible pattern of property ownership and capital utilization, with a high degree of informality with regard to book-keeping and income distribution. In addition, the enterprise in question develops relations with the formal sector. The nature of this relationship illustrates the kinds of benefits which the formal sector obtains from arrangements such as sub-contracting, while also bringing out the factors which, in the central highlands, limit the subsumption of small-scale enterprise by large-scale capital. Above all, this case shows the new types of economic linkage that restructure the regional economy, generating a more complex pattern of population movement and resource use in which the city is predominantly a centre for servicing small-scale production.

The new regional pattern of economic relations

Small-scale activities represent the attempt by the people of the area around Huancayo to continue to be economically viable without a permanent or long-term migration far from home. From this perspective, much of the contemporary economic activity of Huancayo represents the taking over of the city by its surrounding area.

The recent migration into Huancayo is not so much migration in search of jobs – as was the earlier migration to the textile industry – but a migration to extend or to consolidate particular economic enterprises. This is illustrated by the history of the garment-making industry of the nearby village of Sicaya. According to informants in that trade, this developed quickly after the ending of the seasonal migrations to the coastal cotton plantations. These migrations had been a major source of cash income in the village, with some 200 to 300 people going down every year. After these opportunities declined at the end of the 1940s, women increasingly took to sewing and knitting. Much of this work was organized on a putting-out system by local residents who had saved enough cash to purchase machines and the raw material.

The developing domestic industry was also stimulated by the number of men and women from the village who worked in the textile factories of Huancayo and who, consequently, had privileged access to raw materials. According to the industrialists we interviewed, these women often commuted from Sicaya. With the closure of many textile factories and workshops, some of these Sicaya workers were given machinery in compensation and established their own garment workshops in Huancayo.[15] They became more permanently resident in the city in order to look after their interests there. Among the major garment entrepreneurs in Huancayo in 1972, fifteen were from Sicaya, but they now reside in the city. One of the most important of these had two houses in Sicaya, one in Lima and one in Huancayo. This woman had, at one time, employed sixteen out-workers, although in 1972 she only had five. In Sicaya itself, there were approximately twenty garment entrepreneurs and some two hundred people, each with their own sewing machine, who were contracted to work for them on a putting-out arrangement. The movement of garment entrepreneurs into Huancayo is marked from the 1960s onwards. Our informants claimed that Huancayo provided better access to markets and materials. The scale of the industry is considerable. A great deal of out-work employment is generated and the entrepreneurs travel to distant coastal and highland markets to sell their products.

For the surrounding population, Huancayo became an essential centre that allowed them to continue with a diversified, but near subsistence, economy.

The average size of landholdings in the villages of the area is not sufficient for contemporary levels of subsistence, including, as they do, educational costs and many manufactured items. Agriculture has become almost a complementary occupation for this farming population. In some villages, such as Muquiyauyo or Ahuac, most households engage in some craft, commercial or wage labour activity to complement what they receive from farming (Grondín 1978a, Samaniego, 1978). For some, it is possible to undertake these activities within the village, but most depend on a neighbouring urban centre to obtain some of their work. For Muquiyauyo, this centre is Jauja, but for most of the area it is Huancayo that concentrates the goods and services, enabling people to continue living in the villages while obtaining additional income from their urban contacts.

Many villagers come to the city for odd-job work in construction or in the service industries, to find extra carpentry work, to make a sale and so on. Some of the wealthier villagers remain in the village but have invested in urban property, in bus companies or industrial workshops. The village remains a good base and agriculture provides a basic subsistence and security in a climate of economic uncertainty. The village and the city thus become interrelated as complementary locations permitting the local survival of a population through activities which, by themselves, would not be sufficient for subsistence. In this situation, there develops neither a large urban proletariat, nor an extensive middle class, nor a specialized farming population, but rather a hybrid economic group characterized by its flexible and small-scale exploitation of the resources of the area.

Migration flows

The contemporary migration situation in Huancayo reflects the nature of the interrelationships of the area. Much of the contemporary population of Huancayo is clearly a floating population. We had great difficulty in locating many of the urban sample, simply because those originally appearing in our census had moved on in the intervening month or were away for a period of time. Many traders keep a room in Huancayo for use for some days in the month, but may keep their families elsewhere – in their home village, for example. The city is still, to a certain extent, a temporary dormitory for some of its working population, in which the man sleeps during the week but returns to the village and his family at weekends. However, the increase in transport facilities permits many of these workers to live permanently in the nearby villages. This relative impermanence in the population is reflected in the housing stock: almost half of it is of the lodging-house type, with rooms arranged around an interior courtyard, and 53 per cent of the male population live in rented accommodation. Renting accommodation is mainly a local, small-scale business: 78 per cent of the landlords are resident in Huancayo and 14 per cent of them live in Lima.

Much of the contemporary migration flow in Huancayo and the area around is a temporary exploration of economic possibilities or educational advantages. It does not result in permanent commitments. Of Huancayo's present population, approximately 30 per cent of the adult males (excluding those born in Lima) have spent one or more years in Lima.[16] This return migration from Lima to the highlands is part of a more general pattern: 21.3 per cent of Huancayo's adult male population has lived for a period in the city, migrated away and returned again (Muñoz, 1982: 138–41). What many of these migrants are doing is what people of the central highlands have always done. They use migration as a means to combine flexibly economic resources in different locations and in response to eventualities in the family cycle. Of those who have returned to Huancayo from Lima, many are professionals or white-collar workers who were born in the villages around Huancayo. For them, Huancayo provides a convenient location that allows them to maintain a certain standard of living and to be near to kin and to the economic interests (mainly land) that many retain in the villages. Others, who have worked in Lima or on the coast for a number of years, return when the illness of parents or the need of siblings to go away to obtain education or work requires their presence to help out in a smallholding or in a family business.

The significance of these migration patterns is that they reflect and are made possible by the lack of detailed control over economic organization on the part of government or by large-scale capitalist enterprise. This is also true of Lima, in which a large proportion of the economically active also earn their living from informal activities. Immigration to both Huancayo and Lima is, consequently, different from that of an industrial city like Monterrey in Mexico, in which industrial employment and stable commercial and service activities encourage migrants to commit themselves to the city and to long-term occupational careers (Balán et al., 1973). There is a considerable disarticulation of economic activities both within the central highlands and between Lima and the region. There are, as a consequence, no clearly established occupational careers or inter-firm linkages which lead people in a unilinear direction from one location to another and from one economic activity to another.

Despite the economic dominance of Lima and the economic opportunities present in that city, it thus remains possible for migrants to use the capital city as a temporary economic resource, entering, building up experience or capital and, if relative opportunities change, later returning to the highlands. As was noted above, the relative advantage of Lima in terms of per capita income may have been declining in recent years. This pattern is complemented by the continuing persistence of small-scale economic activities in Huancayo and in the rural areas around. Under these local conditions, it remains possible for people to take up or leave off an activity relatively easily and without a long period of training or commitment. People may move from one job to another but they keep within the same type of activity. The closest resemblance to occupational career patterns that is discernible amongst Huancayo's male population are careers based on moving from town to town, but keeping the same type of job.

Government employees and those of the large firms that maintain branches in Huancayo tend to be in their thirties and to have been born on the coast; they do not expect to spend the rest of their life in the city (Roberts, 1973: Table 5). Many professionals and people on pensions are from the surrounding villages. They have pursued their careers elsewhere, but have finally chosen to settle near their places of origin. Elements of competition and a realistic assessment of their position influence the destination of this kind of migrant. In a survey of Sicaya, we found that migrant professionals were most likely to settle in Huancayo. However, traders from Sicaya were most likely to settle in Lima. Traders in Huancayo were disproportionately from the more remote villages, especially from Huancavelica – and some of these continued to trade with their home area (Table 25). Craftsmen and skilled workers were more likely to come from Huancayo itself or from the nearby villages. Some of them are the residue of the industrial working class of the textile industry.

The relative commitments of these groups to staying in Huancayo varies. The survey showed that those from the smaller places are less likely to expect to move than those from Lima or Huancayo. The attachment of someone to Huancayo depends very much on his career and the stage of life cycle, the nearness of relatives, the relevance of local contacts to the type of work, or changes in the prospects of other members of the family.

The end result of these career strategies is a population in which place of origin makes little difference to the occupation that a person attains (Table 25; See also Muñoz, 1982: 187). Migrants obtain similar jobs to those born in Huancayo because of the ease of access to jobs in small-scale enterprises. Furthermore there has been an out-migration of those born in Huancayo who have relatively high qualifications and who might otherwise have occupied the better-paid occupations in the city. Huancayo has thus become a town of permanent transition: 47.2 per cent of its adult male population stated in the survey that they definitely intended to move from the city and the percentage planning to move is higher amongst the white-collar workers (Muñoz, 1982: 147).

Table 25 *Places of origin and present occupations of male population of Huancayo in 1972 (in percentages)*

Present occupation	Place of birth				
	Huancayo (159)	Villages of Mantaro valley (193)	Other highland villages (226)	Mines (42)	Lima and the coast (73)
Professional and white collar (216)[a]	27	26	27	4	16
Traders and salespeople (158)	28	22	37	4	10
Skilled workers (172)	26	31	30	7	6
Unskilled workers (81)	14	31	48	2	5

[a] No. in parentheses represents number of cases in sample.

Note: The data are taken from the stratified sample. The proportions of the different occupational groups indicated by the number of cases over-represent white-collar workers and traders.

Source: Sample survey of Huancayo, 1972.

The role of the government in the new regional economy

Within this overall pattern, one economic resource has become especially significant – government services and administration, which have considerably expanded in the area since the 1960s. Fourteen per cent of Huancayo's adult male population is now employed by the government in administration, education and in services ancillary to these. The significance of government employment is the greater because it is concentrated among the higher paid of Huancayo's population. If, to these government employees, are added those in Huancayo living off government pensions or the pensions of the big mining companies (some 4 per cent of the adult male population), an appreciable part of the city's income is derived externally. Indeed, this source of income makes possible the continuing economic vitality of the city, providing the cash flow on which much of the commercial and small industrial activity is based. The increasing importance of government and its services in the area's economy is also felt at village level. For some villages, this can become a major source of employment. Thus, Muquiyauyo has some fifty teaching posts in its various primary and secondary schools and, of these, twenty-four are filled by people born in the village, constituting the largest group of those who have attained professional status from Muquiyauyo.

The increasing importance of government and of the salaries that it pays may partly reverse the outflow of capital that has so long characterized this and other areas of the highlands. Also, the trend to small-scale, informally organized businesses is likely to have proportionately reduced the outflow from the area.[17] Partly, this is a question of the relative share of taxes such enterprises pay since many of them escape taxation. Some supporting evidence for this claim is the suggestion made by Gonzales (1982: 203–4), on the basis of banking data, that there is no evidence that the substantial centralization of financial resources in Lima has increased since the late 1940s. The previous economic structure of Huancayo did allow for a greater concentration of profit and its remission to Lima. In the period of the dominance of the importing houses and their agencies, merchants in Huancayo had effective monopolies of trade both in the city and in the area around. Considerable profits were made by some and many of these invested the money in Lima, either in business or in urban land.

In the contemporary situation, these near monopolies have been broken. The products of the national factories substitute imported goods and are not vertically integrated into import–export retailing ventures. Improved communications have allowed even quite small traders to shop directly in Lima. Whereas, previously, village and small town traders bought from the large Huancayo merchants, many of them now make weekly or monthly trips to Lima for their goods. The large merchants in Huancayo, with experience of both periods, specifically complain that access to national producers has enabled the smallest operators to buy reasonably cheaply and has reduced their own profits quite severely. In this situation, the relatively small profits made by local businessmen also make it less likely that they accumulate sufficient to make proportionately as many remittances to Lima as once were made.

Lima-based firms, banks or capitalists no longer exercise the control over the organization of the Huancayo economy that they did when they were responsible for the jobs and relative rates of pay of 3,500 textile workers or for channelling of goods and credit to the large Huancayo firms. The degree of information available both to Lima capitalists and to government over the economy of Huancayo is also less. Government does not, for example, possess accurate estimates of the contemporary textile labour force nor of local production. Nor does it have much information about the potential supply of agricultural goods that come from the area.[18]

This situation limits both government action and planning and the capacity of Lima capitalists to assess the provincial market. The installation of the regional milk processing plant at Concepción near Huancayo with a daily capacity in excess of possible local supply is one example of planning based on lack of information (Long and Sánchez, 1978). The hesitant support that government gave to the highly successful textile co-operative is another example of not possessing adequate information. Lack of detailed knowledge about, and low central control over, Huancayo's economy does not lead to autonomous local development. We have seen many examples of the ways in which central control of credit and the movement of goods limits the endeavours of local entrepreneurs. But what it does mean is that the provincial area retains a vitality and a volatility which makes it a significant source of unanticipated development.

Politically, the dominant groups in Huancayo now have less national influence. The city council has become even more of an adjunct to government administration than in the past, and includes local bank clerks, accountants, architects, doctors and co-operative officials. None of the remaining members of the large-scale business class serve on the council. The mayor of Huancayo was, in 1972, an official from Jauja. So unimportant have local pressure groups become that those wanting to obtain anything from the central government work directly with Lima. Thus, in a recent attempt to have an airport opened near Huancayo, one of the foremost promoters of the scheme – a councillor and medical doctor – was explicit in not wanting to work through the council which he saw as having little weight. Instead, he used contacts made through the local Rotary club to get in touch with a high official of the Ministry of Aviation and arrange a delegation to the minister. The lack of political weight of the city is further demonstrated in its failure to attract any major government plan or subsidy for developments. Unlike other cities, it was even unable to persuade the president in 1972 to attend the quater-centenary celebrations of the city's foundation.

The present political situation is, in fact, the counterpart of the economic situation. Politics flourish in the central highlands, but mainly at the local level and with little manifest co-ordination. For example, despite a national political situation from 1968 to 1976 in which political parties were prevented by the military government from playing a public role in government and administration, avowed members of the APRA political party controlled important positions in Huancayo and its area. Several of the largest agricultural co-operatives were dominated by APRA. Many of the village councils were controlled by APRA members and, even in Huancayo, co-operatives and the town council had APRA members. Apart from APRA, there were also other important sources of local-level political organization, such as the organization of workers against the government sponsored agrarian co-operatives, the opposition of villagers to local agrarian reform and the overt and covert lack of co-operation with government agricultural plans for production and prices shown by small farmers, intermediaries and transporters (Long and Roberts, 1978).

The dominance of the small-scale in the economic and political life of the area deprives government agencies of the means to make effective their control of local life. There was a vast extension of the government presence in the area from 1968 to 1975, especially through the creation of a social mobilization programme – SINAMOS (Sistema Nacional de Apoyo a la Movilización Social). SINAMOS co-ordinated existing programmes of community development and co-operative organization. It used its officials to intervene directly at the village level. Yet during the period of our work in the area, it was evident that the ambitious programmes of SINAMOS had little success and were, in some respects, creating problems for the government by arousing antagonism at the local level. SINAMOS was subsequently dissolved.

In 1972, local officials of the agency felt frustrated because they did not have adequate information on which to base their interventions. In the face of the social and economic heterogeneity of the area, they could devise no framework for consistent polity. In many instances which we recorded these officials were manipulated by local interest groups. In this respect, the lack of strong centralized political organization in the region, based on Huancayo, probably made the work of the military government more difficult.

Conclusion

The penetration of Huancayo by the interests and strategies of people from the villages and small towns has meant that this provincial area has been able to retain a certain economic and social vitality. The average standard of living is one of the highest for the highland areas of Peru and is sufficiently attractive for people to return there to work or to retire. The area has also maintained a steadily growing population, despite the large-scale out-migration to Lima from other areas of the highlands. In all this, the role of the city has been vital.

The significance of Huancayo for the development of the central highlands of Peru is not that expected of large central places. The migration patterns of the area, and those which link highlands and coast, are not hierarchically ordered by stages from the smallest villages to Huancayo and finally to Lima. Economic and political activities in the central highlands display a similar lack of co-ordination and order. This situation bears a certain resemblance to that described as the dendritic pattern in which the national metropolis is linked directly to the small villages of the hinterland, bypassing the provincial centres (Johnson, 1970). However this resemblance highlights certain difficulties with the assumptions of the dendritic model. The history of Huancayo makes clear that effective control of the economy and polity of a provincial area from the metropolis depends on the existence of a dominant provincial class which is both locally resident and committed to the organization and control of the regional economy.

Huancayo did not evolve such a dominant class to enable the city to become an organizing and control centre. Under the agro-mining economy the city prospered without its resident business class controlling regional production. In the more contemporary period, the small-scale pattern of economic growth has undermined central control and planning. Although this 'anarchy', as it often appears to government planners, frustrates long-term planning, it is also a resource which enables local people to retain a degree of control over their environment in a period of rapid change and uncertainty. This resource, and the use to which it has been put, has also been an effective means for local people to cope with some of the disruptive effects of Peru's rapid urbanization.

8

The village economy, agricultural development and contemporary patterns of social differentiation

Decline in the economic significance of the mining sector has not been compensated by the development of agriculture. Despite increasing urban concentration, the rural population has continued to grow, increasing pressure on existing land resources. Using the census definition of 'rural' locations (less than 5,000), there has been an increase in the rural population of Junín in the intercensal years from 1961 to 1972 from 265,458 to 281,890. And by 1980, it was estimated that this rural population had increased to 349,176. (*Indicadores estadísticos*, 1981: Tables 27, 28). Urban growth was more rapid, but many of these 'urban' places were large villages in which a majority of the population still farmed as their major economic activity. The average land-holding in 1972 was 2.4 hectares, but this figure concealed significant inequalities in the distribution of land with 38 per cent of farms in the Mantaro valley zone possessing less than half a hectare (Long and Roberts, 1978: 11). The agrarian reform office estimated that the amount of land needed for basic household subsistence was three hectares; yet about half the households in Junín had less than this minimum holding (*Huancayo Plan Director*, 1976: 36).

Increased demographic pressure was not accompanied by an increase in agricultural production. Agricultural statistics show no evidence of significant improvements between the 1950s and the 1970s, either in levels of production or in productivity of the four main food crops: potatoes, maize, wheat and barley. In the highlands of Junín, the total amount of cultivated land had probably reached its limits by the 1970s and the major new sources of cultivated land were located in the tropical lowlands. Changes in agricultural production were, for that reason, in crops grown in the lowlands: coffee, rice and fruit. The increasing importance of these crops led to some population redistribution through increasing migration of highlanders to the tropical lowlands (Bracco, n.d.). However, the tropical crops still constituted only

169

one-quarter of the value of agricultural production in Junín during the 1970s (*Indicadores estadisticos*, 1981: Table 10).

The failure to raise overall production levels and productivity in the basic food crops occurred despite evidence of the increasing use of chemical fertilizers, insecticides and fungicides in the period from 1950 to 1980. This apparent anomaly is explained by the increasing differentiation of the farming population into two major groups: a commercially-oriented farmer class and a large, impoverished semi-subsistence peasantry. As we showed in chapter six, this tendency towards polarization is most marked in some of the villages of the Mantaro valley which has traditionally been the major area of market-oriented farming in Junín.

In the contemporary period, most of the region's farming population have been forced to subsist on land that is inadequate for their consumption needs. They have managed to survive by pursuing the same strategies as were used in earlier periods: diversifying the household economy and migrating temporarily to centres of work. A central analytical question is why these rural families have continued to retain a village base, often farming miniscule plots of land for little economic return. Alongside this peasant class, lives a class of small-scale entrepreneurs, themselves of peasant background, who farm commercially using modern inputs on medium-sized holdings, and who also often operate as traders, truckers and, occasionally, as small-scale industrialists (e.g., processing timber). As was described in chapters three and six, the origins of this class also lie in the mining economy. Their contemporary role is now more closely tied to the needs of the urban economy of Huancayo and Lima.

In this chapter, we provide case material on two villages to illustrate these social and economic processes. Most of it concerns the village of Matahuasi (see also chapter 6 and Long and Roberts, 1978: chapters 8 and 10). Matahuasi is one of the most prosperous of Junín villages, being located on relatively rich, irrigated land in the centre of the Mantaro valley. We will also use comparative data from the village of Pucará located at the southern end of the Mantaro valley (Solano, 1978; Arce, 1981). The value of farming production in Pucará is lower than that of Matahuasi and the village is less socially and economically differentiated. Pucará has a relatively small amount of cultivated land, although used intensively for vegetable production, but has extensive pasture land.

The survival of the peasant household

In both Pucará and Matahuasi, most farming households have very small landholdings. In Matahuasi, in 1979, 73 per cent of households had less than one hectare of land and 94 per cent (706 households) had less than three hectares

(Benavides and Gamarra, 1980: 27). This extreme land fragmentation is complemented by a high degree of concentration: forty-eight Matahuasinos own 47 per cent of the land (386 hectares). In Pucará, 76 per cent of the households have less than two hectares of land, but the degree of land concentration is much lower. Six per cent of households control more than four hectares of land and their holdings account for 25 per cent of the total cultivated area. In both villages, the majority of the population must seek means of complementing their agricultural production by wage labour, either locally or in urban centres, and by engaging in non-agricultural economic activities.

In Pucará, only a small minority (15.3 per cent) of household heads claimed that they worked exclusively in agriculture (Arce, 1981: 73). Ten per cent of households gave trade as their major occupation. The rest of the households combined some agriculture with trade, craftwork, teaching or wage labour. In Matahuasi, economic diversification is equally marked. However, in this village a larger proportion of households are landless (22 per cent) and their members work either on the farms of others, or as construction labourers, operatives in the local timber mills, or assistants to drivers and traders.

For most of those who own land, agricultural production is not sufficient to meet even the food consumption needs of the families. Consequently, none of these families are composed of purely subsistence-oriented farmers. In Pucará, for example, production has concentrated, in recent years, on growing vegetables for the Huancayo market. These crops provide a source of cash income for most of the yeear, but not sufficient to cover necessary annual expenditures. Arce (1981: 88-9) calculates that over half of Pucará households earn less from agriculture than the amount needed to meet the minimum cash requirements of household consumption. Hence Pucará peasant households obtain a substantial part of their food requirements by purchase. The following items make up an essential part of the local diet: salt, sugar, edible oil, rice, flour, pasta and bread. All are purchased in local stores or in Huancayo. They constitute what Arce calls the 'minimum cash consumption requirement'. This minimum does not take into account other expenditures such as transport, paraffin, clothing and non-essential, but frequently purchased, items such as coca, cigarettes and alcohol. This situation makes it necessary for these peasant households to seek the additional sources of income that we have noted above.

The strategies that households adopt to cope with this situation involve a combination of economic activities. Labour migration is undertaken by adult male household members, while the women remain behind to look after the fields, the small store or to trade produce in the city. The retention of a base in the village is understandable in these circumstances since it keeps consumption needs to the minimum. Figueroa (1978) estimates that the minimum cash requirements of a poor peasant household was approximately thirty soles a day (approximately thirty-five British pence) at a time when unskilled labour could obtain a wage of fifty soles a day working in provincial markets. Since these minimum requirements did not include such expenditures as transport, schooling and housing, survival would be difficult in the city without several members of the household working and even then in better paying jobs.

The villages of the region have, in addition, some communal resources that can be used by individual households. In Pucará, the communal land area – mainly pasture – is considerable and enables households to graze animals which provide both a source of food and a cash income when needed. Communal resources are more limited in Matahuasi but, because of land shortage, they are exploited intensively by poor families. Thus, after the 1969 agrarian reform, Matahuasi's sixty hectares of communal land were farmed collectively by 120 individuals who qualified as *comuneros* under the terms of the reform. These *comuneros* were drawn disproportionately from the poorest strata of the population and included many women.

The survival of the poor peasant household depends on making use of whatever resources are available. Interhousehold co-operation is an important aspect of this strategy. The absence of adult male members of a household means that the remaining members of the household may have to call upon their kin and neighbours for help with particularly demanding tasks. In any event, there are times in the agricultural cycle when even a complete household labour force is unlikely to be sufficient. Harvesting is a case in point, when it is often necessary for households to combine and harvest their crops in rotation to ensure that the produce is brought in speedily. Many other economic activities of these families require a degree of interhousehold co-operation. Several households may combine to collect milk, to process it into cheese and to market it. Likewise, labour migrants may depend on the help of others to find work and accommodation in their destinations. This type of co-operation among the poor is necessary because they are operating at the margins of survival. They cannot afford to take individual risks and must therefore pool resources and information.

Two cases of rural poverty

These themes in the life careers of the poorer peasants can be illustrated by two cases: the first a female head of household in Pucará and the other a male farmer in Matahuasi.

Delia, the Pucará example, is twenty-two years of age and is married to Juan who is away working as a technical instructor in an agricultural secondary school in the neighbouring Department of Huancavelica. Delia has the care of her two small children, and a younger sister who lives with her and travels daily to study in Huancayo. Delia's father is dead and her mother has remarried and is raising a new family. Juan contributes little to the expenses of the household, but whatever savings he can make from his small salary are used for capital expenditures. Thus, the small shop that is the basis of Delia's livelihood was initially financed by Juan with only 600 soles (six pounds sterling) working capital.

Neither Delia nor Juan have land in Pucará, but Juan's mother has a small plot which Delia farms for her. Delia borrows the farming tools from her mother and recruits a daily labour force from among those households which, mainly through her shop, she knows need cash. Operating on behalf of her mother-in-law, she pays the women by the number of sacks of vegetables that they collect and the men by a daily wage plus food and the right to clear away the remaining produce after the harvest has been completed (*payapi*). Delia markets the produce using free animal transport provided by a baptismal godfather. Delia obtains part of the profits of the harvest, but the farm income is mainly for the support of the mother-in-law.

She has other godrelatives in Pucará and Huancayo with whom she maintains close ties. Her Huancayo godparents, who are undertakers, do not have children and have offered to educate one of Delia's daughters. Delia also maintains good relations with certain neighbours and friends. These constitute the clientele of the shop, always making their local cash purchases there; and even Delia's mother-in-law must pay cash for purchases in the shop.

We were allowed to examine the accounts of this shop in the early 1970s and confirmed Delia's claim that her profits were extremely modest, there being no notable increase in the working capital available each year. She bought in bulk in Huancayo, but her turnover was so small that it barely covered the cash consumption requirements of the household. The family did, however, obtain part of their own consumption from the shop. Also, the shop provided some cash flow which was used to lend money to finance her mother-in-law's vegetable production. The major source of profits in the shop was from the sale of alcohol, particularly during the village festivals. The relationships that were made through the shop formed the main basis for the exchange of small services and, as we have seen, a source of labour recruitment. Although Delia makes use of the help of others, such as her neighbours and godrelatives, she is also scrupulous in fulfilling her obligations to them, providing small gifts to her godchildren and assistance whenever needed.

Delia's case is interesting because she has very difficult relations with her consanguineal kin, arising from the accusation that she is the child of an incestuous union. Consequently, she has been forced to foster other relationships in the village and elsewhere, using the shop as a focus. Delia's activities also show the significance of kin and community relationships for aged heads of household. Delia's mother-in-law, who is seventy years old, has no children in Pucará and Delia is, therefore, an essential support for her everyday activities, organizing her farming and representing her interests in communal meetings. Delia often attends meetings to discuss the use of community resources, representing her husband, her sister-in-law, who now lives in Lima, and her mother-in-law. A further important point brought out by this case is that, for poor households with meagre landholdings, economic diversification means survival not capital accumulation. Despite her intense activities, Delia barely makes ends meet and barely fulfils her pressing family commitments.

This point comes out even more strongly in the life-history of Alberto, a small-scale farmer in Matahuasi aged forty-eight years. When we first got to know Alberto, in 1970, he had about three hectares of rather rocky, unirrigated land which he used to cultivate potatoes, maize and beans. He also kept a few cows whose milk was used for family consumption. His family then consisted of four children, his wife and an aged mother. Alberto was a man of ambitions. These were seen in his aspirations for the education of his children and by the fact that he idiosyncratically named his sons, Socrates and Shakespeare. His brother, an engineer working for a Belgian company in Brussels, was his point of reference. Alberto himself had wanted to become a trucker. He worked occasionally as a driver for others and bought a succession of very old vehicles which he hoped to cannibalize to construct a working truck. He succeeded in building trucks, but these never lasted for very long. In the ten years until 1980, he was unable to develop a trucking business. Indeed, during these years, his economic situation noticeably worsened. He had four more children, forcing him to take temporary jobs to finance the growing consumption needs of his family, and he was unable to educate them as he had wished.

In 1980, Alberto and his three eldest children were working in the Satipo area of the tropical lowlands. His wife remained in Matahuasi, looking after the youngest children and the elderly mother, but brought food supplies to them every two weeks or so. Alberto returned frequently to Matahuasi, claiming that his aim was to accumulate money to buy land in Satipo. His need of the labour of his eldest children interfered with their educational prospects. For example, he felt unable to take up the offer of one of the authors, a godparent to the eldest son, to finance his education.

Despite Alberto's lack of economic success, he had a network of relationships in the village, in the mine townships and in the tropical lowlands which had been used throughout his career to find work or start new ventures. Alberto and his household are, however, somewhat isolated from the elite groups in the village. Alberto's family is not from Matahuasi and his wife, who is from the village, is related mainly to the poorer sector of the population.

Community and interhousehold co-operation

Reliance on others leads in these village situations to support for community festivals and other expressions of communal solidarity. Thus, the patron saint's day is celebrated enthusiastically by rich and poor alike. There are also class-based festivals such as the San Isidro fiesta in Matahuasi, which is organized by agricultural labourers and which depicts, through the dance forms and symbolism, their particular way of life. In Pucará, there is an extensive system of spiritual brotherhood (Hermandad Espiritual) that binds non-kinsmen to each other through promises of mutual aid and emotional support. Co-operative practices among the poor seem less strong than they are among some of the entrepreneurial groups that we will discuss in the next sections. However, depending on others and on community institutions creates a sense among these peasant households that their welfare is most securely assured in the local community. Moreover, despite their impoverishment, they do not display much class antagonism towards the richer sections of the village. In these villages, the poor are often kinsfolk to the rich and depend upon them for occasional work and favours.

Peasant households have also shown themselves to be firm believers in experimenting with new forms of co-operation. From 1945 onwards, Pucará households suppported a number of government initiatives to introduce production and service co-operatives (Solano, 1978). In Matahuasi, the new production co-operative that was established following the agrarian reform was likewise supported by the poorer peasant households, whereas the richer families were either opposed or indifferent to it. The interest shown by poor peasants in community enterprise and government agricultural extension projects is not surprising. Living at the margins of subsistence they see as significant any new external input, however small, that could improve local economic opportunities.

These comments should not be taken to imply that co-operation among poor peasants was constant and conflict-free. Indeed, as we have shown in a previous volume (Long and Roberts, 1978), many of these forms of co-operation and reciprocity were used by the more powerful members of the villages to further their specific economic and political interests. Even among the poorer strata, there was a degree of differentiation which pitted some households against others and led to the destruction of some communal ventures. However, most households continued to believe in the value of co-operative strategies and in the possibility of improving their lot collectively as well as individually.

The consolidation of a rural entrepreneurial class

We suggested earlier that the apparent anomaly of stagnant agricultural production with increasing use of modern inputs could be explained by differentiating between a relatively small group of commercially-oriented farmers and the bulk of the peasant population. Data from Pucará and Matahuasi lend support to this argument. In 1971, the vast majority of households in Pucará were farming without much use of modern techniques: 55 per cent of farming households were totally dependent on traditional methods of hand cultivation, without the use of chemical inputs. A further 40 per cent of households used some modern inputs, but these were chiefly insecticides and pesticides (Arce, 1981). Figueroa (1982) argues that these inputs are used to protect the basic staples against the possibility of heavy loss. Chemical fertilizers are not so generally used, suggesting that expansion of agricultural production is not the main aim.

Only a small group of Pucará farmers are fully committed to modern techniques, using mechanical implements, chemical fertilizers, pesticides and insecticides. It is this group of farmers that has made most use of technical aid and government credit. The relatively poor quality soil and the fragmentation of land makes modern techniques difficult to introduce for most farmers.

The situation is different in Matahuasi, where there is a relatively large number of farmers with over four hectares of land and with access to irrigation. There was a rapid increase in the use of fertilizers from 1968 to 1971. This use was concentrated among members of the Matahuasi marketing co-operative who were, almost entirely, the larger farmers of the locality (Long and Roberts, 1978: 278–9). The impact of this increasing use of modern inputs on agricultural production is illustrated by agricultural production data from Matahuasi from the late 1970s (Benavides and Gamarra, 1981). Between 1966 and 1979, the yields of potatoes and alfalfa rose dramatically. Potatoes increased from just over 5.0 tonnes per hectare to 15.0 tonnes. Alfalfa increased from 7.5 tonnes per hectare to 18.5 tonnes per hectare, due to more intensive cultivation. These data are estimates provided by Ministry of Agriculture officials and are biased towards production on the larger, more modern farms. However, the trend is clear and is corroborated by the case studies that follow.

One implication of this improvement in yields is the increasing predominance of forage crops, particularly alfalfa, and potatoes over cereals. Total cereal production had not risen significantly by 1979, although the area in cultivation had remained approximately the same. On the other hand, potato production increased by approximately 6 per cent, although the area under cultivation dropped considerably from some 316 hectares to 141 hectares.

Forage crops expanded their area of cultivation and their total production increased almost fourteen times to over 7,000 tonnes. These figures show that forage crops expanded their area more at the expense of potatoes than cereals, the latter being staple subsistence crops that are cultivated without the use of modern inputs. The suggestion is, then, that these cereal crops are mainly cultivated by the poorer peasant farmers, while the shift towards forage represents the changing strategy of commercial farmers.

The shift to forage has accompanied the rapid development of the dairy industry in the Mantaro valley in the 1970s. Matahuasi is one of the centres of this industry. Its dairy farmers founded the milk marketing co-operative of the valley in 1967. This co-operative subsequently expanded to include a large milk processing plant built with German technical aid, although the plant is now controlled by an association of private milk farmers, many of whom come from Matahuasi and the neighbouring town of Concepción. However, by the mid-1970s, the Mantaro valley was still a relatively insignificant producer of the national milk supply, with, at the most, 3 per cent of the total, but its production was being fostered by government policies which designated the area as an important development zone for dairy farming (Fongal Centro, 1980). In Matahuasi, the number of milk cows rose from 1,208 in 1966 to 4,151 in 1979. 62 per cent of milk cows were owned by what government officials termed medium and specialized milk producers (i.e. owning eleven head of cattle or more).

The change in the pattern of cultivation in Matahuasi does not appear, however, to have been accompanied by increased land concentration. Comparing the data for irrigated landholding in Matahuasi in 1966 and 1979 indicates, at best, a small swing to concentrations of over three hectares (Arroyo, 1967: 38–9; Benavides and Gamarra, 1980: 27). Thus, in 1966, 44 per cent of irrigated land in Matahuasi was owned by thirty-five proprietors with more than three hectares; in 1979, 47 per cent of irrigated land was held by forty-eight proprietors with more than three hectares. Hence, the development of commercial farming in Matahuasi has occurred less through extending hectarage than through more intensive farming practice. The unwillingness of poor peasants to sell land limits the possibility of commercial farmers increasing their hectarage. Furthermore, the costs of modern inputs, together with the labour costs of large-scale farming, are a further deterrent to these small-scale commercial farmers becoming large-scale operators.

Two commercial farmers

The development of commercial farming in the valley area can be illustrated by the life-history of one of Matahuasi's most important dairy farmers. This man,

Saul, was born in Matahuasi in 1919 of parents who were peasant farmers. The land was farmed entirely by family labour and Saul worked alongside his father from early on. He recalls that the family did not have enough money to buy shoes for himself or for his brothers. Up until 1940, he continued helping his father who had now begun to sell some of his produce in Lima. In that year, Saul entered the army and worked his way up to become an officer. He returned to Matahuasi in 1947 to find that his father and brother had been imprisoned, allegedly for buying *cofradía* land which the community claimed should have been incorporated into the communal properties (see chapter 6: 132; Long and Roberts, 1978: 216–18). Using his army rank and influence Saul secured their release and, together with the other purchasers of *cofradía* land, won the case.

From then on, Saul remained farming in Matahuasi. He helped his brother to study agronomy in Argentina, looking after his family and interests while away. Also, inspired by what he had learned in the army, he bought a tractor on credit. Later, his brother returned from Argentina and, together, they farmed the family lands and rented additional extensions. In the 1950s, Saul, his brother and their mother (the father having died earlier) bought all the land that became available near to Matahuasi. Land was difficult to acquire in Matahuasi or nearby and, for that reason, Saul explains, he was forced to go as far afield as Jauja in order to rent land. He estimates that in this period he and his family were farming a total of some 200 hectares of land.

Then, on the death of the mother, he and his brother divided up the property, Saul retaining some thirty hectares, a tractor and a house. He had divorced his first wife some time before and had now marrried a midwife in Jauja whose brother is a medical doctor, but he has no children by this marriage. Saul's wife continues working part-time as a midwife travelling to Jauja and, in 1980, even at the age of sixty-one, she still helped out in the fields when necessary. Saul's only child, a son by his first wife, studied agronomy at the Universidad Nacional del Centro in Huancayo and, since finishing in the late 1970s, has helped his father to administer the farm.

Saul's family was one of the earliest commercially-minded farming families in the locality. His father had bought *cofradía* land out of savings acquired through trading with Huancayo and Lima. Saul continued in this tradition, seizing upon any opportunities to buy or rent land. He also took care to establish himself politically in both the village and the region. He has served as mayor of Matahuasi and has held several other civic offices. He prides himself on the achievements of his period of office and on his campaigns to secure a telephone service, electricity and drinking water for the village. He is a long-term supporter of APRA and has good contacts both in Jauja, where his wife's relatives have influential positions, and in Huancayo. In the 1970s, Saul was one of the first to recognize the possibilities of milk production. He was a founder-member of the milk co-operative and built up his own herd from the one cow he had in 1960 to seventy head in 1981. Of the cattle, thirty-two were cows and seventeen were producing milk.

Saul's farming activities are divided between crop production and dairy farming. He owns forty hectares of land, having succeeded in purchasing an additional ten hectares. He cultivates fifteen hectares of seed potato, which he sells in the Cañete valley – one of the main coastal potato producing regions of Peru. He has seven hectares of maize and ten hectares of beans which he sells by the lot to regional traders. He sows eight hectares with forage, mainly for his own cattle. His milk production is 160 litres a day. He now has four tractors and other mechanical equipment. Apart from family labour, Saul uses six permanent wage labourers. The best paid is the tractor driver, followed by three women labourers who are mainly employed in the constant task of cutting the forage. There are also two fifteen-year-old workers who generally help around the farm. At harvest time, casual labour is employed on a daily basis. This labour is recruited from Matahuasi and neighbouring villages, at times by means of a labour contractor. This casual labour averaged, in 1981, forty-seven workers daily for the three weeks of the harvest. Almost all the workers were women.

A major source of Saul's income is milk production, which we calculated to bring him around 500,000 soles a month (£600 in 1981 prices). The milk is sold to the processing plant of which he is an associate. The potato harvest fetches almost twenty million soles (£23,000). In 1981, he sold 132,000 kilos of seed potato to a regional merchant who marketed it in Cañete. Although the sale price is high, the costs of potato production are considerable. Seed potatoes are expensive to sow, requiring careful treatment and the heavy use of chemical inputs. Harvest labour for the potato is also a heavy requirement, so that almost one-third of the sale price is taken up in costs of production. Beans and maize production is of much lower value, each bringing in less than 100,000 soles. In addition, Saul sells calves, heifers and pigs.

The household gains further income from the wife's job, from the son providing veterinary services to local farmers, and by renting out tractors. Saul is probably the most successful farmer in Matahuasi. The expansion of his activities has been limited by the local shortage of land, but Saul also prefers to diversify his farming activities between arable and dairy farming: the dairy farming provides a regular income for relatively little financial input since the cows are pastured or fed on home-produced forage. Potatoes are a somewhat riskier crop because of the high production costs entailing annual bank loans. Like other commercially-oriented farmers, Saul makes much use of govern-

ment extension services and credit schemes available for valley agriculturalists.

Saul lives in part of the village, away from the main centre, where a number of
the commercial farmers of Matahuasi live. This group associates frequently and
has developed its own festivals to mark the agricultural cycle. Workers are
included in these festivals and are presented with gifts and prizes for good service
(see Long, 1977). These farmers have modernized their installations, and their
houses are also usually well-built and comfortable, contrasting with the traditional, somewhat ramshackle, adobe and tile houses of the rest of the village.

Saul is somewhat exceptional among this group of commercial farmers
because of his specialization in agriculture. His *compadre* Basilio, for example,
who lives in the same locality is not only a farmer but also a trader, trucker and
restaurant owner. Basilio has a herd of twenty milk-producing cows and owns
two trucks which transport minerals from the Huancavelica mines to Pisco on
the coast. He buys up agricultural produce from the district and sells it in the
Lima wholesale market. His daughter runs the restaurant and a niece runs a
general goods store in the neighbouring town of Concepción. Basilio is from a
poor Matahuasi family which had no land, but he earned enough money by
working in the tropical lowlands to buy a small plot. His fortune, however, was
made through marriage to a slightly older woman. This woman brought with
her a considerable amount of land which Basilio worked intensively, reinvesting
the profits to build up his herd and modernize the farm with a tractor and other
equipment. He now owns eighteen hectares of land, but rents a further fifty
hectares outside the village in other parts of the valley. It was Basilio's
middleman activities that, from early on, enabled him to capitalize rapidly on
his wife's resources and to build up his own farming and commercial activities.
His contacts, gained through his trade network, have provided the information, for example, which has enabled him to buy and rent land.

The commercial farming sector in Matahuasi has the capacity to accumulate
capital. The main limitation on this is the reluctance of the poorer peasants to
sell their land; although there are also factors in the internal organization of
these enterprises that inhibit their consolidation. We have already noted the
adoption of diversification strategies among small-scale farming entrepreneurs.
The above examples exhibit similar trends, in which the entrepreneur prefers to
invest in new branches of activity, usually administered by a relative, rather
than to specialize in one type of production. The setting up of new branches of
activity frequently has some spin-off effects for the poorer peasant class, since
new jobs or income opportunities may be created for these latter households. In
the next section we examine in more detail the sets of social relationship that
other types of rural entrepreneurs generate both within the village and beyond.

Entrepreneurs and social networks

Successful rural commercial entrepreneurship depends on the development and consolidation of particular social networks both within and outside the locality. This process shapes village social organization, as well as contributing to the integration of rural and urban locations within the region.

We begin with the example of truckers in Matahuasi. Transport operations are central to the workings of the regional and national economy. Junín, as we have noted, has always been exceptional in Peru for the large number of registered trucks and buses; and some locations, like Matahuasi, have come to be the base for a significant proportion of these truckers. Truckers (*transportistas* or, more precisely, *fleteros* or freight carriers) own their lorries. They convey goods on a single-trip contract basis. Unlike the middleman, the trucker is not concerned with buying and selling, but only with the transportation of goods.

Truckers in Matahuasi are involved in the movement of different types of goods and cover various transportation routes. By far the most important is the movement of agricultural produce from the valley to Lima where it is sold through middlemen in the urban markets. Frequently, on the return trip, the trucker will carry other products, such as consumer-durables and imported foodstuffs destined for the stores and wholesale merchants in Huancayo and the region. These latter contracts are normally obtained through transport agencies and wholesale agents in Lima, after the load from the valley has been discharged. Sometimes, too, they will move timber to the mines of Cerro de Pasco and, from there, will load up with minerals for Lima-Callao, or will bring back building materials (cement and sand) for builders in the valley.

Occasionally, some truckers travel further afield to other southern highland towns (e.g. Huancavelica, Ayacucho, Cuzco), to jungle regions (e.g. Satipo, Pilcomayo, La Merced) to transport fruit, coffee and other tropical products, and to various coastal areas. Thus the type of produce carried varies greatly but, in general, imported foodstuffs and consumer items flow out of Lima and agricultural produce flows in. None of the truckers in Matahuasi are permanently employed by one agency or middleman, and hence they must seek out their contracts on a week-to-week or even daily basis, first in the valley and then in Lima or the mines, after they have unloaded their cargo.

A trucker's operational requirements can be categorized under three broad heads: cash, labour and information. *Cash* in the form of contributions, gifts and loans is required, from time to time, to cover running costs. This is necessitated when the trucker's capital assets are temporarily low. For example, he may take on a contract or series of contracts and have to meet the full running costs before he receives any payment for his work: truckers are normally paid at the destination or completion of their contract. *Labour* breaks down into several types, skilled and unskilled. Although he may drive the lorry himself, a trucker will occasionally take on a co-driver to share in the drive. This is a distinct advantage when he is operating within very tight schedules, involving continuous driving, for long periods, over bad roads. Sometimes, too, he will employ a driver and send him off to complete a contract, while he himself rests up. He will also need a lorry helper who will guard the lorry and load during the owner's or driver's absence, assist when mechanical breakdowns occur and sometimes help with the loading itself. When faced with serious breakdowns or repairs, the trucker will try, where possible, to recruit a mechanic through a personal link. This can help reduce the costs considerably.

Information is a broad category and includes such items as information on the availability of produce or goods for carriage, information on market conditions and contracts in the offing, and general data on the state of roads and on police activity. Information is especially important since buying and selling and transportation contracts are effected on a short-term basis, and truckers must search continuously for other loads during work and non-work activities.

Table 26 summarizes the transactions entered into by one trucker during a six-week period of observation in order to obtain access to these three basic types of resource. Each of these networks based on cash, labour and information constitutes, in Mayer's (1966) terminology, an 'action-set'.[1] That is, each represents a delimited constellation of relationships that are activated on specified occasions for a specified purpose. Although each of the transactions lasts for only a short duration, the original relationships may persist in some other form and may be associated with particular normative contexts (e.g. kinship or associational ties). Action-sets, therefore, may be composed of recognized relationships that are in constant use for innumerable transactions, both before and after the event, or they may remain latent for periods as potential networks.

From Table 26 it can immediately be seen that a majority of individuals providing services live in the same village as the trucker himself (i.e. in Matahuasi): some twelve out of a total of nineteen. Moreover, of those who reside elsewhere, five were born in Matahuasi (Nos. 1, 11, 14, 15 and 12) and, of the remaining two, one (No. 5) is married to a Matahuasino girl and the other (No. 10) lives in a nearby village and maintains close friendship with certain Matahuasinos (e.g. Nos. 7, 18 and 19). The trucker's work necessarily makes him very mobile geographically, bringing him into regular contact with other communities in the valley, with the mines and with Lima. Yet he does not appear to have built up a stable set of external relationships with non-locals, which he can use to obtain resources essential for the operation of his enterprise.

Rather, he utilizes a number of ties with locally resident persons or with persons whose kin networks feed back into Matahuasi. And this holds for less tangible inputs, such as information, too.

Not suprisingly, these local and locally connected relationships are almost entirely with individuals in occupations that are functionally related to trucking: drivers, truckers and mechanics. From these he receives cash, labour and information about fluctuations in supply and demand. This suggests that among these individuals information is not guarded jealously, for they apparently co-operate in the sharing of it.

One advantage of ties with other truckers and drivers is that varied schedules mean that an individual has available, or can obtain information on a wide range of market situations. Secondly, the trucker needs to build up a certain degree of trust and co-operation with others due to the dangers and uncertainties of the road. To get to Lima and several of the mining towns, it is necessary to traverse the main Andean range, climbing to 15,000 feet. Although the road is tarred, it has numerous hairpin bends and heavy traffic, as it is the major access point to the highlands from the coast.

At 13,000 to 15,000 feet, a simple breakdown can represent a major hazard for it frequently snows and drops below freezing-point at night. In addition, such locations are difficult because of the lack of garage facilities. Another hazard is the presence of several police check-points where cargoes are some-times searched and loads weighed. Lorries are often overladen or carry illegal products (e.g. meat from animals not properly slaughtered under government veterinary control, or contraband); consequently, the trucker likes to receive advance warning of police activities before he runs into trouble. Hence, it becomes very useful, if not essential, to have a set of tacit agreements with other truckers to lend mutual assistance whenever needed. While the general code of the road is to stop and give aid to lorries and drivers in difficulty, whoever they may be, the obligation to assist friends and fellow Matahuasinos is stronger.

However, these transactions could be set up with persons of different origins. Indeed it might seem more rational to do this, if the aim was to diversify one's sources of information and aid. How then do we explain the apparent paradox that the trucker's role requires the development of an external network of relations for obtaining loads with the fact that our case study (Pedro Oré) and other truckers in Matahuasi have occupational networks which are predomi-nantly locally-based?

In order to explain this, we need to know more about the particular assets which the participants command. For the purpose of simplicity, we will concentrate on information. During the six weeks of the observation period, we

Table 26 Matrix of resource mobilization through interpersonal ties, *Pedro Oré, transporter, Matahuasi*

| | | | Resource mobilization | | | | | | | | | | | | | | | |
| | | | Cash | | Labour | | | | Information (loads) | | | | | | | | | |
Indiv.	Place of residence	Occupation	Gifts	Loans	Driving	Lorry help	Mechanic, low-skill	Mechanic, high-skill	Agric. prod.	Timber	Fruit	Agencies (Lima)	Agencies (Huamalí)	Mines	Government	Co-operative	Rel. to ego	Member of Club de SS
1	Pilcomayo (jungle)	Timber merchant		X													Friend	Yes
2	Matahuasi	Driver			X	X											Friend	Yes
3	Matahuasi	Odd-job man				X			X								—	—
4	Matahuasi	Driver							X								Affine	Yes
5	Cerro de Pasco	Chemist/ Shopkeeper	X	X										X				
6	Matahuasi	Driver					X	X		X	X						Br.-in-law	Yes
7	Matahuasi	Transporter	X	X			X		X	X	X	X				X	Br.-in-law	Yes

184

No.	Origin	Occupation							Relationship	Regular
8	Matahuasi	Mechanic		X	X		X		Classificatory, mother's brother	—
9	Matahuasi	Mechanic		X	X		X		Classificatory, mother's brother	—
10	Mantaro (valley)	Transporter							Friend	—
11	Lima	Clerk (govt)			X		X	X	Distant matrikin	Yes
12	Humalí (valley)	Small farmer		X	X	X			Brother	—
13	Matahuasi	Secretary to middleman			X	X			Friend	—
14	Lima	Transporter	X	X	X				Classificatory, matrikin	—
15	Lima	Driver	X	X					Affine	—
16	Matahuasi	Transporter			X				Friend	—
17	Matahuasi	Bar owner		X	X				Friend	Yes
18	Matahuasi	Driver		X	X				Friend	Yes
19	Matahuasi	Transporter			X		X		Friend	Yes

Based on six-week period of observation during major maize marketing season.

found that Pedro Oré used the nineteen contacts shown in Table 26 to obtain access to a wider field of information. Each of them acted as 'gatekeepers' to key persons and organizations in the mines, Lima and the highland towns. These contacts included, for example, mine officials, politicians, large-scale farmers and people working in transport agencies.

This emphasizes that within the effective, locally-based network there exists a number of key individuals who mediate between the trucker and the wider interpersonal and institutional systems. Pedro himself, of course, represents for others in his network a similar channel. Anthropologists have used the idea of 'brokers' to describe such individuals who mediate between the community and the outside. They maintain important external connections, know how to handle external administrative institutions, are more acquainted with an urban style of life, or are more cognizant with the workings of the market economy.[2]

The importance of such gatekeeper roles is also shown in a study of the activities of a school teacher in a village in the coastal Chancay valley (Celestino, 1972). This man provided the initial links used by a group of young men who, under pressure from land shortage, sought work in the urban areas of Lima. He also served to establish APRA locally and became a major source for information on modern agricultural techniques. Later, when the same young men returned to the village to share in the benefits of new irrigation agriculture, the teacher helped them to organize themselves and assume power in local government.

The nature of local networks

Table 26 shows two other important aspects of local ties: firstly, that a fair number of Pedro's effective relationships occur with persons related by kinship or affinity; and secondly, that some also occur with members of a local association known as the Club de San Sebastián (Club de SS). This club has as its primary objective the organizing and financing of the major religious festival of the village.[3] Originally, it was created as a sports club and still has its own football and pelotaris teams.

Eleven persons are related to Pedro by kinship and affinity. The full significance of this cannot be appreciated without indicating the range of potential kin from which they have been selected. We recorded sixty-seven persons with whom he acknowledged some kinship tie. However, of these he maintains regular contact with only twenty-three, seeing each of them at least once a fortnight. Most live in Matahuasi and are kin on the mother's side of the family, since his father comes from Huamalí, some six or seven kilometres away. The rest are affines living mainly in Matahuasi. The second generalization is that, by and large, where there are kin in occupations that are functionally related to his role as trucker then these relationships are utilized and consolidated through frequent visiting and social exchanges. Only in the case of a distant uncle do we find someone of similar occupation with whom Pedro has minimal social contact. This arises because of deep-rooted conflict with this segment of the mother's family over the illegitimate selling of land belonging to another uncle in Matahuasi. This dispute also accounts for the poor contact which Pedro and his mother and father have with other kin in Huancayo, who are alleged to be living comfortably in a middle-class suburb off the proceeds from the sale. The remaining kinsmen, with whom he has virtually no contact, are all peasant farmers or urban workers.

Rodrigo (No. 7 on Table 26) is the main broker in Pedro's relations with affines. Several of them are truckers or drivers. Pedro's sister's marriage to Rodrigo has been critical for the development of his ties with these persons and for his occupational career generally. Indeed it was largely through the services of Rodrigo that he was able to get established as a trucker. Initially, they jointly purchased a lorry and operated the business on a co-operative basis. Later, they became independent with their own individual lorries, but retained this pattern of close co-operation. While Pedro provided the capital and mine contacts, Rodrigo provided the business acumen and ties with Lima. In addition to Rodrigo, Pedro's own father constitutes another strategic link in the village to other social groups – to craftsmen (his father was a shoemaker in his youth) and to both peasant and commercial farmers – and he also serves as the chief source of information concerning relatives on the mother's side. As yet, relatively few of these relationships have been crucial for Pedro's transport business but, if he were planning on diversifying to take in the role of agricultural middleman, then they could become important.

Membership of the Club de San Sebastián is given in Table 27. In 1971, there were forty active members of whom fifteen interacted frequently with Pedro. Of these fifteen, three are drinking friends only, and the rest are directly or indirectly involved in commerce or transportation. From the general pattern of occupations and residence, it can be seen that the club constitutes a remarkable pool of resources for the trucker. Sometimes it is described by both members and non-members as being composed of 'proprietarios de camiones, chóferes y negociantes' (lorry owners, drivers and businessmen) or some such formula. Indeed, the fiesta of San Sebastián has, in recent years, undergone a revival due to the participation of wealthy individuals who have lorries at their disposal for transporting bulls for the bull-fight and for bringing the brass band and other entertainers.

The fiesta rejuvenated members' interest in their club and has led to the development of more clearly defined common objectives. Some truckers and businessmen have seized on this as a way of consolidating their own networks

Table 27 *Active members of Club de San Sebastián: social characteristics and patterns of interaction with Pedro Oré*

Indiv.	Place of residence	Occupation	Regular weekly contact	Exchange		
				Information	Labour	Cash
1	Matahuasi	Transporter	+	+	+	+
2	Matahuasi	Retired miner	+			
3	Matahuasi	Building const.	+			
4	Lima	Architect	+	+		
5	Huancayo	Policeman				
6	Matahuasi	Employee, co-op.				
7	Andamarca	Teacher				
8	Matahuasi	Driver	+	+	+	
9	Matahuasi	Driver	+	+	+	
10	Matahuasi	Driver	+	+		
11	Matahuasi	Shopkeeper	+			
12	Matahuasi	Teacher				
13	Matahuasi	Farmer				
14	Matahuasi	Govt. employee				
15	Matahuasi	Middleman	+	+		
16	Pilcomayo	Timber merch.	+			+

#	Place	Occupation				
17	Concepción	Big farmer				
18	Jauja	Big farmer				
19	Lima	Transporter				
20	Matahuasi	Farmer				
21	Cerro de Pasco	Chem./shopkpr	+	+		+
22	Cerro de Pasco	Driver				
23	Matahuasi	Middleman				
24	Matahuasi	Middleman				
25	Matahuasi	Middleman				
26	Matahuasi	Middleman				
27	Matahuasi	Transporter	+	+	+	
28	Matahuasi	Timber merch.				
29	Satipo	Teacher				
30	Lima	Employee				
31	Huancavelica	Miner				
32	Matahuasi	Driver	+	+	+	
33	Matahuasi	Retired policeman				
34	Matahuasi	Farmer				
35	Huancayo	Univ. prof.				
36	Matahuasi	Driver				
37	Tamboraque	Miner				
38	Huancayo	?				
39	Matahuasi	Bar owner	+	+		
40	Mantaro	Transporter	+	+		

and use the symbols of the club publicly in the pursuit of their businesses. Several members, for example, carry the name San Sebastián on the front of their vehicles. Five members have joined together to form a sub-committee of the local agricultural co-operative society, known as El Comité de Transportes San Sebastián, so that they might get contracts to transport fertilizers and other goods from Lima for the co-operative. In order to do this, they had to first engineer their election as members of the co-operative. Although they were not strictly eligible for membership, as they were not practising farmers, their request went through and they now have a virtual monopoly of this service.

The fiesta serves, in numerous ways, to reaffirm relationships among members and tries to project a 'good' public image of businessmen and truckers generally. It also becomes an occasion during which individual entrepreneurs reward their clients and partners through the feasting, dancing and drinking that take place. A number of key roles in the fiesta activities are performed by outsiders, normally wealthy farmers or businessmen. In addition, many non-resident club members, and other Matahuasinos, return to the village from the cities in order to renew their friendships and contacts and to participate in the celebrations. Hence the fiesta is in many ways characterized more by the way in which it integrates Matahuasi with other sectors of both rural and urban Peru than for its positive integrative functions for the village itself.[4] In fact, the fiesta of 1971 depicted more clearly than any other public event during the year where the main lines of cleavage within the village were, since there were conflicts between the club, the municipal authorities and the peasant community over who was responsible for the running of the fiesta.

The evidence points, then, to the club as a dominant arena within which certain types of relationships among entrepreneurs are defined, reinforced and created. These relationships, which derive essentially from collaboration in the organization of the fiesta, are seen by members as being between equals. Hence the development of patron–client relations is specifically vetoed, both in the fiesta itself and in the day-to-day interaction of members. Certain networks of members form themselves into clusters and these individuals co-operate in the provision of various personal services.

The *modus operandi* of other truckers in the valley is similar. A number of individual truckers and drivers, running independent enterprises, co-operate in the exchange of essential services. This, we suggest, tends to avoid some of the uncertainties of performing in a highly competitive field and seems to be a crucial way of obtaining information on supply and demand in widely different contexts. Although a trucker is tied into a local network, his occupational role tends to restrict his effective social ties to individuals of similar commercial interests. For example, few truckers have close relationships with either peasant or commercial farmers in the vicinity. Nor do they show much interest in achieving office in local government: none of them hold, or have held, positions in the municipality. Instead they confine their participation in public affairs to the fiesta organized by the Club. From this they may receive a certain amount of public esteem, but little chance of influencing decisions affecting the village as a whole.

A comparison of truckers with other entrepreneurs

We now want to compare, briefly, the trucker with other types of entrepreneurs in Matahuasi to show that differences in occupational niche lead to the development of different types of social networks. We shall also argue that differences in the material and social assets of entrepreneurs affect this process.

Table 28 gives a breakdown of transportation and marketing enterprises operative in Matahuasi in 1971. From this, a number of contrasts emerge concerning the social characteristics of truckers as against other types. The first point to note is that, with the exception of one person, truckers are all somewhat younger in age, being between thirty-five and forty-five years old. Other types mostly fall into the older age categories. There are three exceptions to this. Number 1 is sixty years old, and has regular contracts with a group of transport agencies in Huancayo where he has political party allies. Unlike other truckers, he does not maintain links with colleagues in Matahuasi, nor is he a member of the Club de San Sebastián. Number 11, who is thirty-five years old, is at present attempting to switch from being a trucker to being a middleman but, as yet, he cannot guarantee a secure living from this, so, from time to time, he has to function as a trucker only. This man is a member of the club and retains close ties with fellow members. Number 10, who is forty-four years old, has recently rented a timber mill from a local Matahuasino, but is not yet financially well established. The availability of grown-up sons or sons-in-law to assist with a business is related to age. All but one of the truckers operate their businesses without such help, as their families are still young.

The last two columns of the Table give details on land ownership and other forms of economic investment. From this, it can be seen that truckers possess little or no land and few other investments. In contrast, timber merchants tend to invest in land (although few inherited this from their parents) and other marketing entrepreneurs combine commercial farming with the running of multiple businesses.

These correlations suggest that different enterprises may be associated with different stages in an entrepreneurial career. From an examination of life-histories it appears that some larger-scale entrepreneurs had previously been

Table 28 *Transportation and marketing enterprises: Matahuasi, 1971*

Principal economic activity	Age of owner in years	Composition of regular labour force	Land in hectares	Other forms of economic investment
Truckers				
1	60	Father and son	¾	—
2	43	Alone with casual workers		—
3	35	Alone with casual workers	⅔	—
4	38	Alone with casual workers	⅓	Small shop run by wife
5	45	Father with occasional help from son	1	—
6	38	Alone with casual workers	—	Owns land in Satipo
Timber merchants				
7	60	Son with employees	8	Operates enterprise with No. 13
8	55	Father and sons	20	—
9	50	Mother-in-law and son-in-law	5	—
10	44	Alone with employees	1	—
Agricultural middlemen				
11	35	Alone with casual workers	4	—
12	55	Father-in-law and son-in-law	6	—
13	47	Mother and sons	7	Operates enterprise with son-in-law (No. 7)
14	58	Alone with employees	5	Land in Tarma and coastal region: six lorries for transporting minerals from mines
Milk traders				
15	47	Father and son	⅔	Small shop run by wife
16	67	Father, sons and employees	10	Restaurant and buses
Petrol transporter				
17	61	Father, daughter and son, and employees	5	Restaurant, shop and garage

truckers or small-scale agricultural middlemen, although the number of successful careers of this type is limited by various contingent factors. Moreover, the points of transition from one type to the other are, we think, often coincident with changes in household composition. To operate successfully as a large-scale agricultural middleman requires a heavier labour input; whereas the trucker can manage by himself with temporary assistance from driver friends. The middleman, for example, needs to have working with him on a permanent basis about two other persons whom he can trust. When the driver and vehicle are off with a load for sale in Lima, he, together with his aides, must be buying and arranging for a labour force to harvest the next load by the time the vehicle returns. His work also requires diligent and extensive search activities to secure contracts. For these reasons, most middlemen manage their businesses in close association with other adult members of their households or immediate families. Those who do not have sufficient family labour available must look elsewhere, as does number 14. This man has no surviving children: his only son was killed in 1969 in a motor accident. Since then he has established close links with certain truckers and drivers of the Club de San Sebastián and is himself a member.

Most entrepreneurs have little difficulty in persuading some of their adult children to collaborate with them. Under the inheritance law, property should be divided equally between all children or other legal heirs, although, in practice, some preference is normally given (either through the making of a will or by the consent of the interested parties) to those who have contributed most in time and labour to their father's farm or enterprise and who have no other realistic alternatives for employment. Thus, the participation of sons, daughters and sons-in-law in an enterprise suits their own economic interests. However, co-operation between siblings and brothers-in-law tends to continue only so long as one of the parents remains alive and in control of the business. After his or her death, the property will be divided and the brothers and sisters, and their spouses, will go their separate ways. There are very few cases where enterprises are kept intact under the joint control of such kinsmen. When young men (brothers or brothers-in-law) wish to collaborate, then they do so by exchanging services, as Pedro does with his relatives, rather than through the joint financing and management of an enterprise.

Underlying this pattern of ostensible co-operation there is potential competition and conflict, and the likelihood of this occurring is greater when individuals share the ownership, decision-making and work tasks of an enterprise. Truckers in Matahuasi attempt to avoid these difficulties by collaborating with kinsmen and others in the exchange of services only, and by emphasizing their membership of the Club de San Sebastián, which places a premium on the value of balanced exchange between status equals, rather than by stressing their obligations as kinsmen.

If we now compare the social networks of truckers and marketing entrepreneurs we find that the latter also maintain important local ties. However, their networks differ in that they tend to have well-developed sets of ties (frequently through kin and affines) with large and medium-scale farmers in clearly delimited zones of the district. They also maintain close contact with groups of agricultural workers who are needed for the harvesting of crops or cutting of timber: these workers are often drawn from neighbouring villages and not from Matahuasi. Both sets of ties are essential prerequisites for the successful operation of their businesses since they must know when, where and with whom they may buy produce and also have an immediate supply of labour for harvesting when the crops mature.

On the other hand, they operate largely independently of each other and the one case we knew of proposed collaboration between two middlemen came to nothing. Other middlemen are seen as a main threat to a business and competition is the dominant feature. Stable external ties with certain wholesale merchants and market traders in Lima or, in the case of timber merchants, with mine administrators are essential. These must frequently be established with non-locals. The task of building up such a network can be a long and involved process and may take years. For this reason, these entrepreneurs normally specialize in the marketing of a limited range of produce (even if this can be a risky venture from the point of view of predicting price levels etc.), although they may combine this with farming or the running of a local business.

Some of these entrepreneurs have used the institution of *compadrazgo* through baptism as a way of consolidating relationships with strategic persons living outside the village, but the possibility of using this method is, of course, limited by the number of children available for baptism. One of the more successful middlemen eventually engineered the placing of his own paid agents in the vegetable market in Lima, but this came only after a long period of manoeuvring for stalls in the market, and probably entailed the careful nurturing of ties with influential politicians in Lima.

Like the trucker, the middleman does not appear to be particularly interested in achieving office in the municipality or in village organizations generally. A few have gained positions of leadership in such associations as the local agricultural co-operative but have failed to hold these when challenged by more organized coalitions of commercial farmers. It is farmers such as Saul who have tended to dominate village politics. One successful businessman has narrowed down his local commercial contacts to a tightly organized set of co-operative relations with his affines, and together they jointly manage a multiple enterprise involving the marketing of agricultural produce, timber milling and farming. This avoids the risks of operating in one specialized field of activity, but very few entrepreneurs are able to establish such a complex business, for it demands heavy capital investments and a set of dependable and fairly numerous relationships. In this particular instance, the family organizes its own annual fiesta during carnival time and invites family members and agricultural workers to join in. Throughout the celebrations the boss maintains patron–client relationships with his workers, who are allowed to take part in the festivities, but must respond to his orders when he requires them to help with the preparations for the dancing and feasting. They must also serve guests and collect up the empty beer bottles afterwards.

In sum, we can conclude that the roles of middlemen, timber merchants and other market entrepreneurs necessitate reasonably well-developed local networks which feed into somewhat different sectors of the community from that of the trucker. In addition, they require stable external relationships sited in specialized niches of the markets outside.

Let us finally turn to consider the shopkeeper. First, we must distinguish between the small as against the large shopkeeper, for each has a different type of clientele. The small shopkeeper is generally found operating in some small neighbourhood of the village, as in the case of Delia, and it is from this area that he or she draws the bulk of the customers. For this reason he or she tends to develop a dense network of ties with neighbours and maintains these by allowing credit purchases. Most of these ties will be with peasant farmers and craftsmen. This shopkeeper also tends to show little concern for wider village affairs: he or she may take advantage of the fiestas to make money, but will not normally want to help to organize them, nor to seek office in municipal government.

On the other hand, the larger shopkeepers, whose shops are located along the main Huancayo–Jauja–La Oroya road, have a more diversified clientele, and serve travellers and visitors from outside. One of these has built up fairly wide-ranging social contacts in Huancayo and Jauja, and sees himself as participating in 'middle class' life there. Large shopkeepers also purchase their supplies directly from agents in Lima, while the small shopkeeper is generally bound by debt relations to wholesalers in Huancayo or Jauja, or to prominent large shopkeepers in Matahuasi itself. Several large shopkeepers maintain friendships with selected truckers who, on occasions, transport their supplies from Lima. But, on the whole, they keep their friendship options open at local level, nor do they maintain extensive networks with kin. They seldom take part in fiestas or hold public office in the village. In many respects, they are the most cosmopolitan in network and outlook of all the entrepreneurs.

Conclusion

This account of contemporary patterns of socio-economic differentiation among village populations of the Mantaro valley suggests that class differences have become more pronounced in recent decades. Although processes of economic differentiation have their historical roots in the mine-based regional economy of previous eras, the impact of urban–industrial development and the modernization of agriculture, together with demographic pressure on land, have accelerated this tendency. This has resulted, in certain localities such as Matahuasi, in the increased polarization of a commercially-oriented entrepreneurial farmer class and a poor peasant population which has been deprived of access to land or which is unable to survive on the basis of minuscule smallholder production.

The cases described in the first part of the chapter characterize the types of livelihood strategies pursued by the rural poor, emphasizing how they aim to maximize their cash-earning opportunities by combining a number of different economic activities (agricultural and non-agricultural) and by utilizing, whenever possible, existing networks of kinship and friendship for interhousehold exchange and for fostering external relationships that might widen their economic options.

Many of the same kinds of normative frameworks (e.g. kinship, affinity, *comunidad* solidarity, and *compadrazgo* ties) are also employed by the rich farmer class, although, as we have argued previously, this class is more able to dictate the terms of exchange and to manipulate the symbols of co-operation and solidarity to entrepreneurial advantage (see Long and Roberts, 1978: 305–21 for a fuller discussion of the relationship between differentiation and co-operation). Moreover, for the more prosperous farmer, diversification of economic activities represents a way of expanding his enterprise by investing capital in various complementary branches, and thus signifies an attempt at maximizing profits rather than merely at satisfying a basic level of consumption requirements.

During the past ten years, improved agricultural services and the opening of the milk processing plant at Concepción have stimulated the emergence of a group of more specialized commercial farmers who depend on modern mechanized forms of production and on wage labour, and who have achieved high levels of productivity. This group is rapidly consolidating itself into a distinct farming bourgeoisie which maintains close business ties and, in certain situations, political alliances with other entrepreneurial groups in the region. From time to time, it has taken steps to secure political control at municipal or provincial level (via membership of APRA), when threatened by the actions of other social classes.

The second part of the chapter focussed on transport and marketing entrepreneurs. The illustrations were drawn from data collected in Matahuasi. One important dimension in understanding the types of strategies and networks of non-agricultural entrepreneurs is that Matahuasi has been characterized, for at least fifty years, by a high rate of out-migration and is one of the Mantaro villages with the largest number of urban migrants. This has had the effect of establishing 'communities of Matahuasinos' in various locations outside the valley. Many of these migrants retain strong links with their village of origin through the ownership of land and a house, and by keeping in contact with fellow Matahuasinos in the towns where they live. Matahuasi has, as we shall see in the next chapter, several active clubs in Lima formed by migrants 'in order that the village should not be forgotten'. These clubs have over the years made contributions towards the financing of village development projects.[5]

This history of migration and the fact that some Matahuasinos now occupy strategic government, professional or commercial positions outside the valley make it possible for individual truckers and traders to invest in local 'village' ties in order to forge external relationships in the cities of the highlands and in Lima itself. Thus migration has had a feedback effect on the development of commercial enterprise in the village. Entrepreneurial networks are thus constructed upon the basis of ties of kinship, affinity and village affiliation, and are extended through *compadrazgo* relationships. Sometimes they are additionally reinforced, as in the case of the truckers, through membership of specific associations such as fiesta clubs.

The particular economic locations and strategies of entrepreneurs affects political involvement at the local level. Material from Matahuasi suggests that, with the exception of the farmers, none of the entrepreneurial categories (i.e. the truckers, traders and shopkeepers) show much interest in assuming office in municipal government, although they may undertake to organize village-level social events, such as the annual religious fiestas. Entrepreneurs, then, who do not depend so much on control of land tend to dissociate themselves from positions of leadership in formal village organizations (the *consejo municipal* and the *comunidad*), lest they become embroiled in intra-village factionalism that might limit their access to certain local groups. So long as municipal, provincial and national governments do not aim to restrict their economic operations, they consider themselves less vulnerable if they remain somewhat on the touchlines. In contrast, commercial and peasant farmers are frequently drawn into local politics and actively seek to protect and further their interests, especially in the face of major state intervention such as that of the Velasco agrarian reform.

9

Regional commitment among central highlands migrants in Lima[1]

The preceding chapters have emphasized the thriving nature of economic and social life in the central highlands which is based on a pattern of small-scale activities and considerable spatial mobility. This dynamic structure continues to exist in the face of increasing centralization of resources in the metropolitan area of Lima-Callao, generating, as was pointed out in chapter seven, a considerable return migration from Lima to the villages of the area and to the city of Huancayo.

Yet, despite this evidence of the region's capacity to retain and attract population, it is clear that, since the 1940s, there has been substantial out-migration and that most of this has been towards Lima. During the apogee of the agro-mining economy, labour migration to the mines and to the plantations was the predominant pattern. The surveys carried out by the project, in 1972, in the villages and in Huancayo itself showed, however, that this type of migration was increasingly replaced by direct migration to Lima (Roberts, 1973: 259; Samaniego, 1974: chapter VII). In this chapter, I look at a sample of migrants from the central highlands who now live in Lima, focussing, in particular, on the nature and significance of their ties with their area of origin.

A main aim of the chapter is to explore the implications of regional and village commitment for urban social life. In so doing, I hope to throw light on the nature of the interrelationships of metropolitan city and province in Peru, arguing that an integrated field of action has evolved in which the analytic distinction between rural and urban becomes redundant. As Doughty has suggested, understanding migrant life in Lima must take account of the general penetration of *provincial* society by urban economic and organizational forms. Migration to Lima does not entail the ruralization of the city because there is nothing uniquely rural about the provinces (Doughty, 1976).

It is necessary to stress these issues because Lima is unusual in Latin America because of the large number of active regional associations in the city. For example, in 1974, there were approximately 4,000 in the city, each of which represented a specific place of origin. Each association is known by the name of a village, town, district or region, and membership is normally confined to persons born in the locality or who have close connections with it (e.g. through marriage or through having lived there). Each association is formally organized and legally registered. They hold periodic meetings, organize sports events and use radio and newspapers to broadcast their activities. These associations have increased in recent years, as more and more provincial areas have sent migrants to Lima.[2] There is scarcely a provincial district which is not now represented by at least one association, and some have five or more associations each identified with a specific neighbourhood (*barrio* or *anexo*) of the district of origin.

The phenomenon of regional associations in Lima has given rise to a lively debate (Doughty, 1970, 1976; Jongkind, 1974, 1979).[3] The major point of contention is whether or not such associations should be seen as primarily urban phenomena, representing the types of voluntary association that apparently arise as a means of establishing social relationships in urban milieux. This is Jongkind's view, who uses survey data to argue also the relative insignificance of associations for migrants in Lima. In contrast, Doughty maintains that such associations are significant vehicles for the expression and strengthening of regional identities in the city. To Doughty, regional associations are based on the interrelationships of city and provinces, and the continuing significance of these relationships for migrants in the city. Doughty (1976) is explicit in rejecting the suggestion that this is a question of unacculturated peasants seeking a means of adapting to urban life. He points out that the term 'provinces' refers to places that are highly differentiated socially and economically. Many, if not most, of the migrants who come to Lima have a range of experiences and competences which are not substantially different from those of native Limeños. To Doughty, the significance of regional identities for migrants is partly cultural, reflecting the values and practices of their home region, and partly political, reflecting the desire of migrants to pressure government to provide resources for their home areas.

In this chapter, I want to raise additional questions about the role of regional associations from a comparative perspective. Firstly, the social and economic structure of regions and localities affect the functioning of associations in Lima. Secondly, associations have not always had the same significance over time, from the point of view of both members and their communities of origin. Lastly, I will suggest why regional associations in Peru flourish, whereas in other similar cultural contexts, like Mexico and Guatemala, they are a less evident part of urban life (Roberts, 1974). The significance of regional associations, I believe, rests upon the same general processes of change that have influenced regionalization in Peru and that have, subsequently, led to increasing centralization.

The data are taken from a comparative study of sixteen regional associations based in Lima, five of which are linked to the district of Matahuasi in the Mantaro valley and the remaining eleven to the district of Ongoy in the Department of Apurimac. The Matahuasi associations have a total membership of 448, of which 95 are returned migrants living in the district. The largest association (Centro Social y Deportivo Matahuasi) has 128 members, all of whom are resident in Lima, and the remaining four associations have between 50 and 100 members each. The membership of two *anexo* associations is divided between migrants in Lima and those who have returned to live in the district. In Ongoy, there is a total membership of 860, with 472 of these currently residing in the district. There are eleven associations representing Ongoy, many of which are associated with particular *barrios* or *anexos* (Altamirano, 1980: 138–9).

As previous chapters have shown, Matahuasi is an economically differentiated *mestizo* community, with a population of about 4,000 in the late 1970s. The urban centre has just over 2,000 inhabitants, and the rest live in the rural hinterland which includes the two *anexos* (subordinate settlements) of Maravilca and Yanamuclo. The main economic base of the district is commercial agriculture and dairying. Its inhabitants are well-known for their long-established trade and transport enterprises. Fifty-seven per cent of the economically active population are farmers or farm labourers and the remainder have non-agricultural occupations, such as traders, truckers, craftsmen and government and other employees. The district has a long history of substantial out-migration, both to the mines and to the major urban centres, including Lima.

The district of Ongoy has twelve *anexos* with a total population, in 1975, of 9,421. There were only 297 people living in the district centre, reflecting a dispersed settlement pattern. It was not until 1975 that a proper access road to the district was built. Before the recent agrarian reform, Ongoy had been dominated by neighbouring haciendas which controlled about two-thirds of the land in the district. The population is predominantly Indian and Quechua-speaking. Most of this population were tenants of the hacienda, providing it with labour in return for land. They also engaged in short-term seasonal migration to the coffee, tea and fruit estates of the tropical lowlands. From the beginning of the twentieth century, people from Ongoy have migrated to Lima, but mostly on a temporary basis. Most households also owned small private plots and had access to community land, both of which resources provided an increasingly insufficient basis for subsistence.

In the early 1960s, before agrarian reform, the district had very little occupational differentiation. Agrarian reform created new opportunities when the haciendas were expropriated and turned into production co-operatives. Livestock production, trade and service activities became more important. In 1975, 75 per cent of the economically active population were classsed as agriculturalists, 5 per cent as cattle farmers and 20 per cent as traders, government employees and craftsmen (Altamirano, 1980: 80).

The account which follows deals mainly with the Matahuasi study, with Ongoy providing a point of comparative reference. The example of Ongoy, although drawn from outside the central highlands, is a useful contrast with Matahuasi because it is relatively undifferentiated economically and has been subordinate, until recently, to local haciendas. This contrast highlights the varying types of village situation that create differences in the history and dynamic of regional associations.

Mantaro valley regional associations in Lima

In this section, I give a general account of the organization and characteristics of Lima-based regional associations from the Mantaro valley as compared with those from Ongoy. In subsequent sections, the analysis concentrates on the history and contemporary characteristics of the main associations from Matahuasi and Ongoy.

There are about forty associations from the northern part of the Mantaro valley in Lima, of which twenty-three are affiliated to the Junín Departmental federation (Federación Departamental de Junín(FDJ)). Each village often has a main association (*asociación matriz*) and several associations representing other parts of the district. These various associations from the same district often do not have much institutional contact with each other in Lima. Seventeen of the associations of the FDJ represent rural neighbourhoods within districts, while the remaining six claim to represent the district as a whole (Altamirano, 1980: 129).

Villages in the central and southern part of the valley are represented by two similar institutions called Asociación Inter-distrital de la Provincia de Huancayo, made up of twenty-seven associations, and the Central de Entidades Regionales del Departamento de Junín, which comprises about thirty. Hence, inter-institutional relations are not limited by the *comunidad–distrito* boundaries. Affiliation of associations to a regional supra-institution allows members to interact extensively with members of other associations, whatever their places of origin.

There are about thirty regional associations in Lima from the general area of

Ongoy (the Pampas valley). Twenty-six of them represent rural neighbour-hoods, while four claim to represent districts as a whole. In contrast to the Mantaro situation, there is no federation uniting them, although the main association of each district has close formal and informal exchanges with the others from the same district. These Pampas valley associations usually have branches in the home village which provide returned migrants with a means for maintaining links with Lima. They serve as a base for recreational activities and for furthering village development.[4] These branches are much less frequent in the Mantaro valley, although Matahuasi has two located in the outlying hamlets.

Members of the Mantaro valley associations come from varied backgrounds and practise a wide range of occupations: skilled workers, technicians, medium- and small-scale traders and professionals (e.g. lawyers, army officers, teachers and university lecturers). They come from both urban and rural localities of the region. This variety of occupations and the fact that they are predominantly Spanish speakers, most having received full primary education, contrasts markedly with the Pampas area. In the Pampas area, most people have Quechua as their first language, have not completed primary school, and are predomi-nantly peasant farmers.

In contrast to migrants from the Pampas area who settle mainly in Lima's squatter settlements, the main residential areas in which Mantaro migrants are concentrated are the middle and middle–lower class districts of Surquillo, Barranco, Pueblo Libre, San Miguel and Lince. At the present time, both the Asociación Inter-distrital de la Provincia de Huancayo and the Cooperativa de Vivienda Huancayo Ltda N.218 are involved in an ambitious project. This project entails the building of the Ciudad Satelite Huancayo (satellite city of Huancayo) in the Zarate district of Lima. The idea is to reproduce in Lima the urban aspect of Huancayo, including the styles of the houses and the names and locations of the streets. By 1977, it was reported that 90 per cent of the available housing plots were already sold; and some of the buyers (all of them from the valley) had started to build their houses. This area also has a stadium where sports, religious and cultural events take place at weekends or during holidays.

The various activities (sports, social, economic, religious and political) in which associations from the Mantaro area are involved are similar to those of Pampas. However, they show more interest in economic, religious and recreational pursuits, with political activities on behalf of the local community being generally less important than in the case of the Pampas associations. This relative lack of political commitment has its origins in the rural setting, since in recent decades people from the Mantaro valley area have been less directly affected by conflict with *hacendados* and by agrarian reform.

The continuing significance of these associations for economic and political aid to their home villages can be illustrated by the contrast between the recent contributions of the Matahuasi and Ongoy associations. All Ongoyino *barrios* continue to benefit from their respective associations. About 90 per cent of aid is destined for the improvement of *barrio* schools (Altamirano, 1980: 149–50). The average contribution made by associations to village development projects has been of the order of £500. This may seem small but, considering that the average wage of association members in Lima is £25 a month, it is, in fact, substantial. Furthermore, this assistance is often the only outside help that the *barrio* or *comunidad campesina* can expect to receive. Ongoy associations have also lobbied government for permission to operate a transport co-operative in Ongoy and have raised about £1,000 for this purpose. In the past, the Ongoy associations have been active in organizing opposition to the *hacendados* of the area; and, more recently, they have been involved in agitating for the implementation of land reform in the province of Andahuaylas. In 1974, for example, several associations assisted village institutions in occupying hacienda land which accelerated the process of agrarian reform.

In the case of Matahuasi, associations continue to provide economic aid to the home district, but the bulk of it has gone to the modernization of the urban centre. Thus, contributions have been made towards the rebuilding of the church, to the installation of a piped water supply, and a smaller amount for improvements to the school buildings. In general, Matahuasino schools maintained less contact with the Lima associations than did those of Ongoy, although the two *anexo* associations of Matahuasi were more likely to concentrate their efforts on school development. Although involved in local-level politics, the Matahuasi associations have not acted recently on behalf of the district as a whole.

Most of the activities undertaken by the Mantaro valley associations, as also for Pampas, are, however, concerned with social-cum-recreational and religious events. All associations sponsor religious celebrations in Lima in veneration of the patron saints of their villages. They observe the main religious festivals of the agricultural calendar of the highlands, such as *carnavales*. They also sponsor return visits to their communities of origin (*caravanas de retorno*), often partly financing village festivals. In these activities, it is clear that the more 'modernized' communities of the Mantaro valley are as active as those of the Pampas area. Indeed, the greater average wealth of their members enables them to sponsor more expensive and more elaborate celebrations.

Associations from both areas also observe national holidays. However, their main social functions are the sports and cultural activities that they organize.

Those organized by the FDJ provide an example of these, although the Pampas associations are less elaborate in their organization.

At every opportunity, one of the twenty-three district associations affiliated to the FDJ sponsor activities. These activities are noteworthy on three counts: their uniformity of character, their frequency and the large number of participants. The most common events are folk dances (*pachahuara*, *los avelinos*, *huaylas* and *huaynos*), sports such as football, *sapo*, volley-ball, and carnival celebrations (*corta-monte*, *jalapato*).

The manner in which football tournaments are arranged in the league (which includes twenty-three football teams and about ten volley-ball or basketball teams) bears much similarity to that of the *minka* (traditional Andean system of reciprocity or mutual aid). Arrangements are based upon a rotating sponsorship of Sunday activities. Each Sunday, one of the twenty-three associations organizes the activities. Members of this association have to present their best selection of music, dance and food, and are responsible for the decoration of the football ground. The entrance fee is about ten pence per person. My data show that the rent for the use of the playing grounds was about £20 per full day and that the money collected was £167 or 50,000 soles, which came from the entrance tickets for over 1,000 spectators, the sale of food and drinks, raffles and voluntary donations.

The rise of the Matahuasi associations

In this section, I want to identify the historical stages in the emergence of Matahuasino associations. One important aspect is that, from the late nineteenth century until the 1940s, Matahuasi faced no major internal or external political conflicts. As documented in earlier chapters, the most significant struggle in which Matahuasi has been engaged this century has been over the sale of *cofradía* land in the early 1940s and its repercussions. These disputes were directly related to the founding of the first Matahuasi association in Lima in 1943. In contrast, villagers in Ongoy have experienced a long drawn-out and bitter conflict over land boundaries with neighbouring haciendas. As early as 1923, migrants from Ongoy in Lima formed the first Ongoy association with the explicit aim of lobbying government on behalf of the community. As Long and Roberts point out (1978:314), the 1920s was a propitious period for highland communities wishing to protect their communal property rights against the encroachment by neighbouring communities and haciendas. The new legislation recognizing the *comunidad indígena*, together with the impact of the pro-Indian (Indigenista) movement, gave legitimacy to these attempts to protect communal resources. It was during this period that many of the first regional associations were formed – some by migrant groups seeking to lobby for official recognition of community rights to land, others by migrants from villages whose control was threatened by such recognition.[5]

My argument, then, is that the impetus for the formation of regional associations in Lima derives, in part, from the weak centralization of the Peruvian political system which accompanied the regionalization of export production. As previous chapters have shown, there are two aspects to this: firstly, until the 1960s, central government did not exercise close administrative control over provincial areas; secondly, the dominant classes in many areas either were not interested in intervening in village politics, or were poorly linked to nationally dominant classes.[6] The Peruvian political system thus encouraged local communities to seek direct access to the centres of power in Lima.

The formalization of Peruvian regional associations made them effective lobbying mechanisms in the absence of any developed political system of representations.[7] Although communities in Mexico, for example, seek direct access to the centres of power, the existence of a strong, vertically organized political system controlled by the governing party (Partido Revolucionario Institucional) makes the institutionalization of direct lobbying through regional associations less likely and less effective.

The general nature of the political system, however, is not a sufficient explanation for the emergence and persistence of regional associations, without taking into account the economic forces developing at the local level. Some of these have already been indicated, such as the interests of local farmers in expanding their production in the face of rival communities or of the encroachment of large-scale landowners. Since these affected localities at different periods and in different ways, such forces and conflicts help to account for the variation in the timing of the formation of regional associations. Yet, we must attempt to explain the persistence of regional associations once their original objectives have been largely achieved. In order to explore this problem, I look at the internal economic and political processes that shape regional associations once they are founded.

Several major features characterized the first Matahuasi association in Lima. It was set up by a group of *comunidad* members and non-members from Matahuasi who, in the main, came from the middle and lower social strata.[8] It addressed itself primarily to the social and economic problems of migrants and newcomers in Lima, but also served as a channel through which the *comunidad* could lobby government in an attempt to gain legal control over the disputed *cofradía* land, which had been sold by the church to a group of more prosperous Matahuasinos.

The Matahuasi association was called Sociedad Auxilios Mutuos Hijos de Matahuasi (SAMHM). It provided economic and social assistance to those Matahuasinos who were not able to find a job or to those who, having found a job, still did not have enough money to survive. Financially, the association relied on voluntary donations from members. They made contact not only with other existing regional associations but also with APRA because some of the members were affiliated to this political party which, at the time, was the most important and best organized in Peru. Joining the new association did not exclude them from membership of the *comunidad indígena*. On the contrary, many of them retained their community rights and continued to hold land in the village.

The association was very successful, at least during its first decade. Its membership was made up of both temporary and permanent migrants. Almost every year the association's representatives arranged a short visit to Matahuasi, often during the religious celebration of the Virgen de la Asunción on 15 August. The celebration of the patron saint's fiesta, which took place every year, was the major community event in Lima, bringing together all classes of Matahuasinos, even migrants of upper status. In 1946, three years after its foundation, the association donated an electric power generator to the *comunidad indígena*. The *comunidad* quickly organized communal work (*faena comunal*) to install the generator. The association was also able to help its members financially. It remained, however, under the control of a group of middle-status migrants. This situation produced, on some occasions, internal cleavages which gradually and directly affected the organization of the association. Hence, the association was not able to assist all of its members needing financial help. Many members complained that the office-holders were only helping their own relatives and close friends, and also alleged that the destination of some of the funds was not clear. Such problems were frequently used as a means of changing the officers.

In 1961, the association began to establish relations with the church committee in Matahuasi (Comité Pro-Templo). Many of its members sent individual contributions for the construction of the new church building. During the 1960s, the construction of the church became the central concern not only of migrant members but also of migrant non-members. It was reported that the total cost of the construction, in 1972, was about two million Peruvian soles (approximately £7,000), of which a large part was donated by Matahuasinos in Lima.

In 1963, a second association called Central Social Maravilca was formed. Its main concern, in contrast to SAMHM, was with sport and recreation, and members were drawn from the families of small-scale agriculturalists from

Maravilca *barrio*. The Maravilca association was independent from SAMHM and, after its formation, became affiliated to the FDJ, which enabled the members to participate actively in Sunday events at a Lima sports ground. In 1965, the third association, called Centro Social Union Yanamuclo, was created by migrants from the Yanamuclo *barrio*. Its objectives were similar to those of the Maravilca association, and its members were also drawn from small-scale agriculturalists.

During the late 1960s, the SAMHM gradually became somewhat disorganized because of internal disputes arising largely from financial difficulties. These difficulties were caused by some members failing to make their monthly contributions. In 1970, the association tried to persuade some upper-status migrants to join the association. Many of these migrants responded favourably and became active members. A member of the upper-status group was nominated as the president of SAMHM. Shortly after this, the new president tried to change the name of the association to Centro Social y Deportivo Matahuasi (CSDM).

This redefinition reflected increasing differentiation among Matahuasi migrants in Lima. On the one hand, there was a group of professionals, often allied with traders and small industrialists, who favoured improving the public buildings and amenities of the district; on the other hand, there were the skilled and semi-skilled migrant workers, who were more likely to return to live in the village than was the first group and who were more interested in developing its economic base. It was this latter group that supported the plans of the district council and of the *comunidad* to press for the recovery of alienated *cofradía* lands. They also pushed for the implementation of agrarian reform. This took place during the first years of the Velasco government (1968–75) when the town council was favourably disposed towards government reform policies. The professional group and their allies were linked to APRA. Indeed, their rejoining the Matahuasi association possibly reflected their lack of alternative vehicles for political expression when parties were banned in the early years of the military regime.

The professional group broke away from SAMHM founding the CSDM. In terms of village politics, this group was linked to the buyers of *cofradía* land and to certain commercial interests, many of whom also supported APRA. Using their contacts in Lima, CSDM members were able to secure a change in the control of the district council so that their allies became dominant. A new *alcalde* (mayor) was installed and the attempts of the *comunidad* to regain its lost land were effectively blocked. In 1973, a migrant from the Yanamuclo *barrio* decided to create a further association which immediately affiliated to the FDJ. As with the other two *barrio*-based associations, the Yanamuclo association had a sports and recreational role rather than an overtly political one.

Two of the Matahuasi Lima associations have branches in the village, but they do not attribute as much importance to these as do the Ongoy associations. Furthermore, the Matahuasi branches are not as active as those of Ongoy in promoting local village development.

General historical tendencies

Certain features of these historical processes can be applied generally to other regional associations. It is usually migrants from the centre of the district or main village population who first establish a regional association in Lima. The first migrants to Lima often come from families living in these centres. These families are the richer ones and are generally more educated. In the case of Matahuasi, the earliest long-distance migrants were drawn from the middle and upper strata of the district. *Anexo* associations are founded later, coinciding with the involvement of the poorer peasant strata in long-distance migration. Secondly, as the outlying hamlets within a district begin to expand economically, their residents come to resent the power and control exercised by the centre over land and various types of services, such as schools or health facilities. Hence, founding an association is one means of seeking better acccess to centres of power and influence. In the case of the Maravilca and Yanamuclo associations from Matahuasi, there are, in fact, signs that their foundation and development are closely related to the desire for political independence from the district.

The split in the main Matahuasi association reflects internal cleavages in the village, particularly between richer and poorer farmers. These divisions are related to the historical process by which Matahuasi has become increasingly differentiated internally, as its commercial and agricultural base has expanded. However, the main impetus for division was the growing importance of differences in occupation and style of life amongst the Lima residents. These differences also coincided with differences in political attitudes and affiliation. The Lima businessmen and professionals tended to be suspicious of the new reform policies of the military government and continued to support APRA, which they saw as favouring small- and medium-sized private enterprise. The politics of the CSDM were then, it seems, less based on village loyalties than on developing class interests.

This brief historical account suggests that the significance of regional associations must be understood in relation both to the dynamics of provincial development and to the emerging pattern of social stratification in the city.

The social characteristics of members of regional associations

In this section, I look, in more detail, at the social composition and activities of the 'upper-status' association (CSDM), comparing it with Ongoy's main association. Since CSDM is Matahuasi's 'elite' association, with few of its members actually intending to return to the village to live permanently it provides an extreme case for exploring the question of why Lima residents should continue to retain regional or village commitments.

The CSDM has 128 registered members who are drawn from households with an average of approximately six persons per household. Eighty-eight per cent of surviving parents of members were born in Matahuasi. Of these parents, only 27 per cent remain in Matahuasi. The rest are largely resident in Lima. In contrast, all the surviving parents of the members of the Ongoy association were born in Ongoy and 57 per cent of them still continue to live there. Seven per cent of the Matahuasi parents are illiterate; 52 per cent have primary education; 34 per cent have secondary school education; and 8 per cent have university education. All are Spanish speakers. In contrast, 64 per cent of the parents of Ongoy members are illiterate, and the rest generally have only a few years of schooling. In the Matahuasi case, about one-third of the economically active parents farm, while the remainder practise a large variety of occupations with a preponderance of traders and white-collar workers, such as school teachers, clerks, an engineer and an economist. In the Ongoy case, over 80 per cent of economically active parents continue to farm, while the occupations of the rest are: trader, shopkeeper and four school teachers.

Matahuasi and Ongoy households in Lima are distinguished by three features. Firstly, an Ongoy household generally consists not only of a nuclear family, but also of some close kinsmen such as brothers or sisters and occasionally migrants from the same *barrio*. Parents, as indicated above, are likely to remain in the village. Kin are present in Matahuasi households too, but they are usually confined to parents or parents-in-law of the household head. Matahuasi households often include servants. There were twenty-seven cases of Matahuasi households containing 'adopted' children (*abijados* or *recogidos*). These children usually came from poorer households who sent them to Lima to obtain an education in return for helping around the house. In the Ongoy case, this is even more marked: there were seventy-two cases of 'adopted' children among the eighty-nine association members. These data on Matahuasi and Ongoy households in Lima suggest that the latter maintain rural–urban relationships more actively than the former.

Secondly, Ongoy members often use kinship relations in order to recruit labour for their economic activities which are often based on small-scale, informal-type enterprises. Self-employed Matahuasinos, on the other hand, prefer to hire labour rather than rely on unpaid family or kin labour. Thirdly, relationships among Ongoy members, both within and between households, seem to be more cohesive and stable than those of Matahuasi households. These latter households are often occupationally heterogeneous. Moreover, there is a clearer separation of work and family spheres than is the case of Ongoyinos. Matahuasinos work in a variety of job situations and work locations, and few of them work together.

Ninety-four per cent of Matahuasi households live in the centre of Lima in middle and lower-middle class zones. The remaining 6 per cent reside in squatter settlements, although, as the literature shows, such areas are not necessarily inhabited by the poorest of urban dwellers. Fifty-nine per cent of these households own their own house and 12 per cent have plots of land for building. These households do not live close to each other. Ongoy members, in contrast, are much more likely to live within easy walking distance of each other; and 81 per cent of them are concentrated in the squatter settlements surrounding Lima, particularly those on the right bank of the river Rimac.

This suggestion that Matahuasinos, as compared with Ongoyinos, have adopted a more individualized pattern of urban life is reinforced by the character of family participation in the associations. Spouses of Matahuasi members participate in the association, mainly in the fiestas, but adolescent and adult children prefer other forms of entertainment such as the cinema. For Ongoyinos, however, the association is much more a centre of family entertainment for parents and children, and a place where relatives and friends gather to exchange gossip about village and urban life.

The Matahuasinos are, in fact, quite middle class in both occupation and style of life. Few members of the Matahuasi association originate from the more rural parts of the district. After completing primary school in the village, some 60 per cent of Matahuasinos continued secondary education in Lima and 20 per cent went on to attend university. Ongoy members are less well-educated with 20 per cent studying secondary education and 3 per cent studying at university. In the Matahuasi association, 44 per cent of members are professionals, 28 per cent are white-collar workers and 22 per cent are small-scale businessmen. The remaining 6 per cent are low-paid wage workers. In the Ongoy association, 48 per cent of members are low-paid workers, 12 per cent are professionals (mostly in the lower-prestige occupations such as nursing assistant or hospital employee) and 28 per cent are white-collar workers. Twelve per cent are petty traders and small-scale businessmen.

Of Matahuasi association members, 59 per cent migrated directly to Lima and 41 per cent migrated in stages. Most of them arrived at about the age of twelve or even earlier. Eight per cent of members considered themselves as temporary migrants: these maintained a double residence in Lima and in Matahuasi, but their life-histories show that they have spent most of their time in Lima. Ninety-two per cent of Ongoy migrants have come directly to Lima and only 8 per cent of them have had other migratory experience. Just over one-third of Ongoy association members describe themselves as temporary migrants. These contrasts bring out the more variegated pattern of economic development in the Mantaro area which presented, early on, a wide range of work opportunities outside the village.

Members of the Matahuasi association had, on average, come to Lima earlier than had those of Ongoy, despite the earlier date of foundation of the Ongoy association. Indeed, 27 per cent of Matahuasi members were already living in Lima at least eight years before the Matahuasi association was founded in 1943.[9] Matahuasi association members are, in fact, older on average than those of Ongoy. Forty-two per cent of Matahuasi members are fifty-one years of age or older, as compared with 18 per cent in the Ongoy case. Young migrants appear to be less interested in the Matahuasi association, although it should be remembered that this pattern would be less true of the other Matahuasi associations. Thus, members of the outlying *barrio* associations from Matahuasi are similar, in some of their characteristics, to members of the Ongoy association.

Social interaction in the city

These comparisons indicate no obvious social or economic reasons for the attachment of Matahuasinos to their association and place of origin. On the surface, they represent a relatively prosperous, well-established urban population that has experienced little difficulty in coping with life in the metropolis.

Part of the explanation for their continuing attachment lies, I suggest, in the pattern of urban life in Lima. This is a city made up, to a very large extent, of a floating population in which large in-flows of migrants are partly compensated by out-flows of returning migrants or of Lima-born people seeking work elsewhere. In addition, stable employment in large enterprises or in government is scarce and the urban economy is somewhat volatile, with seasonal as well as cyclical fluctuations in the demand for labour. Except for the very rich, this milieu has inhibited the development of an urban culture based on clearly demarcated status lines. Regional associations, like the CSDM, become one of the arenas in which middle-class people try to display their status and mark themselves off from other classes.

Members of the Matahuasi association often have their own cars and visit each other during weekdays. For instance, four of the officials of the assocation frequently make short visits to each other. One is a lawyer who deals with the association's legal affairs and is also a close friend of another three who are also professionals. Another example of regular visiting involves three members who are close relatives; two other members see each other regularly because of occupational links as both are small-scale industrialists. The first has a metal smelter and sells his products to the second who owns a shop which specializes in hardware.

Other examples of interactions concern the wives of members who meet regularly. These contacts are reinforced at social gatherings, such as birthdays, weddings and christenings. Compared with Ongoyinos, their conversations tend to revolve more around their own family affairs in Lima. Thus, in general, they talk less about what is going on in Matahuasi. Visits are also used to exchange information on the association's activities, such as meetings and festivals. One feature distinguishing the case of Matahuasi from that of Ongoy is that food is unlikely to be shared on informal occasions among Matahuasinos, and the small amounts of produce sent from Matahuasi are rarely distributed among the group.

Interaction is more frequent and less formal among members of the Ongoy association. Wives of members continuously exchange services. Children of members are sent off to play in the homes of other members. Members do not usually use the post office, but send letters, both personal and official, to the village with returning migrants. People who receive products from the village are expected to share these with close relatives and friends. In both cases, participation is greatest at the social occasions which follow sports events. Here again, though, there are important differences that highlight the contrasting urban life style manifested by Matahuasinos and Ongoyinos.

In the Ongoy case, the celebrations mainly include people from the urban centre of the district of Ongoy. At one such gathering (*gran baile* or grand dance), conversation and the speeches of the officials focussed on the home community and its needs. The formality of the occasion soon gave way to a noisy pattern of interaction interspersed with dancing and reinforced by heavy drinking. A quarrel broke out between a *mestizo* official and other members of the association who felt that, as a *mestizo*, he could not properly represent the interests of the indigenous population. This quarrel was, however, soon settled with the intervention of another association official.

The gatherings in which the Matahuasi members are involved tend to be much larger affairs and bring people together from many villages of the Mantaro valley. Mantaro people in Lima are proud of the 'progressive' reputation of their region and see themselves as a cut above other highland migrants. Hence, their social events tend to exhibit a greater display of status competition, through spending on food and drink and through a friendly inter-village rivalry based on associational membership. A typical event is the football match, often followed by a *gran baile*. I observed many such occasions, but the pattern can be illustrated by a gathering at the 'Buenos Aires' football stadium.

From the early hours of Sunday morning, loudspeakers had been playing popular Andean music from the Mantaro valley (*huaynos*). A football match between two of the twenty-three associations affiliated to the FDJ was taking place in front of about forty spectators. At this time, the president of the FDJ was Venturo, a founder member of the CSDM. Venturo is related to the families of the buyers of *cofradía* land living in Matahuasi and is the tenant of the sports stadium. The association pays him £160 a month for the use of the ground which complements his pension as a retired government employee. Other officers of the association receive commissions from the sale of liquor, soft drinks, sports equipment, and from the printing and distribution of association notices. As the football game proceeded, the number of spectators gradually increased until by late afternoon there were about 1,500 people in the stadium. Loudspeakers announced the sale of typical Andean dishes, such as *patachi* (boiled maize and pork skin) and *caldo de cabeza*. As the official representatives of the various regional associations arrived, their presence was welcomed over the loudspeakers. Music was provided by a highland group called Hermanos Rios, by a well-known folk singer, and by another group of Mantaro valley musicians. Around the field there were many stalls selling beer, soft drinks and food. The spectators were smartly dressed. Men and women interacted freely, conversing both with fellow members and with those from other associations. By about five p.m., the main football match between Matahuasi and its neighbouring village of Molinos was over. CSDM had won and the Matahuasinos joined together to celebrate the event, shouting 'Viva Matahuasi'. However, during the course of the evening, it was regional identity rather than the locality that became more and more emphasized in interaction and during conversations. Some people began dancing the *huaylas*, others played *tiro de sapo* (a type of quoits) in a corner of the field, while others ate traditional foods. The *gran baile* started at about seven p.m., with the younger participants dancing with partners. As one informant commented, the *gran baile* was a 'marriage market'. By eleven p.m., the party was over. The place was quiet with only a few drunks left sleeping on the ground.

The politics of migrant associations

Although it is the social events that occupy much of the time of migrant associations, regionalism and village commitment are ever present and are often important for political purposes. Political activity has been one of the major CSDM objectives, particularly in relation to the internal land dispute between the community and the buyers of *cofradía* land. Recently, since 1975, as the national political climate has become less reformist, more conservative and, consequently, less hostile to APRA, CSDM association activity has increased. As was noted above, several leaders of the association support APRA and during this period they established close relations with the district council of Matahuasi, several of whose council members were also APRA sympathizers. A formal agreement was drawn up allowing the CSDM to negotiate on behalf of the district of Matahuasi for government loans and assistance in implementing a piped water project. Indeed, the president of the village water supply commission was the CSDM representative in Matahuasi.

An important feature of the new political activity of CSDM is the extent to which its members activate their contacts in the different ministries in Lima in favour of village development projects. One official (Venturo) obtained a declaration from the Ministry of Agriculture that Matahuasi had never been declared a land reform area. Likewise, the CSDM negotiated with the Ministry of Health to obtain help with the water supply project. In Matahuasi, several informants believed that the CSDM wished to introduce a *plan regulador* (district plan) to control housing and other developments within the district.

It is important to emphasize that, in all these cases, the CSDM was not merely acting on behalf of the welfare of the whole village, but was taking a political stance as to the direction of political and economic change. By allying itself with the district council, controlled by the richer farmers and shop-keepers of the locality, it had committed itself to a strategy based upon the retention of private enterprise and on the improvement of the service infra-structure as the major forces for economic growth. I attended several meetings of the CSDM at this time, in which members were quite explicit in their identification with the richer farmers of the locality and in their opposition to the *comunidad indígena* (now called *comunidad campesina*). In one instance, they accused the *comunidad* of creating dissent among Matahuasinos. It was stressed that the best farmers were the buyers of *cofradía* land because their use of modern technology was raising productivity in the village. The association officials argued that the *comunidad* was inefficient and backward in its farming practices. This criticism they linked to their support for APRA and its policies. In contrast, the SAMHM, consisting mainly of lower-status migrants, became more closely identified with the *comunidad campesina* in its struggle to secure aid for its production co-operative which had originally been established by the Velasco government.

It seems, then, that especially among members of the CSDM class-based political action is equally as important as any regional or village commitment. In fact, both types of commitment overlap and interplay. This is indicated by the co-existence of the continuing relatively high level of participation in the association, by the strong ongoing links with the village, by the pattern of internal debates about association objectives, as well as by the individualistic and self-interested stance of migrants. This interplay must be understood in terms of the two categories of migrants who are members of the CSDM. The first category is represented by middle and lower-middle status migrants (mainly white-collar workers and small traders) who make up 57 per cent of the membership. The remainder is the upper-status group, comprised of the professionals and businessmen. For the first category of migrant, regionalism and class commitment appear to be equally strong. Regionalism, for example, is used as a source of pride and security and as a means of retaining relations with kinsmen in their home village and province. In the present economic crisis, even white-collar employees depend increasingly on links with the village to supplement their inadequate wages. For the upper-status migrants regional commitment, it seems, is less relevant, although they may appeal to regional and local loyalties when it suits their interests to do so. Although upper-status migrants may unite against opposing interests, the data suggest that they are more individualistically oriented, more competitive and less cohesive as a group than are the lower-status migrants.

Conclusions

In this chapter, I have suggested that regional associations in Lima reflect different aspects of, and different stages in, the consolidation of the Peruvian economy and polity. Hence, not only may different associations have different social functions – some concentrating on exchanges of mutual aid amongst members, others on organizing sports activities, and others being more political in their objectives – but they also highlight different dimensions of structural change affecting Peru in the twentieth century.

The first dimension is the growing competition that developed between estate-based and peasant production, where both sectors sought to expand and protect their land resources. The conflicts that ensued led many villagers to seek allies in Lima and to use regional associations to do so. Secondly, there is the process of internal differentiation within peasant communities which has generated conflicts within districts or villages, often occurring between outlying hamlets (*anexos*) and the centres of administration. This has led to pressures to mobilize political support among migrants in Lima and has also created an interest among these migrants in sending material aid back to their neighbourhoods in the village.

Lastly, class, rather than locality, increasingly seems to be becoming more salient for social and political action, leading both to divisions within established associations and to a new basis for their activity. This class allegiance cuts across the rural–urban divide, reflecting the ways in which provincial areas, not just the city, are becoming urbanized. There have emerged, for example, new types of economic diversification and entrepreneurship in the provinces linked to a small-scale or petty commercial and industrial class. This class is similar in economic interest and ideology to their counterparts in Lima, who now make up a very significant proportion of Lima's economy.

It is this class identity, as much as the pre-existing social networks, that unites rural and urban areas and creates the basis for collaboration between some urban residents and groups in their villages of origin. This coalition of interests is often associated with common political commitments; for example, in the support given to APRA. The regional association can thus become a political vehicle, not merely for fighting local peasant issues, but also for furthering class-based national political strategies. It is important to emphasize that, although these dimensions of change are to a certain extent sequential, they are likely to coincide or overlap in influencing the founding and development of regional associations in Lima. This is shown in the contrast presented between Matahuasi and Ongoy. These cases illustrate why regional associations are diverse in their origins, organization and functions, since contemporary processes of migration include regions of very different levels of socio-economic development and, within regions, people who exhibit different economic and political interests.

10

Confederations of households: extended domestic enterprises in city and country

This chapter focusses on the specific forms of what McGee (1979) has called 'making out', which evolved among a group of Peruvian people whose livelihoods were both rural and urban and both agricultural and non-agricultural.[1] The evidence suggests that the uneven and volatile nature of the capitalist economy led, in this case, to a complex series of linkages between households across space (not merely between the city and the country, but also within the city itself). This spread of livelihood pursuits across space was a reflection of the households' involvement in a variety of economic activities within the context of a very uncertain economic environment.

This dispersed nature of livelihood pursuits affected the character of fieldwork design in two ways. Firstly, working from one or other end of the rural–urban migration process, or on one area within the city, would make it difficult to examine the precise effects of the livelihood pursuits of a household in one location on the livelihood pursuits of households linked to it, but in another location.[2] In this particular case, fieldwork was undertaken first in a specific rural area and then linkages were followed through to various locations until, eventually, the project itself was moved to the Lima *barriadas* and slums, while continuing to focus on people coming from our original community rather than on any one location in the city (cf. Mitchell, 1966; Philpott, 1973).

Secondly, the dispersion of livelihood pursuits, combined with the flexible nature of household composition as people move in pursuit of their various interests, can make the use of statistical data gathered at any one moment extremely distorting. The main body of the evidence provided here, therefore, relies on the detailed examination of case studies.

I suggest that the spreading out of the various sources of livelihood through the maintenance of ties between a variety of households takes the form of what I term 'confederations of households'. These confederations are subject to a process of schism and reformulation, as alliances are broken and new alliances are formed. This process results partly from the changing labour and consumption requirements of each household, as its composition changes through the life cycle, and partly from historical conditions deriving from changes in the Peruvian economy which have the effect of stimulating certain forms of livelihood while driving others to the wall.

The background to Huasicanchino migration

At an altitude of just over 12,400 feet above sea level, Huasicancha is populated predominantly by sheep- and llama-herders who rely on subsistence crops cultivated in sheltered valleys for the bulk of their food.[3] There are just over 400 families in the village. There are about the same number of families again who have migrated from the village and yet still refer to themselves as Huasicanchinos. They continue to involve themselves in one way or another in village affairs (Smith and Cano, 1978). These migrants are concentrated in the provincial town, Huancayo, and in the national capital, Lima. In 1972, a number of men worked in the nearby Cercapuquio mine or moved further away and worked in other mining centres. But, generally speaking, mine migration was not as significant for Huasicancha as it was elsewhere in the central highlands (see chapter 6).

Historically, migration from Huasicancha has been influenced by its geographical position and by the fluctuating fortunes of the large livestock hacienda whose boundaries, until 1970, reached up to the edge of the village itself. Geographically, Huasicancha is located to the south and west of the commercialized Mantaro valley, in the centre of which lies Huancayo. To the south of the village, roughly a two-day mule journey away, lie the Huancavelica mines, once the second largest in colonial Spanish America. From the earliest times, a barter economy consistent with the vertical ecology of the Andes existed for these people (Murra, 1978). Enduring interhousehold ties were set up, predominantly with people in the high jungle, some two weeks' journey away to the east skirting to the south of the Mantaro valley. After the Conquest, trade in the supply of meat to the Huancavelica mines was added to the traditional bartering.

From the late nineteenth century, the combination of growth in the demand for wool, which led to the expansion of the hacienda, and also a growth in the demand for cotton, which led to the need for cheap seasonal labour, resulted in increasing migration. This brought migrants down into Peru's coastal desert and eventually to the riverine cotton haciendas of Chincha and Cañete. But, by the end of the nineteenth century, European and North American demand for agricultural produce was overtaken by an interest in mining. The smelting town of La Oroya was set up on the high spine of the mountains between Huancayo and Lima. In 1908, the railway reached Huancayo, turning it into a commercial centre greatly dependent upon the economy of the mines. Thus, when the First World War led to a near doubling of the price of wool and hence to the further expansion of the hacienda, Huancayo's economy was expanding, attracting a few male migrants from the village.

However, really significant year-round out-migration did not occur until the late 1930s when an extensive road construction campaign was carried out through the use of work-teams recruited from the highland villages. The contracts were for two years and gave many Huasicanchinos their first extensive exposure to a wide area of central Peru, while village households began to adjust to the year-round absence of adult males. A number of Huasicanchinos found that their contracts terminated on the coast not far from Lima, and it was these men who became the first significant group of migrants to the capital.

This provides the historical background to Huasicancha migration from which the contemporary patterns of livelihood have emerged.[4] In the remainder of this chapter, I shall describe the features of multi-occupational households in Lima and then the forms of their ties to households in other parts of Peru. It will become clear that the spread of different sources of income in the city is an extension of the logic which ties the city-based household to other Huasicancha households in other parts of the country. The way in which I shall do this is to discuss the general features of livelihood for Huasicanchinos in Lima. I shall then discuss, again in general terms, the nature of the ties between Huasicanchino enterprises. There are domestic enterprises which may seek out such ties, but fail to maintain them, and others endeavouring to extricate themselves from such ties. These do not receive any detailed treatment in this chapter.

Multi-occupational households in Lima

Migrants from Huasicancha, arriving in Lima during the 1950s, sought out relatives or friends living in one of a number of inner city locations called *corralones*. These are makeshift huts put up on vacant lots in the central area of Lima. During the 1950s and 1960s ex-residents moved out to a number of locations on the fringes of the city.[5] As the city expanded, the earlier settlements were embraced while, over time, houses were built out of more permanent materials. Such areas are neither inner city slums, like the *corralones* and *callejones* of the city core, nor are they shanty towns, like the *barriadas* (shanty towns) constructed on the city's periphery throughout the 1960s.

Huasicanchino ex-residents, then, can be found in one of three different kinds of settlement. Today there exist two *corralones* entirely inhabited by ex-residents of the community. One was started in 1948 and is now in the heart of Lima's upper-class residential area, Miraflores. The other was started in the early 1960s and is on the other side of the city's motorway, near the bus depots and market. Other ex-residents are found in concrete buildings, settled in the late 1950s and located beside the road to Lima's airport. The land was 'invaded', but all Huasicanchinos now have legal title to their houses. Finally ex-residents can be found in one of two *barriadas* on the edge of Lima, where land 'invasions' occurred in the late 1960s and early 1970s. Structures here are less permanent and titles to land are non-existent. The distance of these *barriadas* from the city centre is substantial, the journey taking anything from one hour to one and a half hours by bus.

Those who arrived in the city during the 1950s usually began earning their livelihoods in economic activities characterized by considerable uncertainty, such as selling cold drinks near to the markets, or assisting others on a day-to-day basis. In many cases, ex-residents continue to depend on such hazardous forms of livelihood. But, during the 1950s, it was found that the hazards of ambulant fruit selling could be alleviated somewhat if others from the community were similarly involved. Increasingly, ex-residents were introduced to fruit selling and especially, between November and January, strawberry selling. While many Huasicanchinos in Lima, especially those recent arrivals of between sixteen and twenty-six years of age, continue to depend on fruit selling for a large proportion of their income, others have used fruit selling as a base to branch off into other activities which they undertake while continuing to sell fruit. Still others have gradually moved away from their initial commitment to fruit selling and are now committed to the operation of a truck, the manufacture and repair of vending tricycles, the operation of small buses in the city and so on. I am not interested here in those who are almost entirely dependent upon fruit selling, nor in those who have committed themselves through investment to one enterprise, such as the *transportistas* or the *taller* owner (making tricycles). Together these two groups may constitute 50 per cent of the Huasicanchino ex-residents in Lima.[6]

The fruit seller is, in most cases, attempting to build up an extensive set of sources of income which will have the effect of tying his or her household into a network of other households. Many continually fail in this attempt. At the other extreme, there are people attempting to sever their ties and to concentrate their capital into one operation. They may succeed; they may not. Indeed they may appear to have succeeded for one or two years and then find they are driven back into dependency on previously neglected ties. This makes it difficult to make any clear distinctions or to assess the numbers of Huasicanchinos involved in multi-occupational enterprises. Nevertheless, I believe that this kind of operation provides the core for the economic rationale of the Huasicanchino enterprises in Lima. What follows is a case study of a representative multi-occupational household in Lima.

Vicente Hinojosa is thirty-eight years old and he came to Lima over twenty years ago.[7] He was the third child among seven. On arrival in the city he moved to what was then the only concentration of Huasicanchinos – an inner city *corralon* (squatting on a vacant lot in the central area). He alternated between the quarters of his elder sister's husband and his father's brother, both of whom were early Lima migrants. Vicente no longer lives in the *corralon*. His sister is now dead and his uncle has moved elsewhere, but Vicente keeps up ties with the *corralon* and has another younger unmarried sister living in a shack there. His eldest brother, Victor, still lives in Huasicancha. Each year, Victor comes down to Lima after he has planted his crops in the village and sells strawberries. He stays with Vicente or with one of the other two brothers living in Lima. If he finishes work late and does not want to travel out to his brothers, he stays the night with the unmarried sister.

The *corralon* has seventeen shacks in it, all inhabited by Huasicanchinos. Vicente is one of seven men who use the facilities of the inner city location, but do not actually live there. Since 1959, he has lived with his wife and four children in a *barriada* outside Lima. When he originally arrived in Lima he sold soft drinks in a poor market area. He then turned to fruit selling, progressing from ambulant basket seller to the more mobile tricycle seller as the years went by. Today Vicente pursues a multitude of activities. He has a contract to provide a certain number of strawberry-pickers to a hacienda near Lima each season. Throughout the year, he uses his old pre-war Ford pickup to transport fruit from the central wholesale market to the *corralon* where he and other Huasicanchinos keep their tricycles for easy access to fruit retailing in the central area. (Most of the *corralon* residents themselves are ambulant sellers or are involved in some occupation which – usually due to irregular night hours – makes it difficult for them to move to a *barriada*, even if they wanted to). Vicente therefore spends very important parts of the day at the *corralon* and most of his interaction with other Huasicanchinos centres around there, rather than the *barriada* where the nearest other Huasicanchinos live two or three streets away. He is at the *corralon* from 8.00 a.m. to 9.30 a.m. and often again at about 6.00 p.m. or 7.00 p.m. During this time, inevitably, village and migrant news is discussed and information exchanged.

Although Vicente spends from about 9.30 a.m. to 3.00 p.m. or 4.00 p.m. touring the streets with his tricycle, he is also involved in a number of other activities in the city. On the opposite side of Lima from the Hinojosa's *barriada* there is another, somewhat older, shanty town where a number of Huasicanchinos live. Beyond there can be found an area of small irrigated plots of land. With five other Huasicanchinos – four of whom live in the older shanty town - the Hinojosa family own and farm a plot of land. Although their ambition is to grow entirely cash crops, each year family demands make it necessary for them to grow a combination of subsistence and cash crops, with an emphasis on the former. Still further removed from the city, a truck journey of a least one and a half hours from the centre, Vicente has a small piggery. It comprises what at first appears to be a random pile of old bedsteads and bits of chicken wire, within which are found eight to ten surprisingly healthy-looking pigs which are largely fed on the spoilage from the fruit selling. What with his other commitments, Vicente cannot get to the piggery each day. But he is in partnership with seven other Huasicanchinos who also have makeshift sties and they take it in turn to make the daily visits.

During the strawberry season, which runs from November to the end of January and thus coincides with post-sowing slack periods in the village, Vicente spends the early morning supervising strawberry-picking on a hacienda near Lima. He pays the owner a set price and then sub-contracts to others who pick a controlled amount which they then sell on the streets of Lima during the remainder of the day. The business is fraught with conflicts since the *hacendado* has to unload large amounts of fruit when prices are low and often wishes to preserve his plants from overpicking when a sudden drought has driven prices up. He relies, therefore, on somebody who can control his workforce and who can expand or contract this force quite easily. Vicente uses both seasonal migrants from the village and residents of the inner city slum in order to carry out this task.

Finally, it is the younger, more recent, migrants who are most keen on social occasions and football playing. Since Vicente is a saxophone player, he is in much demand for such occasions. He spends virtually every Saturday night and Sunday, especially during the summer months, playing in a band, either in a second, city location, which has become the centre of such activities, or in one of the more recently formed shanty towns where the younger migrants are found.

Guillermina, Vicente's wife, is thirty-four and married Vicente in 1956 in Huasicancha. She works with him in their small arable plot of land and occasionally sells fruit from baskets (she never uses the tricycle). She does not work with the pigs and says that she only goes there very occasionally (although the wives of Vicente's other partners often do work there). Most of her working days are spent at the *barriada* residence, where she takes in washing from other households, although this is a very irregular source of income. All four children attend school. The oldest, a boy of fourteen, often takes over the ambulant fruit selling from his father in the afternoons, especially when demand is good or when, for some reason, Vicente has been slow on his rounds. The next two children are girls and Guillermina is continually listening for information in the *barriada* which would provide them with small, once-off jobs such as baby minding for a day or helping the neighbour with the market stall. The organization of all such occupations, in which Vicente is not directly involved himself, is in the hands of Guillermina. Both as a result of this and as a result of her involvement in the management of all the consumption dimensions of the household, she is the figure who gives the unit its organic integrity. It is almost as though Vicente's extroversion with respect of household affairs is based upon the secure foundation of Guillermina's management of affairs internal to the household itself.

While Guillermina maintains informal contacts with other Huasicanchinos in the *barriada* as well as with neighbours in her *manzana* (street), Vicente has daily contact with one inner city *corralon* and almost daily contact with another *barriada* besides his own, where his business partners live. He also has contact with another inner city location and on most weekends he finds himself in one or other of the more recently developed shanty towns. During any one year, the Hinojosa household has ties with village households whose members often stay with them while in the city, or contract with Vicente to pick strawberries, and from whom the family receives occasional sacks of subsistence items for consumption within the household.

The multiple sources of livelihood of the Hinojosa household may give the false impression that here are especially fortunate or even exceptionally astute Lima migrants. It is important that I dispel such an illusion. By most terms of reference the Hinojosa family would be termed as closer to the lumpenproletariat than to operators of small but permanent enterprises producing commodities, such as the tailor, cobbler, or mechanic, or even the *transportistas*, tricycle manufacturers and shopkeepers who are Huasicanchinos and to whom I have already referred. The Hinojosa operations lack the consolidation and capital-deepening which is characteristic of such petty commodity producers. Indeed, the family is constantly in the process of discussing and planning yet another branch to the domestic enterprise while at the same time, as a result of what they call 'unforeseen circumstances', withdrawing from some other branch.

On the other hand, the Hinojosa household is apparently able to draw on a greater variety of resources than those migrants – generally younger than Vicente, but not necessarily so – who rely almost entirely on one unstable occupation. In this respect, the Hinojosa family probably do not quite qualify as members of Marx's 'ghostly figures' outside the domain of conventional political economy.[8] If the Hinojosas appear to be especially fortunate *vis-à-vis* these other self-employed poor, it has much to do with the kind of organizational ties the household has which 'extend back' from the present operations of the enterprise. I use the term 'extend back' in two senses. There is an extension back in time to commitments to other households which began when Vicente and then his household migrated to Lima, and even well before that, as a result of commitments within the village itself. Secondly, the extension back is away from the market 'face' of the enterprise to the personal ties which are essential to the continued survival of the household as a viable livelihood earner from one year to the next.

The result of this latter dimension is that the rationality of the Hinojosa's own domestic enterprise is suffused with the rationality of the other domestic enterprises with which it shares ties. I refer to these kinds of arrangements as 'confederations of households'. In this sense, the Hinojosa domestic enterprise, extended though it appears to be, must be seen as just part of a greater set of relationships that may embrace enterprises situated in such widely separated economic areas as Huancayo, the refinery of La Oroya and the village of Huasicancha, as well as other areas of Lima itself.

Confederations of households: rural and urban

Traditionally, the household in Huasicancha was rarely such a well adjusted balance between needs and supplies that it could exist without building 'bridges outwards so that it may fulfil various needs' (Bailey, quoted in Epstein, 1973: 207). Not only were there the broader ties stemming from a vertically organized ecology, such as existed between the corn and coca growing jungle and the highland village, but also there was a narrower ecological range within the village based on interhousehold ties formed between those with predominant access to arable produce and those with predominant access to livestock resources. Interhousehold ties also existed as a result of differences in surplus labour available from one household to another. Traditionally, these ties were not found within the framework of an extended or corporate family structure, but rather operated through complex sets of ties which may or may not have been with kin and which were variously referred to as *uyay*, *minka*, *partidario*, *huaccha* and *michipa*. There is no space to go into these here, but I simply wish to stress that, although kinship may have acted as an important path along which these kinds of ties often moved, they were, and are, by no means confined to kin.[9]

Migration has, in recent years, become a means of broadening the economic base of the village domestic enterprise. The existence of interhousehold ties has meant that migration has not been a single-household affair, but has more generally occurred within the context of confederations of households. In such cases a modern version of vertical ecology takes place in which interdependence between climatic zones is replaced by ties between a range of economic 'zones'. [10] Arrangements are made between those whose major source of income derives from sheep farming, arable farming, entrepreneurial selling and wage labour. The various combinations are almost infinite. These differing economic activities are, in turn, reflected in differing locations of residence – the village, the mountain *estancia* (shepherd's corral and hut), the provincial town, the mines, Lima's inner city and Lima's *barriadas*.

Once again, as in the city, there is variation in the extent and nature of these interhousehold ties. While, as I have said, past experience has contributed to a continuance of attempts to gain footholds in a variety of economic niches, the composition of these niches varies from one confederation of households to another. There remain few households in Huasicancha, however, which do not have one or more economic ties to ex-residents in Huancayo, La Oroya or Lima. Nevertheless, economic polarization has occurred sufficiently that there are a small but significant number of households who are attempting to concentrate their resources at the expense of horizontal ties with their neighbours. And, matching their situation at the other end of the economic scale, there are a number of households who consistently fail to build up any lasting reciprocal relation with others, and rely largely on selling their labour, in one form or another, to the small number of households of the former kind. I have dealt with this process elsewhere (Smith, 1979) and am concerned here only with the 'middle peasant' households which are similar in their organization to the Hinojosa household.

Tomás and Ana Maria Palayo have just set up their own household. The Palayos are not especially wealthy and Tomás' father is not among those men remembered for having been especially prosperous at the height of his economic activity. Tomás had five years of primary schooling which he received in the village and, like 90 per cent of his peers, he can read and write. After his schooling, he spent four years in Lima at the house of his brother, where he contributed his labour to the running of his brother's domestic enterprise and also sold fruit and strawberries on his own account. He feels that this experience was especially useful because, he says, it has allowed him to 'learn the ropes' of fruit and strawberry selling while also enabling him to put aside a little cash. At eighteen, he returned to the village to get married. That was in 1966. Six years later, they had their own house, a modest flock of sheep and two small children to feed. Although the demands on Tomás' time are essentially seasonal, it is true to say that he spends at least 70 per cent of his time in the occupation of arable farmer. Since he is one of seven brothers of a not especially wealthy father, this activity is by no means a reflection of his share in the patrimony. In fact, his own holding of arable land is very small – about 2·8 hectares of very steep and rocky hillside.

Ana Maria brought no land with her. She is the illegitimate daughter of a widow who has just one surviving son from her *convivencia* (recognized partnership without formal marriage). Her mother has a sizeable herd of sheep but, six years after her marriage to Tomás, Ana Maria remained uncertain as to what her share of this flock is. Her half-brother has recently begun to spend more time at the *estancia*, no doubt to emphasize his own contribution to the flock, but Ana Maria spent virtually all her working life prior to her marriage shepherding the flock. Her mother recognizes her as her daughter and, if the greater part of this flock is indeed the progeny of Ana Maria's mother's animals and not of the mother's husband, Ana Maria should be able to claim at least one hundred sheep of the flock. Ana Maria, however, divides up her shepherding time between her mother's *estancia*, to which she has direct economic claims, and that of Tomás' brother Maglorio (see below) where her obligations to contribute some work are less direct, but are related to the extended economic ties of the couple's household, as I shall show.

Apart from shepherding, Ana Maria works the arable plots which they farm and processes food consumed from these plots: winnowing, milling and cooking grain, drying and cooking beans and so on. She also spins wool, which is woven, for household use, by a neighbour. She conducts all the household purchasing in the village and local markets, but travels less to the market town of Huancayo than does Tomás. Apart from cooking, cleaning up and child care, Ana Maria's work throughout the year is largely devoted to farming, of which marginally more time is spent on arable farming than shepherding (a ratio of 3:2)[11].

The form of the Palayos' domestic enterprise, however, is very much a function of the sources outside the immediate household on which it depends for its livelihood. In other words, the way in which labour is apportioned within the Palayo household is not just influenced by the goods and land which the couple received through inheritance. It is also strongly influenced by the composition of productive activities engaged in by those others with whom the Palayos have economic ties. Because of the limited network resulting from Ana Maria's upbringing on the lonely *estancia*, and her small number of family ties, these interhousehold connections are actualized through Tomás.

It is something of an over-simplification to suggest that the Palayos are arable farmers only to the extent that their own siblings are not so. But it does help to make the useful point that their involvement in non-farm sources of income is largely dependent upon their relationships to others who are variously committed to non-farm occupations. This will become clearer if I summarize the position of Tomás' siblings. But I should point out that, although these close family relationships give an extra resilience to the confederation of households which has evolved in this case, there are plenty of examples of confederations that are less reliant on sibling relationships.[12]

Tomás' eldest brother, Teófilo, is forty years old. For the past ten years, he has been a shop assistant in a Japanese hardware store in Huancayo. His six younger brothers consider him to be fortunate in having a regular and reasonably secure income and Teófilo is at least superficially the most affluent of the brothers, with a large adobe house in the provincial town. He is the only one of the brothers earning a regular wage and there is a sense in which Teófilo's livelihood is a mirror-image of Tomás', the younger brother. Teófilo recognizes a need to diversify the sources of his income, just as does Tomás, but for him his wage income provides the predominant form of support, complemented by other non-farm, largely seasonal activities gained through ties with other domestic enterprises, one of which is Tomás'.

The next eldest son, Grimaldo, lives in Lima. Like Vicente Hinojosa in the first of the case studies, Grimaldo lives in a *barriada* but, through his diverse economic activities, he has ties with migrants spread throughout the city. He is a fruit seller. He also has a small plot of land some way out of the city where, in partnership with others, he has a household-plant nursery. When Grimaldo was eighteen, he finished school and went to Huancayo. His small income in various jobs during that time helped to support Teófilo, the eldest brother, who was then attempting to finish secondary school. After Teófilo finished school, however, Grimaldo moved on, getting a job for a couple of years in the mines of La Oroya and eventually arriving in the inner city location which I have already described in the first case study.

When any of the brothers go to Lima, it is with Grimaldo that they lodge and he, in turn, keeps a number of livestock with another of the brothers, Maglorio, who is well-known in the village as a good herder. Teófilo does the same thing, having over one hundred head of sheep distributed among villagers. Tomás works the fields of both these migrant brothers. The land which Grimaldo farms just outside Lima was bought partially with his own capital deriving from the fruit selling business, but also with capital derived from the wages of Teófilo.

The next eldest brother, Maglorio, as I have just mentioned, is predominantly a livestock herder, and Tomás and Ana Maria work some of his arable land for him. The next brother is a carpenter in the village and is the only one with a saleable skill. Although he is a farmer in the village, he has, on occasion, migrated to Lima where he has had little difficulty getting work on construction sites. The next brother, Liberato, is, at present, the least successful, being a porter in Huancayo market for much of the year, and so far he has not managed to establish any significant relationships with his brothers. Tomás' ties to this brother are, in many ways, very interesting. The two of them might well have come into conflict with one another, but for the fact that Liberato married a woman with a large flock of sheep and is more intensely tied into a confederation revolving around his affines. These two brothers were talking of going into rabbit farming together, and Liberato was planning on migrating for two years to earn some extra cash for this purpose.

To this cast of characters, there is space only to provide illustrative scenes. At one point, Tomás needed some emergency cash and Teófilo, in Huancayo, gave him the job of illicitly getting rid of some black-market goods around Huancayo. On another occasion, Teófilo, who was in the village for a fiesta, remarked that having his livestock distributed all over the place was too inconvenient for his accounts and business operations, and that he would like to consolidate. Grimaldo, the brother in Lima, on the other hand, is finding that he cannot provide the necessary labour to keep his various city enterprises going and is constantly calling upon an increasingly reluctant group of village brothers to help him out. It is the combination of all these various kinds of contradictions and pressures which gives the confederation its form and influences the activities of the different domestic enterprises which make it up.

The form of household production – what tasks are performed, as well as the division of labour – cannot only be explained by reference to the internal demographic and capital resources of the household. These variations must also be traced to the influence on household production of the changing developments in Peruvian capitalism (Smith, 1979). However, I have chosen not to concentrate on this determinant here; rather, I have tried to reveal the relationship between a household's position within a network of interlocking ties and the types of livelihood in which its members get involved. These interhousehold ties have a strong influence on the specific form that the household economy takes in each case.

In October 1972, for example, Tomás decided, for the first time, not to migrate to Lima for the strawberry selling season. Whether he went or not, he said, depended on whether Liberato decided to migrate for two years to get capital for the rabbit farm. It also reflected, I would argue, a deeper trend which was that Tomás' position within this particular confederation was pushing him increasingly into subsistence production in the village. This trend belies his stated plans to go into a partnership with Liberato to form a rabbit farm since, in fact, Liberato's migration is having the effect of further pushing Tomás towards agricultural labour. He now has Liberato's fields to add to those he already tills. Secondly, any arrangement he might one day make with this, his youngest brother will certainly threaten his existing arrangements with others in the confederation. Indeed, Tomás, like Vicente Hinojosa, has many plans, but resembles a man rushing round a bonfire on a windy night trying to get the tinder to light – just as one project takes hold, another is extinguished.

Conclusions

This chapter gives some idea of the variety of socio-economic forms which can arise when non-farm resources become an important element in the reproduction of the peasant farm. This statement is apparently self-contradictory. But it serves to emphasize the difficulty of seeing any single trend in the transformation of the peasant farm. On the one hand, family farms are maintained; on the other, participation in non-farm occupations ransom their survival at the expense of their continual loss of autonomy and possibly the eventual total proletarianization of their members. In this particular example, the way in which households link up with one another to form a confederation against the attack on their viability provides just one expression of this paradoxical process.

I shall limit myself here to saying something about the conditions in which confederations exist, the dynamics of their fragmentation and reformulation and, finally, I shall comment on the economic rationality of such enterprises.

In the cases which I have presented here, it is clear that the common feature of the domestic enterprise throughout history – be it in the city or in the village – has been the extreme instability of any single source of support. In the village, livestock rearing became increasingly threatened by the expanding hacienda (Smith and Cano, 1978) and arable cropping at such high altitudes was subject to great variations. In the city, the unpredictable nature of fruit selling was reduced as more Huasicanchinos became involved in the activity; it nevertheless remained a risky occupation.[13]

Confederations – of which migration became but one dimension – were a means of minimizing risk and uncertainty by embracing different forms of productive enterprise over a wide area, such as occurred in the past when interhousehold relationships attempted to take advantage of the Andean vertical ecology. However, over time, these confederations have generated their own rationality and I have attempted to show this in the case study of the Hinojosa family which was, as it were, that part of the iceberg most visible in the city. Indeed, in studying the workings of any one confederation, so interrelated are the various households which make it up, that it becomes difficult to isolate the household unit as the most suitable unit for study. While production and consumption decisions do take place within these units, the factors taken into account have much to do with the situation of other members of the confederation. Hence the degree of risk to be undertaken in a particular operation depends on the comparable risks faced by others of the confederation (not simply the degree of risk, but whether or not it is a risk of the same kind e.g. being laid off versus over-extending capital invested in stock). Similarly, investment in capital equipment will depend upon the cash needs of other confederation members, since such needs would prevent the tying up of cash in equipment.

The same is also true with respect to the way in which the domestic enterprise makes use of labour. Were this simply a function of the enterprise's commitment to the domestic unit as a pool of labour, a kind of Chayanovian rationality might prevail. But, as the cases clearly illustrate, each domestic enterprise adjusts the strategy of its labour use to conditions arising in the other units of the confederation. Factors affecting the use of labour, therefore, are neither perfectly Chayanovian, nor perfectly capitalist.

What this means is that the internal rationality of any one domestic enterprise is crucially a function of its relationship to others. The specific features of each of these others feed back on the original unit, making it very hard – for both operators and ethnographer alike – to envisage the domestic unit apart from these linkages.

Nevertheless, this interdependence should not be overstated. The kin ties and strong sentiments of community membership of Huasicanchinos provide institutional channels through which production relations are expressed. One such institution is the confederation. This is a dynamic relationship experiencing fragmentation and reformulation resulting from the changing economic requirements of each household unit (for labour, for capital, for access to differing sectors of the economy etc.). One enterprise might release itself from the confederation or there may be an overall slackening of obligations among members. Some families may then seek new sets of alliances or, for one reason or another, remain isolated from such intricate ties.

To get at the causes of this dynamic process, it is important to recognize the connection between the imperatives of household production and the social institutions which are used to meet those imperatives. Such imperatives are essentially of two kinds. Firstly, a division of labour on the basis of family roles within the domestic unit affects the interhousehold relationships as the family progresses through its generational cycle (Chayanov, 1966). This puts the confederations in a perpetual state of schism and reformulation. One household hitherto able to provide extra labour to other members, for example, may find one son marrying and setting up on his own, while another (perhaps precisely through the connections offered by the confederation) goes off to the mines. This changes the relationships both to confederates needing labour and to this household's previous ties to wage labour and the mining sector which can now be replaced by the unmarried son.

Secondly, there are imperatives which derive from beyond the household and refer to the other set of linkages (besides the confederations) enmeshing the household unit, namely those tying it to specific sectors of the Peruvian economy. As changes occur in the composition of the Peruvian economy, so households linked to differing sectors of the economy are affected differentially, and this affects the schisms which occur in confederations.

The emergence of a contradiction between the imperatives of the household enterprise and the institution of the particular confederation into which that household is tied usually expresses itself in the form of a succession of failures to meet obligations to other confederate members. This often begins as a reflection of changes in household composition as described above, but may then be exacerbated as the household begins to initiate new alliances, thus introducing itself into a new, and more appropriate, confederation. In other cases, the enterprise cannot, or will not, activate new alliances but gradually releases itself from any confederation. Needless to say, other households are unable so easily to discard the obligations accrued through the confederation and hence remain involved, as one informant put it, 'like a fly in a web, struggling to be free and each time getting more caught'.

This last statement suggests that confederations of households are not always equally advantageous to all members. This, together with the fact that developments in particular sectors of the economy affect enterprises differentially, suggests that the institution of confederations of households may give rise to exploitation between households. The idiom of reciprocity appropriate to the confederations acts to disguise this process and, in some cases, explains the continued participation of the more prosperous members. In another, more detailed, study I have examined the extent to which it is possible for these confederations to allow exploitation of one household by another (Smith, 1975).

Once a particular enterprise becomes more productive than its associates, it faces two conflicting tendencies. On the one hand, not only does the confederation continue to offer labour, for example, at a cheaper rate than the open market, but also other households may attempt to keep the enterprise within the net of obligations as a means, however ineffectual, of in some way benefiting from the more productive enterprise. Such a situation constrains the enterprise from leaving the confederation. On the other hand, the greater productivity of the unit encourages its members to adopt a more strictly capitalist rationale, trying to lock up cash and labour within the enterprise, where returns are greater, rather than in the confederation as a whole. Such incipient capitalists can be seen to be beginning to isolate themselves from other households, often through a series of events whose logical outcome is not entirely clear to them.

In certain branches, the resources on which the operation is based are quite finite. This is the case, for example, for livestock farming, where pasture is limited. In such circumstances, the expansion of the incipient capitalists acts to restrict further the resources for others, increasing their instability and thus encouraging them to maintain their risk-spreading confederations. The anti-social character of these enterprises is thus manifested in the combination of their attempt to minimize interhousehold obligations and their predatory expansion. The conflicts which arise therefrom act as one of a number of factors placing a strict limitation on the long-term success of any one incipient capitalist enterprise.

I believe that the evidence provided by this very small sample suggests that the economic rationality of small-scale enterprises in the informal sector are extremely complex and varied. While it makes it extremely difficult to apply abstract models – for example of simple petty commodity production (Friedmann, 1980; Kahn, 1980: 130–50) – to such enterprises, I do not think that it renders the task of uncovering such economic rationality fruitless. It merely implies a demand for greater empirical information.

Before suggesting observations, albeit minimal, about the rationality of these enterprises, I wish to distinguish here between rationality, logic and rationale. By the logic of a particular form of production, I am referring to imperatives emergent from the structural features of that form of production. This is connected to, but on a quite distinctive analytic plane from, the decisions made by participants, which I refer to as their economic rationale. The developmental logic of a particular form of production is only partly a function of the decisions of participants in that form of production. Likewise, inasmuch as participants cannot be aware of all the historical and conjunctural forces which bear on the development of the form of production in which they are engaged, so, too, their economic rationale is only partly emergent from the economic rationality of the form of production.[14] There is a distinction between the ineluctable logic of capitalism and the rationale with which each capitalist makes a decision.

This distinction is important for understanding the household units discussed here (and I am concentrating only on those having some connection with the confederations discussed above, not on all Huasicanchino households in the informal sector). In any discussion of domestic production, it is useful to distinguish between the production of use values, the production of commodities and the sale of labour for a wage. Like most peasant households, many Huasicanchino households engaged in all three forms of livelihood, in varying degrees. With the penetration of capitalism the peasant jack-of-all-trades has not been replaced by a more specialized peasant, but by a more diversified one. Nevertheless, the social cost of the skills and equipment necessary for this diversification has increased relative to any one household's buying power. Confederations tie households into these three forms of livelihood, while allowing each household to take best advantage of local conditions for one or other of them. In a sense, households participating in confederations have diversified while at the same time specializing.

This makes for some difficulty in assessing the various characteristics of the household as an economic unit. Where the entire source of livelihood for a household is derived from wage labour, it may be possible to draw some conclusions about the economic rationality of that unit. Where a male labourer in a household migrates to the mines, while women maintain the farm production for that household, the situation is rendered more complicated. But, in the cases discussed here, there are household units all of whose members are engaged entirely in wage labour or commodity production, but which are nevertheless subsidized by the production of use values through linkages with the confederation. Thus, many household enterprises ostensibly engaged in one main livelihood – such as petty commodity production in the city – are, in fact, closely tied to the logic of another – such as subsistence production of use values in Huasicancha. The variety of 'mixes' possible for each household makes the assessment of its logic as an economic enterprise a complicated task.

Nevertheless, the confederations provide linkages between different sectors of the economy and, in each sector, surplus is extracted more or less efficiently and in a variety of ways. This means that household enterprises strongly committed to one sector of the economy may be able to take advantage of other sectors, both because of the greater productivity of their sector and, also, because of the fact that they make use of use values produced within the confederation itself. Thus, despite demands to spread investments, there are always some households attempting to withhold resources from circulation throughout the confederation. The need to invest capital within the enterprise acts to push such an enterprise away from confederations. But its frequent need for cheap labour, often for once-off jobs and often where remuneration for work done may be delayed and, even then, take a variety of forms – all these are factors pulling such an enterprise back into the household confederation.

At the other extreme are those households who find it increasingly difficult to maintain the obligations of the confederation. As one operator in Lima began to lose contract business for his small workshop, he was unable to continue to offer seasonal jobs to family members of two confederate households in Huasicancha. They, in turn, began to lose interest in caring for his land or livestock. He therefore had to send his son back to the village. The loss of the skilled labour of the son led to a further reduction in business, eventually resulting in the collapse of the workshop and in the household's inability to participate in any confederation.

Between these two extremes, the confederations maintain their resilience; the economic rationality of each unit depending upon the 'mix' of its operations, its linkages to other units and the constraints of the economy at large. It would be misleading to discern an historical trend towards the polarization of enterprises or the increasing separation of manufacturing and commercial from agricultural ventures. And this may often be so despite the intentions of participants. It was precisely those informants most firmly embedded in confederations who most strongly voiced the economic rationale of individual (household) accumulation with no obligations to those beyond the household. In contrast, it was those whose past five years' history revealed a trend towards increasing accumulation within the enterprise, towards the use of wage labour and a growing trend towards avoiding the reciprocal ties of the confederation of which they were members who most vigorously contrasted the immorality of capitalism with the need for Huasicanchinos to stick together and share their personal strength resourcefully.

These conclusions clearly raise a host of questions for further investigation. This chapter has concentrated on revealing the complexity of the economic relationships which exist among Huasicanchino domestic enterprises, in this case not just located within the city but extending across different sectors of the economy and covering a wide geographical area.

11

Regional development in peripheral economies

In this chapter, we aim to place the foregoing accounts within a broader framework of analysis by exploring the usefulness of a regional focus for understanding processes of development in Latin America. In particular, we examine how far the central highlands region has retained its identity and economic vitality in the face of the continuing centralization of the Peruvian economy.

In chapter one, we argued for adopting a production rather than a marketing and exchange approach to regional analysis. From the case materials presented it should now be clear why we chose to do so. The business class of the city of Huancayo did not depend significantly in any historical period upon its ability to control local markets. Its members made little attempt, for example, to monopolize trade in agricultural or craft products. Rather, their main source of wealth derived from the services they provided the mining economy, their investments in enterprises and, to a lesser extent, their monopolies on the sale of imported manufactures. A similar process occurred at village level, since the main source of capital for local entrepreneurship was savings from work in the mining or plantation economy.

Consequently, the development of a periodic market system in the area cannot be interpreted simply as the outcome of widespread and locally based commercial development and a resulting increase in intra-regional specialization. This market system was consolidated in the 1920s and 1930s, with itinerant traders circulating between markets held in different places on different days of the week (Arguedas, 1957). The main stimulus for the development of this market system was the earnings derived from the rapid increase in wage labour in the mines and plantations and the accompanying increased monetization of the local economy. Later, the importance of this periodic market system declined as the economy became more closely integrated into the urban economy of the coast through migration and the

235

marketing of various foodstuffs. Even the smallest of villages of the area have been able to establish direct marketing relationships with Lima in the contemporary period, and thus are rarely dependent upon any larger local centre. Furthermore, within villages, different producers and traders often use different direct outlets for their goods. Indeed, our surveys of the different local markets demonstrated that outside traders from larger centres play a relatively unimportant role.

It is for these reasons that we place so much emphasis on the analysis of the changing interrelations between different sectors of production as a means of understanding a region's development and identity. Focussing on production is also interesting because it directs attention to transformations in the local economy that acquire their own dynamic and become sources of variation in regional and national development. Changes in production give rise to new class interests and reshape class organization; the conflicts and alliances that result impose their imprint on a region, limiting its range of economic options or, perhaps, opening up new possibilities.

Thus, we use the notion of region as a heuristic device to draw attention to the ways in which local institutions and economic practices in a given area are shaped by direct and indirect involvement with a dominant form or forms of production. Unlike the use of region in market-place oriented analysis, we are less concerned with identifying clearly demarcated geographical units, since the hinterland upon which dominant enterprises depend for labour and other resources can be highly dispersed or may be spatially compact. Instead, we prefer to identify and differentiate regions by reference to the systems of linkages that develop over time between dominant forms of production and the settlements, social groups and economic enterprises within their zones of influence.

Uneven development and capitalist and non-capitalist forms of production

The interdependencies between new forms of production and pre-existing ones are indeed crucial factors shaping the structure of regions in underdeveloped countries, since the survival of certain pre-existing forms has been part of the logic of accumulation on a world scale. This view is consistent with that of De Janvry and Garramon who argue that 'the objective needs of sustained capital accumulation . . . in the centre imply (1) market expansion in the centre and (2) cheapening of raw materials and of specific wage goods through imports from the periphery . . . and increased rate of profit on exported capital to the periphery . . . In the periphery, cheap exports of raw materials and of specific wage goods and high rates of profit result from suppressing (1) the value and price of the labour force . . . and (2) the price of exportables' (De Janvry and Garramon, 1977: 215). An important element in their argument is that the cheapening of labour is produced by what they call 'social disarticulation' (cf. Amin, Vol. 1, 1974: 15–17).[1] Social disarticulation means that even though semi-subsistence farmers may participate in the modern economy through producing export crops or through temporary wage labour, this sector of the population does not significantly participate in the consumption of modern goods. Indeed, the exclusion of labour from such consumption, which includes modern social and economic infrastructure as well as consumer goods, is what basically cheapens the cost of this labour. In chapter three, we showed how modern mining enterprise in the cental highlands profited from such cheap peasant labour.

Export-oriented production in underdeveloped countries has been closely geared to the needs and functioning of the central economies. Whilst the predominant type of production has changed with time (i.e. the change from extraction of precious to non-precious metals, or from agricultural to industrial production), the persistence of the centre–periphery relationship in the world economy has entailed that the system of production in the periphery often retains the same basic tendency: the cheapening of production costs through the way in which the export sector relates to 'traditional' and semi-subsistence forms of production.

It would be wrong, however, to focus upon the centre–periphery distinction to the exclusion of other countervailing tendencies. It is clear, for example, that economic growth, diversification and the expansion of internal markets has taken place, and continues to take place, in peripheral economies, despite their dependence on the centres of capitalist production. To focus on the way in which existing forms of production are *adapted* to capitalist production runs the danger of underemphasizing the extent to which new forms of economic opportunity are *created* in the periphery. Assadourian (1982) argues that the insertion of the Latin American economies into the European system had, from colonial times, the consequence of increasing the amount of exchange-value (expressed in commodity circulation) as against use-value in the economy. Hence, increasing commercialization of the colonial economies not only facilitated accumulation in the centre, but increased the possibilities for accumulation at the periphery. Integration into the European economy, therefore, set in motion a process of economic differentiation and diversification in the peripheral economies which, within certain limits, led to capital accumulation at the provincial level. Indeed, the more closely that a Latin American region or country was tied into the European economy, the more likely it was that substantial economic differentiation and diversification would occur. As Assadourian (1982) points out, in criticizing Frank's (1969) view, isolation from the metropolitan economy could only lead to a return to subsistence-based production, not to a more balanced type of economic growth. On the other hand, the external appropriation of most of the surplus led to a weak development of the internal market and hindered the development of capitalist production outside the export sector. Manufacturing industry was slow to develop in Latin American countries, as was capitalist farming for the domestic market.

This is the structural context which has determined the specific character-istics of the systems of production that developed in the various regions of Latin America. They were, in different ways, organized around the securing and maintenance of cheap labour. This is clearly brought out in the discussion by Palerm (1976: 26–43) of the articulation between mines, haciendas and indigenous communities in colonial Mexico. Palerm argues that the dominant economy was mining and that the economy of haciendas and communities was directly and indirectly regulated to the benefit of the mining centres. Thus, haciendas were often owned by mine owners and were run to produce low-cost products for the mines and their resident populations. The low cost of these products increased the profitability of mining operations and tended to set price levels for commercial production of foodstuffs in a situation where the mining centres constituted the major urban populations. Hence, the apparent low returns from hacienda production were not due to an inefficient or tech-nologically backward production system, but to the priority which mining had in the colonial system in which agricultural production was also burdened with state and church taxes.[2] In turn, the haciendas made use of the indigenous communities as a cheap labour reserve, as a source of land and as a source of agricultural techniques.

The Mexican hacienda made use of a variety of forms of labour which included slavery, share-cropping, tenant farming, forced labour and wage labour. These forms were combined in different periods and under different conditions to meet the demands of the market and to provide a low-cost product. Indeed, Palerm points out that in those areas where there were no indigenous communities, such as in the northern mining zones, the large haciendas created a dependent network of smallholders, ranchers and share-croppers. Thus mining shaped the nature of regional economies, producing new patterns of settlement in unpopulated regions and definitively altering the nature of Indian settlement in the densely populated areas of the central plateau. In fact, Palerm (1976: 41) suggests that the indigenous community, as it developed in the colonial period, could almost be regarded as an institution planned to ensure the economic efficiency of the haciendas. Palerm makes the point that it is the colonial regime that made possible, through legal and fiscal controls and incentives, this close articulation between mines, haciendas and communities.

The clearest regional expression of such a colonial system of production was the Bajio area of north central Mexico (Brading, 1971; Wolf, 1957). There, the large and extremely profitable mining sector brought into being flourishing industrial and commercial centres, highly commercialized haciendas relying on debt peonage, and stimulated small-scale commercial farming on more marginal lands. This was the area of 'open' communities in which ethnic distinctions were eroded and which created a freer more mercantile ethos which, by the end of the colonial period, was seen as a direct threat to the colonial administration itself.

An example of this type of analysis outside Latin America, and extending more into the contemporary period, is Geertz's (1963a) study of Dutch colonial rule in Indonesia, which examines the impact of the plantation system on peasant agriculture and on local urban development. Geertz shows the ways in which this system of production both built upon, and partially transformed, the household economy of peasant farmers: 'The Javanese cane worker remained a peasant at the same time that he became a coolie, persisted as a community-orientated household farmer at the same time that he became an industrial wage labourer . . . And, in order for him to maintain this precarious and uncomfortable stance not only did the estate have to adapt to the village through the land-lease system and various other "native-protection" devices forced on it by an "ethical" colonial government, but, even more comprehensively, the village had to adapt to the estate' (Geertz, 1963a: 89–90).

Geertz uses the term 'involution' to describe the specific pattern of change and adaptation which took place in local-level economic and social practices. By 'involution' he means the process by which existing social patterns become internally more elaborate and intricate. This occurs in relation to land tenure, cropping arrangements and work organization, but is also manifested in the character of village and religious institutions. One important economic consequence of this adaptational process is that increasingly more labour can be absorbed into peasant agriculture and petty trade. Thus, in the economic, as in other spheres, the incorporation of Indonesia into the world economy does not promote full rationalization at local level leading to capital accumulation, proletarianization and 'modern' forms of political and social organization. Geertz argues that this involutionary process continued to affect the development of Indonesia even after the end of colonial rule and the decline of the plantation economy.

The main aim of our discussion so far has been to argue the case for viewing production and changes in production as the central issues in characterizing regional structures and patterns of development. The analysis of production draws attention to the impact of the international economy on peripheral regions in a more complex way than does the analysis of exchange and distribution. In particular, it explains the persistence and even emergence of seemingly 'archaic' forms of production with capitalist expansion. This focus also raises the question of the extent to which different forms of production (both dominant and subordinate) have a reciprocal effect on each other, leading to regionally specific patterns of social and economic development. It also helps to explain how a pattern of economic dualism can persist despite intense exchanges between sectors of high and low labour productivity – a situation characteristic of the Peruvian economy, as we showed in chapters three and seven.

Regional systems of production

Hirschman's (1977) generalized linkage approach offers a useful statement concerning the question of how differences in systems of production affect social structure. He draws upon the staple theory of economic development which concentrates on the way national or regional economies are shaped by the specific production or extraction requirements of the primary products exported to world markets. These requirements include income distribution, processing and transport functions (Hirschman, 1977; Brookfield, 1975: 93–7).

Hirschman's view is a more comprehensive one of the impact of staples. Thus he extends the linkage concept to include the consumption patterns generated by the staple and to take account of whether or not a staple stimulates the development of the state and its fiscal mechanisms. He is interested in whether the staples are owned nationally or not and whether they are owned by a few or a large number of owners, claiming that such factors will shape institutional developments such as the readiness of the state to create fiscal apparatus. Hirschman's major point is that we should pay more attention to the dialectical process that is involved in the expansion of any system of production. This production process creates new class interests and the possibility of contradictions between them. An expanding system of production entails clashes of interest between those committed to the new forms of production and those whose position is threatened by their growth. For example, labour may be attracted away from older forms of production by high wages, and these older forms may find that the policies advocated by the new interests, such as tariff reform, are counter to their own. One can extend this approach by taking into account the types of labour required for different types of staple and industrial production, the political institutions needed to obtain such labour and the implications of these processes for the existing agrarian structure and for the types of class struggle that take place.

Hirschman in fact labels his approach a 'micro-Marxist' one, thus emphasizing the importance he attaches to the political and ideological forces brought into being by the rise of a new system of production and which, in turn, shape economic development itself. This approach is interesting for developing a regional analysis since it implies that within the general framework of the expansion of capitalism one can identify variations in the nature of regional economic and political development consequent upon differences in the labour, capital and technical requirements of particular processes of production. As Morse (1975) points out, the issue is the particular *system* of production and not the inherent production characteristics of crops or other staple products: coffee, for example, is produced under a wide variety of different forms of production and on farms of very different size. Wheat production in the Mid-West of the United States, during the nineteenth century, was based on homesteads, a thriving system of small towns, middlemen and an active popular political participation (Rothstein, 1966); yet, the differences between the Mid-West and the development experiences of Argentina and Chile, where wheat has also been an important staple, indicate that it is mistaken to see wheat production as necessarily encouraging 'egalitarian' and 'democratic' patterns of organization.

A system of production, then, acquires its specific characteristics from the socio-political context in which it evolves. Thus, prevailing legal and political institutions sanction certain forms of labour recruitment and organization, facilitating or discouraging the use, for example, of slave labour, debt peonage or wage labour. Likewise, the nature and strength of the state determine the ways in which the production entrepreneur controls his labour supply, adopting paternalistic and despotic strategies in the face of a weak state or relying on more indirect or market forms of labour control when the state actively supports the expansion of economic enterprises. Another variable of importance is thus the nature of the labour supply, its location and characteristics. For example, the establishment of large-scale production in countries such as Peru took place in the context of a pool of relatively abundant indigenous labour living in independent smallholder communities. In Brazil, in contrast, first slave and then free wage labour had to be imported to meet the needs of sugar and coffee production because of sparse population and poor communications.

Apart from such social and political variables, which contribute to the diversity of production forms evolving around the same product, there are certain ecological and technical constants which constrain the organization of production. The extraction of minerals in a highland area often occurs in zones distant from population concentration and which, because of altitude and terrain, are not suited to cultivation. Mining areas are, consequently, functionally linked to areas of peasant farming, often at a considerable distance, which provide both foodstuffs and a supply of relatively permanent labour. Tropical export crops, on the other hand, are located in lowland areas. In the case of many of these crops, foodstuff cultivation is possible on or near the plantations, although fluctuating and seasonally based labour demands still link plantations to peasant cultivation. This creates, as the earlier quotation from Geertz indicates, an annual production cycle that includes both export and subsistence crops using different technologies.

The technical requirements of some forms of production are inevitably more sophisticated than those of others. Thus, where the value per unit of weight of the product is low (e.g. crude ore or sugar cane), it is likely that fairly sophisticated and high-cost technologies will be used to reduce weight close to the place of production, creating, among other things, a permanently settled, concentrated and task-differentiated workforce. In contrast, some products (e.g. coffee) require only a few simple operations (drying and bagging, for instance) and their value per unit of weight justifies the producer himself transporting them to market. This last situation makes it easier for small-scale entrepreneurs to both enter into production and to retain control over it, including diversification into commerce and transport operations, than is the case in mineral and sugar production (Hirschman, 1977: 77–80).

The historical context of regional diversity in Latin America

A system of production approach is not sufficient to understand the variety of regional systems without taking into account the particular historical context in which 'regions' emerged. It was during the agro-mining stage of the incorporation of Latin America into the world economy that the regional unit as a system of production, and 'regionalism' as a political force, achieved their fullest development. But, when generalizing this type of analysis to peripheral areas, it is essential to consider not simply their integration into the world economy but also the nature and extent of that integration. Latin America is exceptional among underdeveloped areas both for its very early incorporation into the world economy and for the intensity of its commercial exchanges with capitalist countries, although even within Latin America there are areas which have played only a minor role in the export economy.

Recent historical work has emphasized the diverse ways in which regions and sub-regions of Latin America developed under the stimulus of the world market in the nineteenth and early twentieth centuries. More important in generating this diversity than the wide range of products then required by the European markets was the fact that they were produced under widely differing sociopolitical conditions. These included differences in labour supply, land tenure and degree of political centralization.[3] One result of this was to reinforce regionalism, creating divergent patterns of development within, as well as between, countries. Thus, Moreno and Florescano (1974) point to the bypassing of pre-existing colonial trade axes as a result of the direct trade relationships that developed in nineteenth century Mexico through ports and frontier towns between British traders and regional elites. Provincial regional centres, such as Guadalajara and, later, Monterrey and Merida, grew more rapidly than did Mexico City. It was only at the end of the nineteenth century, with the centralization imposed by strong central state authority and reinforced by the railway network, that Mexico City recovered its predominant role.

Regional variations were important even under the apparently highly centralized pattern of development in late nineteenth century Argentina. Balán (1978) argues that Argentinian export growth, even though it mainly benefited the landed elites of the Buenos Aires area, still created economic opportunities for regionally located bourgeoisies. The examples he uses are the sugar planters of Tucuman and the wine traders and growers of Mendoza (Balán, 1979). Political stability was an important condition of capitalist expansion; but this stability depended on alliances between the dominant Buenos Aires groups and provincial oligarchies whose support was granted in return for some share in the benefits of the agro-exporting boom. In Tucuman, for example, sugar production became a profitable venture in the late nineteenth century, with the development of large markets in the urban agglomerations of the Buenos Aires region. These opportunities were created through the construction of a railway, through protective tariffs and through securing, by legislation and police activity, a labour supply. These concerns involved the planter class in national politics (Balán, 1978).

The Argentinian case, as Balán points out, is exceptional because of the nation's rapid integration and development as a capitalist economy, due to the weakness of previous economic and social structures and to the scale of export growth, railway construction and international immigration of free labour. Yet, the diverse patterns of regional growth and the class interests and conflicts that they created have continued to be reflected in patterns of regional inequality. As he puts it: 'spatial systems have "strong memories" carrying with them, so to speak, traces of social relationships established in previous times' (Balán, 1978: 152).

Hence, there is a strong case for arguing that the regional diversity created by the burst of export-led growth in the nineteenth and early twentieth centuries is one of the crucial factors explaining the forms of national political integration that developed in most countries of Latin America by the 1940s. Even the centralizing regime that developed in Brazil under Getulio Vargas (1930–54) reflected the heterogeneity of regional economic interests. Vargas' populist strategy included labour legislation which was based, in part, on the concerns of the São Paulo industrialists. This legislation was not, however, made effective in regions such as the north-east where the dominant land owners kept their labour force tied to them through extra-economic measures. Lopes (1978), in fact, argues that populist politics represented, in part, the continuing strength of regional interests in national political life.

A similar line of argument could be used to understand Peruvian development in the late nineteenth and early twentieth centuries. The development of distinct regional identities in regions such as Trujillo, the central highlands and the Arequipa and Puno regions brought into play heterogeneous economic and political forces which underlie the shifts and compromises that hindered the development of a strong modernizing central state. This process was reflected, for example, in the emergence and continuing strength of the Peruvian populist party APRA which was based on the diverse class interests created by regionalized expansion of export production. This party was particularly strong in the Trujillo region but also had important bases of support in the central highlands.[4]

The most successful case of an 'independent' pattern of regional development in Peru was, however, that of Arequipa. We noted in chapter three that, in contrast to the central highlands, Arequipa had higher levels of locally generated productive investment and a more extensive administrative infrastructure. The dominant class of Arequipa was based on the control of wool production. The railway opened up the whole southern region to the commerce of Arequipa and the city became the place of residence of important merchants and landowners. Foreign capital was important in the initial development of the city and region but, by the beginning of the First World War, a significant group of national entrepreneurs had emerged from amongst local families (Flores Galindo et al., 1977a). Wool trade and production, unlike mining, did not lend itself to monopolization by foreign capital.

Livestock-raising often remained based on traditional forms of production and new techniques had limited success. The dispersed nature of production throughout the southern highlands and the dependence of many producers on credit created opportunities for a local merchant class which could establish relationships throughout the region. Commercial production of sugar and cotton in the coastal valley areas of Arequipa allowed for the consolidation of modern estates which became another basis for Arequipa's capitalist class. This class had to struggle to maintain its control over local resources in the face of the attempts of foreign companies to establish monopolies. However, in contrast to the situation we described for the central highlands, the Arequipa oligarchy was successful in maintaining sufficient political cohesion to defend their position both locally and nationally (Flores Galindo et al., 1977b).

In the twentieth century, the pattern of regionalized economic growth begins to be eroded by the strength of centralizing forces in the Latin American economies. These forces result from the increasing importance of industry and the development and integration of the internal market for industrial products. By the late 1970s, almost all Latin American countries had a greater share of their Gross Domestic Product contributed by industry than by agriculture. Thus, industrial growth has tended to concentrate in one or two of the largest national centres, attracted by the presence there of consumer demand, by an available infrastructure and by the advantage of proximity to the centres of political power. Yet, although industrial growth has mainly been capital intensive it has, as many commentators have pointed out, generated income opportunities in other sectors of the urban economy, including petty trade, workshop production and personal services, such as domestic employment (Roberts, 1978b: chapter 5). It is this concentrated pattern of economic growth that underlies the increasing flow of migrants from provincial areas to the major urban centres.

Increasing centralization tends to break down the coherence of regional systems of production because: (a) the urban–industrial centre establishes direct linkages, through migration and the flow of goods, with villages and towns within a region; (b) the dominant regional forms of production, such as mining and plantations, do not expand local income opportunities sufficiently to keep pace with population increase and to counter the attraction of urban–industrial centres; and (c) because the new enterprises, established by private or government initiative, in provincial regions are highly capital intensive, often with few labour or product linkages within the area.

However, the impact of centralization on provincial regions, by under-mining local labour-intensive production activities, often generates regionally based opposition to government policies. For example, in Arequipa, new industrial plants are highly capital intensive and, in milk processing, concentrate production, negatively affecting small-scale dairy farmers. This situation has provoked widespread and serious political disturbance in the region that has challenged both the military government and the subsequent civilian government.

The transformation of the regional economy of the central highlands

The linkage approach can now be applied to summarize the data for the central highlands in the modern period.

As early as 1914, some 80 per cent of Peruvian copper production came from the central highlands and was concentrated in two large companies, Cerro de Pasco and Backus and Johnston. As we have seen in chapter three, modern mining in the area, as elsewhere in Latin America, was large-scale and mainly controlled by foreign capital. This type of situation is often analysed in terms of its enclave characteristics. However, such a characterization adopts too narrow a conceptualization of linkage effects, stressing the self-contained nature of enclave production.[5]

The linkages of the mining enterprise within the regional economy were, firstly, in terms of a substantial servicing requirement associated with the building of infrastructure, the transport of minerals to smelting centres and railheads, of equipment and raw material for the mines, and the provision of various foodstuffs for the resident mine population. Secondly, the mines needed a relatively stable and skilled male labour force. The size of this labour force was less than than required by agricultural export-oriented production (e.g. cotton). Moreover, the relatively small size of these mining populations, and the proximity of the villages from which they were drawn, meant that only a limited internal market for commercial foodstuffs and manufactures was created. Indeed, there is little evidence that either the railway or the mines greatly increased agricultural production in the Mantaro area.

This situation had, as a first consequence, the emergence of a locally dominant class based primarily on services and not on the control of production, either in agriculture or industry. In chapter four, we described the social and economic characteristics of this business class which, in general, showed little interest in developing production and in securing and controlling labour for this purpose. This situation resulted in a fragmented economic and political structure in which the dominant class in Huancayo did not develop strong local commitments.

Secondly, the recruitment of mine workers and the nature of mine work shaped social and economic organization at the village level, as was shown in chapters five and six. The village economy had to adjust to the relatively permanent absence of men, while the inflow of earnings from wage labour diversified the village economy through small-scale craft and trading activities. Hence, there developed a cropping system that could be handled by female labour and interhousehold exchange. The inhospitable conditions of the mining centres, many of which were located at 12,000 feet or higher, discouraged the permanent settlement of miners and their families. After a number of years of work, most miners would expect to return to their village of origin and, thus, retained rights to land and to community membership.

These processes, in turn, reinforced the predominant pattern of smallholder farming of low productivity. In this context, capital accumulated through trade, transport or savings on mine wages was not likely to be invested in developing and consolidating agricultural or industrial production at the local level. Instead, investments were channelled into transport and trading activities and into improving the social infrastructure of localities by building schools, water and electricity systems and by providing improved health facilities and new public buildings. Education had the additional advantage of securing skilled and white-collar work in the mine centres. Although these activities created work at the local level and improved the general standard of living, they also shifted the focus of village life towards external opportunities and urban status criteria, such as education, modern styles of dress and modern household accoutrements.

This regional pattern of loosely-integrated class relationships and commitments represents the particular imprint that the mining economy made on the central highlands. This imprint continued to influence local responses when the region became more closely integrated with the coastal urban economy, as industrialization concentrated productive activity and income opportunities in the Lima-Callao area. This integration was facilitated by the close geographical proximity of the central highlands to Lima.

Mining in Peru has become increasingly capital intensive in recent decades thereby decreasing the proportion of employment opportunities outside agriculture. In the case of the Cerro de Pasco Corporation, there have been sharp increases in productivity but, as we noted in chapters three and seven, employment has dropped relative to its high point in 1950. The impact of the mining economy on the central highlands has thus lessened in recent years. In its place, as we saw in chapter seven, there is the increasing importance of state employment in administration and other services. These activities have been complemented by the proliferation of small-scale productive and service activities catering mainly for the local peasant population and for state employees. Some of these small-scale activities continue to link into the Lima economy, but new connections are developing with the tropical lowlands consequent upon state investment and planned and unplanned colonization there.

Nevertheless, despite these tendencies towards an increasing economic fragmentation on the one hand, and a greater dependence on central government on the other, local people still fight to maintain distinctive regional and local identities which are founded upon the institutions, organizational practices and resources stemming from the previous mine-based system of production. This struggle to retain a regional identity in the face of state intervention can be illustrated by looking at developments in the central highlands, following the agrarian reform of 1969.

Agrarian reform and contemporary trends in the central highlands

The 1969 reform aimed to restructure agrarian property and production relations in Peru. The implications of the reforms were an increased administrative centralization of the Peruvian economy, combined with an increase in the state's role in planned agricultural and industrial development (Cotler, 1975: 44–78). Caballero (1980: 76–81) outlines the main features of the military government's development strategy, stressing its intention to promote centralized production co-operatives in the expropriated estates and to introduce such co-operatives even in those peasant communities where farming was organized on an individual household basis. This move towards collectivization in agriculture was reinforced by the creation of regional planning areas to coordinate agricultural and industrial development. Finally, the state organized the participation of the rural population by creating a framework of institutions through which decisions were passed downwards, and support for government policies was passed upwards. These reforms can be seen, then, as reinforcing the increasing centralization of the Peruvian economy following industrialization and the creation of a more integrated national market.

The reforms have, in general, failed in their objectives (Caballero, 1981: 81–5). A basic reason for this failure was that they ran counter to the pattern of economic and social relationships which underpinned both large- and small-scale economic enterprise. Caballero (1980: 91) points out that the viability of the highland estates prior to the reform depended, to a great extent, on their making use of a combination of wage labour and various forms of rent (share-cropping, labour services): the estate and the peasant smallholding coexisted without large-scale production being able to displace the small-scale. Poor soil, difficult climatic conditions and the lack of capital investment made it almost impossible for large, rationally administered enterprises to flourish in this situation. The household, as a family enterprise combining its resources in a flexible manner, has, as we have seen, been more able to respond to the austere economic conditions of the highlands, both by offering labour to mines, plantations and highland estates, and by making use of the economic opportunities generated by the expansion of the regional and national economy.

In the case of the central highlands, two aspects of social organization have been particularly significant in determining the fate of the reform measures: the continuing importance of community-based forms of co-operation and the vitality of small-scale household-based enterprise.

As we have shown in a previous volume (Long and Roberts, 1978), one of the major consequences of the evolution of the mining economy was the revitalization of community organization. Communal traditions of interhousehold co-operation and exchange acquired new meaning and social significance with the expansion of migrant labour and the opportunities that opened up for trade and agricultural production in the new work centres. Villagers collaborated to improve local facilities by building roads, schools and other public works. In cases that became famous nationally, such as that of the hydro-electric project of Muquiyauyo constructed in 1908, the villages of the region acquired a reputation for their progressive character (Grondín, 1978a; Adams, 1959). Migrants' clubs in Lima, as Altamirano has shown in chapter nine, contributed to village development as well as providing a system of mutual aid and support for those in the city. One enduring aspect of regional organization, then, has been the strongly institutionalized system of community-based forms of co-operation. This co-operation contributed to a degree of group social mobility in that the standards of living and educational levels of particular villages were raised. The main provinces of the central highlands – Jauja and Huancayo – had, by 1972, some of the highest educational levels in Peru. Indeed, migrants to Huancayo, who were predominantly drawn from the Department of Junín, had higher levels of education than did migrants to Lima (Muñoz, 1982). Education led to better employment prospects, especially with the expansion of state services in the area. This propensity for communities, and groups within them, to take the initiative in improving local infrastructure made this area particularly susceptible to the appeals of Fernando Belaunde when he first campaigned for the presidency in 1962. Belaunde's programme, as we pointed out in the first chapter, stressed community self-help and the value of modernizing farming and local services in highland areas.

The second aspect of regional organization is, in some respects, in conflict with the emphasis on community co-operation. The region is characterized, as we have seen, by a thriving small-scale entrepreneurial sector. This sector developed on the basis of the opportunities created by the expansion of mining. Small-scale entrepreneurs in farming, trade and transport entered into coalitions with two other main classes. The poorer peasant farmers often supported local entrepreneurs in their attempts to expand the local economy by opening up communications and achieving administrative independence (Long and Roberts, 1978: 316–21). And the business class, based in Huancayo during the apogee of the mining economy, provided the small-scale entrepreneur with some political support at national level for local projects and was the main source of credit and of wholesale supplies. These coalitions were unstable since, on the one hand, the small-scale entrepreneurial class, which was often based in the villages, competed with the poorer peasant class for resources such as land and water and, on the other hand, the monopolies of the business class restricted the ambitions of the small-scale entrepreneur. The small-scale entrepreneurial class became the backbone of APRA support in the region. APRA had, by the 1950s, become committed to the advancement of the small-property owner, was against collectively organized agrarian reform, and also remained opposed to the control of the economy by foreign interests and oligarchic groups.

By the time of the 1969 agrarian reform, the basis for the coalitions between these different classes had been eroded. The mining economy was no longer as dynamic a source of income opportunities as it had been in the past. Consequently, the small-scale entrepreneur was, to some extent, made more dependent on the exploitation of local resources and was thus brought into sharper competition with the poorer peasant classes over their use. The business class had, by this time, largely abandoned the central highlands as an economic base. The economy of Huancayo, as we have seen, became more sharply organized around small-scale, local enterprise and government services. This was the context that determined the responses of the central highlands population to the agrarian reform that restructured the *puna* livestock estates and peasant community institutions. These responses were, in the main, negative and, by 1982, it was clear that the reform period had had no substantial impact on either living standards or patterns of livelihood in the central highlands.

The 1969 agrarian reform expropriated the major livestock estates of the central highlands. By the end of 1980, there were six SAIS (Sociedades Agrarias de Interés Social) in operation in Junín, which covered 520,246 hectares of pastureland that had formerly belonged to private estates. These SAIS included only about 2,000 hectares of arable land. In addition, twenty-seven agricultural production co-operatives, CAPS (Cooperativas Agrarias de Producción), were formed in the Department which contained approximately 15,000 hectares of arable land and 56,000 hectares of pasture. These CAPS are located mainly either in the higher altitude zones or in the tropical lowlands. The lands for the CAPS came, in the main, from the smaller mixed farming estates of the Department. However, the amount of arable land redistributed in this way was less than 15 per cent of the total arable land of the Department. Hence, the land redistributed by agrarian reform is located mainly in highland pastoral areas and is marginal to the existing centres of population concentration in the valleys.

The SAIS and the CAPS have attempted to make farming practices in their estates more economically rational than had previously been the case. Thus, they have sought to exclude animals not belonging to the co-operative, thereby ending the practice of shepherds tending both estate sheep and sheep belonging either to themselves or to kin in neighbouring villages. Likewise, the new units have preferred to use wage labour in all their production activities, rather than to rely on share-cropping or on obtaining labour services in exchange for rights to pasture or to arable plots. The restriction on the use of the co-operative land applies even to those communities which are formal beneficiaries of the land redistribution. Thus, although villagers can participate in the running of the new production co-operatives, as members of assemblies that nominate administrators and debate policy, they have no individual rights to land. Indeed, as many commentators have pointed out, they have less access to this land than they had previously under the arrangements whereby, formally and informally, they pastured animals and grew crops under a variety of share-cropping and renting systems.

The villagers share directly in the benefits of the land redistribution as their communities are allocated part of the profits of the co-operative for community projects, such as schools, roads, health clinics. The full-time workers in the co-operative benefit to the extent that their wages and conditions of work have improved over those which they received under the old estate system. The co-operatives were obliged, however, to contribute to the payment of the expropriation compensation and to reinvest part of their profits. Moreover, the natural conditions (e.g. soil types and climate) determining their profitability have not changed, while they have taken on more fixed obligations, such as a commitment to using wage labour and to paying the agrarian debt. The consequence has been that realized profits have been poor.

Villagers have complained that they have received little community benefit and what they have received is only the type of service, such as schooling, that the state is obliged to provide anyway. Land redistribution in Junín, through the SAIS or the CAPS, has done nothing to change villagers' perceptions of land shortage. In 1979, for example, the armed forces were sent in by the government to dislodge villagers from the lands of the SAIS Túpac Amaru, which they had occupied in order to farm them by individual households (Martinez, 1980: 128).

In Junín, there is little evidence that large-scale land redistribution has revitalized the peasant economy in the areas where it has taken place. Because of the factors noted above, redistribution did not directly stimulate peasant farming nor did it lead to the expansion of other economic activities, such as trade or crafts. Indirect evidence for this is suggested by the rates of population increase and decrease in Junín during the 1970s. The pattern is one in which the highland villages, most associated with the land reform, either decline in population or are stagnant; the valley villages, less affected, show a moderate increase; and the towns especially Huancayo, together with the tropical lowlands, show a substantial increase. Agrarian reform did nothing, then, to arrest the decline of the economically-depressed pastoral communities. Statistics on livestock production for the 1970s are not complete or entirely reliable, but those available suggest that livestock production hardly increased in these years. Thus, total production of livestock for Junín was estimated at 273,400 heads in 1970 and, by 1976, it was 274,850 (*Indicadores estadísticos de Junín*, 1981).

The impact of agrarian reform on villages in the arable farming zones of Junín has been slight. The new statutes aimed at reorganizing peasant community institutions but the projected production and service co-operatives were not fully implemented. Only in a few cases were co-operatives actually installed and made to work effectively on the basis of collective labour. As we documented earlier, even in cases where communal arable land was farmed collectively, there were considerable tensions among members as to the amount of time worked and the sharing out of the product (Long and Roberts, 1978: 224–37). A serious limitation on the success of these enterprises was the fact that community land represented only a fraction of the total arable land in these villages. Most arable land was owned and farmed by individual households: community land was frequently also distributed among households. In those cases where community land was farmed collectively, as in the case of Matahuasi, those who worked it were drawn from the poorest families who had no other sources of livelihood. Thus, the small amount of communal land and the economic impoverishment of those who worked it combined to ensure that the *empresa comunal* (community enterprise) was unable to become a nucleus of expansion for collective forms of production. Existing communal enterprises were encouraged by government extension agencies to modernize their production by using machinery and chemical inputs. But, in many cases, this resulted in increasing indebtedness, due to the relatively small amounts of land cultivated and to the high costs of inputs.

The most significant outcome of the reform period was, in fact, the stimulus it gave to the small-scale private farmer. Government policy in the 1970s stressed agricultural modernization by providing loans for agricultural inputs and by encouraging foodstuff production for the internal market by relaxing control over food prices (Samaniego, 1980a). Furthermore, the reduction in real wages during this period led to a shift in consumer preferences from industrialized foodstuffs to fresh foods, such as potatoes. The people best placed to take advantage of these trends were the richer peasant farmers of Junín. They were, as we noted in chapter eight, involved in the running of multiple enterprises in farming, trade and other services which gave them a basis for capital accumulation. They had little difficulty in raising loans and had sufficient land to farm intensively and profitably. They also had easy access to marketing networks. The tendency in the 1970s, then, was towards a greater differentiation at village level. A class of small-scale commercial farmers consolidated itself, while the situation of the majority of the peasant population became more precarious as increasing numbers attempted to subsist on an unchanged land base. Diversification of the household economy continued, as did migration. In this situation, the richer farmers were able to rent additional land and, at times, to make outright purchases since the land market in peasant communities continued to be active during the whole reform period.

The consequences for agricultural production are, it appears, contradictory. On the one hand, there is, as we saw in chapter eight, evidence for increasing productivity in certain activities such as milk, forage and potato production. On the other hand, most of the land still remains under the control of subsistence-oriented peasant farmers who have to struggle to make ends meet, complementing farming with temporary labour migration. Productivity amongst these latter groups is unlikely to have improved and, given factors such as soil depletion and their incapacity to invest in modern inputs, productivity may well have declined. Overall, there are, in fact, signs of a decrease both in the area of land cultivated in the Department of Junín and in the levels of agricultural production. Between 1970 and 1976, the area of arable land in cultivation dropped from 213,348 hectares to 160,695 hectares. The trend is uniform for cereals, vegetables and potatoes. Even forage shows a slight decline (*Indicadores estadísticos de Junín*, 1981: Tables 8 and 9). A significant factor in this decline is the rising importance of commercial production of foodstuffs on the coast (Samaniego, 1980a). The Junín peasant farmer is unable to compete in productivity and prices with the coastal enterprise that increasingly feeds the major Peruvian cities. The only highland agricultural class that expands economically is the rich peasant and this class does so mainly by complementing coastal production. For example, Junín specializes in seed potatoes for the coast. This rich peasant class has also profited from the completion, in 1973, of the milk pasteurization unit in the Mantaro valley. Members of this class constitute the main milk producers of the valley and the plant, which is controlled by them, supplies the growing urban populations of the region.

These tendencies in Junín's agrarian structure have had the consequence of concentrating population increasingly in either the urban centres or in the areas of new colonization in the tropical lowlands. Areas such as Satipo, whose population increased by an average of approximately 9 per cent per year in the 1960s and 1970s, provide opportunities for the poorer peasant farmer to work permanently or temporarily in coffee or fruit production. In 1977, between one-third and one-half of the permanent migrant population in the tropical lowlands of Junín came from other provinces of Junín and about one-third came from Huancavelica (Bracco, n.d.: 51). The villages of the Mantaro valley contributed a good proportion of these migrants as did the *puna* villages. Long's current re-study of Matahuasi shows, for example, that several families that had been engaged in farming in the community in 1971 had shifted their activities to the tropical lowlands, although still retaining a base in the community.

The growth of Huancayo's population has been considerable in recent years, its rate of increase averaging nearly 6 per cent from 1961 to 1980. In 1980, it was estimated that Huancayo, with a population of 211,600, contained almost 25 per cent of the Department's population, as against just over 12 per cent in 1961. By 1980, Huancayo was some four and a half times larger than the next largest town, Tarma. The urban hierarchy of Junín had become substantially modified by that date, reflecting the increasing importance of new economic opportunities in the tropical lowlands. Thus, the second and third largest towns, Tarma and Satipo, are both important commercial and service centres for the lowland areas. In contrast, the traditionally important urban centres, such as Jauja, show less population growth. Significantly, the mining centre of La Oroya lost population in the period from 1961 to 1980. This pattern of urban growth indicates, then, the beginnings of a shift in regional income opportunities away from mining to the agrarian economy of the tropical lowlands. This shift is not a great one, however, and in the 1970s tropical agriculture in Junín showed little more economic dynamism than did temperate agriculture.

The growth of Huancayo is not based on any fundamental change in its economic structure. Small-scale enterprise, mainly in the services, continues to flourish in the city. Thus, in the 1970s, the officially registered service and commercial enterprises in the city numbered over 4,500 establishments. There were, in addition, about 1,300 stalls in the markets of Huancayo. The Sunday market (*feria dominical*) of the city had almost 2,000 stalls and employed some 3,800 people. In the late 1960s, a plan for an industrial park was drawn up for the city by the Ministry of Industry. Such parks have been successfully implemented in such cities as Arequipa and Trujillo. The Huancayo industrial estate was, however, slow to get off the ground. By 1977, the government had not yet approved the final plan for the park which still lacked electricity in June 1980. An official analysis showed that the firms likely to establish themselves in the short term were very small-scale and heavily concentrated in the timber and carpentry trades. The average number of workers per firm was estimated to be about seven (Ministerio de Industria, Huancayo, 1977).

In 1980, the economy of Huancayo still remained based on the government and commercial services it provided to the region's peasant population. The city's role as a government centre had in fact increased with the reforms of the military government. Apart from education and health services, administration and provision of a variety of social services, Huancayo operated as the control centre for government planning and extension services. The city was a market and transport centre for the highlands and also provided the small-scale production and repairs required by the low-income consumers of the area.

The legacy of the mining economy for contemporary social organization is, however, still apparent in these trends in rural and urban economic activity. The majority of the population continues to survive by combining agricultural and non-agricultural sources of income. Migration remains an integral part of these strategies and still involves much of the population in retaining a base in their home villages. Village co-operative institutions, fortified during the mining period and given a progressive caste, are still seen by many as a significant source of security. On the other hand, the small-scale entrepreneurs have extended their activities considerably in both rural and urban areas. In the absence of a politically more powerful local class, only the state and its functionaries can constrain the activities and interests of this class of petty entrepreneurs. This situation is not conducive to a coherent regional political stance in which powerful local interests combine to pressure government to invest in extensive local development. Equally, the fragmentation of interests makes it difficult for centrally planned policies to be successfully implemented. Various reform projects of the state have, as we noted, not found any strong local support. The most successful cases of development in recent years have, in fact, been those undertaken by small-scale private initiative, such as the settlement of the tropical lowlands or the rapid increase in milk production.

One of the most striking signs of continuity in the region's basic structure is the similarity in voting patterns between 1963 and 1980. In the 1963 election, there was a plurality support for Acción Popular and for Fernando Belaunde as President. In 1980, they gained a clear majority. The election returns show the basic division between the small-scale enrepreneurial class who, in the main, are APRA supporters, and the majority of the peasant population who continued to support the progressive and co-operative manifesto of Acción Popular. In 1980, Acción Popular obtained approximately 58 per cent of the vote in Junín, as compared with the 14 per cent obtained by APRA. The remainder of the vote was distributed among thirteen parties, with the Popular Christian party gaining 7 per cent of the vote (*El Comercio*, 23 June, 1980). The APRA vote was strongest in the province of Huancayo and weakest in the least socially and economically differentiated provinces, such as Junín.

Conclusion

Our aim in this concluding chapter has been to raise a number of central issues concerning regional analysis in underdeveloped economies. By focussing upon production and by developing the notion of a regional system of production, we have attempted to show how a region acquires its characteristics through the interplay of dominant and subordinate economic interests. Adopting this perspective necessitates extending the range of social phenomena that are commonly considered relevant for understanding the structure and development of regions. This inevitably means that any constant set of geographical, cultural or administrative criteria have limited usefulness for defining regional structures and mapping their changes over time.

Instead, we have concentrated upon the social and economic impact of the major production activity of our area and the economic interests associated with it. This has entailed looking at the mobilization and organization of resources necessary in relation to both dominant and subordinate production activities. This involved delineating existing production relations and analysing the mechanisms for the appropriation and distribution of the social product in the different economic sectors. In addition, it was necessary to take account of the division of labour and allocation of responsibilities between the members of the labour force, especially between men and women.

Consideration of these matters inevitably led us to explore the external linkages associated with particular production processes. Some of the important linkages we identified were with other sectors of the regional economy or with other local production units producing the same or different commodities. Other economic linkages tied the region to other areas of Peru, especially to the coast and Lima, and some of these linkages were generated by state fiscal policy, such as food pricing. In some instances, it was necessary to follow linkages into the international arena in order to understand how various constraints on production and economic activities stemmed from decisions at that level, although the scope of this study prevented an adequate account of these factors.

Our methodological approach, then, has combined several different levels of analysis. On the one hand, it has been concerned with problems relating to the penetration and expansion of capitalism in underdeveloped economies, determining the repercussions of the international economy at provincial and local level. On the other hand, our account has focussed upon the analysis of various types of local-level economic management units, such as the household or the small-scale enterprise. It has sought to discover the internal logic of their operation, how they articulate with large-scale enterprise, and how they shape the processes and outcomes of regional and national development. Moreover, since linkage analysis involves a concern with reproduction processes (i.e. the mechanisms by which particular processes of production and systems of linkages are maintained and reconstituted), we have also considered various organizational, ideological and cultural factors relevant to the reproduction process.

A final dimension of importance in our analysis has been that, since linkage analysis places emphasis on tracing out the connections between different economic sectors, it necessarily also entails analysis of the interrelationships between different social groups and classes. These relationships are dynamic ones, involving the emergence of particular political, social and religious institutions or groupings that may serve, on the one hand, to consolidate the position of dominant interests, or, on the other hand, to defend that of subordinate groups. It has been necessary, then, to provide some account of the social interests of the various actors and groups involved and to analyse how their interrelationships have changed over time.

Our regional approach has tried, then, to make apparent the connections between seemingly discrete forms of economic, social and political activity. This focus offers a means of understanding the diversity of situations created by capitalist development. Capitalist development does not come evenly to countries like Peru. Its impact is concentrated in certain regions where modern enterprises of considerable scale and technological sophistication draw upon the labour and organization of populations that are primarily committed to satisfying subsistence needs. The pattern of linkages that emerges between these different actors will vary according to specific historical and socio-political conditions. The pattern is likely, however, to have enduring consequences for regional organization and change, affecting the ways in which local populations accommodate to the increasing fragmentation of regional economies and their growing dependence on metropolitan centres.

As we have emphasized, the understanding of these processes requires detailed historically-based research. Such research should provide answers to questions such as why certain types of peasant-based organization persist in some areas and not in others, why some areas are more integrated economically and culturally and/or may resist centralizing forces more effectively than others, or why modern capitalist enterprises are successful in terms of labour recruitment and in creating linkages into the local economy in some areas but not in others. The effort required is a painstaking one, but it is necessary if we are to avoid the pitfalls of applying uniform theoretical models of change, and of using them for planned development. A great deal of planned development, in fact, fails to take sufficient account of why people persist with economic and social strategies that, on the face of it, run counter to so-called 'progressive' modernization policies and to the inevitable trend of capitalist development.

Notes

1 Regional development in an export economy

1 We refer here to the approaches developed mainly in economics, geography and anthropology which place more emphasis than we do on specifically spatial dimensions. See, for example, the discussions in Richardson (1978: 17–24), Berry (1967) and Smith (1976). We return in Chapter 11 to discussing other approaches to regional analysis.

2 Central-place analysis has been developed by geographers as a quantitative model for characterizing and explaining the flows of goods and services in a given area and for identifying the economic functions of the component settlements. Here, however, we are mainly concerned with the patterns of social and political organization that accompany spatial distributions of the central-place type.

3 These kinds of changes are discussed for Colombia in Magdalena León de Leal and Deere (1980), giving particular emphasis to the changes in the division of labour within the household affecting the role of women. Deere (1982) and Deere and De Janvry (1981) provide a similar analysis for the Cajamarca area of the northern highlands of Peru.

4 See Thorp and Bertram (1978) for a detailed account of the evolution of the Peruvian economy from 1890–1977 which pays particular attention to the performance of the export industries.

5 See Fitzgerald (1979) for a comprehensive analysis of the structure of the Peruvian economy bringing out its dualistic nature and the problems this poses for capital accumulation and the role of the state. Here, the term 'dualism' is used in the macro-economic sense as referring to marked differences in levels of production and productivity between economic sectors. As is shown in subsequent chapters, this concept of dualism does not imply the absence of strong economic and social relationships between, for example, the small-scale 'traditional' sector and the large-scale 'modern' sector.

6 The description by Klaren (1973) of the sugar estates of the Chicama valley shows how these became economic enclaves in which provisioning and transport as well as production were organized by the company. Scott (1976) analyses the ways in which the sugar estates organized labour contracting through the *enganche* system (see chapter 3) which often acted against the interest of local military commanders who were eager to conscript peasants for public works projects.

7 For a technical assessment of the zone's resource potential, see Latin Project (1968).

2 The development of a regional economy in the central highlands

1 The harshness of mining conditions at high altitude meant, as Fisher (1977: 7) points out, that the mining centres did not develop as self-sufficient units with their own farms and ranches. Consequently, a whole range of supplies had to be transported from the low-lying valley areas.

2 A fuller periodization of changes in the area's economy during the colonial period is provided by Samaniego (1980b). He analyses change in three periods. The first is until the mid-seventeenth century when traditional reciprocity continued as a basis for the household economy, while the Spanish authorities and landowners exercised control through tribute and labour service. The second period continues until the mid-eighteenth century and is marked by the formation of livestock haciendas in the *puna* region, the expansion of foodstuff production by landowners and immigrant Spaniards in the valley and the consequent expulsion of the native population from part of their lands. Samaniego stresses the importance of mining to these developments through the demand for foodstuffs. He also emphasizes the differentiation that results within the villages and describes the beginnings of *mestizaje* (intermarriage of Spanish and Indian). The third period sees the decline of landlord production and the expansion of household-based cultivation, due to the ending of large-scale mining in Huancavelica. The more scattered mining in the Pasco region favoured small-scale agricultural producers prepared to establish direct links with the miners and to trade over the longer distances.

3 Larson (1972), in her study of merchants in sixteenth century Potosí, shows that trade continued despite fluctuations in mining production. Also, in later periods, when economic conditions reduced the demand for large-scale mining production, mining continued through the activities of individual workers who dug up the ores and processed them through small-scale furnaces. These activities and the inputs they required were a stimulus to commerce and craft activity over a wide region.

4 The comparison between Jauja, the major town of the northern end of the valley, and Huancayo, in the nineteenth century, is necessarily a complex one. One important factor in their relative fortunes appears to be that they tended to be identified with different sides in the civil war and that, during that war and the war with Chile, Jauja and its elite bore the brunt of the war expenditure in the region. There is also some evidence, from verbal accounts, that the elite of Jauja in the early twentieth century did show a more conservative stance towards the development of commerce and industry. One important factor in this difference is that Jauja had less land available for development than Huancayo. At the end of the nineteenth century, new developments in Jauja often meant the purchase and conversion of existing property. In Huancayo, they often involved the development of waste land.

5 The main haciendas with owners resident in Huancayo appear to have been: Tucle of Bernarda Piélago; Antapongo of the Giráldez family; Punto of Jacinto Cevallos; Hanta of Vicente Palomino; Ocorayoc of José María Lora; Callanca of María Ibarra; Ila of Mercedes Torres de Marín (Tello Devotto, 1971: 79). The largest land concentration in the province was probably the haciendas of the Valladares family (Laive, Ingahuasi etc.), but the Valladares did not reside in Huancayo.

6 Lack of time prevented us reading the Actas of Huancayo for every year from 1875. Consequently, we sampled every tenth year and made a detailed analysis and summary of proceedings throughout the year. We were able to examine the Actas of some of the councils near Huancayo (Sicaya, Cacchi and Ahuac). Sicaya and Ahuac, which are part of Huancayo province, did not show any significant interventions by the Huancayo authorities. At these district levels, however, the local authorities did use the free labour of outlying hamlets to benefit the central village. This intervention was related to the economic strategies of the prosperous smallholders that controlled these districts (Samaniego, 1974).

7 Adams (1975) develops a general model of the evolution of power structures, distinguishing between power domains and levels of articulation. His major variable in explaining why power structures become more centralized is the input of energy into a particular system.

8 During the colonial period, also, there were periods when the unitary structure tended to break down in the face of weakening economic links with the European economy. In these periods, there is some evidence for decentralization of economic and political activity based on small-scale enterprise (Arce, 1981: 12–15).

3 The Mining Corporation and regional development.

1 A detailed analysis of the development of mining in the central highlands is provided by DeWind (1977) and Laite (1981).

2 DeWind (1977: 85–6) points out that open-pit mining using diesel-powered rotating mills, power shovels and huge haul truckers could produce eighteen times more ore per worker than the underground system of the Cerro de Pasco mines.

3 *Extracto estadístico*, various years under category Minas metálicas. A proportion of these workers would be working outside the central highlands region. Also, these numbers will include temporary workers such as those employed in construction.

4 Analysis of the Huancayo survey data shows that, of those who had once been in Huancayo and had subsequently left, the majority before 1940 were white-collar workers who went mainly to Lima (Muñoz Vargas, 1982: 161). A similar pattern emerges from life-history data collected in various villages of the valley. See Roberts (1973) and Samaniego (1974) for an analysis of the social characteristics of out-migrants from the Mantaro area.

5 The administrative staff of the mines, who were mainly ex̣ ̣ ̀riate North Americans and Europeans, earned high salaries which accounted for ₹ ̣ut 20 per cent of the company payroll, more in fact than that for the *empleados*. Staff salaries, however, did not feed, in any substantial way, into the local economy. Some of these salaries were spent on local goods and on servants, but a large percentage of their earnings was remitted abroad in the form of savings or went on purchases at mine-owned stores. Figures taken from the company payroll for 1961 (see DeWind, 1977: 183).

6 The tax revenues of Huancayo's provincial council in 1951 (approximately 326,000 dollars) can be compared with the 6,790,000 dollars which the Cerro de Pasco Corporation paid to its employees in the same year (DeWind, 1977: 181).

4 Class relations, local economies and large-scale mining

1 These payments were made in Huancayo by the Cercapuquio mine and other mines of the southern Sierra. Since most mines were located in remote places, it was convenient to have such financial arrangements centred in Huancayo.

2 This businessman bought about 200 to 300 mattresses each month at the height of demand and these purchases continued from 1947 to 1955. The small-scale manufacturer could have sold directly to the Cerro de Pasco Corporation, but preferred to be paid in cash directly by the businessman; the Cerro de Pasco Corporation paid accounts like these with some delay.

3 See DeWind (1977: 126–34) for a discussion of the importance of small- and medium-sized mining companies, of which there were approximately one hundred in the 1960s, for the operation of large companies.

4 These other industries were food processing (mainly flour mills) and beverages. There were also three furniture factories, three sawmills, two shoemaking factories and several candle and soap makers.

5 It is likely that businessmen and women of foreign origin had interests in other establishments also. The Patrón de Comerciantes shows them as partners in many businesses of this time; it was also the practice for establishments to be registered under the name of a Peruvian to avoid difficulties over the requirement that a certain proportion of businesses be Peruvian owned. The figure of 40 per cent was calculated on the basis of foreign surnames, such as Japanese and Chinese surnames. Some names were ambiguous as to nationality, but we verified their nationality from other sources.

6 This is not a reliable procedure since the population in 1972 represents only 'survivors' of the 1940–50 population of Huancayo. As a check on the usefulness of the 1972 data, we also analysed other questions designed to trace friends and relatives who had once been in Huancayo and had subsequently left.

7 This description is a general one and must allow for many exceptions. The Department of Huancavelica, for example, includes large and some relatively prosperous villages and one major town – Huancavelica – which, as the educational data for the last century indicate, had long-standing traditions of sending well-qualified migrants to the city.

8 To this day, there is an office of the Chinese Cultural Association in Huancayo. Also, in the 1920s, the municipal council arranged a special meeting with Chinese businessmen to discuss the economic situation. In some of the companies established by the Huancayo Chinese, explicit mention is made of referring any disputes that might arise to the Lima Chinese Association.

9 This vertical integration was most characteristic of Grace and Company, who possessed sugar haciendas and mills, textile mills and retail outlets, although some of the English trading companies also invested in textile operations. Other importing houses established factories to produce paper, shoes and other basic items.

10 The choice of 1927 is dictated by the relatively full data available for that year in the listing of Huancayo businessmen and establishments given by Oscar Chavez in his book *Huancayo* published in 1927. The Chamber of Commerce was founded in 1925 under the presidency of a local landowner and merchant, Federico Tovar.

11 In this period, there does not appear to have been much shortage of cash in the banks to cover this kind of credit. For much of the period, exports were doing well and the profits – especially from sugar and cotton – were handled by the banking system. There was also a good deal of speculative foreign investment in government bonds and in finance in this period. The subsequent industrial development of Huancayo was also to be financed by bank credits. There was no stock-market in Peru, nor were there other public means of raising money, and personal contacts and 'credit-

worthiness' were vital to securing the capital needed to finance industry or business operations.

12 The Patrón de Comerciantes is the state register of businesses and any businesses involving partners, or in cases where the owners wish to establish legal record of their obligations, will be registered. Although the Patrón contains data on the partners, their relative share of the social capital and any changes in the legal status of partners or managers, it does not state the date of termination of the enterprise. From the index we made of the businesses, it was clear that many of them were short-lived and probably had come into existence to allow their principals to make a claim on interesting new economic developments. Thus, a spate of car agencies were established which appear to have been forerunners of the serious competition over securing the agencies of the different makes imported into Peru.

13 He has been one of the few to remain in Huancayo and has deliberately sponsored employees in their own businesses, seeing local enterprise as one of the crucial elements in national development. He had no capital when he came to Peru and established himself mainly by becoming the agent for importing houses.

5 Highland 'puna' communities and the rise of the mining economy

1 This chapter is based on research carried out in 1975. The project was made possible through the collaboration of the Pontificia Universidad Católica of Peru, Lima and the SAIS Túpac Amaru No. 1. The chapter has been translated and amended by the editors. A fuller, earlier version containing a more extended theoretical discussion of the issues is found in Campaña and Rivera (1979).

2 This discussion is reviewed in chapter eleven. De Janvry and Garramon (1977) see cheap labour as part of the logic of capitalist accumulation at the periphery. A similar view is taken by Amin (1974: 50) who argues that: 'the functions of the peasantry of "rural traditional society" are: (1) to provide the mining industry and plantations with cheap labour, (2) to provide supplementary foodstuffs cheaply permitting the reduction in the value of labour power in the pure capitalist sector, (3) to elevate the real value of the luxury consumption of the privileged strata (*comprador* and bureaucratic bourgeoisies) above providing them with low cost services (domestic etc.)'. We would tend to stress the functionality of the peasantry for capitalist accumulation more than Long and Roberts have done in other chapters of this volume.

3 See Julian Laite's discussion (1978a: 72–97) of this issue. The poisonous fumes were eliminated by the Corporation, which was aware that damage to pastoral land was reversible.

4 See the debate between ourselves and Martínez-Alier concerning the survival of the *huaccha* system in *Estudios Rurales Latinoamericanos* (1978), 1,3,175–80, and 2,1,111–21. We call the system that continues in the Cerro de Pasco haciendas that of *regalía* (i.e. concessions supplementing salary).

5 The history and meaning of the term community (*comunidad*) in Peru is discussed by Winder (1978: 209–40). Persons who have legal membership of the *comunidad* entitling them to access to community resources (e.g. land and water) are called *comuneros*.

6 These were due fundamentally to external factors, such as the ending of the Second

World War, increasing investment in industry in Latin America by the United States and the general reduction in world copper consumption which resulted in the laying-off of workers. See Cardoso and Faletto, 1979.

7 Paccha was legally recognized in 1938, Canchaillo in 1941, Usibamba in 1938 and Suitucancha in 1939.

8 All the communities border the haciendas and were affected negatively by the expansion of the Cerro de Pasco estates. A more detailed discussion of SAIS organization is found in Roberts and Samaniego (1978: 241–63). Also see Caicho, 1972; Montoya, 1973; Fonseca, 1975; Althaus, 1975; Rivera, 1976; Campaña, 1976; Gómez, 1976.

9 Category A consists only of Usibamba. Category B is made up of Chacapalpa, Chalhuas, Huacapo, Huancaya, Huari, Huathuay, Llocllapampa, Ondores, Suitucancha, Tanta and Urauchoc; and Category C includes Canchaillo, Paccha, Pachachaca and Sacco.

10 This recent migration from Usibamba is principally due to the effects of agrarian reform and the restructuring of the communities that resulted. Usibamba is the community that has been most radically affected by this reform.

11 The agrarian reform initiated in 1969 included a restructuring of communities through new land tenure arrangements and by encouraging communal production enterprises (see Long and Winder, 1975; and Winder, 1978; 209–40).

6 Migration and social differentiation amongst Andean peasants

1 On the decline of reciprocal exchanges in Latin American peasant culture see Erasmus (1956).

2 The migration patterns found in this region were similar to those found by Skeldon (1977b).

3 The information which follows is based on interviews with Ataurinos living in Ataura and in La Oroya, and on analyses of their life-histories (Laite, 1977).

4 The information which follows is based on interviews with Matahuasinos living in Matahuasi and in La Oroya, and on analyses of their life-histories (Laite, 1977).

5 The groups interviewed in depth were as follows:

A: Males, now resident in Ataura, with migration experience = 15. This is a 1:7 sample of all males resident in Ataura.

B: Males, now resident in Matahuasi, with migration experience = 14. This is a 1:10 sample of all males with migration experience resident in Matahuasi.

C: Ataura-born and Matahuasi-born males living in La Oroya = 47. These are all known Ataurinos and Matahuasinos living in La Oroya. Ataurinos in La Oroya = 22. Matahuasinos in La Oroya = 25.

The significance tests used are those given by Spiegel. For the X^2: HS = Highly Significant, denoting significance at the 1 per cent level. The life-histories were analysed using a life-history programme from the University of Texas which was modified by S. Pursehouse of the University of Manchester.

6 Julio's case is drawn from Long (1977).

7 On dualism, see Boeke (1953) and Higgins (1956). On the critique of dualism, see Frank (1972).

7 Industrialization and the emergence of an informal regional economy

1 Webb (1975) provides figures showing the sharp disparities in income levels between the coast and the highlands. Even leaving Lima aside the ratio between incomes in other coastal provinces and in the highlands was still 2:1. The central highlands, however, include some of the highest income areas of the highlands.

2 From the 1950s, the Cerro de Pasco Corporation did establish forward and backward linkages with industrial enterprises, but these were mainly located on the coast (Thorp and Bertram 1978: 214).

3 The origin of this distinction can be traced to Geertz (1963b) who distinguishes between the 'bazaar' and 'firm' type economies. Subsequently, Hart (1973) made the explicit contrast between the 'formal' and 'informal' sectors in terms of their job characterisitics. See Moser (1978), Long and Richardson (1978) and Roberts (1978a) for overviews of this literature.

4 These data are reported in full in Alberti and Sanchez (1974). Alberti's data include Chilca and El Tambo and thus provide a useful addition to our data which refer to the Huancayo district (the central district of the city) only. The basis for our own Huancayo business sample is the material collected by Alberti and his assistant Rodrigo Sanchez. We would like to thank them for making it available to us.

5 The percentages are calculated on the basis of the capital value of the various businesses as estimated by council inspectors. These estimates are not likely to be a good guide to the volume of business of an enterprise, but provide some relative measure of the evident capitalization, such as amounts of stock, machinery, size of establishment. When extracting these data, we only extracted enterprises with a declared value above a low cutting point of approximately £100. In practice, this means that the above percentages probably *underestimate* the relative weight of commerce and crafts in the total economy. This underestimation is not great. The businesses excluded are predominantly enterprises such as small corner shops, bakeries or shoemakers, and those included are predominantly the businesses of the main city streets. Agricultural enterprises are also excluded; in 1963 their declared value was equivalent to 6 per cent of the total declared. These enterprises are the Huancayo-based agricultural and pastoral hacienda companies and do not include the giant exploitations which are registered in Lima.

6 Automotores San Jorge is the main agent for companies such as Volvo, Chrysler and General Motors. Its declared capital value in the municipal records of 1972 constituted approximately 37 per cent of the value declared for the transport sector.

7 Alberti and Sanchez report a total of 438 clothing workshops, compared with the 98 listed for Huancayo district alone; they list 947 service establishments (bars, restaurants, barbers, etc.), whereas there are some 550 listed in Huancayo. Conversely, there is a much greater concentration of craft workshops (carpenters, tailors, shoemakers) in Huancayo itself. The large stores and specialized services are all concentrated in the centre.

8 These traders were basically *retail* traders; despite its name of wholesale market, only some sixty of the thousand traders in the market were wholesale traders in the sense of purchasing in bulk from producers and selling to retailers. Many of the retailers in the market did, however, purchase directly from the factories, even where this involved a journey to Lima.

9 Since this transport office serves all the province of Huancayo (a larger administrative

unit than the city, including many villages) and, since Huancayo is the Departmental capital, much of this transport registered in Huancayo belongs to people who live in the villages and small towns of the Department. Huancayo does serve, however, as the major repair and service centre for this transport.

10 Social security offers certain advantages. For a relatively small contribution, drugs, medical attention and hospital care can be obtained free. The standard of service is often low and there are considerable periods of waiting, but private care is often prohibitively expensive.

11 There is a slight tendency for the proportions of those surveyed who reported obtaining their first job by their own initiative (as against through friendship or kin ties) to decline with a later date of entry into the city. It is clear that there is no rise in 'impersonal' criteria for recruiting to jobs; of those who entered the city in the last five years, the majority (60 per cent) got their first job through kin, friends or had assured work on arrival. It is the youngest age group that is *least likely* to have obtained their present jobs by looking for work (34 per cent looked for work) and who are most likely to have obtained it through the help of kin (25 per cent).

12 This estimate is a rough one, taken from the individual forms that truckers must fill in; but we have a total set of figures for three months of trucking of foodstuffs from the Mantaro area to Lima, which is classified by origin of the trader and producer. Our studies of traders indicate their preference for dealing with areas with which they have long-standing contact.

13 This information was given directly by the owner of the store, who allowed us to look at his accounts. He was a good friend to us during our stay in the area and we would regard this information as completely trustworthy.

14 The *priostes* received financial help from kin and fellow traders. They will repay this help in turn when others become *priostes*, thus consolidating, over time, social and business relationships. In the case of the potato trader, he made a point of inviting as guests of honour the Huancavelica mine administrators with whom he had contracted for the supply of potatoes.

15 Several of the factories that closed down were devoted to garment production. The largest one had a labour force of 300. According to the former book-keeper, the largest single group of workers came from Sicaya. When these factories closed, the owners often gave the machinery to the workers as part compensation for their legal entitlements. This machinery was used to set up small, home-based industry. One sweater producer, who had worked all his life in the industry, estimated there to be some 250 small-scale sweater producers, most of them clandestine.

16 In the 1940 census, there were 35,408 people born in Junín reported as living in Lima who constituted 11.7 per cent of the total migrants to the city at that date; by 1961, the number from Junín was 62,594 which constituted 8.0 per cent of the migrants in the city at that date (Slater, 1972: 138, 249). Our surveys of the valley villages suggest that these migrants have come disproportionately from the larger villages. It is apparent that migration to Lima is becoming a little less concentrated, as migrants from more remote Departments begin to make up an important proportion of the total number of migrants (Slater, 1972: 249).

17 This claim necessarily excludes the profits of the large-scale enterprises, such as mines or haciendas; in fact, in the recently co-operativized haciendas of the highlands, their obligations to pay off the former owners through bonds may even temporarily accelerate the outflow of capital from the zone.

18 Although the government has recently taken steps to improve its data collection services, the information gathered must be treated with caution. In the census, for example, there was a clear over-reporting of the population and of farm units as migrants returned to 'claim' their rights. We uncovered an estimated over-reporting for one village of some 5 per cent when we used the census forms to select our sample. On visiting the households we found that the householders had once again returned to the city. The bulk of Huancayo's textile production goes unreported in unregistered firms; a great part of the foodstuff production is transported informally to the cities on buses and is sent to migrant relatives. These features, which reflect the mobile and small-scale nature of the area's economy, present inherent difficulties for government attempts to gain information and to plan accurately.

8 The village economy, agricultural development and contemporary patterns of social differentiation

1 In this analysis, we only consider information on loads. Other items might include the current prices for different types of contracts and information on the activities of competitors.

2 See, for example, Geertz's (1960) analysis of the role of Islamic teachers in Indonesia, and Wolf's (1956) study of political and cultural middlemen in Mexico.

3 The Feast of the Christian martyr, San Sebastián, is celebrated on 20 January. Although San Sebastián is not the official patron saint, his fiesta has become the most lavish and long-lasting one in Matahuasi. It now lasts almost a week, during which various activities are organized: bull-fights, dances, sports competitions and processions.

4 Buechler (1970) makes the same point about religious fiestas in Bolivia.

5 This is not an unusual phenomenon for the Mantaro valley. For other cases of this, see Adams (1959) and Escobar (1964). For a full discussion of these associations, see chapter nine. In Matahuasi, membership of clubs is associated with particular socio-economic categories (e.g. with professionals, farm labourers, mine workers).

9 Regional commitment among central highlands migrants in Lima

1 This chapter has been revised and edited for this volume by Norman Long and Bryan Roberts.

2 In his early studies, Doughty (1970), utilizing a variety of sources such as newspapers, radio, specialized magazines and interviews, found about 1,050 formally organized associations in Lima alone. More recently (1976), he estimates there to be as many as 5,000 such clubs, although he warns that these clubs rise and decline with some regularity. The first provincial areas to send migrants to Lima were the nearby and more commercialized areas of Junín, Ancash and Arequipa. Subsequently, more remote and economically less-developed areas, such as Puno, have become more important senders of migrants to Lima. There is a growing literature that bears directly or indirectly on regional associations and migration in Peru. See Mangin, 1959, 1967, 1970, 1973; Long, 1973; Isbell, 1974; Roberts, 1974; Skeldon, 1976, 1977a, 1977b.

3 The major controversy has been between Jongkind and Doughty. Lima's regional associations have attracted attention partly because no other Latin American city

shows such a range of associations or such an active membership. The debate has also been over methodological issues such as the reliability of survey results as compared to the more intensive, but limited, focus of participant observation and case study.

4 In my fieldwork in Ongoy, I identified several kinds of aid provided for *barrios*, such as equipment for schools and sports teams, which were channelled via the branch associations from the Lima association. These branch associations were also politically active in the village, adopting a 'modernizing' stance, often against the reluctance of the central authorities to develop the outlying areas. See Altamirano, 1980: 161–73.

5 In the early part of the twentieth century, the expansion of commercial opportunities for both hacienda and village production led to a series of land conflicts which raised, in an acute form, the question of land boundaries and community rights. These matters are fully discussed in Samaniego (1978) and Winder (1978).

6 This is partly the issue of 'traditional' highland landowners who had little in common with the Lima elite who were tied into the export economy. Provincial elites, such as those of the central highlands, who were tied into the export economy had, on the other hand, little need to control village-level politics.

7 The rise of APRA from the 1920s onwards was to some extent to provide such an alternative structure. Interestingly, in the Mantaro area, the organization of APRA and the political role of the regional associations eventually became intertwined.

8 The *comunidad* in Matahuasi is the institution controlling communal resources, which, in this case, are quite small: approximately 70 hectares of land out of a total of 1,550 hectares (see Winder, 1978).

9 This raises an interesting issue for those who wish to stress that the primary purpose of regional associations is simply that of helping migrants to adjust to urban life. In the case of Ongoy, those who founded the association returned to their region of origin to be replaced by the successive wages of temporary migrants. Hence, we find a greater proportion of temporary migrants among the members of the Ongoy association, than with the Matahuasi case.

10 Confederations of households: extended domestic enterprises in city and country

1 The work of McGee in South East Asia, Lomnitz in Mexico and Gerry and Lebrun in West Africa have focussed attention on what McGee (1979) calls 'making out' in Third World cities (McGee, 1971a, 1971b, 1973, 1977; Lomnitz, 1975; Gerry and Lebrun, 1975). This interest has led to a recent call by various disciplines for the study of the urban poor specifically in terms of the ways in which they undertake casual work (*World Development* (Special Issue), 1978; Moser, 1977; Bromley and Gerry, 1979), rather than studies which focus on their marginality to capitalism (Nun, 1969; Quijano, 1974) or their informal nature in contradistinction to the more formalized economy (Hart, 1973). Such studies do not deny the important influence of large-scale capitalism on the forms of casual work which arise in Third World cities (see especially MacEwen Scott, 1979), but suggest that this influence should not preclude detailed study of the way in which people 'make out' through casual work (a term taken from Bromley and Gerry, 1979: Introduction). See also, for a general discussion of these perspectives: Roberts, 1978a; Jones, 1971; Worsley, 1976.

2 See Connell et al., 1974: 'Most studies of migration in rural areas have been concerned with migrants who have moved away from the areas; hence many of the characteristics of these migrants are undetermined. The migrants have not been followed up at their destination . . . Conversely, urban studies [concentrate] on integration into urban social organizations . . . Consequently between the two groups of studies there is a gap which is rarely bridged.'

3 Fieldwork was carried out throughout 1972 and 1973. It was funded by the Canada Council and the Ministry of Education of the Government of Quebec.

4 A more detailed study of the relationship between the changing forms of petty production in Huasicancha and the historical development of the Peruvian economy from 1870 can be found in Smith (1979).

5 Use of the term 'ex-resident' may seem confusing. It has its advantages, however. It is the term used by the Huasicanchinos, both in town and country, to describe *comuneros* not resident in the village. It also avoids the bias which results from the use of the word 'migrant' for anybody who has arrived in the city, however long ago. Presumably there comes a time when a Lima resident no longer thinks of him- or herself as a migrant, just as eventually some will no longer think of themselves as Huasicanchino ex-residents; although, in this latter case, this would reflect a legal connotation too: lack of the status of *comunero* (legally recognized member of a *comunidad campesina*).

6 The complexity of living arrangements and livelihood activities among the Huasicanchinos makes findings resulting from the administration of a questionnaire extremely difficult to use for the purpose of firm statistics. Questionnaires were administered to 87 households, although what constituted a separate, definable occupation and what constituted 'possession' of productive resources were beyond any hard definition. For this reason, I find the presentation of case studies more helpful. One year was spent in the rural area and eight months were spent in Lima.

7 Names used are pseudonyms.

8 Marx, 1964: 137–8: 'Political economy . . . does not recognise the unemployed worker, the working man so far as he is outside this relationship. Thieves, tricksters, beggars, the unemployed, the starving, wretched and criminal workingman, are figures which do not exist for political economy, but only for other eyes; for doctors, judges, gravediggers, beadles etc. They are ghostly figures outside the domain of political economy.'

9 These arrangements are discussed in some detail in Smith (1975). Briefly they can be summarized as follows:
Uyay: extra-household reciprocal exchange of labour.
Minka: extra-household exchange of labour for goods.
Partidario: literally glosses as 'division'. Refers to arrangements which involve the sharing of produce from a resource controlled by one party but exploited by another. Besides arable land, this may also refer to pregnant animals, where the owner allows another party to a share of the parturition in return for feeding the animal during pregnancy. In the most common form, the receiver takes all the first litter, continues to feed the animal and then returns it with the second litter.
Huaccha: literally 'orphan'. Refers therefore to a person without any inheritance of livestock. Such a person may care for another's flock in return for a share of a year's parturition, then referred to as *huacchas*.

Michipa: a household may care for the animals of another household in amongst its own flock in return for a variety of forms of payment, usually arable goods or work on the arable land.

10 I would be reluctant to take this analogy any further than just a passing illustration.

11 Rations of labour 'time' should be treated with caution when comparing such differing activities as the intensive tasks of arable farming, which precludes subsidiary work, and the less intensive work of shepherding, where child minding and spinning, for example, are often undertaken at the same time.

12 The fact that Huasicancha is predominantly endogamous means that it is possible for a person to apply some kin term or other to virtually anybody with whom he or she has some kind of economic tie.

13 Such benefits include the transmission of skills, informal credit and certain advantages of scale, especially in joint purchasing in the central fruit market. See the brief discussion of this in Grompone, 1981.

14 The economic rationale reflected in decisions of participants is also influenced by ideological and cultural factors. This is not the place to discuss the relationships between the economic logic of the form of production and the ideology of participants. Suffice it to say that the latter is a product of factors far broader than just the contemporary economic rationality of production.

11 Regional development in peripheral economies

1 Amin (1974) elaborates the notion of disarticulation in peripheral economies to emphasize the break in the production–consumption cycle that occurs and to draw attention to the lack of close integration between different economic sectors within peripheral economies.

2 Palerm (1976: 35) cites data on the average yield of wheat in colonial Mexico, as compared with England and Holland, and shows that the Mexican yield on irrigated land was more than twice as great as in these other countries.

3 Although we do not wish to develop this point here, it would be possible to construct a typology of the patterns of regional development in Latin America based upon such factors as the presence of enclave-type production as against smaller-scale, nationally-owned, export-oriented production, and in terms of the characteristics and availability of the labour supply. In some cases, conflicting principles of regional development may be at work, as when an enclave-type system of production is juxtaposed with one based upon national, smaller-scale entrepreneurship. This, for example, seems to have been the case in nineteenth century Sonora, Mexico. See Aguilar, 1977.

4 Despite being banned by the military government which took power in 1968, APRA retained much of its organization intact in areas like the central highlands, drawing support from a wide segment of the rural and urban populations, particularly the middle sectors.

5 The notion of enclave has been used to describe systems of production that are relatively self-sufficient in terms of their production inputs (raw materials, technology, services etc.) and administrative infrastructure; the enclave also produces for the external rather than the internal market. From this point of view, an enclave form of production has relatively weak backward or forward linkages into the surrounding regional economy. Although this type of analysis is not helpful in exploring social

and economic interdependencies at sub-national regional level, it has served to characterize the special situation of those countries in which enclave forms of production have constituted the dominant means of economic expansion. The national implications of enclave development are analysed by Cardoso and Faletto (1979: 48–53) in their contrast between enclave dominated countries such as Peru and Mexico and those such as Argentina and Brazil in which dominant production was nationally controlled and more closely linked to other sectors of the economy. See also Beckford (1972) on plantation economies.

Bibliography

Archives

Actas del Consejo Provincial de Huancayo.

Archivo municipal de Sicaya.

Registro Civil, Patrón de Comerciantes, Consejo Provincial de Huancayo.

Registro Electoral de 1906, Consejo Provincial de Huancayo.

Registro Mercantil, Consejo Provincial de Huancayo.

Adams, R. N., 1959. *A community in the Andes: problems and progress in Muquiyauyo.* University of Washington Press. Seattle and London.

1975. *Energy and structure: a theory of social power.* University of Texas Press. Austin and London.

Aguilar, C. H., 1977. *La Frontera Nómada.* Siglo XXI Editores. Mexico.

Alberti, G. and Sanchez, R., 1974. *Poder y conflicto social en el valle del Mantaro.* Instituto de Estudios Peruanos. Lima.

Alberti, G. et al., 1977. *Estado y clase: la comunidad industrial en el Perú.* Instituto de Estudios Peruanos. Lima.

Alers-Montalvo, M., 1967. *Pucará: un estudio de cambio.* Instituto Interamericano de Ciencias Agrícolas de la OEA. Lima.

Altamirano Rua, T., 1980. Regional commitment and political involvement amongst migrants in Lima: the case of regional associations. Unpublished Ph.D. Thesis. University of Durham.

Althaus, J. de, 1975. Las Comunidades de la SAIS Túpac Amaru: Memoria de Bachiller. Unpublished thesis. Pontificia Universidad Católica del Perú. Lima.

Alvarez, E., 1980, *Política agraria y estancamiento de la agricultura*, 1969–1977. Instituto de Estudios Peruanos. Lima.

Amin, S., 1974. *Accumulation on a world scale*: a critique of the theory of underdevelopment. 2 vols. Monthly Review Press. New York and London.

Anuario estadístico del Perú, 1944–57. Dirección Nacional de Estadística. Lima.

Appleby, G., 1976. Export monoculture and regional social structure in Puno, Peru. In *Regional Analysis*, ed. Smith, vol. II. Academic Press. New York.

1979. Las transformaciones del sistema de mercados en Puno: 1890–1960. *Análisis*, 8–9: 55–71. Lima.

Arce, A., 1981. Peasant enterprise and processes of monetisation in highland Peru: the case of Pucará. Unpublished M.A. thesis. University of Durham.

Arguedas, J. M., 1957. Evolución de las comunidades indígenas. *Revista del Museo Nacional*, 26: 78–151. Lima.

Arroyo, H. R., 1967. *Distrito de Matahuasi*. Instituto Indigenista Peruano. Huancayo.

Assadourian, C., 1982. *El sistema de la economía colonial: mercado interno, regiones y espacio económico*. Instituto de Estudios Peruanos. Lima.

Balán, J., 1978. *Estructura agraria, desarrollo capitalista y mercados de trabajo en América Latina: la migración rural–urbana en una perspectiva histórica*. Estudios Sociales, 10. CEDES (Centro de Estudios de Estado y Sociedad), Buenos Aires.

1979. *Urbanización regional y producción agraria en Argentina: un análisis comparativo*. Estudios CEDES, 2, 2. Buenos Aires.

Balán, J. et al., 1973. *Men in a developing society: geographic and social mobility in Monterrey, Mexico*. University of Texas Press. Austin, Texas.

Beckford, G. L., 1972. *Persistent poverty: underdevelopment in plantation economies of the third world*. Oxford University Press. New York.

Becker, D., 1982. Modern mine labour and politics in Peru since 1968. *Boletín de Estudios Latinoamericanos y del Caribe*, 32: 61–86.

Behrmann, K. and Umbach, A., 1978/9. Strassenhandel in Huancayo ansatze zu einer begrifflichten Klarung. MS. Fakultät Für Soziologie, Universität Bielefeld.

Benavides Zuñigo, R. M. and Gamarra Cisneros, S., 1980. Parentesco y reciprocidad en una sociedad rural de clases. Unpublished Licentiature thesis. Universidad Nacional del Centro. Huancayo.

Berry, B. J. L., 1967. *Geography of market centres and retail distribution*. Prentice-Hall. Englewood Cliffs, New Jersey.

Boeke, J. H., 1953. *Economics and economic policy as exemplified by Indonesia*. Institute of Pacific Relations. New York.

Boletín de estadística Peruana, 1958–62. Dirección Nacional de Estadística. Lima.

Bonilla, H., 1974. *El minero de Los Andes*. Instituto de Estudios Peruanos. Lima.

Bourricaud, F., 1970. *Power and society in contemporary Peru*. Praeger. New York.

Bracco. M., n.d. *La migración eventual a la ceja de selva*. Documento de Trabajo, 24. Centro de Investigaciones Socio-Económicas, Universidad Nacional Agraria, La Molina. Lima.

Brading, D. A., 1971. *Miners and merchants in Bourbon Mexico, 1763–1810*. Cambridge University Press. Cambridge.

Brading, D. A. and Cross, H. E., 1972. Colonial silver mining: Mexico and Peru. *Hispanic American Historical Review*, 52: 545–79.

Bromley, R. J., 1974. The organization of Quito's urban markets: towards a reinterpretation of periodic central places. *Transactions*, 62: 45–70. Institute of British Geographers.

Bromley, R. J. and Gerry, C. (eds.), 1979. *Casual work and poverty in third world cities*. John Wiley and Sons. New York and Chichester.

Brookfield, H., 1975. *Interdependent development*. Methuen. London.

Buechler, H. C., 1970. The ritual dimension of rural–urban networks: the fiesta system in the northern highlands of Bolivia. In *Peasants in cities*, ed. Mangin: 62–71.

Bullon, G., 1942. *Monografía de Ataura*. Lazo Sanchez. Huancayo.

Burgos, H., 1970. *Relaciones interétnicas en Riobamba*. Instituto Indigenista Interamericano, Ediciones Especiales, 55. Mexico.

Caballero, J. M., 1980. *Agricultura, reforma agraria y pobreza campesina*. Instituto de Estudios Peruanos. Lima.

1981. *Economía agraria de la sierra Peruana: antes de la reforma agraria de 1969*. Instituto de Estudios Peruanos. Lima.

Cabieses, H. et al., n.d. *Industrialización y desarrollo regional en el Perú*. Ediciones Economía, Política y Desarrollo. Lima.

Caicho, H., 1972. *La SAIS Túpac Amaru*. Cencira. Lima.

1977. *Las SAIS de la Sierra Central*. Escuela de Administración de Negocios para Graduados (ESAN). Lima.

Campaña, P., 1976. Surcos de cobre: estudio del proceso de recalificación campesina en las comunidades de la SAIS Túpac Amaru. Unpublished Master's dissertation. Pontificia Universidad Católica del Perú. Lima.

Campaña, P. and Rivera, R., 1979. El proceso de descampesinización en la sierra central del Perú. *Estudios Rurales Latinoamericanos*, 1,2: 71–100.

Cardoso, F. H. and Faletto, E., 1979. *Dependency and development in Latin America*. University of California Press. Berkeley, California.

Celestino, O., 1972. *Migración y cambio estructural: la comunidad de Lampian*. Instituto de Estudios Peruanos. Lima.

Celestino, O. and Meyers, A., 1981. *Las cofradías en el Perú: región central*. Verlag Klaus Dieter Vervuert. Frankfurt-on-Main.

Chavarría, J. 1978. The colonial heritage of national Peru: an overview. *Boletín de Estudios Latinoamericanos y del Caribe*, 25: 37–50.

Chavez, O., 1927. *Huancayo*. Huancayo.

Chayanov, A. V., 1966. *The theory of peasant economy*. Translated and edited by D. Thorner et al. for the American Economic Association. Homewood, Illinois.

CIDA (Comité Interamericano de Desarrollo Agrícola), 1966. *Tenencia de la tierra y desarrollo socio-económico del sector agrícola*. Unión Panamericana. Washington, D.C.

COMACRA (Comisión de Apoyo y Coordinación Para la Reforma Agraria), 1971. *Las comunidades integrantes de la SAIS Túpac Amaru*. Ministerio de Agricultura, Lima.

Connell, J. et al., 1974. Migration from rural areas; the evidence from village studies. *Discussion Paper, No. 36*. Institute of Development Studies, University of Sussex.

Cotler, J., 1967–8. The mechanics of internal domination and social change in Peru. *Studies in Comparative International Development*, III, 12: 229–46.

Cotler, J., 1975. The new mode of political domination in Peru. In *The Peruvian experiment: continuity and change under military rule*, ed. A. Lowenthal. Princeton University Press. Princeton, New Jersey.

Deere, C., 1976. Rural women's subsistence production in the capitalist periphery. *Review of Radical Political Economy*, 8,1: 9–17.

Deere, C., 1982. The division of labour by sex in agriculture: a Peruvian case study. *Economic Development and Cultural Change* 30,4: 795–811.

Deere, C. D. and De Janvry, A. 1981. Demographic and social differentiation among northern Peruvian peasants. *Journal of Peasant Studies*, 8,3: 335–66.

De Janvry, A. and Garramon, C., 1977. The dynamics of rural poverty in Latin America. *Journal of Peasant Studies*, 4,3: 206–16.

De Wind, A. W., 1970. A history of the political economy of mining in Peru. Unpublished Master's dissertation. University of Columbia.

1977. Peasants become miners: the evolution of industrial mining systems in Peru. Unpublished Ph.D. dissertation. University of Columbia.

Dirección General de Estadística, 1944. *Censo nacional de población y ocupación de 1940* (12 vols). Lima.

Dirección Nacional de Estadística y Censos, 1966. *Sexto censo nacional de población, 1961.* Lima.

Doughty, P. L., 1970. Behind the back of the city: 'provincial' life in Lima, Peru. In *Peasants in cities* ed. Mangin: 30–46.

1972. Peruvian migrant identity in the urban milieu. In *The anthropology of urban environments*, ed. T. Weaver and D. White. Society for Applied Anthropology Monographs, 11. Washington, DC.

1976. The social life of migrants: the case of provincial voluntary associations in Lima in method and interpretation. Unpublished paper presented to the XLII Congress of Americanists, Paris.

Epstein, S., 1973. *South India: yesterday, today and tomorrow.* Macmillan. London.

Erasmus, C., 1956. Culture, structure and process: the occurrence and disappearance of reciprocal farm labour. *South-Western Journal of Anthropology*, 12: 44–69.

Escobar, G., 1964. Sicaya: una comunidad mestiza de la sierra central del Perú. In *Estudios sobre la cultura andina del Perú*, ed. L. Valcarcel et al. Universidad Nacional Mayor de San Marcos. Lima.

1973. *Sicaya: cambios culturales en una comunidad mestiza andina.* Instituto de Estudios Peruanos Lima.

Espinoza Soriana, W., 1973. *Enciclopedia Departamental de Junín*, vol. I. Huancayo.

Extracto estadístico del Perú, 1923–43. Dirección Nacional de Estadística. Lima. FAO, 1955. *Yearbook of food and agricultural statistics.* United Nations Food and Agricultural Organization. Washington, DC.

Favre, H., 1975. Le peuplement et la colonisation agricole de la steppe dans le Pérou central. *Annales de Géographie*, 84: 415–40.

Ferner, A. M., 1977. The role of the industrial bourgeoisie in the Peruvian development model. Unpublished D. Phil. dissertation. University of Sussex.

1978. A new development model for Peru? Anomalies and readjustments. *Bulletin of the Society for Latin American Studies*, 28: 42–63.

Figueroa, A., 1978. La economía de las comunidades campesinas: el caso de la sierra sur del Perú. In *Campesinado e indigenismo en América Latina*, ed. E. Valencia. Ediciones CELATS. Lima.

1980. Política de precios agropecuarios y ingresos rurales en el Perú. In *Realidad del campo peruano después de la reforma agraria*, ed. C. Amat de León et al. Centro de Investigación y Capacitación. Editora Ital. Lima.

1981. *La economía campesina de la sierra del Perú.* Fondo Editorial, Pontificia Universidad Católica del Perú. Lima.

1982. Production and market exchange in peasant economies: the case of the southern highlands in Peru. In *Ecology and exchange in the Andes*, ed. Lehmann: 123–56.

Fisher, J., n.d. Silver mining and silver mines in the viceroyalty of Peru, 1776–1824. In *Social and economic change in modern Peru*, eds. Miller et al.

1970. *Government and society in colonial Peru: the intendant system, 1784–1814.* Athlone Press, London.

1977. *Silver mines and silver miners in colonial Peru, 1776–1824.* Centre for Latin American Studies, University of Liverpool, Monograph Series, 7. Liverpool.

Fitzgerald, E. V., 1976. *The state and economic development: Peru since 1968.* Department of Applied Economics Occasional Paper, 49. Cambridge University Press. Cambridge.

1979. *The political economy of Peru, 1956–78: economic development and the restructuring of capital.* Cambridge University Press. Cambridge.

1981. The new international division of labour and the relative autonomy of the state. *Bulletin of Latin American Research*, I, 1: 1–12.

Flores Galindo, A., 1974. *Los mineros de la Cerro de Pasco, 1900–1930.* Departamento Académico de Ciencias Sociales, Pontificia Universidad Católica del Perú. Lima.

Flores Galindo et al., 1977a. Oligarquía y capital comercial en el sur Peruano (1870–1930). Mimeo. Departamento Académico de Ciencias Sociales, Pontificia Universidad Católica del Perú. Lima.

1977b. Notas sobre oligarquía y capitalismo en Arequipa (1870–1940). Mimeo. Departamento Académico de Ciencias Sociales, Pontificia Universidad Católica del Perú. Lima.

Fongal Centro, 1980. *Desarrollo de la ganaderia lechera del centro*, vols. I and II. Fondo de Fomento para la Ganadería Lechera del Centro. Huancayo.

Fonseca, C., 1975. Comunidad, hacienda y el modelo SAIS. *América Indígena*, XXXV, 2. Mexico.

Foster-Carter, A., 1978. Can we articulate 'articulation'? In *Towards a new economic anthropology*, ed. J. Clammer. Macmillan, London.

Frank, A. G., 1969. *Capitalism and underdevelopment in Latin America.* Monthly Review Press. New York.

1972. The development of underdevelopment. In *Dependence and underdevelopment*, eds. J. D. Cockcroft et al. Doubleday Anchor. Garden City, New York.

Friedmann, H., 1980. Household production and the national economy: concepts for the analysis of agrarian formations. *Journal of Peasant Studies*, 7, 2: 158–84.

Geertz, C., 1960. The changing role of the cultural broker: the Javanese Kijaji. *Comparative Studies in Society and History*, 2: 228–49.

1963a. *Agricultural involution.* University of California Press. Berkeley, California.

1963b. *Peddlers and princes: social development and economic change in two Indonesian towns.* The University of Chicago Press. Chicago, Illinois and London.

1979. *Meaning and order in a Moroccan town.* Cambridge University Press. Cambridge.

Gerry, C. and Lebrun, O., 1975. Petty producers and capitalism. *Review of African Political Economy*, 3: 20–32.

Godelier, M., 1977. *Perspectives in Marxist anthropology. Cambridge University Press, Cambridge.*

Gómez, J., 1976. *Reforma agraria y campesinado en Cailloma.* Arequipa.

Gongora, M., 1975. *Studies in the colonial history of South Amercia.* Cambridge University Press. Cambridge.

Gonzales de Olarte, E., 1982. *Economías regionales del Perú.* Instituto de Estudios Peruanos. Lima.

Goodman, D. and Redclift, M., 1981., *From peasant to proletarian: capitalist development and agrarian transitions.* Basil Blackwell. Oxford.

Grompone, R., 1981. Comercio ambulante: razones de una terca presencia. *Que Hacer*, 13. Centro de Estudios y Promoción del Desarrollo. Lima.

Grondín, M., 1978a. *Comunidad andina: explotación calculada.* Secretaría de Estado de Agricultura de la República Dominicana. Santo Domingo.

1978b. Peasant cooperation and dependency: the case of the electricity enterprises of Muquiyauyo. In *Peasant cooperation and capitalist expansion*, ed. Long and Roberts: 99–127.

Harris, O., 1978. Complementarity and conflict: an Andean view of women and men. In *Sex and age as principles of social differentiation*, ed. J. La Fontaine. Academic Press. London.

Hart, K., 1973. Informal income opportunities and urban employment in Ghana. *Journal of Modern African Studies*, 11: 61–89.

Higgins, B., 1956. The dualistic theory of underdeveloped areas. *Economic Development and Cultural Change*, 4: 99–115.

Hilliker, G., 1971. *The politics of reform in Peru: the Aprista and other mass parties in Latin America*. Johns Hopkins University Press. Baltimore and London.

Hirschman, A., 1977. A generalized linkage approach to development. In *Essays on Economic Development and Cultural Change in Honor of Bert. F. Hoselitz*, ed. M. Nash. Economic Development and Cultural Change, 25. University of Chicago Press. Chicago, Illinois.

Huancayo Plan Director, 1976. Dirección General de Desarrollo Urbano, Consejo Provincial de Huancayo. Huancayo.

Hutchinson, W. B., 1973. Sociocultural change in the Mantaro valley region of Peru: Acolla, a case study. Unpublished Ph.D. dissertation, University of Indiana.

Indicadores estadísticos, Departamento de Junín, 1981. Instituto Nacional de Planificación, Oficina Regional de Huancayo. Huancayo.

International Development Service, 1953. *Report on the regional development of the Mantaro valley*. Lima.

Isbell, B. J., 1974. The influence of migrants upon traditional social and political concepts: a Peruvian case study. In *Latin American urban research*, vol. 4, eds. W. Cornelius and F. Trueblood. Sage Publications. Beverly Hills and London.

Johnson, E. A., 1970. *The organization of space in developing countries*. Harvard University Press. Cambridge. Mass.

Jones, G. S., 1971. *Outcast London: a study in the relationship between classes in Victorian London*. Clarendon Press. Oxford. Reprinted 1984. Penguin Books. Harmondsworth.

Jongkind, C. F., 1971. La supuesta funcionalidad de los clubes regionales en Lima. *Boletín de Estudios Latinoamericanos y del Caribe*, 11: 11–12. Centre of Latin American Research and Documentation, Amsterdam.

    1974. A reappraisal of the role of regional associations in Lima, Peru. *Comparative Studies in Society and History*, 16,4: 471–82.

    1979. The regional associations in Lima revisited: new data and interpretation of a reinterpretation. Unpublished paper prepared for XLIII Congress of Americanists, Vancouver, Canada.

Kahn, J. S., 1980. *Minangkabau social formations: Indonesian peasants and the world economy*. Cambridge University Press. Cambridge.

Klaren. P. F., 1973. *Modernization, dislocation and Aprismo: origins of the Peruvian Aprista party, 1870–1932*. University of Texas Press. Austin and London.

Krause, G., 1977. *Der sonntagsmarkt von Huancayo and die sozioökonomische struktur des Mantaro-tals in Peru*. Gebr. Mann Verlag, Indiana Beiheft, Ibero-Amerikanisches Institut. Berlin.

Kruijt. D., 1982. Mining and miners in central Peru, 1968–1980. *Boletín de Estudios Latinoamericanos y del Caribe*, 32: 49–60.

Kruijt, D. and Vellinga, M., 1977. The political economy of mining enclaves in Peru. *Boletín de Estudios Latinoamericanos y del Caribe*, 25: 97–126.

1979. *Labor relations and multinational corporations: the Cerro de Pasco corporation in Peru, 1902–1974.* Van Gorcum. Assen.

Laite, A. J., 1977. The migrant worker: a case study of industrialization and social stratification in highland Peru. Unpublished Ph.D. thesis. University of Manchester.

1978a. Processes of industrial and social change in highland Peru. In *Peasant cooperation and capitalist expansion*, ed. Long and Roberts: 72–98.

1978b. Industrialisation, migration and social stratification at the periphery. *Sociological Review*, 26: 72–98.

1981. *Industrial development and migrant labour.* Manchester University Press. Manchester.

Larson, B., 1972. Merchants and economic activity in sixteenth century Potosí. Mimeo. Unpublished M.A. thesis, University of Columbia.

Latin Project, 1968. *Training the Rio Mantaro.* Basle and Lima.

Lehmann, D. (ed.), 1982. *Ecology and exchange in the Andes.* Cambridge University Press. Cambridge.

Lenin, V. I., 1967. *The development of capitalism in Russia.* Collected works vol. 3. Progress Publishers. Moscow.

León de Leal, M. and Deere, C. D., 1980. *Mujer y capitalismo agrario: estudio de cuatro regiones colombianas.* Asociación Colombiana Para el Estudio de la Población. Bogotá.

Lomnitz, L., 1975. *Networks and marginality: life in a Mexican shantytown.* Academic Press. New York.

Long, N., 1973. The role of regional associations in Peru. In *The process of urbanization*, ed. M. Drake et al. The Open University. Bletchley.

1977. Commerce and kinship in the Peruvian highlands. In *Andean Kinship and Marriage*, ed. R. Bolton and E. Meyer. American Anthropological Association Special Publication, 7. Washington, DC.

1979. Multiple enterprise in the central highlands of Peru. In *Entrepreneurs in cultural context*, ed. S. M. Greenfield et al. University of New Mexico Press. Albuquerque.

1980. Mine-based regional economies: Andean examples, historical and contemporary. In *State and region in Latin America*, ed. G. A. Banck et al. Centre for Latin American Research and Documentation. Amsterdam.

Long, N. and Richardson, P., 1978. Informal sector, petty commodity production and social relations of small-scale enterprise. In *Towards a new economic anthropology*, ed. J. Clammer. Macmillan. London.

Long, N. and Roberts, B. R., 1969. Regional structure and entrepreneurial activity in a Peruvian valley. An unpublished research proposal submitted to the SSRC. Mimeo. University of Manchester.

1974. Regional structure and entrepreneurial activity in a Peruvian valley. Final report to the SSRC (unpublished), lodged in the British Lending Library.

(eds.), 1978. *Peasant cooperation and capitalist expansion in central Peru.* University of Texas Press. Austin and London.

Long, N. and Sánchez, R., 1978. Peasant and entrepreneurial coalitions: the case of the Matahuasi cooperative. In *Peasant cooperation and capitalist expansion*, ed. Long and Roberts.

Long, N. and Winder, D., 1975. From peasant community to production co-operative: an analysis of recent government policy in Peru. *Journal of Development Studies*, 12,1: 75–94.

Lopes, J. B., 1978. Capitalist development and agrarian structure in Brazil. *International Journal of Urban and Regional Research*, 2,2: 1–11.

Lopes, J. B. and Brant, V. C., 1978. Extrativismo e decadencia: cidade e campo en Parnaiba. Mimeo. CEBRAP. São Paulo.

MacEwen Scott, A., 1979. Who are the self-employed? In *Casual work and poverty in third world cities*, ed. Bromley and Gerry.

McGee, T. G., 1971a. Catalysts or cancers? The role of cities in Asian society. In *Urbanization and national development*, eds. L. Jakobson and V. Prakash: 157–82. Halstead Press. New York.

1971b. *The urbanization process in the third world: explorations in search of a theory*. John Wiley. London.

1973. 'Peasants in cities': a paradox a most ingenious paradox. *Human Organization*, 32,2.

T. G. McGee and Y. M. Yeung. 1977. *Hawkers in selected southeast Asian cities: planning for the bazaar economy*. International Development Research Centre. Ottawa. Ontario.

1979. The poverty syndrome: making out in the southeast Asian city. In *Casual work and poverty in the third world city*, ed. Bromley and Gerry.

Mangin, W., 1959. The role of regional associations in the adaptation of rural migrants to cities in Peru. *Sociologus*, IX: 23–36. Reprinted in D. B. Heath and R. N. Adams (eds.), *Contemporary cultures and societies of Latin Amarica*. 1965. Random House. New York.

1967. Latin American squatter settlements: a problem and a solution. *Latin American Research Review*, 2,3: 65–98.

(ed.), 1970. *Peasants in cities: readings in the anthropology of urbanization*. Houghton Mifflin. Boston, Mass.

1973. Sociological, cultural, and political characteristics of some urban migrants in Peru. In *Urban anthropology*, ed. A. Southall: 315–50. Oxford University Press. New York and London.

Manrique, R., 1972. La transformación de una empresa industrial textil del sistema capitalista al sistema cooperativo. Unpublished thesis, Universidad Nacional Mayor de San Marcos. Lima.

Marmora, L., 1975. Superpoblación relativa, migraciones, movimientos campesinos y reforma agraria en el Perú (1956–68). *Serie Publicaciones previas, Subarea de Población*, 7. CISEPA, Pontificia Universidad Católica del Peru. Lima.

Martinez, H., 1980. Las empresas asociativas agrícolas Peruanas. In *Realidad del campo peruano después de la reforma agraria*, C. Amat y León et al. Centro de Investigación y Capacitación. Editoria Ital. Lima.

Martínez-Alier, J., 1973. *Los huacchilleros del Perú*. Ruedo Iberico. Paris.

1977. *Haciendas, plantations and collective farms: agrarian class societies – Cuba and Peru*. Frank Cass. London.

1978. El ganado huaccha en las haciendas de la Cerro de Pasco Corporation. *Estudios Rurales Latinoamericanos*, 1,3: 175–80.

Marx, K., 1964. Economic and philosophical manuscripts. *Early writings*, translated and edited by T. B. Bottomore. McGraw-Hill. New York.

1972. *Capital*, vol. 1. Everyman's Library. Dent. London.

Massey, D., 1978. Regionalism: some current issues. *Capital and Class*, 6: 106–25.

Matos Mar, J., 1966. Migration and urbanisation – the barriadas of Lima. In *Urbanisation in Latin America*, ed. P. Hauser. Unesco Liège.

Matos Mar, J. et al., 1969. *Dominación y cambios en el Perú rural*. Instituto de Estudios Peruanos. Lima.

Mayer, A. C., 1966. The significance of quasi-groups in the study of complex societies. In *The social anthropology of complex societies*, ed. M. Banton: 97–122. Tavistock. London.

Meillassoux, C., 1972. From reproduction to production: a marxist approach to economic anthropology. *Economy and Society*, 1,1: 93–105.

Miller, R., n.d. Railways and economic development in central Peru, 1890–1930. In *Social and economic change in modern Peru*, ed. Miller et al.

Miller, R. et al., nd. *Social and economic change in modern Peru*. Centre for Latin American Studies, University of Liverpool, Monograph Series, 6. Liverpool.

Ministerio de Industria, 1977. *Programa parque industrial: perfil dinámico de distribución de empresas*. Ministerio de Industria, Dirección Región VI. Huancayo.

Mitchell, J. C., 1966. Theoretical orientations in African urban studies. In *The social anthropology of complex societies*, ed. M. Banton: 37–68. Tavistock. London.

Montoya, R., 1973. *La SAIS Cahuide y sus contradicciones*. Universidad Nacional de San Marcos. Lima.

Moreno Toscano, A. and Florescano, E., 1974. *El sector externo y la organización espacial y regional de México, 1521–1910*. Cuadernos de Trabajo del Departamento de Investigaciones Históricas. Instituto Nacional de Antropología y Historia, Mexico.

Morse, R. M., 1975. The development of urban systems in the Americas in the nineteenth century. *Journal of Interamerican Studies and World Affairs*, 17,1: 4–26.

Moser, C., 1977. The dual economy and marginality debate and the contribution of micro-analysis: market sellers in Bogota. *Development and Change*, 8,4: 465–90.

1978. Informal sector or petty commodity production. *World Development*, 6,9/10: 1041–64.

Muñoz Vargas, M., 1982. Urbanization, migration and occupational structure in Latin America with special reference to Peru. Unpublished Ph.D. thesis. University of Manchester.

Murmis, M., 1969. Tipos de marginalidad y posición en el proceso productivo. *Revista Latinoamericana de Sociología*, 5,2: 43–120.

Murra, J., 1978. *La organización económica del estado Inca*. Siglo XXI Editores. Mexico.

Nun, J., 1969. Superpoblación relativa, ejercito industrial de reserva y masa marginal. *Revista Latinoamericana de Sociología*, 5,2: 178–237.

ONEC, 1974. *Censos nacionales, VII de población, II de vivienda, 4 de Junio, 1972*. Oficina Nacional de Estadística y Censos. Lima.

Orlove, B. S., 1977. *Alpacas, sheep and men: the wool export economy and regional society in southern Peru*. Academic Press. New York.

Palerm, A., 1976. *Sobre la formación del sistema colonial en México: apuntes para una discusión*. La Casa Chata. Tlalpan, Mexico.

Pareja, P., 1979. Proceso organizativo en las fábricas de tejidos de lana de Huancayo: Los Andes y Manufacturas del Centro. In *Serie Andes Centrales*, 7. Taller de Estudios Andinos, Universidad Nacional Agraria. La Molina.

Pelto, P. J. and Poggie, J. J., 1974. Modes of modernization: a regional focus. In *Rethinking modernization*, ed. J. J. Poggie, Jr and R. N. Lynch. Greenwood Press. Westport, Connecticut.

Peruvian Yearbook, 1956/7. Andean Airmail and Peruvian Times, A. A. Lima.

Philpott, S. B., 1973. *West Indian migration: the Montserrat case*. The Athlone Press. London.

Plan de desarrollo económico y social, 1967–70, 1967. Instituto Nacional de Planificación. Lima.

Plan operativo, 1980. Ministerio de Vivienda y Construcción, Huancayo.

Poggie, J. J. and Miller, F. C., 1969. Contact, change and industrialization in a network of Mexican villages. *Human Organization*, 28,3: 190–98.

Ponce, H., n.d. *Cambios fundamentales en la ocupación del territorio y migración interna en el Perú*. Publicaciones Previas. Subárea de Población, 3. Departamento Académico de Ciencias Sociales, Pontificia Universidad Católica del Perú. Lima.

Portes, A., 1981. Unequal exchange and the urban informal sector. In *Labor, class and the international system*, eds. Portes and Walton: 67–106.

Portes, A. and Walton, J. (eds.), 1981. *Labor, class and the international system*. Academic Press. New York.

PREALC (Programa Regional de Empleo para America Latina y el Caribe), 1976. *Situaciones y perspectivas del empleo en América Latina*. International Labour Office. Geneva.

Preston, D. A., 1975. Dominación interna, los pueblos pequeños, el campo y desarrollo. *America Indígena*, 35: 29–37.

1978. *Farmers and towns: rural–urban relations in highland Bolivia*. Geographical Abstracts Ltd, University of East Anglia. Norwich.

Quijano, A. 1971. *Nationalism and capitalism in Peru: a study in neo-imperialism*, trans. H. R. Lane. Monthly Review Press. New York and London.

1973. Redefinición de la dependencia y proceso de marginalización en América Latina. In *Populismo, marginalización y dependencia*, ed. A. Quijano and F. Weffort. Editorial Universitaria Centroamericana. San José, Costa Rica.

1974. The marginal role of the economy and the marginalized labour force. *Economy and Society*, 3,4: 393–428.

Renique, G., 1978. *La agricultura del valle del Mantaro: estadísticas socio-económicas, 1950–1968*. Taller de estudios andinos: serie andes centrales, 5. Universidad Nacional Agraria. La Molina.

1979. *Desarrollo de la ganadería lanera Peruana y evolución de las explotaciones pecurias*. Taller de estudios andinos: serie ensayos generales, 3. Universidad Nacional Agraria. La Molina.

Richardson, H. W., 1978. *Regional economics*. University of Illinois Press. Urbana, Illinois.

Rivera, R., 1976. La tierra es ancha y de todos: estudio de la reestructuración campesina en la SAIS Túpac Amaru. Unpublished Master's dissertation. Pontificia Universidad Católica del Perú. Lima.

Roberts, B. R., 1973. Migración urbana y cambio en la organización provincial en la sierra central de Perú. *Ethnica: Revista de Antropología*, 6: 237–61 Barcelona.

1974. The interrelationships of city and provinces in Peru and Guatemala. In *Latin American urban research*, vol. 4, eds, W. Cornelius and F. Trueblood: 207–36. Sage Publications. Beverly Hills and London.

n.d. The social history of a provincial town: Huancayo, 1890–1972. In *Social and economic change in modern Peru*, eds. Miller et al.

1978a. The bases of industrial cooperation in Huancayo. In *Peasant cooperation and capitalist expansion*, ed. Long and Roberts: 129–62.

1978b. *Cities of peasants*. Edward Arnold. London.

1980. State and region in Latin America. In *State and region in Latin America*, ed. G. A. Banck et al. Centre for Latin American Research and Documentation. Amsterdam.

Roberts, B. R. and Samaniego, C., 1978. The evolution of pastoral villages and the significance of agrarian reform in the highlands of central Peru. In *Peasant cooperation and capitalist expansion*, ed. Long and Roberts: 241–64.

Rothstein, M., 1966. Antebellum wheat and cotton exports: a contrast in marketing organization and economic development. *Agricultural History*, 41,4: 91–100.

Samaniego, C., 1974. Location, social differentiation and peasant movements in the central sierra of Peru. Unpublished Ph.D. thesis. University of Manchester.

1978. Peasant movements at the turn of the century, and the rise of the independent farmer. In *Peasant cooperation and capitalist expansion*, ed. Long and Roberts: 45–71.

1980a. Perspectiva de la agricultura campesina en el Perú. In *Realidad del campo peruano después de la reforma agraria*, C. Amat y León et al. Centro de Investigación y Capacitación. Editoria Ital. Lima.

1980b. Campesinado en el valle del Mantaro, Perú. *Estudios Andinos, IX*, 16: 31–72.

Sanchez Enriquez, R., 1979. Capitalismo y persistencia del campesinado parcelario: el caso de la sierra central. Mimeo. Taller de coyuntura agraria, 27. Universidad Nacional Agraria. La Molina.

Scott, C., 1976. Peasants, proletarianization and the articulation of modes of production: the case of the sugar-cane cutters in northern Peru, 1940–1969. *Journal of Peasant Studies*, 3,3: 321–42.

Shanin, T. (ed.), 1973. *Peasants and peasant societies*. Penguin Books. Harmondsworth.

1974. The nature and logic of the peasant economy: a generalisation. *Journal of Peasant Studies*, 1,2: 186–206.

Skeldon, R. 1976. Regional associations and population migration in Peru: an interpretation. *Urban Anthropology*, 5,3: 233–52.

1977a. Regional associations: a note on opposed interpretations. *Comparative Studies in Society and History*, 19,4: 506–10.

1977b. The evolution of migration patterns during urbanisation in Peru. *Geographical Review*, 67,4.

Slater, D., 1972. Spatial aspects of the Peruvian socio-economic system, 1925–1968. Unpublished Ph.D. thesis, University of London, London School of Economics.

1979. The state and territorial centralization in Peru, 1968–1978. *Boletín de Estudios Latinoamericanos y del Caribe*, 27: 43–67.

Smith, C. A. 1972. The domestic marketing system in west Guatemala: an economic, locational, and cultural analysis. Unpublished Ph.D. dissertation. Stanford University.

(ed.), 1976. *Regional analysis*, vols. I and II. Academic Press. New York, San Francisco and London.

1981. Regional analysis in world system perspective: critique of three structural theories of uneven development. Unpublished paper presented to Conference for

282   *Bibliography*

Society of Economic Anthropology, Bloomington, Indiana. Mimeo. Department of Anthropology, Duke University, Durham, North Carolina.

Smith, G. A., 1975. The social basis of peasant political activity: the case of the Huasicanchinos of central Peru. Unpublished D.Phil. thesis. University of Sussex.

1979. Socio-economic differentiation and relations of production among petty producers in central Peru, 1880 to 1970. *Journal of Peasant Studies*, 6,3: 286–310.

1980. Rural resistance: community and class consciousness. Unpublished paper presented to interdisciplinary conference on peasant production and the evolution of social systems. University of Iowa. Mimeo.

Smith, G. A. and Cano, P., 1978. Some factors contributing to peasant land occupations: the case of Huasicancha. In *Peasant cooperation and capitalist expansion*, ed. Long and Roberts: 163–90.

Solano Saez, J., 1978. From cooperative to hacienda: the case of the agrarian society of Pucará. In *Peasant cooperation and capitalist expansion*, eds. Long and Roberts: 191–208.

Stavenhagen, R. 1965. Classes, colonialism, and acculturation. *Studies in Comparative International Development*, 1,6: 53–77.

Tandeter, E., 1980. La rente comme rapport de production et comme rapport de distribution: le cas de l'industrie minière de Potosí, 1750–1826. Unpublished thesis. Paris.

1981. Forced and free labour in late colonial Potosí. *Past and Present*, 93: 98–136.

Tello Devotto, R., 1971. *Historia de la provincia de Huancayo*. Casa de la Cultura de Junín. Huancayo.

Thorp, R. and Bertram, G., 1978. *Peru 1890–1977: growth and policy in an open economy*. Macmillan. London.

Tullis, F. L., 1970. *Lord and peasant in Peru: a paradigm of political and social change*. Harvard University Press. Cambridge, Mass.

Vandendries, R., 1975. Internal migration and economic development in Peru. In *Latin American modernisation problems*, ed. R. E. Scott. Illinois University Press. Chicago, Illinois.

Wachtel, N., 1977. *The vision of the vanquished: the Spanish conquest of Peru through Indian eyes, 1530–1570*. Harvester Press. Hassocks, Sussex.

Webb, R., 1975. Government policy and distribution of income. In *The Peruvian experiment*, ed. A. Lowenthal. Princeton University Press. Princeton, New Jersey.

Wils, F., 1979. *Industrialization, industrialists and the nation-state in Peru*. Institute of International Studies, University of California. Berkeley, California.

Wilson, F., 1978. The dynamics of change in an Andean region: the province of Tarma, Peru, in the nineteenth century. Unpublished Ph.D. thesis. University of Liverpool.

1979. Propiedad e ideología: estudio de una oligarquía en los Andes centrales (S. XIX). *Análisis*, 8–9: 36–54. Lima.

1980. The conflict over Indian land in nineteenth century Peru. In *State and region in Latin America*, ed. G. A. Banck, et al. Centre for Latin American Research and Documentation. Amsterdam.

1982. Property and ideology: a regional oligarchy in the central Andes in the nineteenth century. In *Ecology and exchange in the Andes*, ed. D. Lehmann: 191–210.

Wilson, P., 1975. From mode of production to spatial formation: the regional consequences of dependent industrialization in Peru. Unpublished Ph.D. thesis. Cornell University.

Winder, D., 1978. The impact of the *comunidad* on local development in the Mantaro valley. In *Peasant cooperation and capitalist expansion*, ed. Long and Roberts: 209–40.

Wolf, E. R., 1950. An analysis of ritual co-parenthood: *compadrazgo*. *Southwestern Journal of Anthropology*, 6: 1–18.

1956. Aspects of group relations in a complex society: Mexico. *American Anthropologist*, 58,6: 1065–76.

1957. The Mexican bajio in the eighteenth century: an analysis of cultural integration. In *Synoptic studies of Mexican culture*, ed. M. S. Edmundson. Middle American Research Institute, Publication 17. Tulane University. New Orleans.

World Development (Special Issue), 1978. Vol. 6, nos. 9–10. Edited by R. Bromley.

Worsley, P., 1976. Proletarians, sub-proletarians, lumpenproletarians, *marginalidados*, migrants, urban peasants and urban poor. *Sociology*, 10,1.

Yepes, E., 1972. *Perú, 1820–1920: un siglo de desarrollo capitalista*. Instituto de Estudios Peruanos. Lima.

Young, F. W., 1964. Location and reputation in a Mexican inter-village network. *Human Organization*, 21,1: 36–41.

Young, F. W. and Young, R. C., 1960. Social integration and change in twenty-four Mexican villages. *Economic Development and Cultural Change*, 8: 366–77.

Index

Acción Popular, 14, 255
Adams, R.: on population pressure on land resources, 33; on power domains, 42–3
administrative units in Peru, 13; in colony, 26–7; in nineteenth century, 32–3; in Huancayo, 84, 166, 264 n. 9
agrarian reform, 3, 18, 100, 145, 248–53; and APRA, 14, 86; and villages, 99, 167, 201
agriculture, 59–63; importance in national economy, 140–2, 244–5; in Junín, 18–20, 142, 169–72, 252–4; relationship with mining, 25, 48–9, 51–2, 58–9, 92, 238–9; relationship with towns 83; in *puna*, 94; in Mantaro valley, 38–42, 108, 160–1; comparison with Indonesia, 239. *See also* production
agro-mining economy, 71–3
Alberti, G. and Sanchez, R.: on changes in village organization and politics in the Mantaro area, 32, 34, 36; on Huancayo, 148, 264 nn. 4, 7
anexo (sub-district): as basis for local identity, 114, 200, 208, 215
Appleby, G.: on Puno, 7
APRA (American Popular Revolutionary Alliance), 13, 244, 269 n. 4; activities in Mantaro region, 84–6, 167, 206, 214, 267 n. 7; bases of support, 85–6, 178, 186, 207, 250; in textiles, 79; vote (1980) for, in Junín, 255
Arequipa: regional system of, 66–7, 244–5
Arguedas, J. M.: on development of Huancayo, 34, 235
Assadourian, C. S.: on colonial economy, 237–8
aviador (small-scale middleman), 27

Balán, J.: on regional development in Argentina, 243
barrio: as basis for village organization, 26–7, 34, 135–7, 199, 203, 267 n. 4
Belaunde, Fernando (President 1963–8; 1980–): government of, 14, 249, 255
Bolivar, Simon: 1824 decrees of, 32
brokers: political, at village level, 186

Caballero, J. M.: on agrarian reform, 248; on agriculture in highlands, 18
Cacchi: hacienda of, 34
capital: role of foreign, 11–15, 46–8, 78, 244; accumulation of, in region, 44, 104, 110, 156, 174; outflow of, from region, 165
capitalism: development of, 5, 10, 144, 257; in agriculture, 89–90, 125–8; and non-capitalist forms, 9, 88, 91–2, 109, 230–2, 262 n.2; and regional growth, 1–3, 9, 24, 67–8, 104–5, 142–3, 235–48; and rural socio-economic differentiation, 107, 137–9
central highlands, 1–2; definition of, 16; government investment in, 15. *See also* Mantaro valley
centre–periphery: concept of, 237
Cerro de Pasco Mining Corporation, 46–58, 89, 106, 264 n. 2; formation of, 46; haciendas of, 86, 89–90; impact on Huancayo, 71–2; relation to villages, 92–4, 104, 116–21, 262 n. 4; and hydro-electric project, 16; and sub-contracting, 115
Chayanov, A. V.: on differentiation among peasantry, 107; on economic rationality of household, 230
Chilean War, 11, 40, 114
cholo: use of term, 29–30

284

Chupaca, 33, 35, 59; dominant position of, 29–30, 38–9
class: among peasantry, 91, 103, 109–11, 137–9, 170, 175; formation of, in region, 36, 40–3, 67–8, 70, 80–7, 161, 166, 168, 246–55; in colony, 30–1; in nineteenth century, 36; in Peruvian politics, 13–15, 205, 208, 214–16; in regional analyses, 3–4, 7–9, 236–45
cofradía system, 27, 30, 108; sale of lands of, 127, 178, 204
compadrazgo (ritual co-parenthood), 91, 105, 108–9, 194, 196–7
comunero (community member), 92–3, 172, 262 n. 5, 268 n. 5; differentiation among, 99–100, 102, 105
comunidad (community): activities of, 108, 203, 204–6, 262 n. 5; *indígena* and *campesina*, 214; *industrial*, 152. *See also* peasantry
community: differentiation of, 42, 107, 215–16, 262 n. 5; industrial, 15; organization of, in central highlands, 27–8, 30–2, 88, 92, 113, 125, 172, 175; politics of, 204–6; role in development, 2, 105–6, 206, 238–9, 249; and agrarian reform, 100–1, 251–3, 263 n. 11
Concepción, 34, 39, 166
co-operation: forms of, 2, 108–9, 167, 193–5
co-operatives: activities of, in region, 100–1, 148–50, 156–7, 166–7, 194
curaca, 27

De Janvry, A. and Garramon, C.: on cheap labour in agriculture, 88, 236–7, 262 n. 2
development: local projects of, 177, 197, 203, 214; policy, in Peru, 15, 145, 167, 248; regional, 4–9, 44, 241–5, 269 n. 3; uneven, in Peru, 12, 68–9, 144
differentiation: social and economic, 2, 28–31, 38, 107, 215; at periphery, 237–8; in Huancayo, 76, 145–9; in *puna* communities; 99–100, 105–6; in valley communities, 111–39, 170, 253
district: as administrative unit, 2, 26–7, 36; creation of, 8; regional associations of, 199, 204, 208; relations with *comunidad*, 214; votes in, 38–9
domination: nature of, in region, 32–3
Doughty, P.: on regional associations, 199
dualism: nature of, in Peru, 11, 68, 155, 240; urban, 142–3

ecological levels in Peru, 218, 224–5, 229, 241–2

education: growth of, in region, 37–8, 44–5, 249; importance of, in villages, 68, 174; and out-migration, 52, 57, 75, 100, 102, 125, 209–10
enclave: consequences for local economic activity, 105; definition of, 246, 269 n. 5; in mining, 1, 68; and regional development, 269 n. 3
enganche, 51–2, 115–16, 118–19
entrepreneurs: characteristics of, in region, 31, 48, 52, 66–7, 78–9, 105, 130–1, 156–61, 170, 176–97; origins of, in region, 40–1, 235; significance of, in regional politics, 2, 14, 84, 249–50, 255
estates: relation of, to villages, 41, 44, 86, 89–91, 200, 215, 248; significance of, in region, 18–19, 28, 34–6, 66, 250–1. *See also* haciendas, pasture
ethnicity, 5, 28–31; and enterprise, 76–82. *See also mestizaje*
exchange: significance of, 5, 9, 107; types of, in region, 108, 150, 173, 186–90, 249, 268 n. 9. *See also* social relationships

faena (collective labour), 42, 114, 133
family: budget of, in mines, 54–5; development cycle of, 230; employment of, in small-scale enterprises, 145–7, 152–9, 193, 209–10, 223; extended, in villages, 136–7, 224. *see also* household economy, social relationships
farmers: commerical, in nineteenth century, 36–8, 41; significance of, in region, 141, 170, 176–80, 194; and agrarian reform, 252–3. *see also* peasantry
fiestas: functions of, 42; in towns 159, 210; in villages, 108, 134–7; of San Sebastián, 187, 190, 195, 266, n. 3
Fitzgerald, E. V. K.: on dualism, 68, 143, 258 n. 5; on food prices in Peru, 60

Geertz, C.: on bazaar economy, 155; on agriculture, 239

haciendas, 18, 25–6, 77, 238–9; development of, in region, 28, 30, 33–6, 41–3; impact on regional development, 7–8; relation to Huancayo, 71–2, 259 n. 5; relation to villages, 86, 89–92, 200, 203, 218–19, 267 n. 5. *see also* estates, pasture
Hirschman, A.: on linkage theory, 240–2
household economy, 8; in city, 220; in *puna* communities; 105; in valley, 108, 131, 161,

plantations, 59; to tropical lowlands, 169, 200

military government of 1968, 14–15; policies of, 145, 148, 152, 248–52

mining: in central Peru, characteristics of labour force, 57–8; changes in technology of, 55–6, 141; employment in, 20 Table 1, 56, 64 Table 7, 122 Table 17, 146 Table 22; impact on region, 63, 67–9, 89, 95, 138, 246–7, 249, 255; in colonial period, 25–6, 30–1; in nineteenth century, 31–2, 37; in twentieth century, 45–8; organization of, 49–51, 71–2; recruitment of labour for, 51–2, 93, 115–16; wages in, 52, 53 Table 4, 54–5, 118. *See also* production

minka (rewarding people in kind), 108, 224, 269 n. 9

mita (labour service), 26, 113

mobility: social, in central highlands, 93, 100, 111–12, 137–9, 249

Moser, C.: on informal sector, 143

Muquiyauyo, 37, 54, 56–7, 161, 165, 249

national economy of Peru, 10–11, 45, 140–1

Odría, Manuel, 82

Ongoy, 200, 208–12

Orlove, B. S.: on Sicuani, 7

Padilla, Norberto: 1874 report of, 35

Palerm, A.: on the colonial system of production, 238–9

pasture: in central highlands, 18–19, 96–7; control over, by community, 92, 172, 251; effect of La Oroya smelter on, 89, *see also* haciendas, estates

peasantry: as cheap labour, 88; as peasant worker, 68, 99; as producers of food for urban market, 60; characteristics of, in region, 2, 92, 107–8, 171–2, 229, 253; differentiation within, 105, 109–11, 137–9, 170; disappearance of, 102; impact of government policies on, 15–16, 175, 248–52; in city, 199; in colonial period, 28; in nineteenth century, 37; movements, 86, 106, 215; politics of, 14, 85, 255; relation to commercial farmers, 177; relation to mining, 51–2, 58, 93; and household economy, 232–3. *See also comunidad*, farmers, smallholder agriculture

peasant community: *see comunidad*

plantations, cotton, 44, 51, 59, 71, 244

political parties, 13–14. *See also* APRA, Acción Popular

population: growth of, during colonial period, 33; growth of, Huancayo, 36, 39 Table 2, 65, 73, 254; growth of, in Lima, 11, 140; over-reporting of, in census, 266 n. 18; statistics of, for Junín, 16, 44, 65 Table 8, 141, 169; structure of, in *puna* communities, 98 Fig. 1, and land fragmentation, 52

Prado, Manuel, 13, 79

production: as focus of research, 5, 7–9, 236, 256–7; export, 10–11, 237; household, 228, 233; petty commodity, 143, 232; relationships of, 105, 230; system of, in region and elsewhere, 25–6, 31, 70, 89, 140, 238–42, 245; value of, by sector, in Junín, 20 Table 1. *See also* mining, agriculture, industrialization, social relationships

progressiveness, concept of, in central highlands, 33, 35, 212, 249, 255

proletariat: weak formation of, in region, 68, 99–100, 161

Pucará, 170–6

Puno, 12, 44; regional system of, 7, 244

Quijano A.: on economic centralization and marginality, 142

railway: Huancayo–Lima and Huancayo–Huancavelica, 16, 20, 60

reducciones, 26

region: concept of, 3–4, 236, 257; importance of local variations to, 95; in development, 9, 237–45; in urban identity, 199; other definitions of, 6; and class analysis, 7–8

regional associations: *see* migrant associations

Sacco, 102

SAIS (Sociedades Agrarias de Interés Social), 18–19, 90, 95, 250–2

Samaniego, C.: on conflict between haciendas and communities, 89; on population pressure and land resources, 33

Satipo: colonization of, 157, 174; commercial links with, 158–9; growth of, 16, 253–4

share-cropping (*al partir*), 108, 110; on highland estates, 248. *See also* michipa

shepherds: in villages, 226, 269 n. 11; on haciendas, 49, 89–91; and agrarian reform, 251

Sicaya: in colonial period, 28–30; in nineteenth century, 34, 38, 39 Table 2; industry in, 160; migration from, 59, 163, 265 n. 15

SINAMOS (Sistema Nacional de Apoyo a la Movilización Social), 167

small-scale enterprise: characterization of, 143, 149–50, 230–4; in Huancayo, 145–8, 156, 254; in villages, 181, 252–3; networks within, 186–90, 194–5; risks of, 154–5, 229; and politics, 167, 197, 249–50, *See also* social relationships

smallholder agriculture: prevalence of, in highlands, 18. *See also* peasantry

Smith, C.A.: on regional analysis, 5–6, 7

social relationships: significance of, in city, 152, 154; significance of, within villages, 133, 181–97. *See also* exchange, family, production, small-scale enterprise

Sociedad Ganadera del Centro, 41

Sociedad Ganadera de Junín, 41, 49

state: in colonial period, in Peru, 28, 42; in economic development, 240–1; in nineteenth century, in Peru, 32; in Peru, 2, 12; policies of, in Peru, 15–16, 248–9; role of, in Peruvian economy, 9, 144; and regional development, 243–4, 247; and small-scale enterprise, 152; and social services, 145

Tarma: economic changes in, 40–41, 65, 254;

in colonial period, 31; in nineteenth century, 32, 34; landed elite of, 35, 36; links between town and villages, 99

textile industry: in Huancayo, 60, 66, 72–3, 78, 80, 81, 147–8, 151–2, 154, 156–7, 160; workers in, 68, 75, 79, 82–3, 85

Thorp, R. and Bertram, G.: on Cerro de Pasco Corporation, 46–7; on Peruvian economic development, 10

transport: by pack animal, 38, 89; employment in, 20 Table 1, 64 Table 7, 142; improvement in and mining, 46; significance of, for regional economy, 48; and small-scale enterprise, 79, 150, 181–6

uyay, 108, 110, 268 n. 9

Velasco Alvarado, Juan, 15. *See also* military government

villages: of region, 22–4; during colonial period, 27–31; in nineteenth century, 32–5; in *puna* region, 88–106. *See also* Huasicancha, Matahuasi, Muquiyauyo, Pucará, Sicaya

Webb, R.: on regional inequality in Peru, 141

Wilson, F.: on Tarma, 31–2, 34–5, 40–1

wool: as export, 10, 47 Table 3; in regional development, 7, 33, 67, 218, 244; and textile industry, 66

CAMBRIDGE LATIN AMERICAN STUDIES

Cambridge Latin American Studies

N